UNION CEMETERY

Leesburg
Loudoun County
Virginia

The Later Plats

1880-1995

❖II❖

Elizabeth R. Frain

HERITAGE BOOKS
2008

HERITAGE BOOKS
AN IMPRINT OF HERITAGE BOOKS, INC.

Books, CDs, and more—Worldwide

For our listing of thousands of titles see our website
at
www.HeritageBooks.com

Published 2008 by
HERITAGE BOOKS, INC.
Publishing Division
100 Railroad Ave. #104
Westminster, Maryland 21157

Copyright © 1997 Elizabeth R. Frain

Other Heritage Books by Elizabeth R. Frain:

Fairfax County, Virginia Death Register, 1853-1896

Loudoun County, Virginia Death Register, 1853-1896
Elizabeth R. Frain and Marty Hiatt

Loudoun County, Virginia Marriages after 1850: Volume 1, 1851-1880
Patricia B. Duncan and Elizabeth R. Frain

Monocacy Cemetery, Beallsville, Maryland

Union Cemetery, Leesburg, Loudoun County, Virginia: Plats A and *B, 1784-1995*

Union Cemetery, Leesburg, Loudoun County, Virginia: The Later Plats, 1880-1995

All rights reserved. No part of this book may be reproduced or transmitted in any form or by any means, electronic or mechanical, including photocopying, recording or by any information storage and retrieval system without written permission from the author, except for the inclusion of brief quotations in a review.

International Standard Book Numbers
Paperbound: 978-1-888265-10-1
Clothbound: 978-0-7884-7535-1

UNION CEMETERY

LEESBURG, LOUDOUN COUNTY, VIRGINIA

Table of Contents

INTRODUCTION	v
THE HISTORY OF UNION CEMETERY	vi
PLAT C	1
PLAT D	118
PLAT E	171
PLAT NEW	228
APPENDIX A	235
INDEX	239

INTRODUCTION

This is the second and final volume of information from Union Cemetery, Leesburg, Loudoun County, VA. I have followed the same information gathering strategies and form of presentation as in the first volume.

It is interesting to notice the changes in burying customs. In the older plats lots are usually owned by one family. The custom was to buy an entire lot and several generations of one family or the families of several brothers and sisters were buried there, making it easy to group information by families. As time has passed and families have become more transient, half-lots, then individual sites were sold. I have indicated ownership in the lots only when at least 6 sites are owned by one family. I find that once ownership drops below that number, very little is gained by knowing who owns each site.

I have kept the date acquired from each source separate so that I could compare them to be sure of the accuracy of my work. The death and birth dates given are either an agreement between sources or where there was an obvious error in the disagreeing source which could then be eliminated. I have generally accepted the date and other information on the tombstone to be correct. In the cases where I could not decide which was correct, I have listed all the sources involved with the following abbreviations before the information:

- CR Information from the Cemetery Records
- IB Information from the Interment Book
- TS Information from the Tombstone

Please note that Plat NEW (this is the term used by the cemetery) starts over with Lot 1. There is also some duplication of lot numbers between Plats C & D. It can become very confusing if you are looking for a lot number and do not know the Plat.

Should you have family information regarding persons buried in Union Cemetery, or wish to obtain photographs of your family stones, please contact me, Elizabeth Frain at 1 Turley Court, North Potomac, MD 20878.

THE HISTORY OF UNION CEMETERY

The gates of Union Cemetery, donated in memory of Henry T. Fairfax in 1921, proclaim it's establishment in 1851. The Cemetery was legally incorporated by the Virginia General Assembly on February 27, 1852. The original incorporators were James B. Beverly, Thomas P. Knox, Armistead M. Vandevanter, Daniel G. Smith, Charles B. Tebbs, James S. Harris, Asa Jackson, William H. Gray, John Hoffman, Addison H. Clarke, James Garrison, George R. Head, James Steadman, Levin W.S. Hough and Edward Hammat.

The first land acquired by the Cemetery was four acres and 23 perches purchased from Daniel G. Smith and Ellen E. Smith his wife on May 1, 1853 for a total of $414.37. Several months later, on December 10, 1853, an additional 3 roods and 28 poles was purchased from William Drish and Harriett Drish his wife for $92.81. Both of these deeds are recorded in Deed Book 5H in the Loudoun County Court House, Leesburg, VA.

According to Wilbur C. Hall, a member of the Board of Trustees, in his speech before the Rotary Club in Leesburg, VA in January, 1946, no other land was acquired until 1888 when 4 acres were purchased for $700 from Robert H. Gray. Then in 1894 the Cemetery paid $337 to F.W. Shafer for 2.248 acres. In later years several acres were obtained from the Henry T. Harrison heirs both by exchange and purchase.

Mr. Hall also states that the first burial in Union Cemetery was Mrs. Elizabeth Garrison on February 6th, 1853. Her husband, James Garrison was one of the original incorporators of the Cemetery. You will find her listed in Lot 136, Site 3. However her tombstone gives the date of death as February 5, 1854.

There is some belief that there were burials in the Cemetery before it officially became Union Cemetery, but there is no way to prove or disprove this point.

Burials prior to the establishment of Union Cemetery were in the Old Stone Church Cemetery (Methodist), the Episcopal Church Cemetery, the Old Presbyterian Church Cemetery or in private cemeteries located on family property. The name Union which was used for many Cemeteries established during this era, indicates that it is for all religions or people. There are quite a few graves in Union Cemetery which have obviously been moved from earlier resting places as family land was sold or other old cemeteries were allowed to deteriorate, making the cemetery a repository for much earlier history than one would expect. Union Cemetery has become a major burial ground for the county.

The earliest records I have seen are in an Account Book which begins in 1866. This book primarily shows money received from sales of lots and digging of graves, and expenses paid out. The lot owners are named but not the individual to be buried in the grave.

The earliest Minute Book available begins in 1886 and at one of the first meetings a committee is set up to determine the ownership of each lot and to list who is buried in each lot. Apparently before that time no records were kept and the Cemetery Board had no idea of who was where. At the same time they decided to begin the Interment Book which I have copied for the beginning base of this book.

The Cemetery is divided into Plats A, B, C, D, E and NEW. Each plat is divided into Lots, each usually containing 12 burial sites. The lot number suffix "1/2" only means that the number had been used somewhere else but was the next logical number to use.

The Chapel in the center of Plat A was built in 1908. As far as we can tell it was planned from the beginning as no graves were moved or renumbered at that time. Unfortunately the Chapel is being allowed to deteriorate. It is a lovely building which could be used for services in bad weather or when funerals come in from out of town.

UNION CEMETERY
LEESBURG, LOUDOUN CO., VA

Plat C

Lot: 663 Owner: Miscellaneous

Site 1   Mary B. Maddox   No stone   Age: 23 years
         Cause: Tuberculosis   Death: 1929/07/13   Burial: 1929/07/15
Site 2   Lemuel Maddox   No stone   Age: 55 years
         Cause: Tuberculosis   Death: 1930/12/30   Burial: 1931/01/01
Site 3   Mary Lena Maddox   No stone   Age: 52 years
         Cause: Tuberculosis   Death: 1937/05/09   Burial: 1937/05/11
Site 4   Edgar Nichols   No stone   Age: 57 years
         Cause: Enalphatitis   Death: 1929/12/23   Burial: 1929/12/23
Site 5   Carl Reynard Jr.   Cause: Pneumonia   Age: 21 months
         Birth: 1929/08/11   Death: 1931/05/16   Burial: 1931/05/18
         TS: Son of Carl E. & Alma Reynard
Site 6   Clifford L. Kenman   No stone   Age: 3 years
         Cause: Burns   Death: 1933/03/07   Burial: 1933/03/09
Site 6   Child Greenway   Death: 1939/10/21   Burial: 1939/10/23
         Cause: Stillborn   No stone
Site 7   George Robert Polen   Cause: Senility   Age: 74 years
         Birth: 1852/03/04   Death: 1927/02/23   Burial: 1927/02/25
Site 8   Catherine Polen   Cause: Pneumonia   Age: 82 years
         Birth: 1852/02/26   Death: 1935/01/07   Burial: 1935/01/09
         TS: Wife of George Robert Polen
Site 9   Ernest H. Rehker   Cause: Endocarditis   Age: 77 years
         Birth: 1852   Death: 1927/06/10   Burial: 1927/06/12
Site 10 Bettie Ann Jackson   No stone   Age: 7 months
         Cause: Acidosis   Death: 1928/04/12   Burial: 1928/04/14
Site 11 Robert Hardy   No stone   Age: 62 years
         Cause: Hemorrhage   Death: 1931/02/19   Burial: 1931/02/21

Lot: 664 Owner: Miscellaneous

Site 1   Charles E. Greenwade   Died: Leesburg, VA   Age: 83 years
         Birth: 1878/05/27   Death: 1961/11/01   Burial: 1961/11/05
Site 2   Victoria Belle Greenwade   Age: 71 years
         Birth: 1876/02/22   Death: 1947/07/26   Burial: 1947/07/28
Site 3   Virginia Anna Greenwade Cause: Pneumonia   Age: 12 years
         Birth: 1918/09/12   Death: 1931/02/23   Burial: 1931/02/25
Site 4   George Robert Stickle Cause: Nephritis   Age: 85 years
         Birth: 1845/01/08   Death: 1930/09/25   Burial: 1930/09/27
Site 5   Virginia L. Stickle   Cause: C. Rayuguster Age: 79 years
         Birth: 1858/01/31   Death: 1937/04/25   Burial: 1937/04/27
         TS: Wife of G. Robert Stickle

Site 6   James M. Franklin   Cause: Gun Shot   Age: 52 years
         Birth: 1879/08/22   Death: 1932/02/25   Burial: 1932/02/27
Site 7   Harriett R. Breckenridge   No stone   Age: 19 years
         Cause: Heart Disease   Death: 1928/05/28   Burial: 1928/05/30
Site 8   Nelson W. Breckenridge   No stone   Age: 66 years
         Cause: Pneumonia   Death: 1935/05/06   Burial: 1935/05/08
Site 9   Frances A. Breckenridge   No stone   Age: 60 years
         Cause: Myocarditis   Death: 1939/11/10   Burial: 1939/11/12
Site 10 Lillie Mae Hough Cooper   Cause: Eclorimia   Age: 19 years
         Birth: 1913/05/11   Death: 1932/11/07   Burial: 1932/11/10
Site 11 Mary Scott Duryea   Cause: Cholecystitis   Age: 80 years
         Birth: 1847   Death: 1927/09/18   Burial: 1927/09/20

Lot: 665   Owner: D.V. Cummings   Purchased: 1916/09/05
Site   William V. James   TS: In memory of
         Birth: 1924/05/19   Death: 1975/04/25
Site 4   James Volney Cummings   Age: 30 years
         Birth: 1916/07/30   Death: 1947/04/20   Burial: 1947/04/22
Site 6   Doris Lee Holliday   Age: 14 years
         Birth: 1927   Death: 1941/12/21   Burial: 1941/12/23
Site 8   Lola Frances James   Died: Prince George, MD   Age: 63 years
         Birth: 1904/12/23   Death: 1966/01/30   Burial: 1966/02/03
Site 9   Louise E. & Infant Daughter Bjornson   Age: 19 years
         Birth: 1922   Death: 1941/08/31   Burial: 1941/09/02
         Cause: ? of Hip   TS: Wife of Ben Bjornson
Site 10 David V. Cummings   Cause: Pneumonia   Age: 49 years
         Birth: 1873/05/01   Death: 1923/04/21   Burial: 1923/04/24
Site 11 M. Elizabeth Cummings   Cause: Coronary Thrombosis   Age: 60 years
         Birth: 1877   Death: 1939/09/18   Burial: 1939/09/20
Site 12 Maude Helen Cummings   Age: 1 month
         Birth: 1916/07/30   Death: 1916/09/03
Site 12 Child James   Cause: Stillborn   No stone
                                    Death: 1949/07/13   Burial: 1949/07/13
Site 12 Baby Girl Holliday   Cause: Stillborn   Died: Arlington, VA
         No stone   Death: 1963/12/09   Burial: 1963/12/11

Lot: 666 E   Owner: Mrs. E.P. Jackson   Purchased: 1916/07/29
Site 9   Albert G. Jackson   Cause: Myocarditis   Age: 75 years
         Birth: 1849/08/31   Death: 1925/10/18   Burial: 1925/10/20
Site 10 Emma Jane Porter Jackson   Age: 79 years
         TS: Age 79 years   Death: 1940/11/08   Burial: 1940/11/10
         Cause: Valvular Heart Disease   On stone with Albert G. Jackson
Site 11 Robert Lee Jackson   Cause: Suicide   Age: 30 years
         Birth: 1886/08/08   Death: 1917/01/31
Site 12 Bernard W. Jackson   Cause: Heart Failure   Age: 32 years
         Birth: 1884/11/17   Death: 1916/07/28

Lot: 666 W   Owner: Herbert Jackson   Purchased:
Site 3   Herbert Griffith Jackson   No stone   Age: 43 years
                                    Death: 1945/06/10   Burial: 1945/06/12

Site 4 Florence Keys Jackson No stone   Age: 58 years
        Died: Arlington, VA   Death: 1964/06/02   Burial: 1964/06/05
Site 5 Ludwell Alex. Keyes   No stone   Age: 76 years
                               Death: 1949/08/15   Burial: 1949/08/17
Site 6 Charlotte Ann Keyes   No stone   Age: 68 years
                               Death: 1946/06/16

Lot: 667 Owner: C.H. Maffett   Purchased: 1923/05/07
Site 4 Bertie F. Maffett   Died: Catlett, VA   Age: 89 years
        Birth: 1874/01/01   Death: 1965/12/10   Burial: 1965/12/12
Site 5 Charles Harry Maffett Died: Leesburg, VA   Age: 84 years
        Birth: 1876/10/06   Death: 1960/10/25   Burial: 1960/10/28
Site 6 A. Fannie Franklin   Cause: Pneumonia   Age: 53 years
        Birth: 1870/01/02   Death: 1923/05/07   Burial: 1923/05/09
        TS: Daughter of Newton & Barbara Burch Franklin
Site 7 Frederick Karl Leissering   Age: 62 years
        Birth: 1884/09/09   Death: 1947/05/08   Burial: 1947/05/10
Site 9 Kathryn E. Lund   Age: 42 years
        Birth: 1907/09/25   Death: 1948/06/26   Burial: 1948/06/28
Site 10 Einor G. Lund   Age: 42 years
        Birth: 1905/07/25   Death: 1948/06/29   Burial: 1948/07/01
Site 12 Alfred Lee Cunningham   Age: 11 days
        Birth: 1928/11/06   Death: 1928/11/17   Burial: 1928/11/18
        Cause: Pneumonia   CR: Henry Maffett's son's child

Lot: 668 E Owner: Herbert Harrison   Purchased: 1924/01/27
Site 7 Mary E. Carter Harrison Cause: Peritonitis   Age: 21 years
        Birth: 1903   Death: 1924/01/28   Burial: 1924/01/30
Site 8 Herbert Lester Harrison Died: Adamstown, MD   Age: 65 years
        Birth: 1892   Death: 1958/03/22   Burial: 1958/03/24
Site 9 Ruth Wilson Harrison Shaffer   Age: 59 years
        Birth: 1912   Death: 1972/06/13
Site 12 Infant of Herbert Harrison   No stone
        Cause: Stillborn   Death: 1933/08/26   Burial: 1933/08/26
Site 12 Child Harrison   Cause: Bronchial Pneumonia Age: 3 days
        No stone   Death: 1937/01/13   Burial: 1937/01/13

Lot: 668 W Owner: Mrs. Jos. Moffett   Purchased: 1925/09/22
Site 1 Mrs. Ruby G. Moffett   Died: Alexandria, VA
        Birth: 1906/03/14   Death: 1971/03/14   Burial: 1971/03/17
        BP: Mrs. Joseph Moffett
Site 2 Joseph L. Moffett   Cause: Suicide   Age: 35 years
        Birth: 1903/09/15   Death: 1939/04/12   Burial: 1939/04/14
Site 3 Joseph E. Moffett   Cause: Cancer   Age: 56 years
        Birth: 1869/06/24   Death: 1925/09/21   Burial: 1925/09/23
Site 4 Florence A. Moffett   Died: Leesburg, VA   Age: 98 years
        Birth: 1871/04/11   Death: 1969/11/13   Burial: 1969/11/17
        TS: Wife of Joseph E. Moffett
Site 5 Merrill Armour   Birth: 1903/04/09   Death: 1974/10/15

Lot: 669 E   Owner: Mary Virginia Henderson   1922/05/26
Site 0   Carroll E. Henderson   Death: 1914/08/05
         Removed from Lot 79E Aug. 5, 1922   No stone
Site 7   C. Benton Rosen   Died: Leesburg, VA   Age: 62 years
         Birth: 1918/11/18   Death: 1981/02/14   Burial: 1981/02/17
         TS: SP 1 US Navy WWII
Site 9   Mrs. H. K. Henderson   No stone   Age: 48 years
         Cause: Tuberculosis   Death: 1922/05/16   Burial: 1922/05/18
Site 10 Dorothy M. Henderson   No stone   Age: 3 months
         Cause: Tuberculosis   Death: 1922/08/04   Burial: 1922/08/06
Site 12 Dorothy Steadman Rollins   Age: 40 years
         Birth: 1932   Death: 1973/09/05   Burial: 1973/09/08
                                Died: Fairfax, VA

Lot: 669 W   Owner: Raymond C. Maffett   Purchased: 1923/09/21
Site 1   Marcellus L. Maffett   Cause: Cholecystitis   Age: 70 years
         Birth: 1853/04/01   Death: 1923/09/21   Burial: 1923/09/23
Site 2   Sarah E. Maffett   Age: 75 years
         Birth: 1854/03/08   Death: 1929/08/09   Burial: 1929/08/11
         Cause: Apoplexy   TS: Wife of M.L. Maffett
Site 3   Raymond Henry C. Maffett   Age: 73 years
         Birth: 1881/11/18   Death: 1955/07/28   Burial: 1955/07/28
         Died: Leesburg, VA   TS: Son of Sarah E. Maffett

Lot: 670 E   Owner: Charles Ruebin Hawes Purchased: 1921/05/10
Site 7   Pearl A. Hawes   Age: 21 years
         Birth: 1908/03/16   Death: 1929/06/13   Burial: 1929/06/15
         Cause: Tuberculosis   TS: Daughter of Charles & Mishia Hawes
Site 8   Mary Hawes   No stone   Age: 59 years
         Died: Leesburg, VA   Death: 1974/04/17   Burial: 1974/04/19
Site 9   Charles R. Hawes   No stone   Age: 67 years
                                Death: 1950/07/01   Burial: 1950/07/03
Site 10 Bessie Lee Hawes   Age: 42 years
         Birth: 1889/07/04   Death: 1931/12/16   Burial: 1931/12/18
         Cause: Cancer   TS: Wife of C.R. Hawes
Site 11 Harry O. Hawes   Cause: Spinal Meningitis   Age: 5 years
         Birth: 1922/07/16   Death: 1928/01/14   Burial: 1928/01/16
         TS: Son of Charles & Bessie Hawes
Site 12 James Elmer Hawes   Cause: Poison   Age: 5 months
         Birth: 1920/12/04   Death: 1921/05/10
         TS: Son of C.R. & Bessie Hawes

Lot: 670 W   Owner: Mrs. Geo. Wortman   Purchased: 1921/12/28
Site 1   Richard T. Wortman   Died: Hagerstown, MD   Age: 69 years
         Birth: 1893   Death: 1962/12/15   Burial: 1962/12/18
Site 2   Henry Wortman   Cause: Malignancy of brain Age: 38 years
         No stone   Death: 1939/10/26   Burial: 1939/10/28
Site 3   George E. Wortman   Cause: Heart Trouble   Age: 63 years
         Birth: 1858/07/31   Death: 1922/12/27

Site 4 Mollie W. Wortman   Cause: N. Carcinoma   Age: 68 years
        Birth: 1868/03/12   Death: 1936/01/19   Burial: 1936/12/21
Site 5 Mrs. Mary E. Carter   Age: 53 years
        Birth: 1900/05/22   Death: 1952/10/07   Burial: 1952/10/09
        TS: Children Virginia, Lee, William

Lot: 671 Owner: John A. Hope   Purchased: 1918/10/15
Site 1 Cora May Hope   Died: Knoxville, MD   Age: 81 years
        Birth: 1883/04/16   Death: 1964/05/18   Burial: 1964/05/20
        TS: Wife of John A. Hope
Site 2 John Alexander Hope   Age: 65 years
        Birth: 1880/07/20   Death: 1946/07/07   Burial: 1946/07/09
Site 4 Mary Pleasant Hope   Cause: Pneumonia   Age: 32 years
        Birth: 1886/01/03   Death: 1918/10/14
        TS: Wife of John A. Hope
Site 10 Paul H. Hope   Died: Leesburg, VA
        Birth: 1916/03/20   Death: 1994/11/11   Burial: 1994/11/14
Site 11 Margaret L. Hope   Died: Leesburg, VA   Age: 67 years
        Birth: 1922/06/02   Death: 1990/02/21   Burial: 1990/02/24
        TS: Married Paul H. Hope August 6, 1938
Site 12 Forrest William (Billy) Hope   Age: 1 1/2 years
        Birth: 1944/04/08   Death: 1945/11/04   Burial: 1945/11/06

Lot: 672 Owner: George W. Hough   Purchased: 1919/01/21
Site 1 J. Frank Fry   Cause: Cancer   Age: 66 years
        Birth: 1865/05/08   Death: 1932/01/13   Burial: 1932/01/15
Site 2 Hannah (Nannie) Ann Fry   Age: 86 years
        Birth: 1866/05/07   Death: 1957/10/03   TS: Wife of J. Frank Fry
Site 4 Mary E. Hough   Cause: Old Age   Age: 79 years
        Birth: 1839   Death: 1918   TS: Wife of J.F. Hough
Site 5 Lydia M. Everhart   Cause: Heart   Age: 38 years
        Birth: 1879/07/23   Death: 1925/08/01   Burial: 1925/08/03
Site 6 Frances E. Everhart   Cause: Gastric Enteritis Age: 33 years
        Birth: 1907/09/17   Death: 1940/01/23   Burial: 1940/01/25
Site 7 Miss Ello Costello   Died: Winchester, VA   No stone
                                 Death: 1988/03/13   Burial: 1988/03/15
Site 8 Marjorie Costello   Age: 80 years
        Birth: 1906   Death: 1987/06/02   Burial: 1987/06/06
        Died: Leesburg, VA   No stone
Site 9 George W. Hough   Age: 75 years
        Birth: 1868/09/28   Death: 1943/06/17   Burial: 1943/06/19
Site 10 Mary Hough   No stone   Age: 55 years
        Cause: Hydrocephalous   Death: 1933/12/05   Burial: 1933/12/07
Site 10 Joanna T. Hough   Age: 80 years
        Birth: 1855/01/15   Death: 1937/07/04   Burial: 1937/07/08
        Cause: C. Astheris   TS: Wife of George W. Hough
Site 11 Joe Hough   Cause: Valvular Heart Disease Age: 77 years
        No stone   Death: 1941/07/10   Burial: 1941/07/12

Lot: 673 Owner: O.H. Tittmann   **Purchased: 1918/01/15**
Site 2   Charles Trowbridge Tittmann   Age: 81 years
         Birth: 1883/02/07   Death: 1964/10/08   Burial: 1964/10/14
         Died: Washington, DC
Site 3   Jean Crosby Tittman   Died: CO   Age: 81 years
         Birth: 1884/05/20   Death: 1965/08/27   Burial: 1965/09/16
Site 4   Dr. Otto Hilgard Tittman   Age: 88 years
         Birth: 1850/08/20   Death: 1938/08/21   Burial: 1938/08/23
         Cause: Valvular Heart Lesions   TS: Born Belleville, Ill
Site 5   Kate T. Wilkins Tittman   Age: 82 years
         Birth: 1855   Death: 1938/02/14   Burial: 1938/02/16
         Cause: Cancer   TS: Born Detroit. Died Leesburg.

Lot: 674 Owner: E.T. Titus   **Purchased: 1920/07/04**
Site 1   Child of Albert Titus   Death: 1950/10/06   Burial: 1950/10/06
         TS: Infant daughter of Albert B. & Margaret A. Titus
Site 2   Edward Farrell Titus   Cause: Bronchial Pneumonia   Age: 33 years
         Birth: 1908/09/03   Death: 1942/05/04   Burial: 1942/05/06
Site 3   Edgar Tunis Titus   Age: 66 years
         Birth: 1873/11/14   Death: 1940/02/19   Burial: 1940/02/21
         Cause: Cirrhosis of Liver & hemorrhage
Site 4   Dorothea Marie Titus   Cause: Coronary Occlusion   Age: 54 years
         Birth: 1886/01/20   Death: 1940/03/14   Burial: 1940/03/16
Site 5   Dorothy Jane Titus   Age: 41 years
         Birth: 1920/01/02   Death: 1961/11/26   Burial: 1961/11/28
         Cause: Cancer   Died: Legnehburg, VA
Site 7   Franklin Dunlap Titus   Cause: Accident   Age: 22 years
         Birth: 1911/09/08   Death: 1934/06/03   Burial: 1934/06/05
Site 8   Albert Burch Titus   Died: Leesburg, VA   Age: 57 years
         Birth: 1916/01/18   Death: 1973/11/01   Burial: 1973/11/03
Site 11   James M. Church   Died: Leesburg, VA   Age: 83 years
         Birth: 1886/12/02   Death: 1970/06/29   Burial: 1970/07/03
Site 12   Belva B. Church   Died: Silver Spring, MD   Age: 93 years
         Birth: 1889/11/11   Death: 1983/09/11   Burial: 1983/09/14

Lot: 675 Owner: R.C. Duff   **Purchased: 1920/02/09**
Site 4   Eugene Iris Spradley   Died: Warrenton, VA   Age: 46 years
         Birth: 1921/09/23   Death: 1967/12/25   Burial: 1967/12/28
         TS: Arkansas S MAJ SIGNAL CORPS WWII
Site 6   Martha Evelyn Spradley   Died: Fairfax, VA   Age: 1 day
         Death: 1963/04/21   Burial: 1963/04/22
Site 7   Virginia Barbara Duff   Died: Elizabethtown, TN   Age: 73 years
         Birth: 1910/08/29   Death: 1983/10/31   Burial: 1983/11/03
Site 8   Robert Cecil Duff   Died: Armond Beach, FL   Age: 81 years
         Birth: 1877/02/17   Death: 1958/08/30   Burial: 1958/09/04
Site 9   Mrs. Martha Boyd Tompkins Duff   Age: 68 years
         Birth: 1882/08/31   Death: 1951/01/07   Burial: 1951/01/12
         TS: Wife of Robert Cecil Duff

Site 10 Robert Cecil Duff Jr.
Birth: 1917/07/04   Death: 1941/12/07   Burial: 1948/03/17
TS: Tennessee PVT 18 AAF BOMB WING WWII
Site 11 Martha Elizabeth Duff   Age: 18 years
Birth: 1920/12/07   Death: 1939/08/15   Burial: 1939/08/17
Cause: Acute Intestinal Obstruction
Site 12 James Duff   Death: 1920/02/08   IB: Infant of R.C. Duff
Site 12 Mary M. Duff   Death: 1922/03/14   No stone
IB: Infant of R.C. Duff

Lot: 676   Owner: Herbert J. Fry   Purchased: 1917/02/13
Site 3 Richard Lee Harris   Cause: Apoplexy   Age: 66 years
        Birth: 1853/05/12   Death: 1917/02/10
Site 4 Sarah Margaret Harris Cause: Cerebral Hemorrhage Age: 71 years
        Birth: 1854/05/23   Death: 1925/04/21   Burial: 1925/04/23
Site 5 Herbert J. Fry   Cause: Pneumonia   Age: 53 years
        Birth: 1884/09/16   Death: 1937/11/17   Burial: 1937/11/19
Site 6 Nellie M. Fry   Died: Leesburg, VA   Age: 85 years
        Birth: 1888/04/17   Death: 1973/08/25   Burial: 1973/08/28
        On stone with Herbert J. Fry
Site 10 Alma P. George Fry   Age: 25 years
        Birth: 1909/11/15   Death: 1935/04/22   Burial: 1935/04/24
        Cause: F. Deptocia   TS: Wife of M.H. Fry
Site 11 Marshall Herbert Fry Died: Berryville, VA   Age: 73 years
        Birth: 1908/10/17   Death: 1982/01/06   Burial: 1982/01/08
Site 12 Ella B. Fry   Died: Leesburg, VA
        Birth: 1916/04/15   Death: 1993/12/25   Burial: 1993/12/28
        On stone with Marshall Herbert Fry

Lot: 677 E   Owner: Mrs. Leah Bitzer   Purchased: 1916/06/15
Site 9 John W. Bitzer   Cause: Cancer   Age: 68 years
        Birth: 1847/10/31   Death: 1916/06/09
Site 10 Mrs. Leonora Goodhart Bitzer   Age: 95 years
        Birth: 1860/12/19   Death: 1956/05/06   Burial: 1956/05/07
                             Died: Tampa, FL

Lot: 677 W   Owner: Mrs. Lucy Rollins   Purchased: 1939/09/01
Site 5 Ida Lucinda Rollins   Age: 95 years
        Birth: 1874/07/17   Death: 1970/04/30   Burial: 1970/05/01
        Died: Leesburg, VA   On stone with Louis Charles Rollins
Site 6 Louis Charles Rollins   Age: 89 years
        Birth: 1868/06/10   Death: 1958/03/10   Burial: 1958/03/12

Lot: 678 E   Owner: H.L. Titus   Purchased: 1915/07/26
Site 7 Robert Gordon Titus   Age: 10 years
        Birth: 1919/01/23   Death: 1929/05/22   Burial: 1929/05/24
        Cause: Accident   TS: Son of H.L. & May Titus
Site 8 Pvt. Charles R. Titus   TS: Virginia PVT 399 INF WWII
        Birth: 1923/12/01   Death: 1944/12/07   Burial: 1948/12/16

Site 9 Carrie Virginia Titus   Died: Berryville, VA   Age: 95 years
        Birth: 1889/07/05   Death: 1984/09/21   Burial: 1984/09/24
        TS: Daughter of George & Phoebe Hough
Site 10 Henry L. Titus   Cause: Intestineptiritis   Age: 62 years
        Birth: 1871/03/08   Death: 1934/01/15   Burial: 1934/01/17
Site 11 Lillie May Gant Titus   Cause: Pneumonia   Age: 37 years
        Birth: 1881/03/28   Death: 1919/01/24
        TS: Wife of Henry L. Titus
Site 12 C.R. Titus   Death: 1915/02/26   Age: 6 months
        IB: Infant of Henry L. Titus   No stone
Site 12 D.T. Titus   Death: 1915/11/27   No stone
        IB: Child of Henry Titus

Lot: 678 W Owner: Bruce McIntosh   Purchased: 1915/02/26
Site 1 Infant son of James McIntosh   TS: Infant son of J.L. & I.B. McIntosh
        Cause: Premature Birth   Death: 1924/02/10   Burial: 1924/02/10
Site 2 James Logan McIntosh   Age: 87 years
        Birth: 1898/09/05   Death: 1986/07/27   Burial: 1986/07/30
                                  Died: Leesburg, VA
Site 3 Irene Bridges McIntosh   Died: Leesburg, VA   Age: 83 years
        Birth: 1897/10/28   Death: 1981/06/10   Burial: 1981/06/13
        On stone with James Logan (Bruce) McIntosh
Site 4 James Logan McIntosh Jr.
        Birth: 1926/01/31   Death: 1945/03/26   Burial: 1948/09/02
        TS: Virginia PFC 354 Inf. 89th Div., WWII, ETO

Lot: 679 Owner: H.J. Houpt   Purchased: 1914/12/07
Site 1 Henry J. Houpt   Cause: Accident   Age: 80 years
        Birth: 1852/04/03   Death: 1932/10/03   Burial: 1932/10/06
        TS: Son of George A. & Susannah Wingert Houpt.
        Born Bedford Co., VA
Site 2 Sarah Louise Houpt   Cause: Apoplexy   Age: 81 years
        Birth: 1850/02/26   Death: 1931/08/31   Burial: 1931/09/02
        TS: Wife of Henry J. Houpt.
        Daughter of Charles & Diana Cleaver. Born Montgomery Co., PA
Site 3 Sallie Ellen Houpt   Died: Leesburg, VA   Age: 79 years
        Birth: 1879/03/07   Death: 1958/03/08   Burial: 1958/03/10
        TS: Daughter of Henry J. & Sarah L. Houpt.
        Born Montgomery Co., PA
Site 5 Mary Emma H. Raush   Died: Leesburg, VA   Age: 88 years
        Birth: 1875/07/26   Death: 1963/09/15   Burial: 1963/09/17
        TS: Daughter of Henry J. & Sarah L. Houpt. Wife of J.V. Raush.
Site 7 Joseph Shafer Whitmore   Died: Leesburg, VA   Age: 84 years
        Birth: 1886/07/22   Death: 1970/08/16   Burial: 1970/08/19
        TS: Son of Michael T. & Emma S. Whitmore
Site 8 Louise Gertrude H. Whitmore   Age: 101 years
        Birth: 1883/08/06   Death: 1984/08/26   Burial: 1984/08/29
        Died: Leesburg, VA   TS: Wife of Joseph S. Whitmore.
        Daughter of Henry J. & Sarah L. Houpt.

Site 10 Myrtle Ferne Truehart   Cause: Tuberculosis   Age: 28 years
        Birth: 1886/02/22   Death: 1914/12/04
        TS: Wife of William C. Truehart.
        Daughter of Henry J. & Sarah L. Houpt

Lot: 680 Owner: John R. McCabe   Purchased: 1915/09/13
Site 1 J. Randolph McCabe   Cause: Accident   Age: 18 years
        Birth: 1897/09/29   Death: 1915/09/11
Site 2 John R. McCabe   Cause: Heart Trouble   Age: 73 years
        Birth: 1858/08/14   Death: 1931/09/08   Burial: 1931/09/10
Site 3 Cora Havener McCabe   Age: 78 years
        Birth: 1874/02/06   Death: 1952/04/27   Burial: 1952/04/30
Site 4 Dorothy Hodson McCabe McCabe   Died: Jacksonville, NC
        Birth: 1906/07/20   Death: 1993/11/04
Site 7 William H. McCabe   Age: 37 years
        Birth: 1903/05/02   Death: 1940/07/14   Burial: 1940/07/16
Site 8 Miss Ethel Gray McCabe   Died: Jacksonville, NC   Age: 83 years
        Birth: 1894/11/17   Death: 1978/10/05   Burial: 1978/10/10

Lot: 681, 682, 683, 684 Owner: J.T. Manning   1915/04/05
Site 0 Mabel Manning   Age: 7 months
        Birth: 1888/08/02   Death: 1889/03/10   Reinterment
Site 0 Mrs. Florence Louise Manning   Age: 51 years
        Birth: 1866/02/25   Death: 1917/08/07   Cause: Heart Trouble
        TS: Wife of J. Forrest Manning
Site 8 Florence Graham Manning   Died: Winchester, VA
        Birth: 1886/02/17   Death: 1973/01/03   Burial: 1973/01/05
Site 1 Marguerite Manning   Died: Hamilton, VA   Age: 69 years
        Birth: 1894/02/16   Death: 1965/10/04   Burial: 1965/10/07
Site 1 Robert D. Manning   Died: Leesburg, VA   Age: 76 years
        Birth: 1908/07/05   Death: 1984/08/21   Burial: 1984/08/24
Site 12 James Forrest Manning   Age: 75 years
        Birth: 1862/09/16   Death: 1938/05/22   Burial: 1938/05/23
        Cause: Chronic Bronchitis/Coronary   TS: Died at Eudora

Lot: 685 Owner: Mrs. H.W. Ballenger   Purchased: 1916/01/17
Site 2 Mrs. Rosa B. Kitchen   Died: Culpeper County, VA   Age: 81 years
        No stone   Death: 1955/01/25   Burial: 1955/01/29
Site 3 Henry W. Ballenger   Age: 71 years
        Birth: 1870/03/28   Death: 1941/09/20   Burial: 1941/09/22
Site 4 Daisy C. Wallace Ballenger   Age: 44 years
        Birth: 1875/11/16   Death: 1919/11/11
        Cause: Tuberculosis   TS: Wife of Henry W. Ballenger
Site 4 Clifton Ballenger   No stone   Age: 41 years
                              Death: 1945/10/04   Burial: 1945/10/06
Site 7 Paul P. Ballenger   Died: Arlington, VA   Age: 62 years
        Birth: 1898/01/07   Death: 1960/09/06   Burial: 1960/09/09
Site 8 Mildred Elona Ballenger   Cause: Heart   Age: 36 years
        Birth: 1900/01/07   Death: 1936/09/11   Burial: 1936/09/13
        TS: Wife of Paul P. Ballenger.

Site 8 Mary V. Ballenger   Death: 1936/09/11   Burial: 1936/09/13
        Cause: Stillborn
Site 9 Lawrence D. Ballenger   Died: Richmond, VA   Age: 58 years
        Birth: 1921/12/04   Death: 1980/02/19   Burial: 1980/02/21
        TS: MM1 US NAVY WWII
Site 11 Paul P. Ballenger   Died: Arlington, VA   Age: 69 years
        Birth: 1920/07/09   Death: 1990/01/22   Burial: 1990/01/24
        TS: US ARMY WWII

Lot: 686 E   Lula G. & George F. Weaver   Purchased: 1937/05/14
Site 9 H. Fredrick Mang   Died: Fairfax, VA
        Birth: 1926/04/11   Death: 1995/12/19   Burial: 1995/12/22
Site 9 Hazel Grimes Mang   Died: Leesburg, VA
        Birth: 1908/05/31   Death: 1983/01/12   Burial: 1983/01/14
Site 10 George F. Weaver   Died: Patuxent, MD
        Birth: 1893   Death: 1978/01/10   Burial: 1978/01/12
Site 11 Lulu G. Weaver   Died: Leesburg, VA   Age: 88 years
        Birth: 1893   Death: 1981/09/29   Burial: 1981/10/01
Site 12 Capt. Robert G. Klotz
        Birth: 1886/09/28   Death: 1937/03/29   Burial: 1937/09/28

Lot: 686W   Owner: Mrs. H. L. Payne   Purchased: 1917/10/19
        Trans: E to Mrs. Emma Raush
        from Mrs. H.L. Payne Herndon   1924/11/06
Site 1 Joseph A. Powers   Died: Leesburg, VA   Age: 81 years
        Birth: 1895/11/10   Death: 1977/08/20   Burial: 1977/08/25
Site 1 Vivienne Reinhart Powers   Died: Falmouth, MA
        Birth: 1902/01/29   Death: 1993/04/02   Burial: 1994/08/13
Site 2 Rachel P. Marshall   Died: Richmond, VA   Age: 78 years
        Birth: 1906/06/20   Death: 1985/02/28   Burial: 1985/03/02
Site 3 Herman L. Payne   Cause: Poison   Age: 42 years
        Birth: 1875/01/10   Death: 1917/10/19
Site 4 Siddie Jane Kerrick Payne   Age: 74 years
        Birth: 1875/03/13   Death: 1949/11/26   Burial: 1949/11/29
Site 5 Hugh E. Atwell   Died: Washington, DC   Age: 73 years
        Birth: 1902   Death: 1975/08/07   Burial: 1975/08/10

Lot: 687 E   Owner: Miscellaneous
Site 8 Dr. James W. Marshall   TS: MD   Age: 51 years
        Birth: 1872   Death: 1923/09/27   Burial: 1923/09/29
        Cause: Brain Tumor
Site 9 Mrs. Katharine S. Marshall   Age: 68 years
        Birth: 1867   Death: 1935/05/02   Burial: 1935/05/17
        Cause: Carcinoma   On stone with Dr. James W. Marshall
Site 11 Pinckney L. Gum   Died: Leesburg, VA   Age: 93 years
        Birth: 1885/03/13   Death: 1979/01/21   Burial: 1979/01/25
Site 12 Mary P. Gum   Age: 55 years
        Birth: 1877/08/12   Death: 1933/03/13   Burial: 1933/03/15
        Cause: Cancer of Uterus   TS: Wife of P.L. Gum

Lot: 687 W Owner: Mrs. S.H. Love Purchased: 1916/06/28
Transfer 1: E to Katherine S. Marshall 1923/10/11
Site 1 Frank T. Dailey Age: 70 years
  Birth: 1876 Death: 1946/05/11 Burial: 1946/05/13
Site 2 Elizabeth M. Love Dailey Age: 77 years
  Birth: 1876 Death: 1954/01/27 Burial: 1954/01/29
  Died: Leesburg, VA On stone with Frank T. Dailey
Site 3 Samuel Henry Love Cause: Heart Trouble Age: 74 years
  Birth: 1844/03/04 Death: 1918/06/23
Site 4 Mrs. Josephine M. Love Age: 84 years
  Birth: 1845/07/03 Death: 1927/03/20 Burial: 1927/03/22
  Cause: Pneumonia TS: Wife of Samuel Henry Love
Site 5 Nora H. Love Age: 62 years
  Birth: 1879 Death: 1942/12/10 Burial: 1942/12/12

Lot: 688 Owner: Est. of P.C. Smith Purchased: 1919/01/04
Site 1 Lillie Bell Calkins Age: 86 years
  Birth: 1871/08/15 Death: 1956/08/29 Burial: 1956/08/29
  Died: Fairfax, VA TS: Mother
Site 3 Philip Clark Smith Cause: Pneumonia Age: 28 years
  Birth: 1891/05/20 Death: 1919/01/14
Site 4 Myrtle Smith Died: Arlington, VA Age: 88 years
  Birth: 1892 Death: 1981/07/18 Burial: 1981/07/21
  TS: Wife
Site 5 Linwood J. Smith Cause: Meningitis Age: 9 years
  Birth: 1917 Death: 1925/10/23 Burial: 1925/10/25
Site 7 Infant of A. Calkins Cause: Stillborn No stone
  Death: 1926/11/30 Burial: 1926/11/30

Lot: 689 E Owner: M.D. Ellmore Purchased: 1919/01/21
Site 0 Virginia Grey Ellmore Cause: Flu Age: 3 years
  Birth: 1916 Death: 1919
  TS: Daughter of M.D. & L.G. Ellmore
Site 9 Rev. Murphy D. Ellmore Age: 42 years
  Birth: 1884 Death: 1926/08/02 Burial: 1926/08/04
  Cause: Peritonitis TS: Husband of Lena G. Rollins
Site 10 Lena Ellmore Died: Lynchburg, VA Age: 86 years
  No dates on stone Death: 1978/07/11 Burial: 1978/07/14

Lot: 689 W Owner: Mrs. G. O. Powell Purchased: 1919/02/07
Site 3 Mrs. Maude M. Ellmore Powell Age: 65 years
  Birth: 1879/09/03 Death: 1945/01/24 Burial: 1945/01/26
  IB: Mrs. George O. Powell
Site 3 George Oden Powell Age: 80 years
  Birth: 1868/12/12 Death: 1947/02/15 Burial: 1947/02/17
Site 5 Ruth Ellmore Powell Died: Winchester, VA Age: 74 years
  Birth: 1907/12/13 Death: 1982/06/18 Burial: 1982/06/23
Site 6 Erma I. Powell Died: Leesburg, VA Age: 78 years
  Birth: 1907 Death: 1986/01/12 Burial: 1986/01/15

Lot: 690 E   Owner: E.H. Robertson   Purchased: 1920/03/01
Site 8   Luther R. Robertson   Died: Washington, DC   Age: 55 years
         Birth: 1910/11/03   Death: 1966/03/10   Burial: 1966/03/13
         TS: Virginia PVT US ARMY WWII
Site 9   Alice L. Robertson   Age: 32 years
         Birth: 1912/01/07   Death: 1945/03/30   Burial: 1945/04/02
Site 10 Carroll Robertson   Cause: Cardiac Failure   Age: 25 years
         Birth: 1915/03/20   Death: 1940/09/16   Burial: 1940/09/18
Site 11 Mrs. Margaret M. Robertson   TS: Wife of E.H. Robertson
         Birth: 1889/08/23   Death: 1920/02/29
Site 12 Eppa H. Robertson   Died: Charlottesville, VA   Age: 92 years
         Birth: 1880   Death: 1978/10/20   Burial: 1978/10/23
         On stone with Margaret M. Robertson

Lot: 690 W   Owner: E. Harry Kimes   Purchased: 1920/11/02
Site 1   Infant Kimes   Cause: Stillborn   No stone
                               Death: 1935/04/28   Burial: 1935/04/28
Site 2   Carl Austin Kimes   Died: Leesburg, VA   Age: 70 years
         Birth: 1907   Death: 1978/04/18   Burial: 1978/04/20
Site 3   Ruth S. Kimes   Died: Winchester, VA   Age: 84 years
         Birth: 1901   Death: 1985/12/08   Burial: 1985/12/11
         On stone with Carl A. Kimes   No death date on stone
Site 4   Harry Egbert Kimes   Died: Leesburg, VA   Age: 75 years
         Birth: 1877   Death: 1956/02/05   Burial: 1956/02/06
Site 5   Mrs. Lillie Jane Kimes On stone with Harry E. Kimes Age: 58 years
         Birth: 1884   Death: 1942/12/22   Burial: 1942/12/24
Site 6   Olaf Douglas Kimes   Age: 13 years
         Birth: 1906/04/23   Death: 1919/10/28
         TS: Son of Harry E. & Lillie J. Kimes

Lot: 691   Owner: Robert L. Sowers   Purchased: 1923/04/23
Site 1   Robert J. Sowers   Died: Leesburg, VA   Age: 88 years
         Birth: 1885   Death: 1973/12/19   Burial: 1973/12/22
Site 2   Beulah F. Sowers   Died: Leesburg, VA   Age: 88 years
         Birth: 1885   Death: 1973/10/13   Burial: 1973/10/16
         On stone with Robert J. Sowers
Site 3   Robert L. Sowers   Cause: Nephritis   Age: 78 years
         Birth: 1847/01/06   Death: 1925/12/14   Burial: 1925/12/16
Site 4   Harriett Ashton Eskridge Sowers   Age: 82 years
         Birth: 1848/04/03   Death: 1930/04/30   Burial: 1930/05/02
         Cause: Prenon   TS: Wife of Robert L. Sowers
Site 5   Lavalette O'Darr Sowers   Died: Paeonian Springs, VA
         Birth: 1882   Death: 1958/12/13   Burial: 1958/12/15
Site 7   Frederick H. Franklin Cause: S. E. of face   Age: 23 years
         Birth: 1907/11/08   Death: 1931/10/02   Burial: 1931/10/04
         TS: Son of Corbin H. & Hattie F. Franklin
Site 8   Hattie Sowers Franklin   Age: 61 years
         Birth: 1876/09/13   Death: 1937/09/15
         Cause: Cancer of Colon   TS: Wife of Corbin H. Franklin

Site 11 Philip D. Sowers   Died: Paeonian Springs, VA   Age: 86 years
        Birth: 1872   Death: 1959/02/14   Burial: 1959/02/16
Site 12 Mrs. Annie Catherine Adrain Sowers   Age: 86 years
        Birth: 1868   Death: 1955/07/29   Burial: 1955/07/29
        Died: Paeonian Springs, VA   On stone with Philip D. Sowers

Lot: 692 E   Owner: W.H. Rollison   Purchased: 1921/09/12
Site 7 Clayton Rollison   Died: Washington, DC   Age: 47 years
                                  Death: 1953/04/04   Burial: 1953/04/07
        Cause: Congestive Heart Failure   No stone
Site 9 William H. Rollison   Cause: Congestive Heart Failure Age: 60 years
        No stone   Death: 1939/12/24   Burial: 1939/12/26
Site 10 Maude F. Rollison   Death: 1921/08/08   Age: 35 years
        Cause: Appendicitis   No stone
Site 11 Laurence Lee Rollison   Death: 1921/09/09   Age: 8 years
        Cause: Accident   No stone

Lot: 692 W   Owner: Miscellaneous
Site 4 Esther M. Brown   Died: Leesburg, VA   Age: 58 years
        Birth: 1933/01/11   Death: 1991/07/19   Burial: 1991/07/22
Site 6 Lucille A. Berry   Died: Leesburg, VA   Age: 59 years
        Birth: 1927/04/13   Death: 1986/06/10   Burial: 1986/06/13

Lot: 693   Owner: Harry Mitchell   Purchased: 1922/01/04
Permission given Jas. W. Wallace to bury 1930/05/14
Site 7 James W. Wallace   Cause: S. Signoid   Age: 69 years
        Birth: 1861/05/22   Death: 1930/10/07   Burial: 1930/10/18
Site 8 Arminda E. Wallace   Age: 68 years
        Birth: 1861/08/06   Death: 1930/04/02   Burial: 1930/04/04
        Cause: Heart Disease   TS: Wife of James W. Wallace
Site 9 Llewellyn T. Mitchell   Died: South Hill, VA   Age: 83 years
        Birth: 1904/12/09   Death: 1988/11/05   Burial: 1988/11/12
Site 10 Eleanor R. Mitchell   Died: Leesburg, VA   Age: 54 years
        Birth: 1907/02/03   Death: 1961/08/23   Burial: 1961/08/27
        On stone with Llewellyn T. Mitchell
Site 11 Annie M. Mitchell   Age: 50 years
        Birth: 1871/11/27   Death: 1922/01/03   Burial: 1922/01/04
        Cause: Pneumonia   On stone with Henry Mitchell
Site 12 Henry Mitchell   Died: Leesburg, VA   Age: 84 years
        Birth: 1872/02/12   Death: 1956/09/29   Burial: 1956/10/01

Lot: 694   Owner: W.T. Fry   Purchased: 1925/05/30
Site 1 James William Stream   Died: Leesburg, VA   Age: 76 years
        Birth: 1899   Death: 1976/07/19   Burial: 1976/07/21
Site 2 Beulah M. Stream   Died: Leesburg, VA   Age: 71 years
        Birth: 1904   Death: 1975/12/23   Burial: 1975/12/28
        On stone with James William Stream
Site 3 Paul Clifton Stream   Died: Hagerstown, MD   Age: 60 years
        Birth: 1927   Death: 1987/12/22   Burial: 1987/12/28

Site 7	William N. Fry	Died: Baltimore, MD	Age: 72 years	
	Birth: 1902	Death: 1974/09/19	Burial: 1974/09/23	
Site 8	William Thomas Fry	Died: Lucketts, VA	Age: 87 years	
	Birth: 1868/11/24	Death: 1956/07/11	Burial: 1956/07/12	
Site 10	Anne May Fry		Age: 44 years	
	Birth: 1880/10/02	Death: 1925/05/30	Burial: 1925/06/01	
	Cause: Gall Stone		TS: Wife of William T. Fry	
Site 11	Charles Frank Stream	Died: Leesburg, VA	Age: 80 years	
	Birth: 1903/04/15	Death: 1984/01/19	Burial: 1984/01/23	
Site 12	Jessie F. Stream	Died: Leesburg, VA	Age: 84 years	
	Birth: 1905/11/29	Death: 1990/04/03	Burial: 1990/04/06	

Lot: 695 Owner: W.H. Howser   Purchased: 1925/06/26

Site 1	James Wilton Thayer	Died: Leesburg, VA	Age: 75 years
	Birth: 1913/01/01	Death: 1988/11/24	Burial: 1988/11/26
Site 2	Beatrice H. Thayer	Died: Leesburg, VA	Age: 69 years
	Birth: 1915/08/19	Death: 1984/09/30	Burial: 1984/10/02
	On stone with James Wilton Thayer		
Site 3	William Henry Howser		Age: 74 years
	Birth: 1870/09/18	Death: 1947/01/13	Burial: 1947/01/15
Site 5	Cora Carena Howser	Died: Ashburn, VA	Age: 76 years
	Birth: 1876/09/21	Death: 1953/08/02	Burial: 1953/08/06
Site 9	Miss Prissilla G. Howser	Died: Leesburg, VA	Age: 73 years
	Birth: 1913/10/30	Death: 1987/06/15	Burial: 1987/06/18
Site 10	Irene H. Howser	Died: Leesburg, VA	Age: 82 years
	Birth: 1906/08/28	Death: 1988/10/11	Burial: 1988/10/14
Site 11	Marshall C. Bush Howser		Died: Leesburg, VA
	Birth: 1901/02/02	Death: 1973/06/19	Burial: 1973/06/22
Site 12	Lloyd M. Howser	Cause: Convulsions	Age: 13 months
		Death: 1925/06/24	Burial: 1925/06/26
	TS: Son of Marshall C. & Irene L. Howser.		
	Age 1 year 1 month 25 days		
Site 12	Dorothy H. Jones		Died: Leesburg, VA
	Birth: 1926/02/13	Death: 1993/11/12	Burial: 1993/11/15

Lot: 696 Owner: I.S. Long   Purchased: 1906/03/28
Transfer 1: To Grace E. Hurst 1926/03/31

Site 2	William (Bill) G. Hurst		Age: 67 years
	Birth: 1914/12/13	Death: 1982/01/07	Burial: 1982/01/10
	Died: Leesburg, VA		TS: US ARMY
Site 3	John Harry Hurst	Cause: Pneumonia	Age: 36 years
	Birth: 1889	Death: 1926/03/30	Burial: 1926/04/01
Site 4	Grace E. Hurst	Died: Leesburg, VA	Age: 87 years
	Birth: 1890	Death: 1978/06/13	Burial: 1978/06/16
	On stone with John Harry Hurst		
Site 5	Henry D. Hurst	Died: Winchester, VA	Age: 65 years
	Birth: 1916/02/18	Death: 1981/08/19	Burial: 1981/08/21
Site 7	Joseph M. Settle		Age: 34 years
	Birth: 1907/12/11	Death: 1942/08/07	Burial: 1942/08/09

Site 8   Myrtle H. Settle   Died: Purcellville, VA   Age: 73 years
         No stone   Death: 1985/02/15

Lot: 697   Owner: Eugene D. Howell   Purchased: 1927/09/10
Transfer 1: To M.L. Beckner 1927/09/10
Site 1   James Howard Keyes   Cause: Arteriosclerosis   Age: 84 years
         Birth: 1857/04/18   Death: 1941/06/03   Burial: 1941/06/05
Site 3   Marcus L. Beckner Sr.   Died: Fairfax, VA   Age: 82 years
         Birth: 1883/07/22   Death: 1966/12/30   Burial: 1967/01/01
Site 4   Ella V. Beckner   Age: 94 years
         Birth: 1888/04/06   Death: 1982/09/16
         On stone with Marcus L. Beckner Sr.
Site 5   Marcus L. Beckner Jr.   Died: Falls Church, VA   Age: 53 years
         Birth: 1920   Death: 1974/02/03   Burial: 1974/02/06
Site 7   Catherine K. Beales   Died: Washington, DC   Age: 85 years
         Birth: 1891/01/29   Death: 1976/07/04   Burial: 1976/07/07
Site 8   Hugh William Cary   Age: 60 years
         Birth: 1915/08/22   Death: 1976/02/14   Burial: 1976/02/17
         Died: Arlington, VA   TS: TEC 5 US ARMY WWII
Site 9   Lillian H. Cary   Age: 77 years
         Birth: 1902/02/26   Death: 1979/02/15   TS: Daughter
Site 10 J. Howard Howell   TS: Son   Age: 59 years
         Birth: 1905/01/21   Death: 1964/04/08   Burial: 1964/04/11
Site 11 Eugene D. Howell   Age: 88 years
         Birth: 1876/05/06   Death: 1964/12/25   Burial: 1964/12/27
         Died: Leesburg, VA   TS: Father
Site 12 Rosa Florence Howell   TS: Mother   Age: 69 years
         Birth: 1879/03/27   Death: 1948/11/05   Burial: 1948/11/07

Lot: 698   Owner: Mrs. Julian R. Lee   Purchased: 1927/09/29
Site 4   Julian R. Lee   TS: Father   Age: 67 years
         Birth: 1886/12/20   Death: 1954/07/04
Site 5   Bessie Keyes Lee   Age: 80 years
         Birth: 1889/10/16   Death: 1969/12/03   Burial: 1969/12/06
         Died: Washington, DC   TS: Mother
Site 12 Ella M. Finch Keys   Age: 65 years
         Birth: 1863/06/10   Death: 1930/03/15   Burial: 1930/03/15
         Cause: Diphtheria   TS: Wife of Howard Keys

Lot: 699 E   Owner: Ernest F. Schulke   Purchased: 1927/06/15
Site 7   Ernest H. Schulke Jr.   Died: Purcellville, VA   Age: 57 years
         Birth: 1910   Death: 1968/02/04   Burial: 1968/02/07
Site 8   Glen Alan Darby   Age: 22 years
         Birth: 1961/10/23   Death: 1984/04/26   Burial: 1984/04/30
         Cause: Ditch cave-in   Died: Fairfax, VA
Site 9   James L. Maddox   Died: Fairfax, VA   Age: 65 years
         Birth: 1904   Death: 1969/05/02   Burial: 1969/05/05
Site 10 Dorthey Schulke Maddox   Age: 55 years
         Birth: 1914   Death: 1969/10/15   Burial: 1969/10/18
         Died: Ashburn, VA   On stone with James L. Maddox

Site 11 Ernest F. Schulke Sr.   Died: Leesburg, VA   Age: 81 years
         Birth: 1874   Death: 1955/12/14   Burial: 1955/12/14
Site 12 Lena Jackson Schulke   Age: 49 years
         Birth: 1877   Death: 1927/06/15   Burial: 1927/06/17
         Cause: Cirrhosis of Liver   On stone with Ernest F. Schulke Sr.

Lot: 699 W   Owner: John Tavenner   Purchased:
Site 3   Ernest Johnson   No stone   Age: 74 years
                                    Death: 1950/05/13   Burial: 1950/05/13
Site 4   John H. Tavenner   Age: 51 years
                                    Death: 1939/10/31   Burial: 1939/11/03
         Cause: Abdominal Hemorrhage   No stone
Site 5   Nancy Lee Tavenner   Cause: Accident   Age: 5 years
         Birth: 1922/12/12   Death: 1928/02/09   Burial: 1928/02/11
Site 6   Viola Johnson Tavenner   Died: Leesburg, VA   Age: 72 years
         Birth: 1898/02/05   Death: 1970/10/26   Burial: 1970/10/28

Lot: 700   Owner: Heirs of Jas. E.. Poole   Purchased: 1927/06/11
Site 1   James E. Poole   Cause: Meningitis   Age: 66 years
         Birth: 1860   Death: 1927/06/11   Burial: 1927/06/13
Site 2   Margaret Virginia Poole   Age: 66 years
         Birth: 1861   Death: 1927/12/26   Burial: 1927/12/28
         Cause: Heart Disease   On stone with James E. Poole
Site 3   William Keith Poole   Died: Montgomery, MD   Age: 94 years
         Birth: 1882/07/03   Death: 1977/06/10   Burial: 1977/06/13
Site 4   Carrie Bell Poole   Age: 79 years
         Birth: 1897/03/31   Death: 1976/08/01   Burial: 1976/08/04
         Died: Sandy Springs, MD   On stone with William Keith Poole
Site 5   Robert Burton Poole   Died: Baltimore, MD   Age: 64 years
         Birth: 1907/02/11   Death: 1972/01/16   Burial: 1972/01/19
Site 7   Floyd Foster Darne   Died: Ryan, VA   Age: 70 years
         Birth: 1888/08/30   Death: 1959/04/07   Burial: 1959/04/10
Site 8   Lillie P. Darne   Age: 68 years
         Birth: 1891/05/13   Death: 1959/09/27   Burial: 1959/09/30
         Died: Annandale, VA   On stone with Floyd Foster Darne
Site 9   Maurice Poole   Died: Arcola, VA   Age: 75 years
         Birth: 1902/06/02   Death: 1977/11/15   Burial: 1977/11/17

Lot: 701   Owner: Miscellaneous
Site 1   John E. Hessick   Cause: Suicide   Age: 24 years
         Birth: 1908/04/17   Death: 1933/02/01   Burial: 1933/02/04
         On stone with Annie C. & Edward W. Hessick
Site 1   Edward W. Hessick   Age: 79 years
         Born 1868/09/24   Death: 1948/03/02   Burial: 1948/03/04
Site 2   Annie C. Hessick   Age: 56 years
         Birth: 1876/10/04   Death: 1933/03/06   Burial: 1933/03/08
         Cause: Myocarditis   On stone with Edward W. Hessick
Site 3   John Carlton Pearson   Age: 73 years
         Birth: 1873/09/17   Death: 1947/09/05   Burial: 1947/09/07
         TS: Husband of Nannie B. Pearson

Site 4	Nannie B. Pearson		Age: 56 years	
	Birth: 1877/06/06	Death: 1933/02/22	Burial: 1933/02/24	
	Cause: Pastinar Cilum.	TS: Wife of John C. Pearson. Age 56 years		
Site 5	George W. Suddith	No stone	Age: 62 years	
	Cause: Myocarditis	Death: 1937/04/24	Burial: 1937/04/26	
Site 6	Effie V. Sudduth	No stone	Age: 87 years	
	Died: Washington, DC	Death: 1963/07/11	Burial: 1963/07/13	
Site 7	J. M. Dripps	No stone	Age: 70 years	
	Cause: Apoplexy	Death: 1934/09/26	Burial: 1934/09/28	
Site 8	Betty Anne Kearns	Cause: C. Chotis	Age: 4 years	
	No stone	Death: 1931/08/08	Burial: 1931/08/10	
Site 8	Child Kern	No stone	Age: 3 years	
	Cause: Myocarditis	Death: 1936/12/15	Burial: 1936/12/17	
Site 9	John Jorman	No stone	Age: 61 years	
	Cause: Pneumonia	Death: 1932/05/05	Burial: 1932/05/07	
Site 9	Betty Kerns	No stone	Age: 1 year	
	Cause: Acidosis	Death: 1932/08/15	Burial: 1932/08/17	
Site 10	Mabel V. Kern	No stone	Age: 28 years	
	Cause: Pneumonia	Death: 1931/04/11	Burial: 1931/04/13	
Site 11	William H. Spinks	No stone	Age: 85 years	
	Died: Leesburg, VA	Death: 1972/02/05	Burial: 1972/02/09	
Site 12	Lena L. Spinks	No stone	Age: 38 years	
	Cause: Pneumonia	Death: 1931/03/02	Burial: 1931/03/04	

Lot: 702   Owner: Miscellaneous

Site 1	C.A. Fling	IB: Infant of Ashby Fling	No stone	
	Cause: Stillborn	Death: 1942/12/23	Burial: 1942/12/23	
Site 1	Infant of Robert Jarmens	No stone	Age: 2 hours	
	Birth: 1947/10/03	Death: 1947/10/03	Burial: 1947/10/05	
Site 2	Infant Ashby Fling	Cause: Stillborn	No stone	
		Death: 1938/10/05	Burial: 1938/10/06	
Site 2	Child Blantz	Cause: Stillborn	No stone	
		Death: 1940/11/04	Burial: 1940/11/06	
Site 3	George L. Broderick	No stone	Age: 73 years	
	Cause: Fractured Skull	Death: 1936/11/08	Burial: 1936/11/10	
Site 4	Elsie Costello	Cause: S. Abortion	Age: 24 years	
	Birth: 1911	Death: 1936/10/28	Burial: 1936/10/30	
Site 5	Raymond L. Repass	No stone	Age: 10 months	
	Cause: Pneumonia	Death: 1935/12/17	Burial: 1935/12/19	
Site 5	Child of Mr. Gordon	Cause: Marasmus Diarrhea	Age: 3 months	
	No stone	Death: 1940/10/01	Burial: 1940/10/03	
Site 7	Clarence D. Bell Jr.		Age: 1 month	
	Birth: 1931/06/09	Death: 1931/07/31	Burial: 1931/08/02	
	Cause: Pneumonia		TS: Son of C.D. & S.E. Bell	
Site 8	Clifford D. Sutphin	Cause: Acidosis	Age: 10 months	
		Death: 1936/09/19	Burial: 1936/09/20	
	TS: Son of K.G. & C.T. Sutphin. Age 10 months			

Site 8   Peggy Ann Sutphin   Cause: Diarrhea   Age: 4 months
                               Death: 1937/08/04   Burial: 1937/08/06
          TS: Child of K.G. & C.T. Sutphin. Age 5 months
Site 9   Boldon D. Sutphin   Age: 62 years
          Birth: 1891/06/01   Death: 1952/07/02   Burial: 1952/07/05
Site 10   Mabel C. Sutphin   Cause: Uremic Poisoning   Age: 37 years
          Birth: 1894/03/14   Death: 1931/06/15   Burial: 1931/06/17
Site 11   Steven Hampton Reavis Died: Leesburg, VA   TS: "Coach"
          Birth: 1969/06/12   Death: 1993/06/24   Burial: 1993/06/26

Lot: 703 Owner: Miscellaneous
Site 1   Child Miller   Cause: Pneumonia   No stone
                               Death: 1939/12/30   Burial: 1940/01/02
Site 1   Child Russell   Cause: Stillborn   No stone
                               Death: 1940/06/30   Burial: 1940/07/01
Site 2   Annie Gregg Smith   Died: Leesburg, VA   Age: 69 years
          Birth: 1884   Death: 1953/12/25   Burial: 1953/12/28
Site 3   George Gregg   Cause: Cerebral Hemorrhage Age: 77 years
          Birth: 1863/09/23   Death: 1941/07/25   Burial: 1941/07/27
Site 4   Mrs. Mary E. Wallace   Age: 79 years
                               Death: 1939/03/22   Burial: 1939/03/24
          Cause: Cerebral Hemorrhage   IB: Mrs. L.K. Wallace No stone
Site 5   William T. Dawson   Age: 73 years
          Birth: 1865   Death: 1940/02/23   Burial: 1940/02/25
Site 6   Cora V. Dawson   Age: 89 years
          Birth: 1872   Death: 1960/02/05   Burial: 1960/02/07
          Died: Waterford, VA   On stone with William T. Dawson
Site 7   William V. Best   Cause: Cellulitis   Age: 70 years
          Birth: 1866   Death: 1936/02/20   Burial: 1936/02/22
Site 8   Phoebe Ann Thompson Best   Age: 79 years
          Birth: 1876   Death: 1955/08/12   Burial: 1955/08/12
          Died: Greenbelt, MD   On stone with William V. Best
Site 9   Mrs. Ella P. Smith   No stone   Age: 73 years
          Cause: Pneumonia   Death: 1936/11/08   Burial: 1936/11/10
Site 10   Lucy A. Jacobs   No stone   Age: 76 years
          Cause: C. D?   Death: 1936/12/04   Burial: 1936/12/06
Site 11   Eugenia F. Mooney   Cause: Cardiac Renal Disease Age: 71 years
          No stone   Death: 1936/12/21   Burial: 1936/12/23
Site 12   Adams   No stone   Age: 24 years
                               Death: 1972/09/03

Lot: 704 Owner: Miscellaneous
Site 1   Ella S. (Ethel Lula) Parsons   Age: 44 years
          Birth: 1898   Death: 1942/03/27   Burial: 1942/03/29
Site 1   Child Hall   Cause: Stillborn   No stone
                               Death: 1948/03/25   Burial: 1948/03/27
Site 2   George William Mock Age: 67 years
          Birth: 1871   Death: 1938/12/06   Burial: 1938/12/08
          Cause: Heart Failure

Site 3	Lucy Lee Palmer Mock		Age: 70 years
	Birth: 1878	Death: 1951/06/07	Burial: 1951/06/09
	On stone with George William Mock		
Site 4	Airlines Corp. Penn.	Cause: Plane Accident	No stone
	Died: Lovettsville, VA	Death: 1940/08/31	Burial: 1940/09/02
Site 5	Morgan Green Spurlock		Age: 40 years
	Birth: 1904/05/26	Death: 1944/07/07	Burial: 1944/07/09
Site 6	Rest Hipe Hottel	Died: L.C.H. Leesburg, VA	Age: 75 years
	No stone	Death: 1962/05/24	Burial: 1962/05/26
Site 7	James Z. Parsons	Birth: 1898	Death: 1985
Site 7	Joseph C. Smith	No stone	Age: 68 years
	Cause: Influenza	Death: 1937/02/23	Burial: 1937/02/24
Site 8	Henry Russell Mock	Cause: Heart	Age: 63 years
	Birth: 1874	Death: 1937/05/14	Burial: 1937/05/16
	On stone with James H. Mock & Mary Elizabeth Mock		
Site 9	James H. Mock		Removed from Waterford
	Birth: 1841/07/14	Death: 1911/10/27	
Site 9	Mary Elizabeth Mock		Removed from Waterford
	Birth: 1845	Death: 1929	On stone with James H. Mock
Site 10	Mrs. M. J. Hottle	No stone	Age: 52 years
	Cause: Cancer	Death: 1938/03/24	Burial: 1938/03/26
Site 11	Annie F. Enery Buttlery	No stone	Age: 18 years
	Cause: Eclampsia	Death: 1938/10/05	Burial: 1938/10/07
site 12	Albert M. Kline Jr.	IB: Child of Al Kline	Age: 1 year
	Birth: 1940/03/24	Death: 1941/03/24	Burial: 1941/03/26
Site 12	Gibson H. Kline		Age: 40 years
	Birth: 1934/03/16	Death: 1974/08/31	Burial: 1974/09/14
	Died: Leesburg, VA		TS: SP 3 US ARMY
Site 12	Albert M. Kline		TS: F1 US NAVY WWI
	Birth: 1900/04/27	Death: 1976/08/26	

Lot: 705 E   Owner: Garnet G. Stewart   Purchased: 1933/11/20

Site 7	William L. Rothrock		Died: Leesburg, VA
	Birth: 1912/01/10	Death: 1994/10/01	Burial: 1994/10/05
Site 10	Charles Lee Gill	Cause: Fractured Skull	Age: 19 years
	Birth: 1914/01/13	Death: 1933/11/19	Burial: 1933/11/21
Site 11	Emma F. Gill		Age: 72 years
	Birth: 1891/09/14	Death: 1964/08/25	Burial: 1964/08/27
	Died: Leesburg, VA		On stone with Luther W. Gill
Site 12	Luther W. Gill	Died: Manassas, VA	Age: 86 years
	Birth: 1887/02/19	Death: 1973/04/17	Burial: 1973/04/20

Lot: 705 W   Owner: George Gill   Purchased: 1931/02/27

Site 1	George W. Gill	No stone	Age: 73 years
	Died: Leesburg, VA	Death: 1963/02/04	Burial: 1963/02/06
Site 2	Essie May Gill	No stone	Age: 50 years
		Death: 1946/09/10	Burial: 1946/09/12
Site 3	George R. Gill 3rd		Age: 1 year
	Cause: Pneumonia	Death: 1938/01/09	Burial: 1938/01/11
	IB: Infant of George Gill		No stone

Site 4   Cora B. Gill   Cause: Cerebral Hemorrhage   Age: 64 years
         No stone   Death: 1931/12/15   Burial: 1931/12/17
Site 5   George W. Gill Jr.   No stone   Age: 75 years
         Cause: Hemorrhage   Death: 1931/02/26   Burial: 1931/02/28
Site 6   Alice Skenker Best   No stone   Age: 48 years
                                   Death: 1957/03/07

Lot: 706 E   Owner: John G. Franklin   Purchased: 1928/04/21
Transfer: W to John K. Kerns & George Scott 1928/04/23
Site 10 Thomas F. Franklin   Age: 34 years
         Birth: 1917   Death: 1951/12/10   Burial: 1951/12/12
Site 11 John G. Franklin   Age: 69 years
         Birth: 1876   Death: 1946/05/12   Burial: 1946/05/14
Site 12 Rebecca Fannie Franklin   Age: 62 years
         Birth: 1876   Death: 1940/05/22   Burial: 1940/05/24
         Cause: Coronary Occlusion   On stone with John G. Franklin

Lot: 706 W   Owner: John K. Kerns & George Scott   1928/04/03
Site 1   John K. Kerns   Cause: Poison   Age: 52 years
         Birth: 1879/02/21   Death: 1931/07/17   Burial: 1931/07/19
Site 1   Sarah I. Kerns   On stone with John K. Kerns   Age: 63 years
         Birth: 1880/01/30   Death: 1943/06/27   Burial: 1943/06/29
Site 1   Baby Boy Beauchamp
         Birth: 1948/10/19   Death: 1948/10/19   Burial: 1948/10/20
         Cause: Stillborn   IB: Stanley H. Beauchamp
Site 3   George E. Scott Sr.   TS: "Father"   Age: 53 years
         Birth: 1892/04/23   Death: 1945/02/12   Burial: 1945/02/14
Site 4   Mary Ruth Scott Creamer   Age: 85 years
         Birth: 1905/10/01   Death: 1991/08/01   Burial: 1991/08/05
                                   Died: Clinton, MD   TS: "Mother"
Site 5   Dorthy Isable Scott Beauchamp   Age: 57 years
         Birth: 1926/03/02   Death: 1983/10/23   Burial: 1983/10/26
                                   Died: Montross, VA
Site 6   Milton L. Scott   Cause: Pneumonia   Age: 42 years
         Birth: 1894/02/18   Death: 1937/01/10   Burial: 1937/01/13
Site 6   Robert Scott   No stone   Age: 33 years
         Cause: Fractured Skull   Death: 1938/10/09   Burial: 1938/10/22

Lot: 707 E   Owner: Mrs. Essie Slack   Purchased: 1929/08/26
Site 7   Baby Slack   No stone   Age: 32 hours
                                   Death: 1949/04/05   Burial: 1949/04/05
Site 9   Clarence E. Slack   Cause: Accident   Age: 33 years
         Birth: 1895/10/15   Death: 1929/08/25   Burial: 1929/09/27
Site 11 Essie I. Slack Redmond   Died: Charles Town, WV   Age: 88 years
         Birth: 1897/08/25   Death: 1986/07/27   Burial: 1986/07/30
Site 12 Golden A. Redman   Died: Washington, DC   Age: 61 years
         Birth: 1898/01/21   Death: 1959/03/23   Burial: 1959/03/25

Lot: 707 W   Owner: R.E. Harper   Purchased: 1931/01/15
Site 1   Helen Lee Corley   Age: 4 years
         Birth: 1926/10/23   Death: 1931/01/14   Burial: 1931/01/16
         Cause: Scarlet Fever   TS: Daughter of James R. & Carrie Corley
Site 2   Raymond C. Heskett   Died: Prince Frederick, MD   Age: 69 years
         Birth: 1910   Death: 1980/06/17   Burial: 1980/06/20
Site 3   Carrie Lee Heskett   Age: 78 years
         Birth: 1905   Death: 1983/12/25   Burial: 1983/12/29
         Died: Frederick, MD   On stone with Raymond C. Heskett
Site 4   Thomas D. Miles   Age: 67 years
         Birth: 1916/01/18   Death: 1983/07/08   Burial: 1983/07/12
         Died: Prince Frederick, MD   TS: US NAVY WWII
Site 5   Elsie M. Palmer   No stone   Age: 85 years
         Died: Annapolis, MD   Death: 1987/10/13   Burial: 1988/07/27

Lot: 708   Owner: Paul G. DeHart   Purchased: 1928/03/10
Site 1   Robert DeHart   No stone   Age: 21 years
         Cause: Diabetes Mellitus Death: 1940/12/29   Burial: 1941/01/01
Site 2   Paul G. DeHart   Cause: Nephritis   Age: 71 years
         Birth: 1859/09/25   Death: 1931/03/30   Burial: 1931/04/02
Site 3   Martha A. DeHart   Age: 57 years
         Birth: 1870/10/24   Death: 1928/04/25   Burial: 1928/04/27
         Cause: Pyelitis   On stone with Paul G. DeHart
Site 5   Claude Henry DeHart   Died: Chantilly, VA   Age: 64 years
         Birth: 1897/02/02   Death: 1961/11/24   Burial: 1961/11/27
Site 6   Mrs. Ruth E. DeHart   Age: 35 years
         Birth: 1900/09/20   Death: 1936/02/15   Burial: 1936/02/18
         Cause: Septicemia   On stone with Claude Henry DeHart
Site 11 Paul L. DeHart   No stone   Age: 4 years
                                  Death: 1925/09/24   Burial: 1924/09/26
         Moved from Lot 211 March 24, 1949, two in same grave
Site 11 L. G. DeHart   No stone   Age: 13 days
         Cause: Pneumonia   Death: 1927/03/17   Burial: 1927/03/19
         Moved from Lot 211 March 24, 1949, two in same grave
Site 11 Margaret M. Simmons   No stone   Age: 28 weeks
         Cause: Malnutrition   Death: 1928/03/18   Burial: 1928/03/20
Site 12 Martha Simmons   No stone   Age: 4 years
         Cause: Pneumonia   Death: 1928/03/10   Burial: 1928/03/12
Site 12 Infant DeHart   Cause: Bronchial Pneumonia   Age: 2 days
         No stone   Death: 1932/12/10   Burial: 1932/12/10

Lot: 709 E   Owner: E.J. Godbold   Purchased: 1930/03/25
Site 9   Edwin Joslyn Godbold   Cause: Angina Pectoris   Age: 70 years
         Birth: 1869   Death: 1939/07/04   Burial: 1939/07/07
Site 10 Mary D. Godbold   Age: 85 years
         Birth: 1871   Death: 1957/03/25
Site 11 Mary H. Godbold   Age: 64 years
         Birth: 1908   Death: 1972/08/16

Lot: 709 W   Owner: Arthur H. McPherson   Purchased: 1930/04/09
Site 3   Arthur H. McPherson   Cause: Carcinoma   Age: 75 years
         Birth: 1861   Death: 1937/09/25   Burial: 1937/09/27
Site 4   Ida C. McPherson   Died: Manassas, VA   Age: 88 years
         Birth: 1880   Death: 1968/08/18   Burial: 1968/08/21
         On stone with Arthur H. McPherson
Site 5   Elmore Lee McPherson   Age: 71 years
         Birth: 1898/02/08   Death: 1969/11/30   Burial: 1969/12/04
         Died: Martinsburg, WV   TS: Virginia PVT US ARMY WWII
Site 6   William Henry Lowe   Age: 70 years
         Birth: 1848   Death: 1931/08/27   Burial: 1931/08/29
         Cause: Cerebral Hemorrhage   TS: "Father"

Lot: 710   Owner: Izetta Gardner Bowers   Purchased: 1927/08/25
Site 3   Harry Samuel Bowers   Cause: Heart Failure   Age: 62 years
         Birth: 1879/04/05   Death: 1940/07/11   Burial: 1940/07/14

Lot: 711 E   Owner: Athoel Daymude   Purchased: 1927/07/01
Site 8   Athoel Edward Daymude Died: Washington, DC   Age: 63 years
         Birth: 1906/01/11   Death: 1969/03/20   Burial: 1969/03/21
Site 9   Mary E. Daymude   Age: 55 years
         Birth: 1903/09/29   Death: 1959/02/25   Burial: 1959/02/28
         Died: Washington, DC   On stone with Athoel E. Daymude
Site 10 Mrs. Luvenia Augusta Daymude   Age: 79 years
         Birth: 1871   Death: 1950/04/12   Burial: 1950/04/16
         On stone with Edward L. Daymude
Site 12 Edward L. Daymude   Cause: Valvular Heart Disease Age: 81 years
         Birth: 1872   Death: 1953/07/18   Burial: 1953/07/20

Lot: 711 W   Owner: W.J. Daymude   Purchased: 1926/11/17
Site 3   James J. Daymude   Died: Prince George Co., MD   Age: 51 years
         Birth: 1923/05/14   Death: 1974/06/11   Burial: 1974/06/15
Site 4   Nettie A. Daymude   Age: 70 years
         Birth: 1898/02/27   Death: 1968/12/01   Burial: 1968/12/04
         Died: Washington, DC   On stone with Willie Jacob Daymude
Site 5   Willie Jacob Daymude
         Birth: 1898/07/23   Death: 1949/02/05   Burial: 1949/02/07
Site 6   Willie J. Daymude Jr. Cause: Surgical Neck   Age: 4 days
         Birth: 1926/11/12   Death: 1926/11/16   Burial: 1926/11/18
Site 6   James Lowe Daymude   Death: 1958/06/09   Burial: 1958/06/10
         Cause: Stillborn   Died: Warrenton, VA   No stone

Lot: 712 E   Owner: Elizabeth T. Reynolds   Purchased: 1926/08/06
Site 7   Alex W. Thompson   No stone   Age: 46 years
         Cause: Pneumonia   Death: 1927/03/23   Burial: 1927/03/25
Site 9   John H. Reynolds   Age: 54 years
         Birth: 1873/01/09   Death: 1927/01/13   Burial: 1927/01/16
         Cause: Tuberculosis   TS: Co. F 1 IDA INF Spanish American War
Site 10 Elizabeth T. Reynolds No stone   Age: 60 years
         Cause: N. Steusis   Death: 1931/11/30   Burial: 1931/12/02

Lot: 712 W Owner: John W. Connor   Purchased: 1926/08/10

Site 3 John William Connor   Age: 69 years
        Birth: 1876   Death: 1945/10/27   Burial: 1945/10/29
Site 4 Hattie E. Connor   Age: 86 years
        Birth: 1884   Death: 1971/07/18   Burial: 1971/07/20
        Died: Leesburg, VA   On stone with John W. Connor
Site 5 Margaret Helen Connor Cause: Malnutrition   Age: 15 years
        Birth: 1910   Death: 1926/08/10   Burial: 1926/08/12
Site 6 William Jerome Connor Cause: C. Spinal   Age: 26 years
        Birth: 1908   Death: 1935/03/16   Burial: 1935/03/18

Lot: 713 Owner: T.R. Tillett   Purchased: 1923/12/26

Site 4 Hugh Albert Tillett   Age: 71 years
        Birth: 1885/01/28   Death: 1957/11/30   Burial: 1957/12/03
        Cause: Old Age   Died: Martinsburg, VA
Site 5 Mary L. Tillett   Died: Hamilton, VA   Age: 93 years
        Birth: 1891/06/02   Death: 1984/08/04   Burial: 1984/08/07
Site 6 Annie Taylor Slack   Cause: Heart Disease   Age: 76 years
        Birth: 1849/05/04   Death: 1926/03/15   Burial: 1926/03/17
Site 7 Harry Randolph Tillett Died: Leesburg, VA   Age: 62 years
        Birth: 1893/01/01   Death: 1955/05/03   Burial: 1955/05/04
Site 8 Eugenia Anderson Tillett   Age: 73 years
        Birth: 1900/06/14   Death: 1973/12/26   Burial: 1973/12/28
        Died: Fairfax, VA   On stone with Harry Randolph Tillett
Site 9 Samuel C. Tillett   Cause: Pneumonia   Age: 79 years
        Birth: 1851   Death: 1930/12/12   Burial: 1930/12/14
Site 11 Orra Lee V. Tillett   Cause: Cerebral Hemorrhage   Age: 80 years
        Birth: 1858   Death: 1939/02/11   Burial: 1939/02/13
Site 12 Jean Berry Tillett   Died: Lynchburg, VA   Age: 50 years
        Birth: 1927/03/22   Death: 1977/09/06   Burial: 1977/09/08

Lot: 714 Owner: J.A. Franklin   Purchased: 1924/01/14

Site 2 Mrs. Winfred Lee Goodhart   Age: 45 years
        Birth: 1897   Death: 1942/05/14   Burial: 1942/05/16
Site 3 Lena D. Franklin   Died: Herndon, VA   Age: 93 years
        Birth: 1883   Death: 1976/12/29   Burial: 1976/12/31
Site 4 John A. Franklin   Cause: Myocarditis   Age: 79 years
        Birth: 1858   Death: 1938/02/01   Burial: 1938/02/03
Site 5 Mrs. Mary Louise Hoskinson Franklin   Age: 69 years
        Birth: 1855/09/10   Death: 1924/01/14   Burial: 1924/01/16
        Cause: Bronchitis   TS: Wife of John A. Franklin
Site 8 Reginald Ernest Marshall Died: Martinsburg, WV   Age: 79 years
        Birth: 1914   Death: 1993/12/23   Burial: 1993/12/28
Site 10 Vernon G. Franklin   Cause: Pneumonia   Age: 39 years
        Birth: 1887   Death: 1927/04/02   Burial: 1927/04/04
Site 11 Roger O. Sowers   IB: Mrs.   Age: 27 years
        Birth: 1909   Death: 1937/07/25   Burial: 1937/07/27
Site 12 Irwin G. Hoskinson   Age: 72 years
        Birth: 1874/04/03   Death: 1946/04/03   Burial: 1946/04/05

Lot: 715 E   Owner: Maj. William Burr Harrison   1922/09/12
Site   Mary B. Harrison   TS: Remains buried in Cuba
           Birth: 1907/12/13   Death: 1953/08/25
Site 8   Lelia W. Harrison   Cause: Cerebral Thrombosis   Age: 58 years
           Birth: 1880/06/09   Death: 1938/11/14   Burial: 1938/11/16
Site 11   Maj. William Burr Harrison   Age: 55 years
           Birth: 1871/02/27   Death: 1926/10/20   Burial: 1926/10/22
           Cause: Cirrhosis   TS: Major US ARMY
Site 12   Sarah Powell Harrison   Cause: Unknown   Age: 14 years
           Birth: 1908/08/02   Death: 1922/09/11   Burial: 1922/09/12

Lot: 715 W   Owner: Geo. C. Carter   Purchased: 1929/06/13
Site 2   George C. Carter   Age: 81 years
           Birth: 1865   Death: 1947/06/07   Burial: 1947/06/09
Site 4   Mary Eyre Carter   Age: 63 years
           Birth: 1865   Death: 1929/10/24   Burial: 1929/10/26
           Cause: Cancer   TS: Wife of George C. Carter of Oatlands.

Lot: 716 E   Owner: F.A. Thompson   Purchased: 1922/03/21
Site 7   John W. Thompson   Cause: Intestria Phthisis   Age: 72 years
           Birth: 1855/02/13   Death: 1928/01/13   Burial: 1928/01/15
Site 8   Franklin Allen Thompson   Age: 83 years
           Birth: 1861   Death: 1945/03/22   Burial: 1945/03/24
Site 9   Mary Geneva H. Thompson   Age: 73 years
           Birth: 1873   Death: 1946/11/20   Burial: 1946/11/22
           On stone with Franklin Allen Thompson
Site 10   Miss Maud E. Thompson   Age: 44 years
           Birth: 1905/02/07   Death: 1949/05/07   Burial: 1949/05/09
Site 12   Etta M. Thompson   Cause: Influenza   Age: 29 years
           Birth: 1892/04/17   Death: 1922/03/20   Burial: 1922/03/21

Lot: 716 W   Owner: J.W. Perry   Purchased: 1936/03/07
Site 1   Adley C. Cooper   Died: Leesburg, VA   Age: 76 years
           Birth: 1892/11/18   Death: 1966/02/07   Burial: 1966/02/10
site 2   Mary Perry Cooper   Age: 68 years
           Birth: 1892/11/18   Death: 1973/10/22   Burial: 1973/10/25
           Died: Leesburg, VA   On stone with Adley C. Cooper
Site 3   Louise Perry Rawlings   Age: 24 years
           Birth: 1912   Death: 1937/03/27   Burial: 1937/03/29
           Cause: Auto Accident   TS: Wife of Leith Rawlings
Site 4   John William Perry   Age: 70 years
           Birth: 1875/12/22   Death: 1946/07/31   Burial: 1946/08/02
Site 5   Maud C. Perry   Age: 57 years
           Birth: 1878/12/26   Death: 1936/03/07   Burial: 1936/03/09
           Cause: C. ditistion   On stone with John William Perry

Lot: 717   Owner: Charles Beall   Purchased: 1919/07/05
Site 1   Charles Richard Beall   Died: Washington, DC   Age: 79 years
           Birth: 1879/05/22   Death: 1958/06/10   Burial: 1958/06/13

Site 2   Orra L. Beall   Age: 77 years
         Birth: 1885/10/02   Death: 1963/08/20   Burial: 1963/08/22
         Died: Washington, DC   On stone with Charles Richard Beall
Site 3   Virginia Beall Weeks   Age: 55 years
         Birth: 1908/05/23   Death: 1964/03/15   Burial: 1964/03/18
         Died: Washington, DC   On stone with William A. Weeks
Site 5   William A. Weeks   Died: Washington, DC   Age: 61 years
         Birth: 1906/03/17   Death: 1967/11/17   Burial: 1967/11/21
Site 10 Alvarado Hardy   Age: 75 years
         Birth: 1856/11/15   Death: 1932/06/14   Burial: 1932/06/17
         Cause: Arteriosclerosis   TS: Husband of Hattie Jane Hardy
Site 11 Mrs. Hattie Jane Hardy TS: Wife of Alvarado Hardy Age: 68 years
         Birth: 1852/06/19   Death: 1921/03/06   Cause: Paralysis
Site 12 Leonard Gray Hardy   Age: 29 years
         Birth: 1890/07/25   Death: 1919/07/04
         TS: Son of Alvarado & Hattie Jane Hardy

Lot: 718   Owner: Benj. J. Fletcher   Purchased: 1919/01/06

Site 0   James H. Fletcher   Age: 3 years
         Birth: 1916/07/20   Death: 1919/01/06
         Cause: Flu   TS: Son of B.J. & Bertha Fletcher
Site 8   Mary Fletcher Storke   Died: Edgewater, MD   Age: 86 years
         Birth: 1899/08/16   Death: 1985/12/21   Burial: 1985/12/27
Site 9   Nina Fletcher Forry   Died: Falls Church, VA   Age: 81 years
         Birth: 1904/03/09   Death: 1985/10/01   Burial: 1985/10/04
Site 10 Benjamin James Fletcher Died: Leesburg, VA   Age: 72 years
         Birth: 1880/12/16   Death: 1953/12/09   Burial: 1953/12/11
Site 11 Bertha F. Fletcher   Died: Leesburg, VA   Age: 81 years
         Birth: 1879/10/02   Death: 1961/07/11   Burial: 1961/07/13

Lot: 719   Owner: Edwin E. Garrett   Purchased: 1918/04/30

Site 4   Edwin Enoch Garrett Jr. Died: Richmond, VA   Age: 69 years
         Birth: 1905   Death: 1975/04/27   Burial: 1975/05/01
Site 5   Edwin Enoch Garrett   Birth: 1870/10/21   Death: 1957/01/10
Site 6   Agnes Dibrell Garrett   Died: Leesburg, VA   Age: 79 years
         Birth: 1877/12/22   Death: 1957/12/11   Burial: 1957/12/14
Site 8   Margaret F. Garrett   No stone   Age: 72 years
         Died: Richmond, VA   Death: 1976/04/23   Burial: 1976/04/26
Site 9   William Francis Garrett   Age: 53 years
         Birth: 1866/01/10   Death: 1919/12/05   Cause: Heart Trouble
Site 10 Rosa Virginia Garrett   Age: 78 years
         Birth: 1869/04/25   Death: 1947/10/20   Burial: 1947/10/22
         TS: Nee Cox.   On stone with William Francis Garrett
Site 11 Catherine Cox Garrett   Died: Leesburg, VA   Age: 60 years
         Birth: 1895/03/15   Death: 1955/04/18   Burial: 1955/04/18
         On stone with William Francis Garrett & Rosa Virginia Garrett

Lot: 720   Owner: Wallace George   Purchased: 1917/01/18

Site 1   Annie, Child of Wallace George   Stone unreadable
         Birth: 1905/04/11   Death: 1905/05/28   Burial: 1905/05/29

Site 1   Norman George   Age: 18 months
         Birth: 1922/09/15   Death: 1923/07/11   Burial: 1923/07/13
         TS: Son of Wallace & Sallie E. George
Site 2   Edward Clayton George   Age: 2 months
         Birth: 1920/08/08   Death: 1920/11/01
         Cause: Auto Intoxication   TS: Son of Wallace & Sallie E. George
Site 3   Wallace George Sr.   Cause: Old Age   Age: 92 years
         Birth: 1845/04/19   Death: 1938/03/13   Burial: 1938/03/15
Site 5   Sallie E. George   Age: 46 years
         Birth: 1881/07/23   Death: 1928/03/22   Burial: 1928/03/24
         Cause: Valins Disease   TS: Wife of Wallace George
Site 6   Wallace West George Sr. Died: Washington, DC   Age: 56 years
         Birth: 1903   Death: 1960/06/17   Burial: 1960/06/19

Lot: 721   Owner: John W. Shry   Purchased: 1916/08/07
Site 0   Harry Thornton Shry   Age: 2 years
         Birth: 1922/08/12   Death: 1924/07/13   Burial: 1924/07/14
         Cause: Accident   TS: Son of Charlie A. & Helen Shry
Site 3   Priscilla E. Shry   Age: 75 years
         Birth: 1849/12/23   Death: 1925/07/13   Burial: 1925/07/15
         Cause: Tuberculosis   TS: Wife of J.W. Shry
Site 5   J.W. Shry   Birth: 1850/05/09   Death: 1933/03/29
Site 7   Harry T. Shry   Died: Winchester, VA   Age: 89 years
         Birth: 1881/08/11   Death: 1971/05/28   Burial: 1971/05/28
Site 8   Edith Virginia Shry   Died: Paeonian Springs, VA   Age: 74 years
         Birth: 1881/12/01   Death: 1956/07/06   Burial: 1956/07/06
Site 10 Charles A. Shry   Cause: Endocarditis   Age: 55 years
         Birth: 1875/02/26   Death: 1931/01/21   Burial: 1931/01/23
Site 11 Lillian Helen T. Shry   Age: 67 years
         Birth: 1882/03/29   Death: 1949/11/14   Burial: 1949/11/16

Lot: 722   Owner: Geo. W. Titus   Purchased: 1916/03/18
Site 0   Roger Titus   TS: Son of G.W. & Ellen Titus Age: 42 years
         Birth: 1877/01/02   Death: 1919/05/30   Cause: Consumption
Site 0   George W. Titus   Cause: Apoplexy   Age: 78 years
         Birth: 1844/12/16   Death: 1922/09/18   Burial: 1922/09/19
Site 1   William F. Titus   Died: Leesburg, VA   Age: 69 years
         Birth: 1913/12/12   Death: 1983/04/06   Burial: 1983/04/09
Site 2   Annabel H. Titus   Age: 76 years
         Birth: 1912/08/19   Death: 1988/10/16   Burial: 1988/10/19
         Died: Leesburg, VA   On stone with William F. Titus
Site 10 Mrs. India R. Titus   On stone with George W. Titus Age: 64 years
         Birth: 1878/08/29   Death: 1943/04/20   Burial: 1943/04/22

Lot: 723   Owner: V.T. Bly   Purchased: 1918/10/16
Site 9   Merwyn Cluxton Bly   Died: Fairfax, VA
         Birth: 1898/03/20   Death: 1995/01/17   Burial: 1995/06/13
Site 10 Coral Erickson Bly   Age: 59 years
         Birth: 1922/03/03   Death: 1981/01/18   Burial: 1981/06/28
         On stone with Robert Tuthill Bly

Site 10 Robert Tuthill Bly Died: Riverside, CA Age: 79 years
 Birth: 1902/12/06 Death: 1979/12/20 Burial: 1981/06/28
Site 11 Mrs. Chloe Cluxton Bly Age: 78 years
 Birth: 1874/01/14 Death: 1952/03/10 Burial: 1952/03/12
 TS: Wife of Vincent Tuthill Bly
Site 12 Vincent Tuthill Bly Age: 83 years
 Birth: 1868/03/15 Death: 1951/07/28 Burial: 1951/07/30

Lot: 724 Owner: Mrs. A.F. Shry   Purchased: 1916/12/01
Site 2 William Nelson Shry No stone Age: 9 months
 Cause: Intestinal Death: 1923/09/25 Burial: 1923/09/27
Site 3 A. F. Shry Cause: Accident Age: 60 years
 Birth: 1856/08/29 Death: 1916/11/29
Site 4 Catherine V. Shry Age: 64 years
 Birth: 1855/10/27 Death: 1919/11/10
 TS: Wife of Andrew F. Shry. Age 64 years 14 days
Site 5 Viola Shry Age: 76 years
 Birth: 1901 Death: 1977/08/26 Burial: 1977/08/30
 Died: Petersburg, VA TS: Wife of James W. Shry
Site 6 James W. Shry Died: Leesburg, VA Age: 83 years
 Birth: 1892 Death: 1975/11/27 Burial: 1975/12/01
Site 7 Victor C. Snoots Age: 26 years
 Birth: 1898/08/02 Death: 1925/07/09 Burial: 1925/07/11
 Cause: Appendicitis TS: Husband of Beatrice Snoots
Site 12 Alfred F. Shry Age: 3 years
 Birth: 1914/11/11 Death: 1917/11/04

Lot: 725 Owner: J.W. George   Purchased: 1916/05/17
Site 2 James W. George Cause: Myocarditis Age: 84 years
 Birth: 1847/11/07 Death: 1932/03/16 Burial: 1932/03/18
Site 4 Mrs. Flora Louisa George TS: Wife of James W. George
 Birth: 1853/09/10 Death: 1916/12/16
Site 5 Charles G. George Died: FL Age: 84 years
 Birth: 1876 Death: 1963/04/09 Burial: 1963/04/13
Site 6 Mary E. George Age: 99 years
 Birth: 1879 Death: 1979/03/19
 On stone with Charles G. George
Site 7 Infant of E.C. & B.C. Gibson No stone
 Cause: Stillborn Death: 1925/05/18 Burial: 1925/05/19
Site 8 Edward C. Gibson Died: Aldie, VA Age: 80 years
 Birth: 1883 Death: 1964/06/16 Burial: 1964/06/18
Site 9 Bessie George Gibson Age: 75 years
 Birth: 1882 Death: 1957/11/10 Burial: 1957/11/12
 Died: Leesburg, VA On stone with Edward C. Gibson

Lot: 726 Owner: Mrs. M.W. Howard   Purchased: 1919/01/04
Site 1 William Spencer Howard TS: Husband of Annie Blanche Hughart
 Birth: 1846 Death: 1919/12/06

Site 2   Oden Hughart Howard   Cause: Flu   Age: 31 years
         Birth: 1887   Death: 1919/01/04
         TS: Husband of Madeline Weeks.
         Son of Annie Blanche Hughart & W.S. Howard
Site 3   Mrs. Annie Hughart Howard   TS: Wife of William Spencer Howard
         Birth: 1857/03/14   Death: 1920/10/29   Burial: 1920/10/31
Site 3   Sarah Page Howard   Age: 49 years
         Birth: 1884/10/01   Death: 1934/03/16
         TS: Daughter of Annie Hughart & William Spencer Howard
Site 4   Josephine Page Howard   Died: Baltimore, MD   Age: 72 years
         Birth: 1911/06/11   Death: 1983/10/02   Burial: 1983/10/05
         TS: Daughter of William A. & Sara Wharton Howard
Site 5   Maj. William Alanson Howard   Age: 79 years
         Birth: 1882/02/14   Death: 1959/04/27   Burial: 1959/04/29
         Died: Baltimore, MD
Site 6   Sara Wharton Howard   Age: 78 years
         Birth: 1879/09/16   Death: 1958/09/15   Burial: 1958/09/17
         Died: Pikesville, MD   TS: Wife of William Alanson Howard

Lot: 727   Owner: Mrs. J.H. Williams   Purchased: 1919/04/11
Site 1   Alexander R. Johnson   Age: 62 years
         Birth: 1888/05/12   Death: 1950/12/25   Burial: 1950/12/28
Site 2   Lena I. Johnson   Age: 82 years
         Birth: 1888/07/19   Death: 1971/04/14   Burial: 1971/04/17
         On stone with Alexander R. Johnson
Site 4   Daisey H. Myers   Died: NC   Age: 80 years
         Birth: 1893/04/12   Death: 1973/07/22   Burial: 1973/07/27
Site 5   Rev. Charles Claude Myers   Age: 76 years
         Birth: 1879/10/24   Death: 1957/08/22
Site 6   Mary Agnes Williams Myers   Age: 60 years
         Birth: 1882/04/07   Death: 1943/06/13   Burial: 1943/06/15
Site 7   Sarah Elizabeth (Betty) Rutter   Age: 82 years
         Birth: 1849/11/24   Death: 1930/12/14   Burial: 1930/12/16
         Cause: Nephritis
Site 8   Joseph Ernest Williams   Died: Leesburg, VA   Age: 84 years
         Birth: 1891/01/22   Death: 1975/05/07   Burial: 1975/05/10
Site 9   Ada Williams   Age: 88 years
         Birth: 1895/02/06   Death: 1983/03/23   Burial: 1983/03/26
         Died: Baltimore, MD   On stone with Joseph Ernest Williams
Site 10 Harry Lacy   Age: 42 years
         Birth: 1909   Death: 1951/12/12   Burial: 1951/12/15
Site 11 John H. Williams   Cause: Apoplexy   Age: 58 years
         Birth: 1860/10/09   Death: 1919/04/10
Site 12 Mattie L. Williams   Age: 78 years
         Birth: 1855/08/18   Death: 1934/06/03   Burial: 1934/06/05
         Cause: Myocarditis   TS: Wife of John H. Williams

Lot: 728   Owner: Mrs. J.W. Plaster   Purchased: 1919/10/23
Site 1   W. E. Plaster   No stone   Age: 49 years
         Cause: Suicide   Death: 1936/06/19   Burial: 1936/06/21

Site 3 James W. Plaster   Cause: Cancer
        Birth: 1836/04/04   Death: 1919/10/30
Site 4 Sarah Marie Plaster   Age: 88 years
        Birth: 1853/10/20   Death: 1941/04/25   Burial: 1941/04/27
        On stone with James W. Plaster
Site 7 David Dixon Plaster   Age: 48 years
        Birth: 1892/09/29   Death: 1940/04/27   Burial: 1940/04/29
Site 8 Leiter Virginia Plaster   Age: 53 years
        Birth: 1893/08/23   Death: 1945/05/15   Burial: 1945/05/16
        On stone with David Dixon Plaster

Lot: 729 E   Owner: J.N. Sampsell   Purchased: 1922/06/19
Site 8 Yulie M. Sampsell   Death: 1989/07/29   Burial: 1989/08/02
                               Died: Orlando, FL   No stone
Site 9 J. Nixon Sampsell   Cause: Heart   Age: 68 years
        Birth: 1866   Death: 1935/09/22   Burial: 1935/09/24
Site 11 Mrs. Maiza M. Sampsell   Age: 61 years
        Birth: 1872   Death: 1933/03/28   Burial: 1933/04/01
        Cause: Myocarditis   IB: Mrs. J.N. Sampsell

Lot: 729 W   Owner: C.T. Sampsell & Mrs. Bessie Bruck 1922/06/19
Site 1 Frank C. Sampsell   Cause: Tuberculosis   Age: 54 years
        Birth: 1875   Death: 1929/07/11   Burial: 1929/07/13
Site 2 Mary B. Sampselle   Died: Manassas, VA   Age: 97 years
        Birth: 1875   Death: 1973/02/22   Burial: 1973/02/24
Site 3 Nannie Lavinia S. Marriott   Age: 75 years
                               Death: 1956/11/16   Burial: 1956/11/17
        Cause: Congestive Heart Failure
Site 6 Frances R. Sampselle   Died: Fairfax, VA   Age: 87 years
        Birth: 1902   Death: 1990/05/16   Burial: 1990/05/19

Lot: 730 E   Owner: Mrs. Alice Greene   Purchased: 1924/06/06
Site 8 Henry H. Gibbs   Age: 72 years
        Birth: 1878   Death: 1949/11/21   Burial: 1949/11/24
Site 9 Bessie V. Gibbs   Age: 88 years
        Birth: 1877   Death: 1965/07/21   Burial: 1965/07/24
        Died: Fairfax, VA   On stone with Henry H. Gibbs
Site 10 Jean Hazel   Age: 8 years
        Birth: 1923/12/07   Death: 1932/05/24   Burial: 1932/05/26
        Cause: Pneumonia   TS: Daughter of Calvert & Marion Hazel
Site 11 Frank I. Greene   Cause: Dropsy   Age: 55 years
        Birth: 1870   Death: 1925/02/20   Burial: 1925/02/22
Site 12 Mary Alice Greene   Died: Bethesda, MD   Age: 82 years
        Birth: 1873   Death: 1956/01/14   Burial: 1956/01/14

Lot: 730 W   Owner: Miscellaneous
Site 3 Edward Hugh Atwell   Died: Hyattsville, MD   No stone
        Birth: 1932/11/03   Death: 1995/04/04   Burial: 1995/04/07
Site 4 Edward C. Fletcher   No stone   Age: 72 years
                               Death: 1951/01/25   Burial: 1951/01/28

Site 6　Zofia Chwalowski　　No stone　　　　　　　　Age: 50 years
　　　　Died: Leesburg, VA　 Death: 1986/06/24　　　Burial: 1986/06/27

Lot: 731　Owner: Mrs. Wm. B. Casilear　　Purchased: 1924/03/15
Site 2　Raph A. Casilear　　　　　　　　　　　　　　Age: 2 years
　　　　Birth: 1924/12/24　　Death: 1926/11/09
　　　　Cause: Burns　　　　　　　　On stone with William B. Casilear
Site 3　William B. Casilear　Cause: Pneumonia　　 Age: 46 years
　　　　Birth: 1878/03/23　　Death: 1924/03/14　　 Burial: 1924/03/17
Site 4　Mrs. Kate Casilear Lowenbach　　　　　　　 Age: 77 years
　　　　Birth: 1886　　　　　 Death: 1963/12/04　　Burial: 1963/12/06
　　　　　　　　　　　　　　　Died: Leesburg, VA
Site 6　Helen C. Lofgren　　 Died: Washington, DC
　　　　Birth: 1911/01/07　　Death: 1968/01/06　　 Age: 56 years
　　　　　　　　　　　　　　　　　　　　　　　　　　Burial: 1968/01/08
Site 11　Martha E. Casilear　Died: Sugar Run, VA　 Age: 50 years
　　　　 Birth: 1930　　　　　Death: 1981/03/19　　 Burial: 1981/03/20

Lot: 732 E　Owner: T.L. & Ann M. Orrison　　　　 1925/07/16
Site 8　Della E. Newton　　　　　　　　　　　　　　Age: 63 years
　　　　Birth: 1918/01/24　　Death: 1981/06/23　　 Burial: 1981/06/26
　　　　Died: Richmond, VA　　　　　　　　　　　　 TS: "Mother"
Site 9　Ann Orrison Carson　　　　　　　　　　　　 Age: 90 years
　　　　Birth: 1883/01/22　　Death: 1973/08/27　　 Burial: 1973/08/29
Site 10　Boxter Duncan Orrison　　　　　　　　　　 Age: 52 years
　　　　 Birth: 1873/03/06　 Death: 1925/07/16　　 Burial: 1925/07/18

Lot: 732 W　Owner: Est. of S.J. Johnston　　Purchased: 1925/08/24
Site 2　Infant Son of Samuel J. & B.N. Johnston
　　　　　　　　　　　　　　　Death: 1920/05/15　　Burial: 1920/05/16
Site 2　Samuel J. Johnston　 Cause: Arteriosclerosis　Age: 71 years
　　　　Birth: 1853/08/30　　Death: 1925/05/29　　 Burial: 1925/05/31
Site 3　Stuart James Johnston　Cause: Appendicitis　 Age: 5 years
　　　　Birth: 1902/06/08　　Death: 1907/11/25
　　　　Moved from Lot 173 Oct. 1925.　　　　　　　No dates on stone
Site 3　Infant of John Allen & H.M. Johnston　　 Cause: Premature Birth
　　　　Birth: 1947/01/10　　Death: 1947/01/10　　 Burial: 1947/01/11
Site 3　Infant of John A. Johnston　　　　　　　　 Age: 11 hours
　　　　No stone　　　　　　 Death: 1948/12/19　　 Burial: 1948/12/21
Site 4　Alice Rebecca Johnston　Cause: Meningitis　 Age: 3 years
　　　　Birth: 1906/07/28　　Death: 1910/04/16
　　　　Removed from lot 173 Oct 1925　　　　　　 No dates on stone
Site 4　Beulah Neel Johnston　Cause: Tuberculosis　 Age: 2 years
　　　　Birth: 1916/11/09　　Death: 1919/01/15
　　　　Removed from lot 173 Oct. 1925　　　　　　No dates on stone
Site 5　Beulah Neel Johnston　Died: Leesburg, VA　 Age: 96 years
　　　　Birth: 1878/12/12　　Death: 1975/07/27　　 Burial: 1975/07/28

Lot: 733 E　Owner: James L. Higdon　　Purchased: 1926/08/28
Site 7　Lula Virginia Powers　Died: Alexandria, VA　Age: 70 years
　　　　Birth: 1890/03/14　　Death: 1958/06/07　　 Burial: 1958/06/10

Site 8 Raymond L. Crouch Cause: Fractured Skull Age: 2 years
        Birth: 1909/12/25   Death: 1931/04/26   Burial: 1931/04/28
Site 9 James L. Higdon   Cause: Nephritis   Age: 81 years
        Birth: 1854/04/05   Death: 1935/05/23   Burial: 1935/05/25
Site 10 Martha Alice Higdon Cause: Nephritis   Age: 73 years
        Birth: 1858/05/30   Death: 1927/04/27   Burial: 1927/04/29
Site 12 Archie R. Newton   Died: Leesburg, VA   Age: 81 years
        Birth: 1905/03/06   Death: 1986/05/05   Burial: 1986/05/08

Lot: 733 W Owner: Mrs. Mary R. Loy Purchased: 1927/02/01
Site 1 Robert S. Painter   Cause: Cancer of Liver Age: 48 years
        Birth: 1886/10/04   Death: 1935/03/17   Burial: 1935/03/19
Site 2 Edna B. Painter   Age: 86 years
        Birth: 1897/04/23   Death: 1983/08/08   Burial: 1983/08/11
        Died: Leesburg, VA   On stone with Robert S. Painter
Site 4 Ernesy L. Baker   Died: Frederick, MD   Age: 89 years
        Birth: 1894/03/04   Death: 1983/05/12   Burial: 1983/05/16
Site 5 Mary Loy Baker   Age: 92 years
        Birth: 1895/08/03   Death: 1987/10/04   Burial: 1987/10/07
        Died: Wheaton, MD   On stone with Ernesy L. Baker
Site 6 Carl A. Loy   Cause: Cerebral Hemorrhage Age: 33 years
        Birth: 1888/08/02   Death: 1927/01/28   Burial: 1927/01/29

Lot: 734 E Owner: Bessie V. Coughlin Purchased: 1928/04/25
Site 7 William M. Coughlin Cause: Apoplexy   Age: 55 years
        Birth: 1873/04/17   Death: 1928/04/24   Burial: 1928/04/26
Site 8 Bessie Virginia Coughlin Died: Leesburg, VA Age: 69 years
        Birth: 1884/12/14   Death: 1954/03/16   Burial: 1954/03/18

Lot: 734 W Owner: Mrs. Minnie Myers Fletcher 1928/05/22
Site 1 Arthur C. Harding Sr. Died: Leesburg, VA   Age: 66 years
        Birth: 1910/05/24   Death: 1976/10/13   Burial: 1976/10/15
Site 2 Eleanora Gray Harding
        Birth: 1915/09/07   Death: 1994/12/20   Burial: 1994/12/22
        Died: Leesburg, VA   On stone with Arthur C. Harding
Site 3 Mary Virginia Curtin Died: Leesburg, VA   Age: 68 years
        Birth: 1906/05/22   Death: 1975/03/07   Burial: 1975/03/10
Site 4 Charlotte Ellen Harding Died: Leesburg, VA Age: 8 years
        Birth: 1945/05/31   Death: 1953/10/14   Burial: 1953/10/21
        BP: Lists last name as Fletcher. No Fletcher on stone.
Site 5 Minnie Ellen Fletcher   Age: 74 years
        Birth: 1873/08/03   Death: 1948/06/04   Burial: 1948/06/06
Site 6 Charles F. Fletcher Cause: Septasimia   Age: 50 years
        TS: Aged 50 years   Death: 1928/05/20   Burial: 1928/05/22

Lot: 735 E Owner: Mrs. John M. Long Purchased: 1929/02/02
Site 7 Robert Joseph Long   Age: 75 years
        Birth: 1903/05/01   Death: 1979/04/25

Site 8   Ruby Kerwin Long   Age: 69 years
         Birth: 1907/01/13   Death: 1976/02/08   Burial: 1976/02/11
         Died: Leesburg, VA   On stone with Robert J. Long
Site 11 Bessie D. Long   Age: 89 years
         Birth: 1879/02/18   Death: 1968/04/03   Burial: 1968/04/05
         Died: Leesburg, VA   On stone with John W. Long
Site 12 John W. Long   Cause: Influenza   Age: 53 years
         Birth: 1876/09/05   Death: 1929/02/02   Burial: 1929/02/04

Lot: 735 W   Owner: Mrs. Henry Mason Wortman   1929/03/04
Transfer 1: To M.F. Snider 1929/03/04

Site 0   Eugenia C. Thomas   No stone   Age: 40 years
         Cause: Tuberculosis   Death: 1923/10/12   Burial: 1923/10/14
Site 1   Robert Lee Fleming   Died: Prince Georges Co., MD Age: 54 years
         No stone   Death: 1962/10/23   Burial: 1962/10/25
Site 1   Katherine Fleming   Died: Manassas, VA   No stone
         Birth: 1913/12/27   Death: 1993/11/14   Burial: 1993/11/17
Site 2   Ernest Glenwood Snider Sr.   No stone   Age: 73 years
         Died: Alexandria, VA   Death: 1955/05/03   Burial: 1955/05/04
Site 3   Marion Franklin Snider Cause: Arterio Occlusion   Age: 72 years
         Birth: 1860/02/02   Death: 1932/10/26   Burial: 1932/10/29
Site 4   Elizabeth Ann Dawson Snider   Age: 74 years
         Birth: 1854/10/03   Death: 1929/03/02   Burial: 1929/03/04
         Cause: Pneumonia   On stone with Marion Franklin Snider
Site 5   Grace Elizabeth Fleming Cause: Myocarditis   Age: 28 years
         Birth: 1905/10/26   Death: 1934/04/06   Burial: 1934/04/08
Site 6   Grace Leslie Fleming   No stone   Age: 65 years
                                Death: 1947/05/19   Burial: 1947/05/21

Lot: 736 E   Owner: Mrs. Mary E. McPherson   1933/02/08

Site 7   Grace Lee Roberts   Age: 60 years
         Birth: 1902/09/12   Death: 1963/08/09   Burial: 1963/08/12
         Died: Staunton, VA   TS: Mother
Site 8   Earl Franklin McPherson Cause: Fractured Skull   Age: 29 years
         Birth: 1911/08/22   Death: 1940/12/29   Burial: 1941/01/01
Site 9   John W. McPherson   Age: 75 years
         Birth: 1857   Death: 1933/02/05   Burial: 1933/02/07
         Cause: Malnutrition   TS: Father
Site 11 Mary E. McPherson   Age: 92 years
         Birth: 1873   Death: 1965/12/04   Burial: 1965/12/07
         Died: Arlington, VA   TS: Mother

Lot: 736 W   Owner: William E. Gaines   Purchased: 1932/08/11

Site 3   William E. Gaines   Died: Leesburg, VA   Age: 70 years
         Birth: 1901/04/19   Death: 1972/03/12   Burial: 1972/03/14
Site 4   Nellie R. Gaines   Age: 76 years
         Birth: 1898/09/04   Death: 1975/01/11   Burial: 1975/01/13
         Died: Leesburg, VA   On stone with William Gaines

Site 5   Peggy Lou Gaines   Age: 1 years
         Birth: 1930/10/15   Death: 1932/07/27   Burial: 1932/07/29
         Cause: Acidosis   TS: Daughter of William & Nellie Gaines
Site 6   Vivian A. Gaines   Died: Winchester, VA No death date on stone
         Birth: 1925/06/29   Death: 1990/05/10   Burial: 1990/05/12

Lot: 737 E   Owner: Mrs. J. L. Talbot   Purchased: 1932/11/03
Site 9   John Leland Talbot   Cause: Angina Pectoris   Age: 62 years
         Birth: 1870/11/03   Death: 1932/11/03   Burial: 1932/11/05
Site 10 Charlotte Mosley Talbot   Age: 82 years
         Birth: 1885   Death: 1968/05/12   Burial: 1968/05/14
         Died: McLean, VA   On stone with John Leland Talbot
Site 12 Helen J. Talbot   Died: Arlington, VA   Age: 55 years
         Birth: 1909/05/08   Death: 1965/06/16   Burial: 1965/06/19

Lot: 737 W   Owner: R.W. Stocks   Purchased: 1933/02/24
Site 1   Mrs. Mary E. Stocks   Age: 78 years
         Birth: 1855/11/13   Death: 1934/05/01   Burial: 1934/05/03
         Cause: Pneumonia   TS: Wife of Richard J. Stocks
Site 2   Mrs. Letitia M. Cooper   Age: 70 years
         Birth: 1865/05/01   Death: 1935/11/13   Burial: 1935/11/15
         Cause: Cerebral Hemorrhage   TS: Wife of Joseph H. Cooper
Site 3   Joseph Henry Cooper   No stone
                                 Death: 1950/05/29   Burial: 1950/06/01
Site 4   Clara Cooper Stocks   Age: 86 years
         Birth: 1900   Death: 1986/12/08   Burial: 1986/12/11
         Died: Leesburg, VA   On stone with Richard W. Stocks
Site 5   Richard W. Stocks   Died: Leesburg, VA   Age: 60 years
         Birth: 1899   Death: 1960/04/04   Burial: 1960/04/06
Site 6   Helen M. Stocks   Age: 18 months
         Birth: 1931/07/29   Death: 1933/02/24   Burial: 1933/02/26
         Cause: Acidosis   No stone
Site 6   Infant daughter of R.W.& Helen Stocks   Age: 2 days
         Birth: 1934/07/29   Death: 1934/07/31   Burial: 1934/07/31
         Cause: H. U. Development   No stone

Lot: 738 E   Owner: Robert E. Harper   Purchased: 1931/01/16
Site 7   Robert Edwin Harper   Age: 77 years
         Birth: 1876/08/30   Death: 1953/02/17
Site 8   Mary Ellen Harper   Age: 79 years
         Birth: 1874/12/03   Death: 1954/10/22
         On stone with Robert Edwin Harper

Lot: 738 W   Owner: George Herndon   Purchased: 1938/06/03
Site 1   George W. Herndon   Age: 84 years
         Birth: 1858   Death: 1943/03/14   Burial: 1943/03/16
Site 2   Martha F. Herndon   TSDeath: 1938   Age: 72 years
         Birth: 1862   Death: 1934/11/13   Burial: 1934/11/15
         Cause: Cerebral Hemorrhage   On stone with George W. Herndon

Site 3 Randolph Herndon   Age: 57 years
        Birth: 1885   Death: 1943/01/24   Burial: 1943/01/26
Site 4 Nannie C. Smith   Died: Leesburg, VA   Age: 76 years
        Birth: 1898   Death: 1974/11/03   Burial: 1974/11/06
Site 5 Shelby Herndon   Age: 51 years
        Birth: 1895/4/   Death: 1946/03/03   Burial: 1946/03/05
Site 6 Rebecca Sevilla Herndon   Age: 48 years
        Birth: 1897/04/29   Death: 1948/01/17   Burial: 1948/01/19

Lot: 739 E   Owner: Arnold Phillips   Purchased: 1939/02/03
Site 7 William Bryant Philips Jr.   Age: 15 years
        Birth: 1943/12/03   Death: 1959/06/27   Burial: 1959/06/29
                                 Died: Montgomery, MD
Site 8 Charles Alan Ricketts   Died: Dickson, MD   Age: 7 years
        Birth: 1957/08/30   Death: 1965/07/06   Burial: 1965/07/09
Site 9 Arnold Phillips   Died: Crawfordville, FL Age: 85 years
        Birth: 1901/12/14   Death: 1987/05/29   Burial: 1987/06/01
Site 10 Mazzie H. Phillips   Age: 77 years
        Birth: 1903/08/15   Death: 1981/04/27   Burial: 1981/04/30
        Died: Roanoke, VA   On stone with Arnold Phillips
Site 11 Avery James Phillips   Died: Clarksburg, MD   Age: 27 years
        Birth: 1929/07/05   Death: 1956/08/01   Burial: 1956/08/03
Site 12 Child John M. Phillips   Cause: Pneumonia   Age: 8 months
        Birth: 1937/05/16   Death: 1938/02/06   Burial: 1938/02/08

Lot: 739 W   Owner: C.R. Hollandsworth   Purchased:
Site 3 Ceveria Ross Hollandsworth   Age: 54 years
        Birth: 1902   Death: 1958/10/28   Burial: 1958/10/31
        Cause: Suicide   Died: Leesburg, VA   TS: Father
Site 4 Daisy Gertrude Hollandsworth   Age: 81 years
        Birth: 1906   Death: 1988/04/27   Burial: 1988/04/30
                                 Died: Leesburg, VA   TS: Mother
Site 5 Philip James Hollandsworth   Age: 5 years
        Birth: 1930/10/28   Death: 1936/01/11   Burial: 1936/01/13
        Cause: Pneumonia   TS: Son
Site 6 Kirby Winston Hollandsworth   Age: 29 years
        Birth: 1933   Death: 1963/01/13   Burial: 1963/01/16
        Died: Bethesda, MD   TS: Son

Lot: 740 E   Owner: C.W. Stewart   Purchased: 1934/03/01
Site 7 Charles Oscar Costello   Died: Middletown, VA   Age: 58 years
        Birth: 1931/01/25   Death: 1989/01/27   Burial: 1989/01/30
Site 8 Harvey J. Stewart   Died: Winchester, VA   Age: 93 years
        Birth: 1898   Death: 1992/02/25   Burial: 1992/02/29
Site 9 Gertrude Leach Cooley Stewart   Age: 68 years
        Birth: 1900   Death: 1969/01/02   Burial: 1969/01/06
        Died: Montgomery, MD   On stone with Harvey J. Stewart
Site 10 Mrs. Bessie Wyncoop Stewart   Age: 70 years
        Birth: 1882   Death: 1952/07/02   Burial: 1952/07/05

Site 11 Chas. Walter Stewart   Age: 79 years
        Birth: 1866/04/09   Death: 1946/03/25   Burial: 1946/03/27
Site 12 Florence Miriam Stewart Cause: Arteriosclerosis   Age: 66 years
        Birth: 1869/08/25   Death: 1935/01/11   Burial: 1935/01/15

Lot: 740 W Owner: Mrs. O.A. Costello   Purchased: 1930/12/01
Site 5 Oscar A. Costello   Died: Winchester, VA   Age: 71 years
        Birth: 1907/01/28   Death: 1978/09/28   Burial: 1978/10/01
Site 6 Bessie Louise Costello Burger   Age: 75 years
        Birth: 1912/11/15   Death: 1988/10/13   Burial: 1988/10/16
        Died: Steavens City, VA   On stone with Oscar A. Costello

Lot: 741 Owner: Miscellaneous
Site 1 Mrs. Fannie Jewell   Age: 72 years
        Birth: 1872   Death: 1945/05/08   Burial: 1945/05/10
Site 2 Walter L. Jewell   Age: 82 years
        Birth: 1876   Death: 1962/01/20   Burial: 1962/01/23
        Cause: Cancer   Died: Washington, DC
Site 3 Isabelle Hershbach   No stone   Age: 76 years
                                Death: 1949/12/05   Burial: 1949/12/07
Site 4 John Spencer Best Sr.   No stone   Age: 52 years
                                Death: 1959/05/01   Burial: 1959/05/05
        Cause: Cirrhosis of Liver   Died: Washington, DC
Site 5 Edward Leith   Age: 30 years
        Birth: 1919   Death: 1949/08/30   Burial: 1949/08/31
Site 6 Lawrence G. Rinker   No stone   Age: 79 years
                                Death: 1948/01/06   Burial: 1948/01/08
Site 7 Joseph Seaton   No stone   Age: 70 years
        Cause: Cancer   Death: 1942/09/04   Burial: 1942/09/06
Site 9 George W. Kitts   No stone   Age: 81 years
        Cause: Arteriosclerosis Death: 1941/10/09   Burial: 1941/10/11
Site 10 Herman F.J. Soden   Age: 60 years
        Birth: 1880/06/22   Death: 1941/07/14   Burial: 1941/07/16
Site 11 John H. Williams   No stone   Age: 69 years
                                Death: 1941/05/29   Burial: 1941/05/31
Site 12 Infant J. O. Gandolph   Death: 1942/09/03   Burial: 1942/09/03
        Cause: Stillborn   No stone
Site 12 Ray Osburne Keys   No stone   Age: 4 days
        Cause: Hemorrhage   Death: 1942/10/01   Burial: 1942/10/02

Lot: 742 Owner: Miscellaneous
Site 2 Baby Girl Carter   No stone
                                Death: 1949/07/05   Burial: 1949/07/05
Site 2 John Dennis Leith   IB:Child of John D. Leith Age: 1 month
        No stone   Death: 1951/03/30   Burial: 1951/04/01
Site 3 Child Williams   No stone   Age: 2 days
                                Death: 1948/03/01   Burial: 1948/03/03
Site 3 Child Clifton Leith   No stone   Age: 1.5 hours
                                Death: 1949/04/19   Burial: 1949/04/21

Site 4	Charles L. Scott	Died: Washington, DC	Age: 49 years
	Birth: 1913/11/17	Death: 1963/07/22	Burial: 1963/07/24
Site 5	Child of Robert B. Ridley		No stone
	Cause: Stillborn	Death: 1945/06/10	Burial: 1945/06/10
Site 5	Child Kappa	No stone	Age: 1 day
		Death: 1948/01/30	Burial: 1948/02/02
Site 6	Calvin D. Coates		Age: 33 years
	Birth: 1911	Death: 1944/11/30	Burial: 1944/12/02
Site 7	Pactheia J. Skidmore	Died: Paeonian Springs, VA	Age: 74 years
	No stone	Death: 1959/05/02	Burial: 1959/05/06
Site 8	Archie Lee Quesenberry		Age: 29 years
	Birth: 1915	Death: 1944/06/20	Burial: 1944/06/22
Site 9	Lee Child of James Early		Age: 1 hour
	No stone	Death: 1944/04/05	Burial: 1944/04/05
Site 9	Baby Girl Ashton	No stone	Age: 30 minutes
		Death: 1944/07/05	Burial: 1944/07/05
Site 10	Marshall E. Costello		Age: 69 years
	Birth: 1874/10/16	Death: 1944/02/11	Burial: 1944/02/13
Site 11	Mrs. Louisa F. Costello		Age: 68 years
	Birth: 1877/02/16	Death: 1945/12/01	Burial: 1945/12/03
	On stone with Marshall E. Costello		
Site 12	Steave S. Beach		Age: 58 years
	Birth: 1888	Death: 1943/09/05	Burial: 1943/09/07

Lot: 743 Owner: Miscellaneous

Site 1	Columbus Berkley Frye	Died: Hillsboro, VA	Age: 40 years
	Birth: 1943/09/03	Death: 1983/09/19	Burial: 1983/09/23
Site 5	Irene Virginia Hawes	Died: Leesburg, VA	Age: 51 years
	Birth: 1937/11/30	Death: 1989/08/07	Burial: 1989/08/11
	Wed W.T. Hawes July 22, 1957		
Site 6	Mrs. Annie Belle Jarmans		Age: 65 years
	TS: Age 71 years	Death: 1949/12/14	Burial: 1949/12/16
Site 7	Child of James Leith	No stone	Age: 10 hours
		Death: 1949/10/12	Burial: 1949/10/12
Site 7	Judy Ann Allison	No stone	Age: 3 days
	Died: Leesburg, VA	Death: 1967/02/14	Burial: 1967/02/16
Site 8	William Calvin Allison		Age: 72 years
	Birth: 1879	Death: 1952/02/18	Burial: 1952/02/20
Site 9	Mrs. Georgia Belle Allison		Age: 65 years
	Birth: 1883	Death: 1949/09/23	Burial: 1949/09/25
	On stone with William Calvin Allison		
Site 10	John W. Wilklow	Died: Hamilton, VA	Age: 83 years
	Birth: 1879/05/18	Death: 1963/02/20	Burial: 1963/02/22
Site 11	Myrtle Virginia Wilklow		Age: 59 years
	Birth: 1889/11/17	Death: 1948/10/08	Burial: 1948/10/10
	On stone with John W. Wilklow		
Site 12	Welby Foster Wilklow	Died: Leesburg, VA	
	Birth: 1908/10/09	Death: 1993/02/21	Burial: 1993/02/25
	TS: Loving son & brother		

Lot: 744 E   Owner: Delbert Rollison   Purchased: 1947/11/12
Site 7	Jeannette Ann Rollison		Age: 6 years
	Birth: 1940/06/08	Death: 1946/10/03	Burial: 1946/10/05
Site 8	Dinah Lee Rollison		Age: 2 months
	Birth: 1947/09/06	Death: 1947/11/10	Burial: 1947/11/12
Site 9	Delbert Rollison	Died: Hyattsville, MD	Age: 58 years
	Birth: 1915/03/12	Death: 1973/11/30	Burial: 1973/12/04
Site 10	Nellie B. Rollison		Died: Washington, DC
	Birth: 1917/11/26	Death: 1993/06/17	Burial: 1993/06/19

Lot: 744 W   Owner: Raymond M. Jordan   Purchased: 1948/08/09
Site 2	Mary Elizabeth Jordan		Age: 48 years
	Birth: 1900	Death: 1948/08/07	Burial: 1948/08/09
Site 2	Harry Jordan Sr.	No stone	Age: 77 years
	Died: Lovettsville, VA	Death: 1980/01/05	Burial: 1980/01/08
Site 3	Katherine Marie Flynn	No stone	Age: 53 years
	Died: McLean, VA	Death: 1954/01/08	Burial: 1954/01/11
Site 4	Raymond M. Jordan	Died: Gettysburg, MD	Age: 70 years
	Birth: 1917	Death: 1987/10/04	Burial: 1987/10/07
Site 6	Thomas Jordan	No stone	Age: 93 years
		Death: 1951/03/30	Burial: 1951/04/02

Lot: 745 E   Owner: Paul L. Stewart   Purchased: 1936/06/27
| Site 9 | Paul Stewart | Died: Leesburg, VA | Age: 73 years |
| | Birth: 1903/04/05 | Death: 1977/03/15 | Burial: 1977/03/18 |

Lot: 745 W   Owner: Wilmer W. Stuart & Helen G. Stewart
Purchased: 1936/06/27
Site 5	Wilmer W. Stewart		Died: Arlington, VA
	Birth: 1907/02/27	Death: 1991/06/22	Burial: 1991/06/25
Site 6	Helen G. Stewart		
	Birth: 1911/02/20	Death: 1993/06/23	Burial: 1993/06/26
	Died: Arlington, VA	On stone with Wilmer W. Stewart	

Lot: 746   Owner: J.R. Lintner   Purchased: 1936/09/12
Site	Roy B. Lintner	Birth: 1905/02/14	Death: 1972/10/12
Site 1	Dorthy Maynard Lintner	Died: Washington, DC	Age: 61 years
	Birth: 1918/05/09	Death: 1980/03/19	Burial: 1980/03/21
Site 2	Julius Ross Lintner	Died: Leesburg, VA	Age: 86 years
	Birth: 1875	Death: 1962/01/21	Burial: 1962/01/23
Site 3	Mrs. Mary Stonestreet Lintner		Age: 90 years
	Birth: 1879	Death: 1967/09/07	Burial: 1967/09/11
	Died: Leesburg, VA	On stone with Julius Ross Lintner	
Site 4	Newell Vanmeter Lintner		Age: 34 years
	Birth: 1908/05/31	Death: 1942/07/27	Burial: 1942/07/29
Site 5	J. Harris S. Lintner	Cause: Tuberculosis	Age: 33 years
	Birth: 1903/05/09	Death: 1936/09/12	Burial: 1936/09/14
Site 6	Henrietta Stanley Lintner	Died: Leesburg, VA	Age: 76 years
	Birth: 1906	Death: 1983/11/04	Burial: 1983/11/12

Site 6   Jules R. Lintner Jr.   Died: Leesburg, VA
         Birth: 1906/10/22   Death: 1995/12/18   Burial: 1995/12/22
Site 7   Frederick Wilhelm Lintner   Age: 77 years
         Birth: 1911/03/27   Death: 1990/06/21   Burial: 1990/07/02
         Died: ID   TS: 1st Lt. US ARMY WWII

Lot: 747 E   Owner: Hugh B. Jones   Purchased: 1936/02/05
Site 7   M.L. Jones   Death: 1936/02/17   No stone
Site 8   Frances Lee Jones   Cause: Pneumonia   Age: 3 months
         Birth: 1935/10/13   Death: 1936/02/05   Burial: 1936/02/07
Site 9   Hugh Bell Jones   Died: Fairfax Co., VA   Age: 46 years
         Birth: 1909/04/28   Death: 1956/04/18   Burial: 1956/04/19
Site 10 Emma Marie Jones   Age: 54 years
         Birth: 1911/11/03   Death: 1966/06/19   Burial: 1966/06/23
         Died: Washington, DC   On stone with Hugh Bell Jones
Site 11 Walter T. Harrison   Died: Paeonian Springs, VA   Age: 88 years
         Birth: 1870/04/02   Death: 1958/09/12   Burial: 1958/09/14
Site 12 Lillie Lee Harrison   Age: 79 years
         Birth: 1870/11   Death: 1953/12/03   Burial: 1953/12/05
         Died: Fairfax, VA   On stone with Walter T. Harrison

Lot: 747 W   Owner: W.T. Moran   Purchased: 1941/08/07
Site   Harmony Thomas Moran   TS: Buried in Moran Cemetery
Site 1   Thomas Edward Bodmer   TS: "Father"   Age: 65 years
         Birth: 1876/01/25   Death: 1942/06/23   Burial: 1942/06/25
Site 2   Henrietta Bodmer   Age: 78 years
         Birth: 1888/08/22   Death: 1967/02/09   Burial: 1967/02/11
         Died: Leesburg, VA   TS: "Mother"
Site 3   Alice Bond Paxson Moran   Age: 87 years
         Birth: 1853/08/18   Death: 1941/08/07   Burial: 1941/08/09
         Cause: Cardiac Failure
Site 5   William Thomas Moran   Died: Leesburg, VA   Age: 75 years
         Birth: 1894/11/10   Death: 1970/03/31   Burial: 1970/04/02

Lot: 748 E   Owner: Eva H. Cooksey   Purchased: 1952/12/22
Site 7   Lawrence Thomas Cooksey   Age: 54 years
         No names/dates on stone Death: 1952/12/22   Burial: 1952/12/24
Site 8   Eva H. Cooksey   No names/dates on stone   Age: 90 years
         Died: Leesburg, VA   Death: 1989/07/02   Burial: 1989/07/05
Site 9   J. Robert Cooksey   Age: 40 years
                                Death: 1936/05/14   No names/dates on stone
Site 9   Lawrence Hickam Cooksey
                                Death: 1957/05/03   No names/dates on stone
Site 11 George Robert Hughes   No names/dates on stone   Age: 72 years
         Died: Leesburg, VA   Death: 1956/01/11   Burial: 1956/01/11

Lot: 748 W   Owner: B. H. Smith   Purchased: 1935/09/05
Site 1   Joseph M. Frye   Died: Leesburg, VA   Age: 98 years
         Birth: 1871/06/01   Death: 1970/04/01   Burial: 1970/04/03

Site 2	Grace C. Frye		Age: 88 years
	Birth: 1887/07/31	Death: 1976/06/24	Burial: 1976/06/26
	Died: Baltimore, MD	On stone with Joseph M. Frye	
Site 3	John W. Smith	Died: Leesburg, VA	Age: 80 years
	Birth: 1885/10/10	Death: 1965/07/28	Burial: 1965/07/31
Site 4	Benjamin Harrison Smith		Age: 57 years
	Birth: 1888/09/19	Death: 1946/08/08	Burial: 1946/08/10
Site 5	Anna Jett Smith		Age: 64 years
	Birth: 1901/04/22	Death: 1966/04/23	Burial: 1966/04/26
	Cause: Cancer	Died: Leesburg, VA	
Site 6	Frances S. Smith		Age: 69 years
	Birth: 1863/06/13	Death: 1935/09/10	Burial: 1935/09/12
	Cause: Heart Lesion	TS: Wife of Joseph D. Smith	

Lot: 749 E   Owner: Rata D. Norris   Purchased: 1937/06/07

Site 7	Charles R. Norris	Cause: Cancer	Age: 67 years
	Birth: 1864/12/23	Death: 1932/09/08	Burial: 1932/09/10
Site 8	Rata J. Norris		Age: 85 years
	Birth: 1868/11/12	Death: 1954/08/24	
Site 11	William W. Norris		Age: 63 years
	Birth: 1894/06/04	Death: 1957/09/07	
Site 12	Margaret E. Norris	Birth: 1900/06/28	Death: 1969/02/25

Lot: 749 W   Owner: Vincenzo Raneri   Purchased: 1933/10/14

Site 1	Carmelo Raneri	CR:Removed No stone	Age: 35 years
	Died: Charlottsville, VA	Death: 1965/12/18	Burial: 1965/12/21
Site 6	Sebastiana Raneri		Age: 37 years
	Birth: 1894/08/21	Death: 1933/07/03	Burial: 1933/07/06
	Cause: Bronchial Pneumonia		Died: Leesburg, VA
	On stone with Vincenzo Raneri	TS: Born Italy, Died Leesburg, VA	
Site 6	Vincenzo Raneri		Age: 85 years
	Birth: 1889/01/31	Death: 1974/07/11	Burial: 1974/07/13
	Died: Martinsburg, WV	TS: Born in Italy; died Martinsburg, WV	

Lot: 750 E   Owner: John F. Thompson   Purchased: 1932/06/01

Site 11	John F. Thompson	Died: Leesburg, VA	Age: 76 years
	Birth: 1896/10/24	Death: 1975/08/13	Burial: 1975/08/16
Site 12	Mary Louise Thompson		Age: 36 years
	Birth: 1895/08/11	Death: 1932/05/30	Burial: 1932/06/02
	Cause: M.of Pancreas	TS: Wife of John F. Thompson	

Lot: 750 W   Owner: Charles Thompson   Purchased: 1932/06/01

Site 1	Charles W. Thompson Sr.		Age: 53 years
	Birth: 1905	Death: 1958/11/03	Burial: 1958/11/06
		Died: Washington, DC	
Site 2	Viola Thompson		Age: 78 years
	Birth: 1905	Death: 1983/09/12	Burial: 1983/09/14
	Died: Fredericksburg, VA	On stone with Charles W. Thompson	

Lot: 751 E   Owner: W.H. & Blanche Johnson   1931/01/15
Site 8   William Henry Johnson Jr.   Age: 39 years
         Birth: 1906/04/01   Death: 1945/12/07   Burial: 1945/12/10
Site 9   William H. Johnson   Cause: Hyposticue Congestion   Age: 80 years
         Birth: 1848/11/04   Death: 1930/06/13   Burial: 1930/06/15
Site 10 Betty Ann Rogers Fornshill   Age: 35 years
         Birth: 1930/06/20   Death: 1965/11/19   Burial: 1965/11/22
         Died: Alexandria, VA   On stone with Kenneth B. Fornshill
Site 10 Kenneth B. Fornshill   Died: Fairfax, VA   Age: 58 years
         Birth: 1930/11/04   Death: 1989/02/24   Burial: 1989/02/28
Site 11 Kenneth D. B. Fornshill Died: Washington, DC   Age: 49 years
         Birth: 1906/12/28   Death: 1956/03/15   Burial: 1956/03/15

Lot: 751 W   Owner: W. Henry Hardy   Purchased: 1929/12/02
Site 3   Earl W. Hardy   Died: Leesburg, VA   Age: 66 years
         Birth: 1907   Death: 1973/12/27   Burial: 1973/12/30
Site 5   William H. Hardy   No stone   Age: 83 years
         Died: Leesburg, VA   Death: 1961/08/17   Burial: 1961/08/19
Site 6   Lucenda May Hardy   Cause: Tuberculosis   Age: 43 years
         Birth: 1886/11/24   Death: 1929/11/30   Burial: 1929/12/02

Lot: 752 E   Owner: Mrs. Eva Gertrude Warren   1929/11/16
Site 7   Mabel S. Peters   Age: 28 years
         Birth: 1910/10/16   Death: 1938/10/24   Burial: 1938/10/26
         Cause: Lung Abscess   TS: Wife of Carl B. Peters
Site 8   Lily Lorraine Peters   No stone   Age: 16 years
                                 Death: 1951/08/27   Burial: 1951/08/30
Site 9   Benjamin E. Warren   Age: 48 years
         Birth: 1882/07/12   Death: 1929/11/16   Burial: 1929/11/18
         Cause: Accident   TS: "Father"
Site 10 Mrs. Eva Gertrude Warren   No stone   Age: 82 years
         IB:Mrs. Ben Warren   Death: 1952/01/01   Burial: 1952/01/03

Lot: 752 W   Owner: Ervin P. Athey   Purchased: 1929/07/31
Site 1   Ervin Preston Athey   Died: L.C.H. Leesburg, VA   Age: 70 years
         Birth: 1888   Death: 1958/04/23   Burial: 1958/04/26
Site 2   Maude L. Athey   Age: 82 years
         Birth: 1896   Death: 1979/07/09   Burial: 1979/07/12
         Died: Leesburg, VA   On stone with Ervin Preston Athey
Site 4   Harry Thomas Athey   Age: 1 years
         Birth: 1930/12/11   Death: 1932/01/11   Burial: 1932/01/13
         Cause: Acidosis   TS: Son of E.P. & M.L. Athey
Site 5   Alta Leona Athey   Age: 3 years
         Birth: 1928/05/22   Death: 1931/11/24   Burial: 1931/11/26
         Cause: Pneumonia   TS: Daughter of J.W. & N.M. Athey
Site 6   Frances Leona Athey   Age: 5 years
         Birth: 1924/09/27   Death: 1929/07/30   Burial: 1929/08/02
         Cause: Pneumonia   TS: Daughter of E.P. & M.L. Athey

Lot: 753   Owner: Edgar Peacock   Purchased: 1925/11/27
Site 1   Edgar Peacock   Cause: Cancer of Bladder   Age: 78 years
         Birth: 1857   Death: 1935/11/22   Burial: 1935/11/24
Site 2   Mary Catherine Peacock   Died: Leesburg, VA   Age: 93 years
         Birth: 1862   Death: 1955/08/10   Burial: 1955/08/10
Site 11 Arthur Raymond Peacock   Age: 73 years
         Birth: 1887   Death: 1960/07/02   Burial: 1960/07/04
                                    Died: Waterford, VA
Site 12 Lola M. Grubb Peacock   Died: Paeonian Springs, VA Age: 56 years
         Birth: 1897   Death: 1953 /08/24   Burial: 1953/08/26

Lot: 754 E   Owner: G.F. Hickam   Purchased: 1925/11/02
Site 7   George F. Hickam   Age: 44 years
         Birth: 1913/04/06   Death: 1957/10/06
         TS: Virginia TEC 5 761 Army Postal Unit, WWII
Site 10 Addie R. Hickam   Cause: Cerebral Hemorrhage Age: 42 years
         Birth: 1883/04/22   Death: 1925/10/30   Burial: 1925/10/31
Site 10 George Fred Hickam   Died: Pulaski, VA   Age: 91 years
         Birth: 1876/02/08   Death: 1967/04/24   Burial: 1967/04/25

Lot: 754 W   Owner: Mrs. Louise S. Jackson Purchased: 1947/08/18
Site 2   Dr. Harold Maurice Jackson   Age: 65 years
         Birth: 1912/05/20   Death: 1977/12/13   Burial: 1977/12/15
                                    Died: Leesburg, VA   TS: M.D.
Site 3   Maurice Stanley Jackson   Age: 65 years
         Birth: 1882/05/08   Death: 1947/08/18   Burial: 1947/08/20
Site 4   Mrs. Louise S. Jackson   Died: Staunton, VA   Age: 80 years
         Birth: 1894/04/27   Death: 1974/05/01   Burial: 1974/05/03
Site 6   William Stanley Jackson   Died: Fairfax, VA   Age: 55 years
         Birth: 1914/09/15   Death: 1970/07/07   Burial: 1970/07/10
         TS: Virginia PFC 86 Mountain Infantry, WWII

Lot: 755 E   Owner: Miscellaneous
Site 8   Lucille Anna Thornton   Died: Washington, DC   Age: 65 years
         Birth: 1919/10/28   Death: 1984/12/01   Burial: 1984/12/05
Site 12 Anne E. McQuade Jobe   Age: 54 years
         Birth: 1931/03/23   Death: 1985/04/13   Burial: 1985/04/18

Lot: 755 W   Owner: W.C. James   Purchased: 1924/09/25
Site 1   Julian Reid Mays   Died: Martinsburg, WV   Age: 73 years
         Birth: 1893/09/01   Death: 1967/07/30   Burial: 1967/08/01
Site 2   Imogene James Mays   Age: 94 years
         Birth: 1890/06/24   Death: 1984/08/10   Burial: 1984/08/12
         Died: Berryville, VA   On stone with Julian Reid Mays
Site 4   Arthur A. James
         Birth: 1883   Death: 1938   Burial: 1987/09/04
Site 4   Edna C. James   Died: Leesburg, VA   Age: 83 years
         Birth: 1904   Death: 1987/09/01   Burial: 1987/09/04
         Cause: Heart   On stone with Arthur A. James

41

Site 4   William Carlyle James   Cause: Heart Trouble   Age: 69 years
         Birth: 1859/08/27   Death: 1929/05/12   Burial: 1929/05/14
Site 5   Emma Cecelia James   Age: 80 years
         Birth: 1859/12/30   Death: 1940/05/22   Burial: 1940/05/24
         Cause: Infirmities of Age   On stone with William Carlyle James

Lot: 757   Owner: J.E. Tavenner   Purchased: 1921/05/03
Site 1   Benjamin E. Tavenner   Age: 72 years
         Birth: 1882   Death: 1954/12/15
Site 2   Paul Washington Tavenner   Age: 69 years
         Birth: 1879   Death: 1948/04/17   Burial: 1948/04/19
Site 4   Minnie B. Tavenner   Age: 71 years
         Birth: 1876   Death: 1947/04/19   Burial: 1947/04/21
Site 5   William W. Moffett   Cause: Myocarditis   Age: 74 years
         Birth: 1859   Death: 1934/04/21   Burial: 1934/04/23
Site 6   Janie S. Tavenner Moffett   Age: 85 years
         Birth: 1867   Death: 1952/07/01   Burial: 1952/07/02
Site 9   James Eden Tavenner   Cause: Tuberculosis   Age: 76 years
         Birth: 1837   Death: 1921/05/03
Site 10 Mrs. Mary Jane Tavenner   Age: 83 years
         Birth: 1845   Death: 1921/07/15
         Cause: Old Age   CR:Mrs. James E. Tavenner
Site 11 Omar E. Tavenner   Age: 74 years
         Birth: 1868   Death: 1943/09/15   Burial: 1943/09/17
Site 12 John W. Tavenner   Age: 72 years
         Birth: 1874   Death: 1947/02/23   Burial: 1947/02/25

Lot: 758 E   Owner: Mrs. Samuel Thrift   Purchased: 1919/07/28
Site 7   Melvin P. Thrift   Cause: Pneumonia   Age: 42 years
         Birth: 1899   Death: 1941/12/03   Burial: 1941/12/05
Site 8   Samuel Thrift   Cause: Pneumonia   Age: 69 years
         Birth: 1861/02/09   Death: 1930/02/22   Burial: 1930/02/25
Site 9   Mrs. Lucie E. Thrift   Age: 66 years
         Birth: 1863/05/08   Death: 1929/04/26   Burial: 1929/04/28
         Cause: Hemorrhage   IB:Mrs. Sam Thrift
Site 10 Chester R. Thrift   Age: 41 years
         Birth: 1902   Death: 1943/10/04   Burial: 1943/10/06
Site 11 Virginia R. Thrift   On stone with Chester R. Thrift Age: 40 years
         Birth: 1904   Death: 1945/10/04   Burial: 1945/10/06
Site 12 Leonard E. Thrift   Died: Arlington, VA   Age: 68 years
         Birth: 1892/08/05   Death: 1961/03/12   Burial: 1961/03/16
         On stone with Blanche E. Thrift born 1884/01/03-no record of her death

Lot: 758 W   Owner: W.D. Davis & Joseph M Thompson 1921/12/26
Site 1   Joseph M. Thompson   Age: 78 years
         Birth: 1871/04/22   Death: 1949/06/12   Burial: 1949/06/14
Site 2   May Louise Thompson   Died: Chevy Chase, MD   Age: 74 years
         Birth: 1881/03/08   Death: 1956/02/23   Burial: 1956/02/24

Site 3 Helen Heckel   No stone   Age: 58 years
        Died: Clearwater, FL   Death: 1972/11/13   Burial: 1972/11/17
Site 5 William Dana Davis   Cause: Pneumonia   Age: 84 years
        Birth: 1843/06/13   Death: 1928/05/29   Burial: 1928/06/01
Site 6 Louisa Davis   TS: Wife of William D. Davis Age: 73 years
        Birth: 1848/06/16   Death: 1921/12/20   Cause: Appendicitis

Lot: 759 Owner: T.W. Belt   Purchased: 1919/01/21
Site 2 Paul Belt   No dates on stone   Age: 45 years
        Cause: Hemorrhage   Death: 1921/12/24   Burial: 1921/12/25
Site 3 Townsend N. Belt   Cause: Cancer   Age: 76 years
        Birth: 1844   Death: 1921/07/05
Site 4 Annie Thrift Belt   Age: 63 years
        Birth: 1845   Death: 1919/02/24
        Cause: Pneumonia   On stone with Townsend N. Belt
Site 5 Samuel Phillips Belt   Age: 65 years
        Birth: 1881/05/28   Death: 1947/02/07   Burial: 1947/02/09
Site 6 Nellie Carr Belt   Age: 93 years
        Birth: 1884/09/30   Death: 1977/08/29   Burial: 1977/09/01
        Died: Washington, DC   On stone with Samuel Phillips Belt
Site 8 Townsend W. Belt Jr.   Age: 48 years
        Birth: 1882/03/30   Death: 1928/06/23   Burial: 1928/06/25
        Cause: Pneumonia   No stone
Site 10 Mary B. Holton   No stone   Age: 67 years
                               Death: 1949/04/09   Burial: 1949/04/11
Site 11 Benjamin T. Belt   Age: 59 years
        Birth: 1889   Death: 1947/12/07   Burial: 1947/12/09
Site 12 Moselle R. Hood   Died: MD
        Birth: 1904/07/11   Death: 1995/11/26   Burial: 1995/11/29

Lot: 760 Owner: Jos. G. Littig   Purchased: 1906/05/13
Site 3 James Gittings Littig Cause: Arteriosclerosis Age: 77 years
        Birth: 1845/07/30   Death: 1922/10/21   Burial: 1922/10/22
Site 4 Lula Ashby Littig   TS: Wife of James G. Littig Age: 64 years
        Birth: 1850/04/27   Death: 1916/05/14   Cause: Stomach Trouble
Site 5 Louise Littig Dudley   Age: 92 years
        Birth: 1888/08/17   Death: 1981/04/17   Burial: 1981/04/18
        Died: Richmond, VA   On stone with Aldrich Dudley Sr.
Site 6 Aldrich Dudley Sr.   Died: Alexandria, VA   Age: 78 years
        Birth: 1886/09/12   Death: 1965/03/31   Burial: 1965/04/02

Lot: 761 Owner: A.M. & J.C. Ely   Purchased: 1917/03/24
Site 1 Alexander M. Ely   Cause: Tuberculosis   Age: 68 years
        Birth: 1859/09/11   Death: 1928/07/31   Burial: 1928/08/02
Site 2 Mrs. Elizabeth L. Richmond Ely   Age: 57 years
        Birth: 1866/10/15   Death: 1917/03/23
        Cause: Diabetes   TS: Wife of Alexander M. Ely
Site 3 Manny Lee Ely   CR: Child of Richmond Ely   Age: 5 months
                               Death: 1929/03/23   Burial: 1929/03/25
        Cause: Pneumonia   No stone

Site 4   Anne R. Norman   Died: Louisville, KY   Age: 54 years
         Birth: 1928   Death: 1980/02/03   Burial: 1980/02/07
         On stone with Lawrence L. Norman & Mary Ely Norman
Site 5   Lawrence L. Norman   Died: Escondido, CA   Age: 75 years
         Birth: 1902   Death: 1977/12/15   Burial: 1977/12/19
Site 6   Mary Ely Norman   Age: 66 years
         Birth: 1903   Death: 1968/05/23   Burial: 1968/05/25
         Died: Leesburg, VA   On stone with Lawrence L. Norman
Site 8   Melvinia Orlena Bales (Mallie O.) Ely   Age: 56 years
         Birth: 1869/07/23   Death: 1925/02/25   Burial: 1925/02/26
         Cause: Cancer   TS: Wife of John C. Ely
Site 9   John C. Ely   Cause: Cancer   Age: 63 years
         Birth: 1868/02/06   Death: 1931/02/24   Burial: 1931/02/26
Site 11 Daniel Floyd Hagins   Age: 79 years
         Birth: 1862/10/04   Death: 1941/12/09   Burial: 1941/12/11
Site 12 Mrs. Almeda Jane Hagins   Age: 74 years
         Birth: 1864/06/10   Death: 1938/12/22   Burial: 1938/12/24
         Cause: Cerebral Hemorrhage   On stone with Daniel Floyd Hagins

Lot: 762 Owner: L.D. Kirby   Purchased: 1919/03/05
Site 1   Lucille Kirby Weadon   Died: Takoma Park, MD   Age: 76 years
         Birth: 1910/02/02   Death: 1986/05/29   Burial: 1986/06/02
Site 3   Luther Delbert Kirby   Cause: Coronary Thrombosis   Age: 60 years
         Birth: 1879/03/14   Death: 1939/04/06   Burial: 1939/04/08
Site 4   Fanny Lee Dyke Kirby   Age: 43 years
         Birth: 1877   Death: 1919/03/03
         Cause: Flu   On stone with Luther Delbert Kirby
Site 4   Irene Myers Kirby   Age: 82 years
         Birth: 1890/07/10   Death: 1973/06/24   Burial: 1973/06/27
         Died: Falls Church, VA On stone with Luther Delbert Kirby
Site 5   Woodrow Wilson Kirby   Died: Winchester, VA   Age: 68 years
         Birth: 1916/09/17   Death: 1981/05/05   Burial: 1981/05/08
Site 8   Harrison Gibson Kirby   Died: Alexandria, VA   Age: 54 years
         Birth: 1911/02/24   Death: 1972/03/25   Burial: 1972/03/27
Site 9   Paxton Marshall Kirby   Died: Leesburg, VA   Age: 86 years
         Birth: 1880   Death: 1967/05/03   Burial: 1967/05/06
Site 10 Mrs. Jennie Strother Kirby   Age: 38 years
         Birth: 1883   Death: 1921/03/04
         Cause: Blood Poisoning   On stone with Paxton Marshall Kirby
Site 11 Anna May Kirby   No stone   Age: 14 months
         Cause: Pneumonia   Death: 1935/01/08   Burial: 1935/01/09

Lot: 763 Owner: C. Henry Ellmore   Purchased: 1918/02/26
Site 3   Charles Henry Ellmore   Age: 67 years
         Birth: 1884   Death: 1952/11/21   Burial: 1952/11/24
Site 4   Bertha Aldridge Ellmore TS: Wife of Henry Ellmore   Age: 30 years
         Birth: 1886   Death: 1918/02/25   Cause: Peritonitis
Site 5   Thomas James Flanagan   Died: Clarksburg, WV   Age: 92 years
         Birth: 1883/05/01   Death: 1975/10/14   Burial: 1975/10/17

Site 6   Pearl Ellmore Flanagan   Age: 96 years
         Birth: 1883/05/24   Death: 1980/10/07   Burial: 1980/10/11
         Died: Clarksburg, WV   On stone with Thomas J. Flanagan
Site 7   Roland C. Cochran   Died: Sterling, VA   Age: 75 years
         Birth: 1896/09/15   Death: 1971/10/24   Burial: 1971/10/27
Site 8   Ethel E. Cochran
         Birth: 1897/02/06   Death: 1993/06/09   Burial: 1993/06/11
         Died: Culpepper, VA   On stone with Roland C. Cochran

Lot: 764   Owner: Mrs. Charles A. Ellmore   Purchased: 1917/04/14
Site 3   Charles A. Ellmore   Cause: Pneumonia   Age: 71 years
         Birth: 1845/12/03   Death: 1917/04/14
Site 4   Sarah Cecelia Ellmore   Age: 89 years
         Birth: 1856/12/14   Death: 1946/06/26   Burial: 1946/06/28
         On stone with Charles A. Ellmore
Site 6   Mary Virginia Ellmore   Died: Leesburg, VA   Age: 66 years
         Birth: 1886/07/10   Death: 1953/07/30   Burial: 1953/08/01
         On stone with Charles A. Ellmore & Sarah Cecelia Ellmore
Site 8   William H. Ahalt Sr.   Died: Leesburg, VA
         Birth: 1918/10/09   Death: 1992/12/31   Burial: 1993/01/04
Site 10 Robert Franklin Ellmore Died: Leesburg, VA   Age: 61 years
         Birth: 1895   Death: 1956/11/28   Burial: 1956/11/29
Site 11 Susie T. Ellmore   Age: 86 years
         Birth: 1900   Death: 1986/07/30   Burial: 1986/08/02
         Died: Leesburg, VA   On stone with Robert Franklin Ellmore

Lot: 765   Owner: C.D. Hammerly   Purchased: 1917/08/24
Site 1   Elizabeth W. Hammerly   Died: Leesburg, VA   Age: 85 years
         Birth: 1880/09/10   Death: 1965/12/25   Burial: 1965/12/27
Site 3   Charles Decatur Hammerly   Age: 83 years
         Birth: 1850/07/18   Death: 1933/09/28   Burial: 1933/09/30
         Cause: Nephritis
Site 4   Mary Lewis Murray Hammerly   Age: 60 years
         Birth: 1857/02/23   Death: 1917/08/23
Site 5   Jane Hammerly Armack   Age: 37 years
         Birth: 1885/01/08   Death: 1922/03/14   Burial: 1922/03/15
Site 6   Adelaide Jessie Hammerly   Died: Leesburg, VA   Age: 89 years
         Birth: 1887/10/11   Death: 1977/07/21   Burial: 1977/07/23
Site 7   Jesse M. Hammerly   Died: Leesburg, VA   Age: 89 years
         Birth: 1893/06/12   Death: 1983/02/26   Burial: 1983/03/01
Site 9   Ruth Hammerly   Died: Leesburg, VA   Age: 86 years
         Birth: 1895/01/31   Death: 1981/07/26   Burial: 1981/07/28
Site 10 Margaret J. Hammerly   Died: Leesburg, VA   Age: 71 years
         Birth: 1881/11/29   Death: 1953/06/10   Burial: 1953/06/12
Site 12 Nellie Blanch Hammerly   Age: 95 years
         Birth: 1883/08/07   Death: 1979/03/22

Lot: 766 E   Owner: V.C. Davis   Purchased: 1919/03/28
Site 10   Mrs. Myrtle Gulick Davis   Age: 24 years
          Birth: 1886   Death: 1919/03/22
          Cause: Flu   TS: Wife of Virgil C. Davis

Lot: 766 W   Owner: Mrs. John Frank Gulick   1919/03/28
Site 1   John Frank Gulick   Cause: Cerebral Hemorrhage   Age: 68 years
          Birth: 1858/06/17   Death: 1927/06/05   Burial: 1927/06/07
Site 2   Mrs. Flora Gertrude Saffer Gulick   Age: 85 years
          Birth: 1867/04/16   Death: 1952/07/07   Burial: 1952/07/09
          TS: Wife of John Frank Gulick
Site 3   Gladys Gulick   Cause: Appendicitis   Age: 35 years
          Birth: 1898   Death: 1934/10/18   Burial: 1934/10/20
Site 4   John Allen Gulick   Age: 50 years
          Birth: 1895/07/31   Death: 1946/05/15   Burial: 1946/05/17
Site 6   Myrtle Thompson Gulick   Age: 78 years
          Birth: 1883/03/18   Death: 1961/12/07   Burial: 1961/12/10
          Died: Leesburg, VA   On stone with John Allen Gulick

Lot: 767   Owner: Jackson Minor   Purchased: 1920/03/27
Site 1   Infant of Jackson Minor   No stone
          Cause: Stillborn   Death: 1924/02/07   Burial: 1924/02/07
Site 2   Jackson Minor   Cause: Cancer of Stomach   Age: 58 years
          Birth: 1865/08/05   Death: 1924/05/03   Burial: 1924/05/05
Site 3   William T. Minor   Cause: Heart   Age: 78 years
          Birth: 1858   Death: 1936/01/04   Burial: 1936/01/06
Site 4   John Brown Minor   Age: 76 years
          Birth: 1872/05/15   Death: 1948/08/10   Burial: 1948/08/12
Site 6   Dora Bell Gray James   Cause: Heart Trouble   Age: 23 years
          Birth: 1907/05/05   Death: 1931/04/27   Burial: 1931/04/29
Site 7   John W. Miner   Age: 26 years
          Birth: 1926/05/09   Death: 1952/09/30   Burial: 1952/10/03
Site 8   Miss Nellie W. Minor   Age: 72 years
          Birth: 1877/07/09   Death: 1949/09/25   Burial: 1949/09/28
Site 10   Mrs. Mary E. Minor   Birth: 1835/01/12   Death: 1920/03/17
Site 11   Mrs. Anna Belle Gray   Age: 82 years
          Birth: 1861/05/11   Death: 1943/11/26   Burial: 1943/11/28
Site 12   Geo. T. Gray   Cause: Adentis   Age: 66 years
          Birth: 1861/08/26   Death: 1928/03/28   Burial: 1928/03/31

Lot: 768   Owner: Mahlon & Jno. M. Morris   1921/07/05
Site 1   John M. Morris   Died: Winchester, VA   Age: 88 years
          Birth: 1885/10/24   Death: 1973/11/03   Burial: 1973/11/06
Site 4   John C. Hopkins III   Died: Washington, DC
          Birth: 1970/02/24   Death: 1970/02/27   Burial: 1970/03/02
Site 5   Mrs. Rose Lee Morris   Died: Arlington, VA   Age: 64 years
          Birth: 1888/10/22   Death: 1953/02/03   Burial: 1953/02/06
Site 6   John M. Morris   TS: Son of J.M. & R.L. Morris   Age: 2 years
          Birth: 1919/06/15   Death: 1921/07/04

Site 7	John Philip Everhart	Died: Leesburg, VA	Age: 83 years
	Birth: 1889/09/01	Death: 1972/11/26	Burial: 1972/11/29
Site 8	Anne Morris Everhart		
	Birth: 1899/03/23	Death: 1993/04/10	Burial: 1993/04/13
	Died: Leesburg, VA	On stone with John Philip Everhart	
Site 9	Ethel M. Morris	Died: Leesburg, VA	Age: 89 years
	Birth: 1892/08/08	Death: 1982/08/05	Burial: 1982/08/07
Site 11	Mahlon Morris	Died: Leesburg, VA	Age: 98 years
	Birth: 1857/05/07	Death: 1955/05/26	Burial: 1955/05/26
Site 12	Mrs. Catherine Elizabeth Morris		Age: 84 years
	Birth: 1859/02/11	Death: 1943/03/07	Burial: 1943/07/09
	On stone with Mahlon Morris		

Lot: 769 E   Owner: William H. Saunders   Purchased: 1924/09/11

Site	Edna Saunders Chatfield	Birth: 1885	Death: 1972
Site 8	Shirley Oswalt Chatfield	Died: Centerville, VA	Age: 38 years
	Birth: 1937	Death: 1976/10/20	Burial: 1976/10/25
Site 9	Frederick R. Chatfield Jr.		Age: 47 years
	Birth: 1924/12/07	Death: 1972/03/03	Burial: 1972/03/11
Site 10	Frederick Rupert Chatfield		Age: 71 years
		Death: 1958/05/09	Burial: 1958/05/12
	Cause: Arteriosclerosis	Died: Washington, DC	No stone
Site 11	William Henry Saunders	Cause: S. Aderosis	Age: 77 years
	Birth: 1856/04/18	Death: 1933/07/21	Burial: 1933/07/23
Site 12	Mrs. Golda C. Norris Saunders		Age: 83 years
	Birth: 1862/05/10	Death: 1945/09/08	Burial: 1945/09/10
	On stone with William Henry Saunders		

Lot: 769 W   Owner: E.H. Drake & Eliz. C. Smith   1924/11/22

Site 1	Mrs. Elizabeth (Lizzie) Carter Smith		Age: 80 years
	Birth: 1871/12/12	Death: 1952/05/31	Burial: 1952/06/03
	TS: Wife of Edward S. Smith		
Site 3	Edward S. Smith		Age: 55 years
	Birth: 1870/03/05	Death: 1924/11/16	Burial: 1924/11/18
	Cause: Accident	TS: Husband of Lizzie Carter Smith	
Site 4	Dr. Eugene H. Drake	Died: Leesburg, VA	Age: 77 years
	Birth: 1884	Death: 1962/01/29	Burial: 1962/01/31
Site 4	Elsie C. Drake		Age: 93 years
	Birth: 1883	Death: 1977/01/18	Burial: 1977/01/21
	Died: Leesburg, VA	On stone with Eugene H. Drake	
Site 5	Eugene Harvey Drake Jr.		Age: 33 years
	Birth: 1913	Death: 1946/05/13	Burial: 1946/05/15
Site 6	Joseph C. Drake	Cause: Suicide	Age: 22 years
	Birth: 1915	Death: 1938/01/01	Burial: 1938/01/03

Lot: 770   Owner: Eva Hutchison et. al.   Purchased: 1926/03/23

Site 1	Margaret Elgin Matthews		Age: 79 years
	Birth: 1878/07/07	Death: 1958/03/27	Burial: 1958/03/29
	Cause: Old Age	Died: Paonian Springs, VA	

Site 2   Gordon M. Hutchison   Age: 27 years
         Birth: 1914/12/30   Death: 1942/06/15   Burial: 1942/06/17
         TS: Son of B.B. & Eva M. Hutchison
Site 5   Benjamin Barbour Hutchison   Died: Arcola, VA
         Birth: 1883/11/26   Death: 1960/05/19   Burial: 1960/05/21
Site 6   Mrs. Eva Matthews Hutchison   Age: 50 years
         Birth: 1884/01/08   Death: 1934/05/06   Burial: 1934/05/08
         Cause: Reguntatis   TS: Wife of B.B. Hutchison
Site 8   Cecile Hutchison Matthews   Age: 85 years
         Birth: 1886/10/20   Death: 1971/07/07   Burial: 1971/07/09
         Died: Leesburg, VA   TS: Wife of Charles B. Matthews
Site 9   Charles Balthrop Matthews   Age: 44 years
         Birth: 1882/01/12   Death: 1926/06/08   Burial: 1926/06/11
         Cause: Nephritis   TS: Son of C.B. & Rose S. Matthews
Site 11 Dr. John Burr Piggott   Died: Fairfax, VA   Age: 73 years
         Birth: 1911/11/03   Death: 1985/10/14   Burial: 1985/10/23
         TS: Son of Belle Matthews Piggott & Fenton L. Piggott. D.V.M.
Site 12 Belle M. Piggott   Age: 46 years
         Birth: 1880/02/25   Death: 1926/03/22   Burial: 1926/03/24
         Cause: Uremia   TS: Daughter of C.B. & Rose S. Matthews

Lot: 771   Owner: John G. Hopkins   Purchased: 1939/11/18
Site 2   Emma Skipwith Hopkins Died: Washington, DC   Age: 93 years
         Birth: 1895   Death: 1989/06/12   Burial: 1989/06/14
Site 3   John Guthrie Hopkins   Died: Millersville, MD   Age: 101 years
         Birth: 1854   Death: 1956/08/19   Burial: 1956/08/20
Site 4   Mary Enos Hopkins   Cause: Old Age   Age: 82 years
         Birth: 1857   Death: 1939/11/18   Burial: 1939/11/20
Site 5   John Hopkins   Died: MD   No stone
         Birth: 1916/12/02   Death: 1993/10/24   Burial: 1993/10/27

Lot: 772 E   Owner: Richard Herndon   Purchased: 1941/05/19
Site 7   Child Herndon   Cause: Stillborn   No stone
                                 Death: 1943/10/07   Burial: 1943/10/07
Site 11 Mrs. Emma Eugene Herndon Brown   Age: 77 years
         Birth: 1872   Death: 1949/08/01   Burial: 1949/08/03
Site 12 Richard T. Herndon   Age: 80 years
         Birth: 1861   Death: 1941/05/19   Burial: 1941/05/21

Lot: 772 W   Owner: Mrs. H. H. Trundle   Purchased: 1938/01/06
Site 2   John Lewis Bryan   Age: 88 years
         Birth: 1859/10/15   Death: 1947/12/18   Burial: 1947/12/20
Site 3   Rolanda (Tinia) Hancock Bryan   Age: 79 years
         Birth: 1859/01/14   Death: 1939/01/05   Burial: 1939/01/07
         Cause: Influenza Pneumonia   On stone with John Lewis Bryan

Lot: 773 E   Owner: Mrs. Margaret Moxley   Purchased: 1929/12/26
Site 7   Evelyn E. Moxley   Age: 77 years
         Birth: 1900   Death: 1977/10/16   Burial: 1977/10/20
         Died: FL   TS: Wife of William T. Moxley

Site 8   William T. Moxley   Died: Washington, DC   Age: 58 years
         Birth: 1907   Death: 1965/12/10   Burial: 1965/12/14
Site 9   Thomas Oden Moxley   Cause: Cancer   Age: 64 years
         Birth: 1866/07/21   Death: 1929/12/26   Burial: 1929/12/28
Site 10 Margaret D. Moxley   Age: 101 years
         Birth: 1882/09/27   Death: 1984/07/05   Burial: 1984/07/07
         Died: Leesburg, VA   TS: Wife of Thomas Oden Moxley

Lot: 773 W   Owner: William E. Virts   Purchased: 1930/04/12
Site 1   Dorothy Catherine Virts   Died: Frederick, MD   Age: 63 years
         Birth: 1902/09/09   Death: 1969/08/22   Burial: 1969/08/26
Site 2   Howard F. Virts   Died: Baltimore, MD   Age: 79 years
         Birth: 1905/12/20   Death: 1985/03/27   Burial: 1985/04/01
Site 3   William Edgar Virts   Died: Frederick, MD   Age: 85 years
         Birth: 1878   Death: 1963/11/04   Burial: 1963/11/08
Site 4   Mrs. Susannah Virts   Age: 73 years
         Birth: 1883   Death: 1956/05/19   Burial: 1956/05/19
         Died: Frederick Co., MD   On stone with William E. Virts
Site 5   William E. Virts Jr.   Age: 13 years
         Birth: 1917/04/17   Death: 1930/03/29   Burial: 1930/04/01
         Cause: Auto Accident   TS: Son of W.E. & S.V. Virts

Lot: 774 E   Owner: George Emory Fouche   1941/11/07
Site 9   Hubert Alvin Fouche   Died: Arlington, VA   Age: 60 years
         Birth: 1905/04/13   Death: 1965/11/24   Burial: 1965/11/27

Lot: 774 W   Owner: Mrs. George W. Popkins   1935/03/30
Site 1   Rev. George Washington Popkins   Age: 75 years
         Birth: 1855   Death: 1931/02/09   Burial: 1931/02/11
         Cause: Hemorrhage
Site 2   Laura W. LeFever Popkins Cause: Coronary Thrombosis Age: 81 years
         Birth: 1860   Death: 1940/12/24   Burial: 1940/12/26
         On stone with George Washington Popkins
Site 3   Edwin W. Popkins   Age: 51 years
         Birth: 1897/06/12   Death: 1949/12/12   Burial: 1949/12/14
Site 5   Ruth H. Popkins   Age: 60 years
         Birth: 1893/09/24   Death: 1954/12/16
         On stone with Edwin W. Popkins

Lot: 775 E   Owner: Durward S. Keatts   Purchased: 1933/03/21
Site 10 Dorothy Keatts   No stone   Age: 22 years
         Cause: Accident   Death: 1933/03/21   Burial: 1933/03/23

Lot: 775 W   Owner: Charles M. Newton   Purchased: 1937/03/02
Site 1   William Fontaine Waddell   Age: 33 years
         Birth: 1902/04/28   Death: 1937/02/08   Burial: 1937/02/10
         Cause: Cerebral Thrombosis
Site 2   Mrs. Margaret Newton Waddell   Age: 81 years
         Birth: 1903/09/03   Death: 1985/02/10   Burial: 1985/02/12
                                    Died: Arlington, VA

Site 5 Charles M. Newton   Died: Arlington, VA   Age: 83 years
        Birth: 1877/06/27   Death: 1960/06/29   Burial: 1960/07/02
Site 6 Ethel B. Newton   Died: Arlington, VA   Age: 99 years
        Birth: 1884/09/18   Death: 1984/05/23   Burial: 1984/05/25

Lot: 776   Owner: Mrs. Rose Loy   Purchased: 1934/07/10
Site 4   William H. Loy   Cause: A. V.Perashymty   Age: 66 years
         Birth: 1867/02/23   Death: 1934/10/13   Burial: 1934/10/15
Site 5   Rosa S. Belle Loy   TS: Wife of William H. Loy   Age: 77 years
         Birth: 1972/11/01   Death: 1950/01/15   Burial: 1950/01/17
Site 6   Leighton W. Loy   Age: 40 years
         Birth: 1906/03/30   Death: 1946/12/24   Burial: 1946/12/26
Site 10 Mollie V. Loy   Age: 84 years
         Birth: 1864/07/21   Death: 1948/04/09   Burial: 1949/04/11
         TS: Loving sister of Maggie A. Loy Umbaugh
Site 12 Mrs. Maggie A. Loy Umbaugh   Age: 75 years
         Birth: 1862/01/27   Death: 1937/06/06   Burial: 1937/06/08
         Cause: M. A?   TS: Loving sister of Mollie V. Loy

Lot: 777   Owner: Herbert H. James   Purchased: 1935/09/23
Site 1   William B. James   Died: Leesburg, VA   Age: 60 years
         Birth: 1933/02/23   Death: 1994/01/09   Burial: 1994/01/18
Site 2   Herbert Harwood James Died: Leesburg, VA   Age: 67 years
         Birth: 1888   Death: 1955/11/05   Burial: 1955/11/05
Site 4   Cora Lee James   Age: 72 years
         Birth: 1890   Death: 1962/10/03   Burial: 1962/10/06
         Died: Leesburg, VA   On stone with Herbert Harwood James
Site 5   Arthur D. James   Cause: Auto Accident   Age: 20 years
         Birth: 1915/07/23   Death: 1935/09/21   Burial: 1935/09/23
Site 6   Berkeley Lee James   Age: 55 years
         Birth: 1922   Death: 1977/10/29   Burial: 1977/11/01
         Died: Sterling, VA   TS: PFC US Army WWII
Site 7   Victor Nelson Jackson Died: Leesburg, VA   Age: 62 years
         Birth: 1895/02/17   Death: 1957/11/28   Burial: 1957/12/01
         TS: Virginia SFC 422 SVC Park Unit MTC, WW I
Site 8   Mable J. Jackson   Died: Leesburg, VA
         Birth: 1913/08/01   Death: 1992/02/18   Burial: 1992/02/20
Site 9   James Robert Brady   Died: Fairfax, VA   Age: 56 years
         Birth: 1914   Death: 1970/07/26   Burial: 1970/07/28
Site 10 Helen J. Brady   Age: 62 years
         Birth: 1920   Death: 1982/05/12   Burial: 1982/05/15
         Died: Alexandria, VA On stone with James Robert Brady

Lot: 778 E   Owner: Herbert H. James   Purchased: 1936/10/15
Site 7   John Daniel Spinks   Age: 94 years
         Birth: 1849   Death: 1943/08/28   Burial: 1943/08/30
Site 8   Mrs. Nancy Catherine Spinks   Age: 79 years
         Birth: 1856/11/28   Death: 1937/03/11   Burial: 1937/03/13
         Cause: Pneumonia   IB:Mrs. John Spinks

Site 9   Catherine L. Johnson   Age: 64 years
         Birth: 1894   Death: 1958/07/15   Burial: 1958/07/18
         Died: L.C.H. Leesburg, VA   On stone with Mac C. Johnson
Site 10 Mac C. Johnson   Died: Leesburg, VA   Age: 73 years
         Birth: 1881   Death: 1955/03/07   Burial: 1955/03/07
Site 11 Marcus Clarence Hopkins   Age: 66 years
         Birth: 1877/01/12   Death: 1937/01/22   Burial: 1937/01/24
         Cause: Arteriosclerosis
Site 12 Annie Elizabeth James   Cause: Cancer of Uterus   Age: 76 years
         Birth: 1860/06/18   Death: 1936/10/03   Burial: 1936/10/05

Lot: 778 W   Owner: Mrs. Harvey Cockrell   Purchased: 1934/01/20
Site 1   Harvey M. Cockrell   Died: Sterling, VA   Age: 62 years
         Birth: 1903   Death: 1965/05/20   Burial: 1965/05/22

Lot: 779 E   Owner: George D. Redmon   Purchased: 1940/05/22
Site 9   George D. Redmon   Died: Leesburg, VA   Age: 83 years
         Birth: 1893   Death: 1976/10/13   Burial: 1976/10/17
Site 10 Myrtle L. Redmon   Age: 73 years
         Birth: 1891   Death: 1964/12/14   Burial: 1964/12/16
         Died: Ashburn, VA   On stone with George D. Redmon
Site 12 Martha Ellen Redmon
         Birth: 1924/09/19   Death: 1940/05/21   Burial: 1940/05/24

Lot: 779 W   Owner: Albert Tillett   Purchased: 1941/06/25
Site 1   Robert Franklin Flynn   No stone   Age: 77 years
                                  Death: 1950/11/07   Burial: 1950/11/09
Site 2   Mrs. Elizabeth Anne Flynn   No stone
                                  Death: 1952/11/18   Burial: 1952/11/20
Site 4   Albert L. Tillett   Died: Leesburg, VA   Age: 74 years
         Birth: 1903/06/11   Death: 1978/01/08   Burial: 1978/01/10
Site 5   Florence E. Tillett   Age: 60 years
         Birth: 1903/02/02   Death: 1963/11/19   Burial: 1963/11/22
         Died: Leesburg, VA   On stone with Albert L. Tillett
Site 6   Howard C. Tillett   Age: 10 years
         Birth: 1930/12/02   Death: 1941/06/23   Burial: 1941/06/25
         Cause: Lightning   TS: Son of A.T. & F.E. Tillett

Lot: 780 E   Owner: Charles H. Gill   Purchased: 1937/03/08
Site 8   Glen Perry Cole Jr.   Died: L.C.H. Leesburg, VA   Age: 1/2 day
         Birth: 1958/09/16   Death: 1958/09/17   Burial: 1958/09/18
Site 9   Charles Henry Gill   Age: 72 years
         Birth: 1885   Death: 1957/10/25
Site 10 Mrs. Pearl Gertrude Gill   Age: 42 years
         Birth: 1895   Death: 1937/03/06   Burial: 1937/03/08
         IB:Mrs. Charles Gill   On stone with Charles Henry Gill
Site 11 Charles W. Gill   Died: Leesburg, VA   Age: 67 years
         Birth: 1914   Death: 1982/01/24   Burial: 1982/01/28

Site 12 Vava Reed Gill   Died: White's Ferry, VA   Age: 62 years
         Birth: 1920/01/03   Death: 1982/06/10   Burial: 1982/06/13
         Cause: Suicide   On stone with Charles W. Gill

Lot: 780 W Owner: Eugene Harrison   Purchased: 1937/03/17
Site 3   Eugene Harrison   Died: Annandale, VA   No stone
         Birth: 1908/04/13   Death: 1994/10/21   Burial: 1994/10/25
Site 4   Miss Shirley Arlene Harrison   Age: 35 years
         Birth: 1934/08/05   Death: 1970/02/23   Burial: 1970/02/26
                                 Died: Fairfax, VA
Site 5   Alma L. Harrison   Cause: Pneumonia   Age: 3 weeks
         Birth: 1937/02/21   Death: 1937/03/17   Burial: 1937/03/19
Site 6   James E. Harrison   Cause: Pneumonia   Age: 6 years
         Birth: 1932/04/17   Death: 1938/03/24   Burial: 1938/03/26

Lot: 781 Owner: Miscellaneous
Site 1   Annie Lottie Wright   Died: Linden, VA   Age: 55 years
         Birth: 1907/11/25   Death: 1963/07/24   Burial: 1963/07/28
Site 2   Martin J. Timon   No stone   Age: 63 years
         Died: Leesburg, VA   Death: 1963/01/29   Burial: 1963/01/31
Site 3   James William Jarmanes Died: Marshall, VA   Age: 54 years
         Birth: 1907/01/05   Death: 1962/02/25   Burial: 1962/05/14
         Removed from Upperville, VA.
         TS: Virginia PVT TRP A 2 Cavalry RTC WWII
Site 8   Judith H. Gunnells   Died: Leesburg, VA
         Birth: 1916/09/16   Death: 1994/05/19   Burial: 1994/05/21
Site 10 Judith Ann Gunnells   Died: Leesburg, VA
         Birth: 1939/10/23   Death: 1993/02/10   Burial: 1993/02/13

Lot: 782 Owner: Miscellaneous
Site 1   Alvirty Vermillion   Died: L.C.H. Leesburg, VA   Age: 84 years
         No stone   Death: 1958/07/18   Burial: 1958/07/23
Site 2   Benjamin F. Leith   Died: Leesburg, VA   Age: 84 years
         Birth: 1883   Death: 1964/06/04   Burial: 1964/06/07
Site 3   Maude Mae A. Leith   Died: Leesburg, VA   Age: 53 years
         Birth: 1903   Death: 1957/12/08   Burial: 1957/12/10
         Cause: Stroke   On stone with Benjamin F. Leith
Site 4   James Michael Russell   Age: 11 years
         Birth: 1951/11/14   Death: 1962/10/26   Burial: 1962/10/29
         Died: Washington, DC   TS: "Son"
Site 5   Lester Russell   Died: Leesburg, VA   Age: 64 years
         Birth: 1909   Death: 1974/03/04   Burial: 1974/03/07
Site 6   Hilda Estella Russell   Died: Leesburg, VA   Age: 58 years
         Birth: 1914   Death: 1973/07/25   Burial: 1973/07/28
         Cause: Heart   On stone with Lester Russell
Site 7   Earl Vandon Howser   No stone   Age: 73 years
                                 Death: 1950/03/04   Burial: 1950/03/06
Site 8   Daniel Lee Shiflett   No stone   Age: Infant
         IB:Child of J.E. Shiflett Death: 1950/06/09   Burial: 1950/06/11

Site 9 Child Buttery   No stone   Age: Stillborn
                                Death: 1951/02/24   Burial: 1951/02/24
Site 9 Robert Franklin Hancock   Age: 3 months
        No stone   Death: 1951/03/23   Burial: 1951/03/23
Site 10 Child Farmer   No stone   Age: 12 hours
                                Death: 1950/09/24   Burial: 1950/09/25
Site 11 Elizabeth Mae Fletcher   Age: 31 years
        Birth: 1926/10/06   Death: 1958/08/27   Burial: 1958/09/03
        Died: Washington, DC   TS: Children Linda, Brenda, Danny Jenkins
Site 12 Miss Betty Pauline Flynn No stone   Age: 26 years
        Died: Washington, DC   Death: 1955/02/18   Burial: 1955/02/19

Lot: 783 Owner: Miscellaneous

Site 1 Mamme R. Gilley   Age: 55 years
        Birth: 1914   Death: 1968/06/30   Burial: 1968/07/03
        Died: Charlottesville, VA   On stone with Charles M. Gilley
Site 2 Charles M. Gilley   Died: Ramson, WV   Age: 75 years
        Birth: 1914   Death: 1990/01/14   Burial: 1990/01/17
Site 3 William E. Powell Sr.   Died: Leesburg, VA   Age: 73 years
        Birth: 1914/07/03   Death: 1988/02/02   Burial: 1988/02/05
Site 4 Georgia Bell Allison (Nanny) Powell   Age: 70 years
        Birth: 1917/04/08   Death: 1987/07/02   Burial: 1987/07/06
        Cause: Heart   Died: Woodbridge, VA
        On stone with William E. Powell Sr.
Site 5 Elmer B. Biggs   Died: Leesburg, VA
        Birth: 1921/01/18   Death: 1992/08/30   Burial: 1992/09/02
Site 6 Margaret Biggs   On stone with Elmer B. Biggs
        Birth: 1917/12/07   Death: 1972/08/24
Site 7 Charlie W. Marion   Died: Winchester, VA   Age: 51 years
        Birth: 1913/02/25   Death: 1964/11/12   Burial: 1964/11/14
Site 8 Ora Lee Marion Bowman Died: Manassas, VA   Age: 72 years
        Birth: 1904   Death: 1976/10/27   Burial: 1976/10/30
Site 9 Vida L. Herndon   Died: Fairfax, VA
        Birth: 1932/12/08   Death: 1994/07/22   Burial: 1994/07/26
Site 10 John Louis Jarmans   Died: Winchester, VA   Age: 57 years
        Birth: 1910   Death: 1971/05/26   Burial: 1971/05/29
Site 11 Etta M. Jarmans   Age: 52 years
        Birth: 1913   Death: 1965/11/08   Burial: 1965/11/11
        Died: Leesburg, VA   On stone with John Louis Jarmans
Site 12 Margaret V. Morris   Died: Leesburg, VA   Age: 64 years
        Birth: 1900   Death: 1965/01/14   Burial: 1965/01/17

Lot: 784 Owner: Miscellaneous

Site 1 Allean Catherine Jennings   Age: 58 years
        Birth: 1905/01/01   Death: 1963/11/20   Burial: 1963/11/22
                                Died: Leesburg, VA
Site 2 Robert H. Biggs   Died: Leesburg, VA   Age: 69 years
        Birth: 1896/05/17   Death: 1965/10/11   Burial: 1965/10/14

Site 3   Cora L. Biggs   Age: 82 years
         Birth: 1896/07/15   Death: 1978/10/25   Burial: 1978/10/28
         Died: Leesburg, VA   On stone with Robert H. Biggs
Site 4   Louise Hough   Died: Leesburg, VA   Age: 81 years
         Birth: 1883/02/13   Death: 1966/01/26   Burial: 1966/01/29
Site 5   Claude Lee Springs   Age: 22 years
                              Death: 1963/06/28   Burial: 1963/07/01
         Cause: Auto Accident Died: Loudoun Co., VA   No stone
Site 7   James E. Kirkpatrick   Age: 27 years
         Birth: 1935   Death: 1963/04/12   Burial: 1963/04/15
Site 8   Mary L. Smallwood   Died: Williamsburg, VA Age: 79 years
         Birth: 1883/12/12   Death: 1963/05/19   Burial: 1963/05/23
Site 9   Harm Gant   No stone   Age: 84 years
         Died: Waterford, VA Death: 1967/05/26   Burial: 1967/05/28
Site 10 Howard P. Smallwood Died: Martinsburg, WV Age: 73 years
         Birth: 1903   Death: 1976/08/27   Burial: 1976/08/29
Site 10 Harry Smallwood   No stone   Age: 78 years
         Died: Alexandria, VA Death: 1992/06/10   Burial: 1992/07/28
Site 12 Ray C. Dawson   Died: Gaithersburg, VA Age: 63 years
         Birth: 1925/01/22   Death: 1989/01/18   Burial: 1989/01/21

Lot: 785 E   Owner: George Stavrakas   Purchased: 1942/02/17
Site 7   Dorothy A. (Dolly) Cooper   Age: 84 years
         Birth: 1898   Death: 1983/01/01   Burial: 1983/01/04
         Died: Leesburg, VA   On stone with David W. Cooper
Site 8   David W. Cooper   Died: Leesburg, VA   Age: 69 years
         Birth: 1896   Death: 1966/06/23   Burial: 1966/06/26
Site 9   John Wesley Cooper   Age: 82 years
         Birth: 1867   Death: 1949/10/17   Burial: 1949/10/19
Site 10 Mrs. Dorcas Ann Cooper   Age: 80 years
         Birth: 1869   Death: 1949/07/13   Burial: 1949/07/15
         On stone with John Wesley Cooper
Site 11 George A. Stavrakas Died: Washington, DC Age: 68 years
         Birth: 1900/04/23   Death: 1969/03/31   Burial: 1969/04/04
Site 12 Ruth Hannah C. Stavrakas   Age: 38 years
         Birth: 1903/06/12   Death: 1942/02/14   Burial: 1942/02/16
         Cause: Pulmonary Tuberculosis

Lot: 785 W   Owner: Maude S. Harris   Purchased: 1942/02/23
Site 1   Thomas E. Mercer   Died: Frederick, MD Age: 22 years
         Birth: 1949/07/06   Death: 1971/11/22   Burial: 1971/11/24
Site 2   Milton A. Harris   Age: 45
         Birth: 1925/06/16   Death: 1970/05/08   Burial: 1970/05/13
         Died: SC   TS: Maryland EM 2 US NAVY Korea
Site 3   Milton E. Alonzo Harris   Age: 54 years
         Birth: 1885/06/20   Death: 1942/02/22   Burial: 1942/02/25
Site 4   Mrs. Maude S. Harris   Age: 81 years
         Birth: 1884/06/13   Death: 1965/12/08   Burial: 1965/12/10
         Died: Frederick, MD   On stone with Milton E. Harris

Site 5 Joseph E. Mercer   Died: Frederick, MD   Age: 58 years
        Birth: 1918/08/19   Death: 1976/02/09   Burial: 1976/02/11

Lot: 786 E   Owner: Henry Kerns   Purchased: 1938/07/25
Site 7   Walter H. Kerns   No stone   Age: 61 years
         Died: Leesburg, VA   Death: 1983/05/28   Burial: 1983/05/31
Site 9   Robert J. Kerns   Died: Fairfax, VA   Age: 61 years
         Birth: 1905/04/25   Death: 1966/05/29   Burial: 1966/06/01
Site 10 Lewis H. Kerns, Sr.   Died: Leesburg, VA   Age: 62 years
         Birth: 1903/06/02   Death: 1965/07/28   Burial: 1965/08/01
Site 11 William Henry Kerns   Died: Sterling, VA   Age: 76 or 79
         Birth: 1881   Death: 1958/07/30   Burial: 1958/08/02
Site 12 Lillie Marshall Kerns   Age: 54 years
         Birth: 1883   Death: 1938/07/25   Burial: 1938/07/27
         Cause: Cerebral Embolism   On stone with William H. Kerns

Lot: 786 W   Owner: William H. Harding   Purchased: 1939/11/15
Site 1   Infant of Mr. William Harding   No stone
         Cause: Stillborn   Death: 1942/09/08   Burial: 1942/09/08
Site 2   William Walter Kenneth Harding   Age: 69 years
         Birth: 1920/06/08   Death: 1989/11/12   Burial: 1989/11/16
         Died: Martinsburg, WV   TS: US ARMY
Site 3   Pvt. Donald O. Harding   Burial: 1948/09/01   No stone
Site 4   William Harding   No stone   Age: 79 years
         Died: Leesburg, VA   Death: 1966/06/21   Burial: 1966/06/23
Site 5   Edna C. Harding   Age: 56 years
         Birth: 1889/11/11   Death: 1947/05/08   Burial: 1947/05/10
Site 6   Leslie Harding   Cause: Accident   Age: 17 years
         Birth: 1922/11/24   Death: 1939/11/14   Burial: 1939/11/16

Lot: 787 E   Owner: Miscellaneous
Site 9   Antoine J. Mauran   Age: 81 years
         Birth: 1871/10/31   Death: 1952/09/01   Burial: 1952/09/04
Site 10 Mrs. Retta Douglas Mauran   Age: 69 years
         Birth: 1868/02/06   Death: 1937/08/04   Burial: 1937/08/08
         Cause: Myocarditis   TS: Wife of Antoine J. Mauran
Site 11 Anna P. Kyle   Age: 97 years
         Birth: 1893/05/25   Death: 1990/11/29   Burial: 1990/12/01
         Died: Gettysburg, PA   On stone with David N. Kyle
Site 12 David Nathionale Kyle   Died: VA   Age: 72 years
         Birth: 1888/03/13   Death: 1960/03/04   Burial: 1960/03/06

Lot: 787 W   Owner: Mrs. J. H. Weaver   Purchased: 1936/11/04
Site 1   James H. Weaver   Age: 84 years
                                  Death: 1958/04/29   Burial: 1958/05/02
         Died: G.W.U. Hosp. Washington, DC   No stone
Site 3   Gertrude W. Groot   No stone   Age: 46 years
         Died: Washington, DC   Death: 1963/04/11   Burial: 1963/04/15

Site 6 Virginia Charon Killinger   Age: 57 years
        Death: 1956/08/04   Burial: 1956/08/06
        Cause: Heart Disease   Died: Washington, DC   No stone

Lot: 788 Owner: Mrs. M. M. Solomon   Purchased: 1935/11/02
Site 2 John Edwin Solomon   Died: Leesburg, VA   Age: 74 years
        Birth: 1915/06/12   Death: 1989/07/23   Burial: 1989/07/26
Site 3 Matthew M. Solomon   Cause: Myocarditis   Age: 66 years
        Birth: 1869   Death: 1935/10/31   Burial: 1935/11/02
Site 4 Fannie S. Solomon   Age: 71 years
        Birth: 1875   Death: 1948/06/10   Burial: 1948/06/12
        TS: Wife of Matthew M. Solomon
Site 6 Miss Ollie Mae Solomon Died: Ashburn, VA   Age: 59 years
        Birth: 1896/05/02   Death: 1955/10/01   Burial: 1955/10/01
Site 9 C. Lester Solomon   Died: Washington, DC   Age: 89 years
        Birth: 1898   Death: 1988/04/25   Burial: 1988/04/29
Site 10 Daisy M. Solomon   Age: 81 years
        Birth: 1902   Death: 1983/09/22   Burial: 1983/09/24
        Died: Arcola, VA   On stone with C. Lester Solomon
Site 11 William M. Solomon   Died: Leesburg, VA   Age: 65 years
        Birth: 1895/01/01   Death: 1961/09/16   Burial: 1961/09/19
Site 12 Bertha K. Solomon   Died: Leesburg, VA   Age: 83 years
        Birth: 1903/12/21   Death: 1987/08/04   Burial: 1987/08/07

Lot: 789 E Owner: Mrs. James Jackson   Purchased: 1935/03/01
Site 7 Lauretta U. Jackson   Age: 74 years
        Birth: 1898/09/15   Death: 1972/10/20   Burial: 1972/10/23
        Died: Winchester, VA   On stone with Powell C. Jackson
Site 7 Powell C. Jackson   Died: Winchester, VA   Age: 65 years
        Birth: 1911/03/02   Death: 1976/08/28   Burial: 1976/08/31
Site 8 James H. Jackson   Died: Leesburg, VA   Age: 61 years
        Birth: 1917/04/23   Death: 1978/09/07   Burial: 1978/09/11
Site 9 James Jackson   Cause: Pneumonia   Age: 48 years
        Birth: 1887/05/15   Death: 1935/01/15   Burial: 1935/01/17
Site 10 Hildur E. Jackson   On stone with James Jackson   Age: 59 years
        Birth: 1888/01/13   Death: 1947/08/22   Burial: 1947/08/24
Site 11 Helen Jackson Pulliam Died: Leesburg, VA   Age: 63 years
        Birth: 1913/03/08   Death: 1976/04/07   Burial: 1976/04/09
Site 12 Matthew Pulliam   Age: 67 years
        Birth: 1910/03/14   Death: 1977/11/07   Burial: 1977/11/10
        Cause: Heart   Died: Leesburg, VA

Lot: 789 W Owner: Mrs. W. P. Coleman   Purchased: 1933/11/09
Site 1 Mary J. Burke   Died: Leesburg, VA   Age: 82 years
        Birth: 1886   Death: 1969/05/31   Burial: 1969/06/03
Site 2 Jean Coleman Miller No stone   Age: 73 years
        Died: Leesburg, VA   Death: 1975/07/17   Burial: 1975/07/19
Site 4 Henry Paris Coleman   Age: 52 years
        Birth: 1905   Death: 1957/10/21   TS: "Son"

Site 5 William P. Coleman   Cause: C. Pancreas   Age: 56 years
        Birth: 1877   Death: 1933/11/09   Burial: 1933/11/11
Site 6 Mrs. Myrtle E. Coleman   Age: 59 years
        Birth: 1883   Death: 1942/07/09   Burial: 1942/07/11

Lot: 790 E   Owner: Miscellaneous
Site 7   James H. Trussell   Died: Frederick, MD   Age: 84 years
         Birth: 1898/06/24   Death: 1982/07/06   Burial: 1982/07/09
Site 8   Edith Jane W. Trussell   Age: 71 years
         Birth: 1917/09/15   Death: 1989/06/29   Burial: 1989/07/01
         Died: Frederick, MD   On stone with James H. Trussell
Site 10 Lenora Hurst Wortman   Age: 70 years
         Birth: 1896   Death: 1966/12/25   Burial: 1966/12/27
         Died: Hillsboro, VA   TS: "Mother"
Site 11 Samuel Gibson Hurst   Age: 78 years
         Birth: 1862/12/08   Death: 1941/05/08   Burial: 1941/05/10
         Cause: Myocardial Degeneration
Site 12 Mrs. Tacie Hurst   Age: 76 years
         Birth: 1861/05/06   Death: 1938/04/10   Burial: 1938/04/14
         Cause: Pneumonia   On stone with Samuel Gibson Hurst

Lot: 790 W   Owner: A. Lee VanDevanter   Purchased: 1937/09/10
Site 1 Howard M. Ryon Sr.   Age: 54 years
        Birth: 1925/07/13   Death: 1979/09/06   Burial: 1979/09/10
        Died: Fairfax, VA   TS: HM 2 US NAVY WWII
Site 3 Albert Lee VanDeventer   Age: 57 years
        Birth: 1894/07/08   Death: 1952/01/14   Burial: 1952/01/16
Site 4 Anne Graham VanDeventer   Age: 95 years
        Birth: 1896/06/21   Death: 1992/04/13   Burial: 1992/04/15
                                  Died: Leesburg, VA

Lot: 791 E   Owner: H.H. Trussell   Purchased: 1931/02/16
Site 7   Betty Jane Trussell   Age: 12 years
         Birth: 1926/12/06   Death: 1938/12/10   Burial: 1938/12/12
         Cause: Diphtheria   TS: Daughter of W.K. & Emma Trussell
Site 7   Child of Herman R. Triman   No stone
         Cause: Stillborn   Death: 1940/05/21   Burial: 1940/05/21
Site 8   Emma J. Trussell   Age: 66 years
         Birth: 1890   Death: 1957/09/11
         On stone with Willie K. Trussell
Site 9   Willie K. Trussel   Died: Prince Georges Co., MD   Age: 73 years
         Birth: 1885   Death: 1959/01/31   Burial: 1959/02/04
Site 10 Harry K. Trussell   Age: 47 years
         Birth: 1922   Death: 1969/11/29   Burial: 1969/12/02
         Died: MD   TS: "Father"
Site 11 Hubert Hanes Trussell   Age: 83 years
         Birth: 1864/10/22   Death: 1946/08/30   Burial: 1946/09/03
Site 12 Fannie M. Trussell   Age: 79 years
         Bieth: 1853/10/22   Death: 1931/02/15   Burial: 1931/02/17
         Cause: Nephritis   TS: Wife of H.H. Trussell

Lot: 791 W   Owner: Miscellaneous
Site 1   Lemuel Perry Smith   Cause: Cerebral Hemorrhage   Age: 89 years
         Birth: 1852/02/24   Death: 1941/05/14   Burial: 1941/05/16
Site 2   Ella Hough Smith   Age: 74 years
         Birth: 1857/04/23   Death: 1931/11/27   Burial: 1931/11/29
         Cause: Cardiac Asthnia   TS: Wife of Lemuel Perry Smith
Site 3   Henry Clay Ward   Age: 85 years
                              Death: 1951/08/21   Burial: 1951/08/23
         Removed to Warrenton, VA Nov. 12, 1954   No stone
Site 3   Frances Smith Shawen   Age: 94 years
         Birth: 1877/12/20   Death: 1972/07/20

Lot: 792 E   Owner: Ruby M. Frye   Purchased: 1930/06/05
Site 7   Millard W. Frye   Cause: Senility   Age: 77 years
         Birth: 1857   Death: 1934/07/04   Burial: 1934/07/04
Site 8   Theresa F. Frye   Cause: Cancer   Age: 60 years
         Birth: 1870   Death: 1930/06/03   Burial: 1930/06/05
Site 9   Frederick H. Tucker Cause: Pneumonia   Age: 59 years
         Birth: 1878   Death: 1938/11/22   Burial: 1938/11/24
Site 10 Viola Frye Tucker   Died: Washington, DC   Age: 86 years
         Birth: 1888   Death: 1975/04/23   Burial: 1975/04/26
Site 11 Ruby M. Frye   Died: Alexandria, VA   Age: 83 years
         Birth: 1899   Death: 1983/05/04   Burial: 1983/05/05

Lot: 792 W   Owner: Mrs. O. Costello   Purchased: 1930/12/01
Site 1   Forrest B. Payne Sr. Died: Leesburg, VA   Age: 73 years
         Birth: 1910   Death: 1983/05/23   Burial: 1983/05/26
Site 2   Mrs. Iva D. Payne   On stone with Forrest B. Payne   Age: 40 years
         Birth: 1910   Death: 1950/07/13   Burial: 1950/07/14
Site 4   Robert Symons   No stone   Age: 71 years
         Died: Alexandria, VA Death: 1962/05/20   Burial: 1962/05/23
Site 5   Oliver T. Costello   Cause: Heart Disease   Age: 58 years
         Birth: 1871/12/31   Death: 1930/12/01   Burial: 1930/12/03
Site 6   Rebecca D. Symons Costello   Age: 90 years
         Birth: 1878/01/14   Death: 1968/03/30   Burial: 1968/04/01
         Died: Leesburg, VA   On stone with Oliver T. Costello

Lot: 793 E   Owner: Mr. & Mrs. T. R. Galleher   1938/06/13
Site 9   Thomas Raymond Galleher   Age: 71 years
         Birth: 1872/04/29   Death: 1943/06/28   Burial: 1943/06/30
Site 10 Elinor Hutchison Galleher   Age: 89 years
         Birth: 1880/03/15   Death: 1969/11/26   Burial: 1969/11/29
                              Died: Montgomery, MD
Site 11 Robert Winfred Welch   Age: 21 years
         Birth: 1951/05/22   Death: 1972/09/16
         TS: Son of Winford J. & Elinor G. Welch
Site 12 Elinor G. Welsh   Died: Harrisonburg, VA
         Birth: 1917/05/27   Death: 1991/07/02   Burial: 1991/07/05

Lot: 793 W   Owner: S.M. Rust   Purchased: 1927/02/16
Transfer 1: W to Elizabeth F. Akers 1943/02/01

Site 1	Fannie Louise Akers	Died: Frederick, MD	Age: 81 years
	Birth: 1904/05/30	Death: 1985/11/01	Burial: 1985/11/04
Site 2	Eliza Agnes Akers	Died: Frederick, MD	Age: 90 years
	Birth: 1896/11/07	Death: 1988/06/08	Burial: 1988/06/11
Site 3	John Brown Akers		Age: 91 years
	Birth: 1904	Death: 1994/01/15	Burial: 1995/04/24
	Died: Frederick, MD		No stone
Site 4	Florence Alma Akers Edwards		Age: 74 years
	Birth: 1895/04/01	Death: 1970/02/07	Burial: 1970/02/10
		Died: Frederick, MD	
Site 5	Elizabeth Florence Akers	Died: Arcola, VA	Age: 88 years
	Birth: 1871/02/03	Death: 1959/07/09	Burial: 1959/07/12
Site 6	James Monroe Akers	Cause: Bronchial Asthma	Age: 71 years
	Birth: 1872/04/07	Death: 1943/01/30	Burial: 1943/02/02

Lot: 794   Owner: Dr. Martin B. Hiden   Purchased: 1928/03/01

Site 5	Keith Babson		Age: 25 years
	Cause: Pneumonia	Death: 1927/02/13	Burial: 1927/02/15
	Removed to Maine Aug. 1927		No stone
Site 8	Dr. Martin Barbour Hiden		Age: 81 years
	Birth: 1886	Death: 1967/09/21	Burial: 1967/09/25
	Died: Warrenton, VA		TS: Surgeon
Site 9	Mrs. Mary Nelson Williams Hiden		Age: 41 years
	Birth: 1886/03/25	Death: 1928/02/28	Burial: 1928/03/01
	Cause: Pneumonia	TS: Wife of Dr. Martin Barbour Hiden of	
	VA. Daughter of Franklin Delano Williams & Ruth Morse Williams of		
	Boston, MA. Mother of Martin Barbour Hiden, Jr., Mary Nelson		
	Williams Hiden, & Franklin Delano Hiden. Born Boston, MA.		
	Died Leesburg, VA.		

Lot: 795   Owner: J.G. Dwyer   Purchased: 1926/08/10

Site 2	John K. Donohoe Jr.	Died: Leesburg, VA	Age: 35 years
	Birth: 1951/10/12	Death: 1987/12/06	Burial: 1987/12/09
Site 3	John G. Dwyer	Died: Arcola, VA	Age: 78 years
	Birth: 1899/01/24	Death: 1978/01/21	Burial: 1978/01/24
Site 4	Daisy M. Dwyer		Age: 77 years
	Birth: 1904/04/25	Death: 1981/11/03	Burial: 1981/11/06
	Died: Ashburn, VA		On stone with John G. Dwyer
Site 5	Maurice J. Dwyer	Died: Leesburg, VA	
	Birth: 1928/04/15	Death: 1994/11/25	Burial: 1994/11/29
Site 12	John G. Dwyer Jr.	Cause: Stomach Trouble	Age: 15 weeks
	Birth: 1926/07/06	Death: 1926/08/09	Burial: 1926/08/11

Lot: 796 E   Owner: Mrs. Ida Fry   Purchased: 1926/10/07

Site 7	Elizabeth E. Fry		TS: Wife of Samuel W. Fry
	Birth: 1855/03/29	Death: 1891/04/18	
	Removed from Oatlands July 31, 1934		

Site 8   Elizabeth J. Fry Edmonston   Age: 49 years
         Birth: 1881   Death: 1929/05/04   Burial: 1929/05/06
         Cause: Cardiac Dilation
Site 9   Samuel W. Fry   Cause: Pneumonia   Age: 79 years
         Birth: 1849   Death: 1929/01/30   Burial: 1929/02/02
Site 10 Ida J. Fry   Age: 67 years
         Birth: 1865   Death: 1932/04/14   Burial: 1932/04/16
         Cause: Hemorrhage   On stone with Samuel W. Fry

Lot: 796 W   Owner: J.M. Swart   Purchased: 1926/09/24
Site 1   William T. Costello   Died: Leesburg, VA   Age: 77 years
         Birth: 1885/09/15   Death: 1963/08/19   Burial: 1963/08/22
Site 2   Mary Ellen Costello   Age: 82 years
         Birth: 1884/09/28   Death: 1967/03/02   Burial: 1967/03/05
         Died: Leesburg, VA   On stone with William T. Costello
Site 3   James M. Swart   Cause: Cerebral Hemorrhage   Age: 74 year
         Birth: 1857/10/10   Death: 1931/11/16   Burial: 1931/11/18
Site 4   Mary J. Smith Swart Cause: Cancer   Age: 73 years
         Birth: 1852/11/03   Death: 1926/09/24   Burial: 1926/09/24
Site 5   Robert W. Swart   Died: Leesburg, VA   Age: 78 years
         Birth: 1886/08/30   Death: 1965/07/09   Burial: 1965/07/11
Site 6   Mrs. Fannie Bell Swart   Age: 57 years
         Birth: 1885/12/15   Death: 1943/02/06   Burial: 1943/02/08
         Cause: Pulmonary Tuberculosis   On stone with Robert W. Swart

Lot: 797   Owner: Mrs. Louise S. Beasley   Purchased: 1922/07/19
Site 4   Paul Willis Garrett Cause: Apoplexy   Age: 60 years
         Birth: 1873/06/14   Death: 1934/04/03   Burial: 1934/04/15
Site 5   Mrs. Mary E. Garrett   Age: 50 years
         Birth: 1869/02/14   Death: 1922/07/18   Burial: 1922/07/20
         Cause: Cancer   IB:Mrs. Paul Garrett   TS: Our Mother
Site 6   Mrs. Rebecca J. Mitchell   Age: 66 years
         Birth: 1841/09/21   Death: 1907/05/06   Cause: Cancer
Site 9   Patricia Wall Beasley   Age: 34 years
         Birth: 1935/02/19   Death: 1969/12/16   Burial: 1969/12/19
         Died: Detroit, MI   TS: Wife of Lucius Scales Beasley
Site 9   Lucius Scales Beasley Died: MI   No stone
         Birth: 1935/01/08   Death: 1995/08/26   Burial: 1995/09/12
Site 10 Oscar Hill Beasley Sr. Died: Alexandria, VA   Age: 74 years
         Birth: 1893/08/25   Death: 1967/10/29   Burial: 1967/11/01
Site 11 Louise Scales Beasley   Age: 93 years
         Birth: 1895/11/17   Death: 1988/11/27   Burial: 1988/12/02
         Died: Media, PA   TS: Wife of Oscar Hill Beasley
Site 12 Louise Mitchell Johnson   Age: 86 years
         Birth: 1874/10/09   Death: 1959/05/04   Burial: 1959/05/08

Lot: 798   Owner: John R. Clemens   Purchased: 1921/12/01
Site 1   John Robert Clemens   Age: 64 years
         Birth: 1876/07/20   Death: 1941/06/26   Burial: 1941/06/28
         TS: Son of William Hendrie & Mary E. Clemens

Site 2 Hattie Jenkins Clemens   Age: 98 years
        Birth: 1880/01/22   Death: 1978/11/06   Burial: 1978/11/09
        Died: Leesburg, VA   TS: Wife of John R. Clemens
Site 6 Emma S. Clemens   Age: 64 years
        Birth: 1909/04/29   Death: 1973/05/30   Burial: 1973/06/01
        Died: Leesburg, VA   TS: Daughter of C.H. & Leona S. Clemens
Site 7 William Hendrie Clemens   Age: 72 years
        Birth: 1850/10/07   Death: 1923/02/10   Burial: 1923/02/13
        Cause: Pneumonia   TS: Born Doylestown, Bucks Co., PA
Site 9 Mrs. Mary E. Clemens   Age: 72 years
        Birth: 1851/02/28   Death: 1923/06/20   Burial: 1923/06/21
        Cause: Cancer   TS: Wife of William Hendrie Clemens
Site 10 Infant daughter Clemens   Death: 1910/12/27
        TS: Infant daughter of J.R. & H.J. Clemens
Site 10 Mary J. Lynch   Age: 1 month
                            Death: 1932/04/04   Burial: 1932/04/06
        CR:Child of Mary Clemens Lynch   No stone

Lot: 799 E   Owner: Samuel E. & C.A. Shryock   1920/12/23
Site 9 Mabel T. Shryock Farnie   Age: 80 years
        Birth: 1886/03/28   Death: 1966/12/25   Burial: 1966/12/28
        Died: Leesburg, VA   TS: Wife of Christopher A. Shryock
Site 10 Christopher A. Shryock Cause: Apoplexy   Age: 67 years
        Birth: 1864/04/07   Death: 1931/11/21   Burial: 1931/11/23
Site 11 Samie E. Shryock   Cause: Pneumonia   Age: 68 years
        Birth: 1855/12/19   Death: 1922/04/02   Burial: 1922/04/04
Site 12 Richard F. Shryock   Cause: Cancer of Stomach   Age: 57 years
        Birth: 1862/09/07   Death: 1920/12/23

Lot: 799 W   Owner: Lester B. Murphy   Purchased: 1920/12/31
Site 1 Clyde Delbert Owens   IB: Child of Milton Owens
        Birth: 1946   Death: 1949/08/26   Burial: 1949/08/28
Site 2 Thaddeus H. Murphy   Died: Winchester, VA
        Birth: 1878/06/21   Death: 1959/02/06   Burial: 1959/02/08
Site 3 James T. Murphy   Age: 85 years
        Birth: 1836/03/13   Death: 1920/12/30   Burial: 1921/01/01
        Cause: Paralysis   TS: CSA
Site 4 Mary Virginia Murphy   Age: 98 years
        Birth: 1842/11/26   Death: 1941/04/01   Burial: 1941/04/05
        Cause: Fracture of Hip   TS: Wife of James T. Murphy
Site 5 Gettie S. Kirby   Died: Winchester, VA   Age: 91 years
        Birth: 1881/06/09   Death: 1973/03/24   Burial: 1973/03/27
Site 6 Mrs. Sarah Catherine Murphy   TS: Wife of L.B. Murphy
        Birth: 1887/01/31   Death: 1921/02/26

Lot: 800   Owner: Family di Zerega   Purchased: 1919/01/14
Site 1 Mrs. Frederica diZerega Died: Leesburg, VA   Age: 93 years
        Birth: 1883/08/10   Death: 1977/03/22   Burial: 1977/03/25
Site 3 Gasquet diZerega   Cause: Pneumonia   Age: 39 years
        Birth: 1879   Death: 1919/01/12

61

Site 4   William Irvine diZerega   Cause: Suicide   Age: 50 years
         Birth: 1868   Death: 1919/02/23
Site 5   Martha Alice diZerega   Cause: Uremia   Age: 50 years
         Birth: 1873/03/09   Death: 1923/10/11   Burial: 1923/10/13
         TS: Wife of William Irvine diZerega. Daughter of Alfred L.B. & Alice
         A. diZerega
Site 7   Dr. James Wallace Gibson   Age: 70 years
         Birth: 1920/08/03   Death: 1987/07/14   Burial: 1987/07/17
         Died: Middleburg, VA   TS: M.D.
Site 9   Henry Berlin Crabites   Died: Middleburg, VA
         Birth: 1907/11/02   Death: 1980/04/27   Burial: 1980/04/30
Site 10 Frederica diZerega Crabites   Age: 81 years
         Birth: 1908/09/15   Death: 1990/11/15   Burial: 1990/11/17
         Died: Winchester, VA   On stone with Henry Berlin Crabites

Lot: 801, 802, 803, 804   Owner: Frank C. Littleton   1919/07/24
Site 2   Frank Campbell Littleton   Age: 78 years
         Birth: 1873/10/06   Death: 1951/10/17   Burial: 1951/10/20
Site 6   Frank Campbell Littleton Jr.   Age: 45 years
         Birth: 1916   Death: 1959/04/08   Burial: 1959/04/10
         Died: Winchester, VA
Site 0   Trowbridge Littleton   Cause: Epilepsy   Age: 14 years
         Birth: 1918/09/28   Death: 1933/07/09   Burial: 1933/09/12
         TS: Son of Frank Campbell & Olive Trowbridge Littleton. Born in
         NY City. Died in Philadelphia, PA
Site 1   Henrietta Olive Trowbridge Littleton   Age: 41 years
         Birth: 1884/06/13   Death: 1924/07/12   Burial: 1924/07/13
         Cause: Heart   TS: Wife of Frank Campbell Littleton. Born
         in NY City. Died in Aldie, VA

Lot: 805   Owner: R.F. Braden   Purchased: 1919/02/28
Site 1   Mrs. Carrie E. Braden
         Birth: 1844/10/06   Death: 1880/07/16   Burial: 1921/03/14
         Transferred from Concaton.   TS: Wife of G.V. Braden
Site 2   Gabriel V. Braden   Cause: Paralysis   Age: 89 years
         Birth: 1841/09/02   Death: 1931/03/01   Burial: 1931/03/03
Site 4   Mrs. Sallie F. Braden   TS: Wife of G.V. Braden Age: 65 years
         Birth: 1853/04/05   Death: 1918/03/01   Cause: Cancer
site 7   Gladys Smoot Braden   Died: Washington, DC   Age: 74 years
         Birth: 1901/12/22   Death: 1976/04/09   Burial: 1976/04/21
site 8   Robert Furr Braden   Died: Rockville, MD   Age: 86 years
         Birth: 1890/05/04   Death: 1976/06/15   Burial: 1976/06/30

Lot: 806 N   Owner: A.L. McGavack   Purchased: 1920/02/26
         Transfer 1: S to W.O. Russell 1921/06/03
Site 4   Andrew L. McGavack   Cause: Cerebral Hemorrhage   Age: 62 years
         Birth: 1869   Death: 1934/03/24   Burial: 1934/03/26
Site 5   A. Llewellyn McGavack   TS: Son of A.L. & Addie A. McGavack
         Birth: 1903/06/14   Death: 1920/02/23

Site 6 Mrs. Adeline (Addie) Virginia McGavack Age: 69 years
        Birth: 1877 Death: 1945/05/16 Burial: 1945/05/18
        TS: Wife of Andrew L. McGavack

Lot: 806 S Owner: Miscellaneous
Site 1 Maude B. Gray Cause: Cancer of Lung Age: 49 years
        Birth: 1891 Death: 1941/09/18 Burial: 1941/09/20
Site 2 Rollie Jay Mallicoat Age: 77 years
        Birth: 1873/10/07 Death: 1951/01/21 Burial: 1951/01/23
Site 8 William Perry Simmons No stone Age: 63 years
        Died: Lucketts, VA Death: 1972/12/05 Burial: 1972/12/08
Site 9 Myron H. Utgaard Died: Leesburg, VA Age: 82 years
        Birth: 1888/12/15 Death: 1971/02/10 Burial: 1971/02/13
Site 9 Mrs. Lucille Schustron Utgaard Age: 51 years
        Birth: 1891/12/12 Death: 1943/02/07 Burial: 1943/02/09
        TS: Wife of H. Utgaard

Lot: 807 Owner: John R. Clemens Purchased: 1921/12/01
Transfer 1: To John R. & Christian H. Clemens
Site 1 Catharine Clemens Foss Died: Leesburg, VA
        Birth: 1935/05/13 Death: 1994/03/23 Burial: 1994/03/26
Site 5 Lois Clemens Kline Age: 52 years
        Birth: 1926/07/06 Death: 1979/05/22
        TS: Wife of H. Wendell Kline. Daughter of C.H. & L.S. Clemens
Site 7 John William Clemens Age: 71 years
        Birth: 1906/12/04 Death: 1978/03/28 Burial: 1978/03/31
        Died: Leesburg, VA TS: Son of John & Hattie Clemens
Site 11 Christian H. Clemens Age: 86 years
        Birth: 1887/08/20 Death: 1974/01/07 Burial: 1074/01/10
        Died: Leesburg, VA TS: Son of W.H. & M.E. Clemens
Site 12 Leona Shroy Clemens Age: 77 years
        Birth: 1889/09/02 Death: 1966/10/31 Burial: 1966/11/03
        Died: Leesburg, VA TS: Wife of Christian H. Clemens

Lot: 808 Owner: Anna S. Connor Purchased: 1926/09/30
Site 3 James Arthur Connor Age: 58 years
        Death: 1926/09/28 Burial: 1926/09/30
        Cause: Cancer of Bladder TS: Husband of Anne Sutherland Connor
Site 5 Ann Sutherland Evans No stone Age: 81 years
        Died: Chevy Chase, MD Death: 1958/11/03 Burial: 1958/11/05
Site 6 Nancy S. Blair Died: MD Age: 72 years
        Birth: 1910 Death: 1983/02/21 Burial: 1983/02/25
Site 7 David Lemmon Age: 83 years
        Death: 1956/02/12 Burial: 1956/02/12
        Cause: Cardiac Failure Died: Washington, DC No stone
Site 8 Mary M. Lemmon No stone Age: 95 years
        Died: Falls Church, VA Death: 1964/06/13 Burial: 1964/06/17

Lot: 809 Owner: Dr. F.N. Kerr Purchased: 1925/12/28
Site   A.A. Stehle Birth: 1871 Death: 1955

Site	Jessie C. Stehle	Birth: 1879	Death: 1963
	On stone with A.A. Stehle		
Site 1	Richard Carson Stehle	Died: Leesburg, VA	Age: 79 years
	Birth: 1912/05/31	Death: 1991/08/23	Burial: 1991/08/27
	On stone with A.A. Stehle & Jessie C. Stehle		
	TS: US AIR FORCE WWII		
Site 4	Floyd Nathaniel Kerr	Birth: 1874/12/25	Death: 1954/03/17
Site 5	Lillian Rhodes Kerr		Age: 71 years
	Birth: 1876/09/30	Death: 1948/11/23	Burial: 1948/11/25
Site 6	Margaret Katharine Kerr		Age: 21 years
	Birth: 1904/03/25	Death: 1925/12/27	Burial: 1925/12/28
	Cause: Pneumonia	TS: Daughter of F.N. & L.R. Kerr	

Lot: 810   Owner: Mrs. Mary P. Orr   Purchased: 1926/08/30

Site 2	William Clayton Orr Jr.	Cause: Pneumonia	Age: 23 years
	Birth: 1911/11/13	Death: 1935/10/03	Burial: 1935/10/05
Site 3	Dr. William Clayton Orr	Cause: Pneumonia	Age: 48 years
	Birth: 1878/08/16	Death: 1926/08/28	Burial: 1926/08/30
Site 5	Mary Page Orr	Cause: Cerebral Hemorrhage	Age: 62 years
	Birth: 1880/05/10	Death: 1941/05/01	Burial: 1941/05/03
Site 7	Dr. William Page Bodmer	Died: Leesburg, VA	Age: 44 years
	Birth: 1914/05/26	Death: 1959/05/20	Burial: 1959/05/22
Site 8	Louise Orr Bodmer		Age: 52 years
	Birth: 1908/08/10	Death: 1961/12/05	Burial: 1961/12/07
	Cause: Suicide	Died: Leesburg, VA	

Lot: 811 E   Owner: L.M. Ferguson   Purchased: 1927/03/19

Site 7	Lulah Blanche Ferguson	Died: Leesburg, VA	Age: 99 years
	Birth: 1883/01/09	Death: 1982/12/12	Burial: 1982/12/16
Site 8	Bertha Jane Ferguson	Died: Fairfax, VA	Age: 92 years
	Birth: 1889/09/10	Death: 1982/07/24	Burial: 1982/07/25
Site 9	Estelle L. Ferguson	Died: Rockville, MD	Age: 82 years
	Birth: 1893/03/23	Death: 1976/01/22	Burial: 1976/01/25
Site 10	Lacey M. Ferguson	Died: Sterling, VA	Age: 77 years
	Birth: 1885/05/03	Death: 1962/09/08	Burial: 1962/09/11
Site 11	Mrs. E. Hazel Ferguson	Cause: Influenza	Age: 35 years
	Birth: 1891/12/03	Death: 1927/03/18	Burial: 1927/03/20

Lot: 811 W   Owner: Mrs. Jas. B. Strawbridge   1927/01/13

Site 3	James Bosler Strawbridge	Cause: Heart Trouble	Age: 66 years
	Birth: 1860	Death: 1927/01/12	Burial: 1927/01/14
Site 4	Mrs. Etta Wharton Strawbridge		Age: 79 years
	Birth: 1865	Death: 1944/09/03	Burial: 1944/09/05
Site 5	Elizabeth Strawbridge	No stone	Age: 81 years
	Died: Leesburg, VA	Death: 1982/12/05	Burial: 1982/12/08

Lot: 812   Owner: Miscellaneous

Site 2	Elton L. Peck	Died: Leesburg, VA	Age: 89 years
	Birth: 1900	Death: 1989/12/05	Burial: 1989/12/07
Site 3	Marion G. Hutchison	Birth: 1895	Death: 1962

Site 4	Oscar C. Hutchison		Age: 80 years
	Birth: 1865	Death: 1945/09/02	Burial: 1945/09/04
Site 5	Ada Leith Hutchison		Age: 77 years
	Birth: 1870	Death: 1949/11/04	Burial: 1949/11/07
Site 6	Lucile Hutchison	Died: Washington, DC	Age: 73 years
	Birth: 1897	Death: 1970/09/30	Burial: 1970/10/03
Site 10	Mrs. Eva Jeanette Crouch		Age: 66 years
	Birth: 1889/11/24	Death: 1956/11/15	Burial: 1956/11/16
	Died: Leesburg, VA	On stone with Clarence Copeland Crouch	
Site 11	Clarence Copeland Crouch		Age: 60 years
	Birth: 1890/05/15	Death: 1951/03/04	Burial: 1951/03/06
Site 12	Henry Pendleton Crouch		Age: 79 years
	Birth: 1858/07/13	Death: 1944/12/04	Burial: 1944/12/06

Lot: 813   Owner: L.H. Elliott   Purchased: 1930/10/22

Site 2	William H. Elliott	Died: Ashburn, VA	Age: 87 years
	Birth: 1904/02/10	Death: 1991/01/29	Burial: 1991/01/31
Site 4	Lewis H. Elliott	No stone	Age: 85 years
	Died: Leesburg, VA	Death: 1964/01/15	Burial: 1964/01/17
Site 5	Sarah Elizabeth Elliott	No stone	Age: 77 years
	Died: Ashburn, VA	Death: 1958/01/16	Burial: 1958/01/19
Site 7	Millard Cunningham	No stone	Age: 9 months
		Death: 1930/10/22	Burial: 1930/10/24
Site 7	Infant Cunningham	Cause: Stillborn	No stone
		Death: 1943/01/08	Burial: 1943/01/08
Site 9	Dolph N. Cunningham	No stone	Age: 58 years
	Died: Ashburn, VA	Death: 1961/02/27	Burial: 1961/03/02
Site 10	Marjorie Cunningham	No stone	Age: 63 years
	Died: Leesburg, VA	Death: 1973/02/27	Burial: 1973/03/02

Lot: 814 E   Owner: Jennie Virginia Bettis   Purchased: 1931/06/20

Site 7	Annie Lee Saunders	No stone	Age: 29 years
	Cause: Apoplexy	Death: 1931/06/18	Burial: 1931/06/20
Site 8	Ruth E. Saunders	Cause: Whooping Cough	Age: 4 months
	No stone	Death: 1932/03/12	Burial: 1932/03/14
Site 8	Child Bettis		No stone
		Death: 1948/12/04	Burial: 1948/12/06
Site 9	William Irving Bettis		No stone
		Death: 1950/09/14	Burial: 1950/09/14
Site 9	Lewis Randolph Saunders		Age: 82 years
	No stone	Death: 1952/01/25	Burial: 1952/01/28

Lot: 814 W   Owner: Mrs. Daisey L. Jackson   1932/04/08

Site 3	Randolph M. Jackson	Cause: Hemorrhage	Age: 42 years
	Birth: 1889/11/08	Death: 1932/04/07	Burial: 1932/04/09
Site 4	Daisy L. Jackson		Age: 92 years
	Birth: 1897/01/18	Death: 1989/12/21	Burial: 1989/12/27
	Died: Winchester, VA	On stone with Randolph M. Jackson	
Site 5	Ronald Glenn Holden	Died: WY	Age: 28 years
	Birth: 1948/11/26	Death: 1977/09/13	Burial: 1977/09/15

Lot: 815 Owner: Mrs. James W. Carr   Purchased: 1934/09/17
Site 9   Robert Gover VanDeventer   Age: 28 years
         Birth: 1906/07/09   Death: 1934/09/15   Burial: 1934/09/17
         Cause: Accident
Site 10 Josephine VanD. Carr   Age: 52 years
         Birth: 1889/01/18   Death: 1941/02/27   Burial: 1941/02/28
         Cause: Carcinoma of Stomach   TS: Wife of James W. Carr
Site 12 James W. Carr   Died: Hillsboro, VA   Age: 81 years
         Birth: 1886/07/23   Death: 1968/01/21   Burial: 1968/01/24

Lot: 816 E   Owner: George W. Hickman   Purchased: 1935/03/30
Site 8   Donald L. Hickman   Cause: Heart   Age: 7 years
         Birth: 1928   Death: 1935/02/18   Burial: 1935/02/20
Site 9   George William Hickman Died: Paeonian Springs, VA Age: 62 years
         Birth: 1893   Death: 1956/06/21   Burial: 1956/06/21
Site 10 Rachel B. Hickman   Died: Leesburg, VA
         Birth: 1901/07/21   Death: 1995/09/10   Burial: 1995/09/13

Lot: 816 W   Owner: D.B. Baker   Purchased: 1935/03/30
Site 3   Harvey Rollins Baker   Age: 65 years
         Birth: 1905/04/27   Death: 1971/02/20   Burial: 1971/02/24
         Died: Leesburg, VA   TS: "Father"
Site 5   Adolphus Bartlett Baker   Age: 69 1/2 yrs
         Birth: 1876   Death: 1945/09/16   Burial: 1945/09/18
Site 6   Frances M. Baker   Age: 76 years
         Birth: 1864   Death: 1940/12/28   Burial: 1940/12/31
         Cause: Nephritis   TS: Wife of Adolphus Bartlett Baker

Lot: 817 E   Owner: Mrs. M.M. Solomon   Purchased: 1934/11/02
Site 9   Naomi M. Muse   Died: Leesburg, VA   Age: 83 years
         Birth: 1890   Death: 1974/01/15   Burial: 1974/01/17
Site 11 James Alexander Hawes   Age: 70 years
         Birth: 1881/09/03   Death: 1951/04/24   Burial: 1951/04/27
Site 12 Ethel M. Hawes   Died: Fairfax, VA   Age: 76 years
         Birth: 1902/03/12   Death: 1979/01/23   Burial: 1979/01/26

Lot: 817 W   Owner: Mrs. George W. Heskett   1935/01/09
Site 3   George W. Heskett   Cause: Myocarditis   Age: 66 years
         Birth: 1875   Death: 1936/01/08   Burial: 1936/01/10
Site 4   Sarah Catherine Heskett   On stone with George W. Heskett
         Birth: 1881   Death: 1954/03/18   Age: 72 years
Site 5   Roger Nathanial Heskett Died: Bolivar, WV   Age: 58 years
         Birth: 1908/03/17   Death: 1966/12/13   Burial: 1966/12/16

Lot: 818 E   Owner: Virgil Poling   Purchased: 1933-10-14
Site 9   Virgil Poling   Cause: Heart Failure   Age: 66 years
         Birth: 1874/11/04   Death: 1939/11/08   Burial: 1939/11/10
Site 10 Laura Virginia Poling   Cause: Arteriosclerosis   Age: 65 years
         Birth: 1872/08/12   Death: 1938/01/19   Burial: 1938/01/21

Site 11 Bena Virginia Poling Mays   Age: 43 years
Birth: 1895/07/21   Death: 1938/08/25   Burial: 1938/09/01
Cause: Pneumonia   TS: Daughter of Virgie & Lula Virginia Poling

Lot: 818 W   Owner: Mrs. Bessie E. Haynes   Purchased:
Site 3   William C. Haynes   Age: 88 years
         Birth: 1862/08/28   Death: 1953/11/13   Burial: 1953/11/17
         Cause: Hyp. Heart Disease   Died: Washington, DC
Site 4   Bessie E. Haynes   Age: 85 years
         Birth: 1870/03/27   Death: 1955/07/13   Burial: 1955/07/16
         Cause: Arteriosclerosis   Died: Montgomery, NY

Lot: 819   Owner: Columbus & Ethel M. Howard   1940/07/31
Site 6   Child of J. F. Howard   Cause: Stillborn
         Birth: 1947/06/21   Death: 1947/06/21   Burial: 1947/06/23
Site 7   Nellie V. Douglass   Died: Leesburg, VA   Age: 62 years
         Birth: 1916/05/04   Death: 1978/12/03   Burial: 1978/12/07
Site 8   Blaine L. Howard   Age: 48 years
         Birth: 1925/10/03   Death: 1973/11/05   Burial: 1973/11/08
         Died: Arlington, VA   TS: Virginia Pvt. US Army World War II
Site 9   Ralph V. Howard   Died: Staunton, VA   Age: 44 years
         Birth: 1923   Death: 1968/02/20   Burial: 1968/02/22
Site 10 Columbus Fletcher Howard   Age: 61 years
         Birth: 1890   Death: 1952/05/03   Burial: 1952/05/06
Site 11 Mrs. Ethel O. Howard   IB:Mrs. Columbus Howard   Age: 48 years
         Birth: 1894   Death: 1943/08/02   Burial: 1943/08/04
         On stone with Columbus Fletcher Howard
Site 12 James A. Howard   Age: 7 years
         Birth: 1932/12/14   Death: 1940/07/29   Burial: 1940/07/31
         Cause: Status Thymo Lyrnetating   TS: Son of C.F. & E.M. Howard

Lot: 820 E   Owner: John W. Kerns   Purchased: 1950/07/28
Site 9   Warren Granville Caylor   Age: 39 years
         Birth: 1911/02/16   Death: 1950/07/28   Burial: 1950/07/28
Site 10 Elizabeth C. McDavid   Died: Leesburg, VA
         Birth: 1936/12/16   Death: 1995/12/18   Burial: 1995/12/21
Site 11 John William Kerns   Died: Leesburg, VA   Age: 39 years
         Birth: 1920   Death: 1960/05/03   Burial: 1960/05/06
Site 12 Sara Louise Kerns   Age: 69 years
         Birth: 1928   Death: 1977/09/26   Burial: 1977/09/29
         Died: Kennett Square, PA   On stone with John William Kerns

Lot: 820 W   Owner: Grover R. Jessee   Purchased: 1951/04/09
Site 5   Grover Roy Jessee   Age: 68 years
         Birth: 1886/04/15   Death: 1954/12/11
Site 6   Mrs. Willie Vera Jessee   Age: 36 years
         Birth: 1914/01/09   Death: 1950/09/07   Burial: 1950/09/09

Lot: 821 Owner: Miscellaneous

Site 1 Harvey Widman   No stone   Age: 91 years
        Died: Staunton VA   Death: 1973/05/24   Burial: 1973/05/26
Site 2 Thomas Walter Johnson No stone   Age: 76 years
        Died: Leesburg, VA   Death: 1976/12/05   Burial: 1976/12/09
Site 3 Martin G. Dunn   Age: 80 years
                               Death: 1979/02/01   No stone
Site 4 Josephine A. Zulcosky Died: Leesburg, VA   Age: 84 years
        Birth: 1905/03/17   Death: 1989/12/15   Burial: 1989/12/19
Site 6 Linda Kay Lane   Age: 17 years
        Birth: 1961/09/07   Death: 1978/09/19   Burial: 1978/09/22
        Cause: Auto Accident   Died: GA
Site 7 Jerry W. Tipton   Died: Fairfax, VA   Age: 33 years
        Birth: 1944   Death: 1978/06/01   Burial: 1978/06/04
Site 8 Mrs. Dorothy Snead Tipton   Age: 56 years
        Birth: 1922/01/08   Death: 1978/09/12   Burial: 1978/09/15
        Cause: Cancer   Died: Purcellville, VA
        On stone with Joseph W. Tipton
Site 9 Joseph W. Tipton   Died: Hamilton, VA
        Birth: 1916/05/02   Death: 1993/06/07   Burial: 1993/06/10
Site 10 Woodrow Bradley   Died: Berryville, VA
        Birth: 1913/04/24   Death: 1993/04/27   Burial: 1993/04/30
Site 11 Taylor William Gibson III   Died: Frederick, MD
        Birth: 1961/04/16   Death: 1995/06/18   Burial: 1995/06/21

Lot: 822 Owner: Miscellaneous

Site 1 Hugh G. Flynn   No stone   Age: 58 years
        Died: Frederick, MD   Death: 1971/02/20   Burial: 1971/02/23
Site 2 Berkley C. Spinks   Died: Charlottesville, VA   Age: 57 years
        Birth: 1917   Death: 1973/08/09   Burial: 1973/08/11
Site 3 Edna V. Spinks   Age: 49 years
        Birth: 1922   Death: 1971/03/18   Burial: 1971/03/20
        Died: Leesburg, VA   On stone with Berkley C. Spinks
Site 4 Kermit E. Cockerille   Died: Winchester, VA   Age: 61 years
        Birth: 1910   Death: 1971/11/30   Burial: 1971/12/03
Site 5 Grace Hough Cockerille   Age: 79 years
        Birth: 1898   Death: 1978/06/25   Burial: 1978/06/27
        Died: Leesburg, VA   On stone with Kermit E. Cockerille
Site 6 James L. Myers   No stone   Age: 67 years
        Died: Toms River, NJ   Death: 1972/12/03   Burial: 1972/12/07
Site 7 Thomas Wayne Wilson   Died: Leesburg, VA   Age: 87 years
        Birth: 1883   Death: 1969/09/27   Burial: 1969/10/01
Site 9 James C. Dawson   Died: Leesburg, VA   Age: 81 years
        Birth: 1901   Death: 1982/06/02   Burial: 1982/06/05
Site 10 Annie E. Dawson   Age: 74 years
        Birth: 1905   Death: 1979/06/10
        On stone with James C. Dawson

Site 12 Ruby Lucille Myers   Age: 47 years
        Birth: 1941/10/09   Death: 1989/03/14   Burial: 1989/03/17
        Cause: Heart Attack Died: Leesburg, VA

Lot: 827   Owner: Miscellaneous
Site 4 Eva C. Cooper   Died: Purcellville, VA   No stone
        Birth: 1902/10/12   Death: 1995/04/27   Burial: 1995/04/28
Site 5 Clarence Leroy Cooper Died: Leesburg, VA   Age: 73 years
        Birth: 1906/09/03   Death: 1979/07/18   Burial: 1979/07/20
Site 6 Lula May F. Cooper
        Birth: 1904/09/28   Death: 1994/07/14   Burial: 1994/07/17
        Died: Leesburg, VA   On stone with Clarence L. Cooper
Site 9 Linda Kirk   Died: MD   Age: 39 years
        Birth: 1953/06/18   Death: 1991/12/26   Burial: 1991/12/28
Site 10 Violet Gill   Age: 80 years
        Birth: 1900/09/19   Death: 1981/03/07   Burial: 1981/03/10
        Died: PA   No stone
Site 11 Mary H. Weed   Age: 48 years
        Birth: 1931   Death: 1979/12/20   Burial: 1979/12/23
        Died: Front Royal, VA   On stone with Lawrence F. Weed
Site 11 Lawrence F. Weed   Died: Rockville, MD   Age: 69 years
        Birth: 1915   Death: 1984/05/12   Burial: 1984/05/14
Site 12 Nannie K. Fanning   Died: Fairfax, VA   Age: 65 years
        Birth: 1913/08/15   Death: 1979/01/15   Burial: 1979/01/18

Lot: 828 E   Owner: W.H. Heskett   Purchased: 1970/01/07
Site 7 William H. Heskett   Age: 75 years
        Birth: 1902   Death: 1977/11/01   Burial: 1977/11/04
        Cause: Cancer   Died: Leesburg, VA
Site 8 Pearl Moxley Heskett   Age: 59 years
        Birth: 1910   Death: 1969/12/11   Burial: 1969/12/14
        Died: Leesburg, VA   On stone with William H. Heskett
Site 10 Asa C. Rusk Jr.   Died: Martinsburg, WV   Age: 61 years
        Birth: 1920/02/27   Death: 1981/07/17   Burial: 1981/07/20
        Cause: Cancer   TS: US Army World War II

Lot: 828 W   Owner: Robert N. Ridgeway   Purchased:
Site 2 Dorothy E. Kearns Bullock Ridgeway   Age: 56 years
        Birth: 1913   Death: 1971/01/22   Burial: 1971/01/25
                             Died: Tappahannock, VA
Site 6 Alfred Bullock   Died: Winchester, VA   Age: 72 years
        Birth: 1905/01/01   Death: 1977/07/03   Burial: 1977/07/06

Lot: 829 E   Owner: Mrs. Welby Tavenner   Purchased: 1955/04/11
Site 8 Charles Welby Tavenner Died: Mountville, VA   Age: 58 years
        Birth: 1897/10/18   Death: 1955/04/09   Burial: 1955/04/11
Site 9 Mary E. Tavenner Hawes   Age: 73 years
        Birth: 1900/09/02   Death: 1973/07/25   Burial: 1973/07/27
        Died: Fredericksburg, VA   On stone with Charles Welby Tavenner

Lot: 829 W Owner: Miscellaneous
Site 4 Ellen May Schmith   Died: Leesburg, VA   Age: 70 years
        Birth: 1915   Death: 1986/05/08   Burial: 1986/05/12

Lot: 830 Owner: Miscellaneous
Site 7 Donald Norman Farmer Died: L.C.H. Leesburg, VA Age: 12 days
        No stone   Death: 1958/05/05   Burial: 1958/05/05
Site 10 Hilda R. Cunningham Donovan   Age: 66 years
        Birth: 1919/12/21   Death: 1986/05/27   Burial: 1986/05/31
        Died: Felton, DE
Site 11 Harold W. Cunningham Died: Frederick, MD   Age: 58 years
        Birth: 1925   Death: 1984/01/30   Burial: 1984/02/03
Site 12 Mary M. Cunningham   Died: Waterford, VA   Age: 53 years
        Birth: 1899   Death: 1953/05/08   Burial: 1953/05/11

Lot: 831 Owner: W.S. & A.J. Quesenbury   Purchased: 1941/03/24
Site 1 William Scott Quesenberry   Age: 69 years
        Birth: 1901/12/03   Death: 1970/11/08   Burial: 1970/11/11
                             Died: Leesburg, VA
Site 4 Carl S. Calhoun   Cause: Stillborn
        Birth: 1944/10/15   Death: 1944/10/15   Burial: 1944/10/15
Site 5 John William Cooper   Age: 61 years
        Birth: 1920/08/29   Death: 1982/01/05   Burial: 1982/01/08
        Died: Fairfax, VA   TS: US Army
Site 7 Mary Katherine Quesenberry   Age: 5 years
        Birth: 1938/06/18   Death: 1944/03/12   Burial: 1944/03/16
Site 8 John H. Quesenberry Died: Leesburg, VA   Age: 80 years
        Birth: 1890/03/21   Death: 1970/06/22   Burial: 1970/06/24
Site 12 Luvenia Quesenberry   Age: 73 years
        Birth: 1867/07/11   Death: 1941/03/07   Burial: 1941/03/10
        TS: Second wife of T.J. Quesenberry

Lot: 832 Owner: Mrs. Francis B. Hickman Purchased: 1940/05/06
Site 3 Lester A. Hickman   Cause: Apoplexy   Age: 51 years
        Birth: 1884/08/31   Death: 1937/01/27   Burial: 1937/01/29
Site 5 Frances B. Hickman   Died: Alexandria, VA   Age: 78 years
        Birth: 1892/08/23   Death: 1979/07/20   Burial: 1979/07/23
Site 6 Doris H. Compher   Died: Alexandria, VA   Age: 78 years
        Birth: 1912/03/24   Death: 1990/12/16   Burial: 1990/12/20

Lot: 833 E Owner: Adolpheus L. Hardy Purchased: 1937/06/12
Site 7 Adolphus L. Hardy   Age: 71 years
        Birth: 1891/05/08   Death: 1962/05/16   Burial: 1962/05/18
        Died: Arlington, VA   TS: Husband of Beulah Hardy
Site 8 Mrs. Beulah Belle Hardy TS: Wife of A.L. Hardy Age: 54 years
        Birth: 1896/09/20   Death: 1950/06/13   Burial: 1950/06/15
Site 9 Mildred May Hardy   TS: Daughter   Age: 26 years
        Birth: 1925/03/06   Death: 1951/01/24   Burial: 1951/01/26
Site 10 Winfred C. Hardy   Died: Bethesda, MD   Age: 52 years
        Birth: 1917/06/16   Death: 1970/06/03   Burial: 1970/06/06

Lot: 833 W   Owner: Harry G. Ball   Purchased: 1938/06/13
Site 1   Mary M. LeRoy   Died: Fairfax, VA   Age: 67 years
         Birth: 1922   Death: 1990/02/14   Burial: 1990/02/14
Site 2   Mary D. Ball   No stone   Age: 61 years
         Died: Washington, DC   Death: 1967/06/05   Burial: 1967/06/08
Site 3   Harry G. Ball   Age: 76 years
         Birth: 1871   Death: 1947/11/26   Burial: 1947/11/28
Site 4   Mrs. Dolly McPherson Ball   Age: 79 years
         Birth: 1872   Death: 1952/07/07   Burial: 1952/07/09
         On stone with Harry G. Ball
Site 5   George H. Ball   TS: Beloved son   Age: 50 years
         Birth: 1897   Death: 1948/07/07   Burial: 1948/07/09
Site 6   William E. Ball   No stone   Age: 53 years
                                Death: 1957/05/09

Lot: 834 E   Owner: Mrs. Douglas N. Myers   1936/02/05
Site 9   Charles Edwin Elliott Cause: C. Rectal   Age: 74 years
         Birth: 1861/10/16   Death: 1936/02/05   Burial: 1936/02/07
Site 10 Mrs. Emily Cox Elliott   Age: 80 years
         Birth: 1862/09/15   Death: 1942/11/19   Burial: 1942/11/21

Lot: 834 W   Owner: E.P. Frye   Purchased: 1942/05/30
Site 2   Edward Pennrose Frye   Died: Leesburg, VA
         Birth: 1927/02/07   Death: 1991/05/22   Burial: 1991/05/25
         TS: Married March 27, 1951   On stone with Edna Q. Frye
Site 3   John William McCann   Age: 63 years
         Birth: 1921/08/22   Death: 1983/02/27   Burial: 1985/03/02
         Died: Ashburn, VA   TS: US Army WWII Korea
Site 4   Mary Louise McCann   Died: Ashburn, VA   Age: 68 years
         Birth: 1920/08/20   Death: 1989/02/04   Burial: 1989/02/06
Site 5   Edward Penn Frye   Age: 55 years
         Birth: 1894/02/23   Death: 1947/03/21   Burial: 1947/03/23
Site 6   Mrs. Mary Naomi Frye   TS: Wife of E.P. Frye   Age: 50 years
         Birth: 1891/06/28   Death: 1942/05/28   Burial: 1942/05/30

Lot: 835   Owner: Joseph H. Turley   Purchased: 1937/05/17
Site 1   Harry A. Turley   Cause: Accident   Age: 30 years
         Birth: 1907/03/09   Death: 1937/05/15   Burial: 1937/05/17
Site 3   Joseph Howard Turley   Age: 79 years
         Birth: 1877   Death: 1955/12/01   Burial: 1955/12/02
         Cause: Heart Failure   Died: Pawtucket, RI
Site 4   Alice W. Alloway Turley   Age: 58 years
         Birth: 1881   Death: 1939/10/19   Burial: 1939/10/21
         Cause: Cancer of Lung   On stone with Joseph Howard Turley
Site 5   John Gouldey Turley   TS: Sgt US Army   Age: 70 years
         Birth: 1909   Death: 1979/04/16

Lot: 836   Owner: Vernon L. Orrison   Purchased: 1934/11/12
Site 1   John C. Tavenner   Died: Washington, DC   Age: 79 years
         Birth: 1882/08/08   Death: 1961/10/06   Burial: 1961/10/10

Site 2   Mrs. Sadie R. Tavenner   Age: 84 years
         Birth: 1886/07/01   Death: 1970/07/13   Burial: 1970/07/16
         Died: Winchester, VA   On stone with John C. Tavenner
Site 3   Robert Henry Orrison   Cause: Angina Pectoris   Age: 64 years
         Birth: 1870   Death: 1934/11/15   Burial: 1934/11/17
Site 4   Edith Alma Tavenner Orrison   Age: 70 years
         Birth: 1879   Death: 1950/02/04   Burial: 1950/02/06
Site 12 Virginia Rose Orrison   Died: Arlington, VA   Age: 52 years
         Birth: 1917   Death: 1970/04/25   Burial: 1970/04/27

Lot: 837 E   Owner: J. Richard Moran   Purchased: 1937/04/24
Site 7   Nora M. Moran   Cause: Myocarditis   Age: 27 years
         Birth: 1910   Death: 1937/06/06   Burial: 1937/06/08
         TS: Daughter   On stone with Sarah E. & Joseph Richard Moran
Site 8   Sarah E. Moran   Cause: P. Tuberculosis   Age: 60 years
         Birth: 1877   Death: 1937/04/23   Burial: 1937/04/25
         TS: Mother   On stone with Joseph Richard Moran
Site 9   Joseph Richard Moran   Age: 74 years
         Birth: 1873   Death: 1941/10/27   Burial: 1941/10/29
         Cause: Fracture of Hip   TS: Father
Site 10 Joyce A. Thompson   No stone   Age: 4 months
         Cause: Meningitis   Death: 1942/08/12   Burial: 1942/08/14
Site 11 Mrs. Gustave Elizabeth Moran Fox   Age: 39 years
         Birth: 1905/02/13   Death: 1944/12/25   Burial: 1944/12/27
Site 12 Clifford K. Rollins   Age: 61 years
         Birth: 1887/06/03   Death: 1948/11/25   Burial: 1948/11/27

Lot: 837 W   Owner: Clark L. Fry   Purchased: 1934/10/30
Site 1   Kaye Irene Fry   TS: R.C. & B.H. Fry   Age: 14 hours
         Cause: Premature Birth   Death: 1941/01/31   Burial: 1941/02/01
Site 3   Clark L. Fry   Died: Winchester, VA   Age: 95 years
         Birth: 1876/02/12   Death: 1971/05/25   Burial: 1971/05/28
Site 4   Mrs. Bertha Magaha Fry   Age: 55 years
         Birth: 1878/12/14   Death: 1934/10/30   Burial: 1934/11/01
         Cause: Diabetes Millitus   TS: Wife of Clarke L. Fry
Site 5   Roger Clifton Fry   Died: Leesburg, VA   Age: 70 years
         Birth: 1904/06/04   Death: 1974/07/04   Burial: 1974/07/07
Site 6   Bela McCann Fry   Died: Leesburg, VA   Age: 76 years
         Birth: 1911/05/06   Death: 1988/03/26   Burial: 1988/03/29
         On stone with Roger Clifton Fry

Lot: 838   Owner: C.C. Saffer   Purchased: 1931/03/13
Site 1   Walton Riticor Saffer   Died: Winchester, VA   Age: 59 years
         Birth: 1906/10/09   Death: 1966/07/25   Burial: 1966/07/27
Site 2   Mrs. Caroline Porter Saffer   Age: 60 years
         Birth: 1909/07/21   Death: 1969/11/21   Burial: 1969/11/25
         Died: Aldie, VA   On stone with Walton Riticor Saffer
Site 4   Claude C. Saffer   Cause: Heart   Age: 62 years
         Birth: 1873/12/26   Death: 1936/10/18   Burial: 1936/10/20

Site 5	Olive May Riticor Saffer	Age: 63 years	
	Birth: 1876/10/18	Death: 1940/05/08	Burial: 1940/05/10
Site 6	Claude Hunton Saffer	TS: Mother	Age: 25 years
	Cause: Auto Accident	Death: 1931/03/12	Burial: 1931/03/14
Site 7	Clinton Stuart Saffer		Age: 79 years
	Birth: 1909/07/29	Death: 1988/08/27	Burial: 1988/08/30
	Died: Leesburg, VA		TS: Sgt US Army WWII

Lot: 839   Owner: Mrs. Martha J. Galleher   Purchased: 1928/10/31

Site 3	William R. Galleher	Cause: Heart Lesion	Age: 68 years
	Birth: 1860/06/02	Death: 1928/10/31	Burial: 1928/11/01
Site 4	Mrs. Martha Jordan Galleher		Age: 85 years
	Birth: 1860/08/28	Death: 1945/12/20	Burial: 1945/12/22
Site 5	Agnes Barbara Galleher		Age: 65 years
	Birth: 1892/05/25	Death: 1957/07/19	
Site 6	Kenneth L. Weed		Age: 61 years
	Birth: 1920/05/27	Death: 1982/05/11	Burial: 1982/05/14
	Died: Arlington, VA		TS: US Army
Site 7	Reginald Lee Nixon		Age: 85 years
	Birth: 1879	Death: 1964/08/23	Burial: 1964/08/26
	Died: Leesburg, VA		TS: Husband
Site 8	Naomi G. Nixon	Died: Leesburg, VA	Age: 96 years
	Birth: 1884	Death: 1980/06/27	Burial: 1980/07/01
	TS: Wife	On stone with Reginald Lee Nixon	
Site 9	Bernard L. Minor	Died: Winchester, VA	Age: 60 years
	Birth: 1921/07/24	Death: 1982/02/15	Burial: 1982/02/17
Site 11	Paul W. Ferguson	Died: Leesburg, VA	Age: 76 years
	Birth: 1887	Death: 1964/08/30	Burial: 1964/09/01
Site 12	Stella Galleher Ferguson		Age: 65 years
	Birth: 1888	Death: 1954/05/24	
	On stone with Paul W. Ferguson		

Lot: 840 E   Owner: Mrs. C.B. Sutton   Purchased: 1928/09/04

Site 7	Rev. Charles B. Sutton	No stone	Age: 76 years
	Cause: Arteriosclerosis	Death: 1933/07/10	Burial: 1933/07/12
Site 8	Mrs. Iola Estelle Sutton	No stone	Age: 68 years
	Cause: Heart Lesion	Death: 1928/08/12	Burial: 1928/08/14
Site 9	Mrs. Irva Sutton Cloud		Age: 57 years
	Birth: 1885-07-23	Death: 1943/11/19	Burial: 1943/11/21
	On stone with James Walter Cloud		
Site 10	James Walter Cloud		Age: 64 years
	Birth: 1878/07/03	Death: 1942/09/10	Burial: 1942/09/12

Lot: 840 W   Owner: Henry Moland   Purchased: 1931/06/24

Site 4	Charles Henry Moland	Birth: 1882	Death: 1957/07/15
Site 6	Edna E. Moland		Age: 74 years
	Birth: 1892	Death: 1967/01/25	Burial: 1967/01/28
	Died: Baltimore, MD	On stone with Charles Henry Moland	

Lot: 841 E   Owner: Miscellaneous
Site 7   George L. Fletcher   Died: Fairfax, VA   Age: 63 years
         Birth: 1913   Death: 1977/12/17   Burial: 1977/12/20
Site 8   Helena R. Fletcher   Age: 84 years
         Birth: 1903   Death: 1988/04/11   Burial: 1988/04/13
         Died: Leesburg, VA   On stone with George L. Fletcher
Site 9   Raymond E. Grimes   Died: Mount Holly, NJ   Age: 80 years
         Birth: 1909/08/09   Death: 1990/01/15   Burial: 1990/01/19
Site 10 Amos B. Slaymaker   Cause: Cerebral Hemorrhage   Age: 57 years
         Birth: 1870/04/23   Death: 1927/05/15   Burial: 1927/05/17
Site 11 Ada Fred Slaymaker   Age: 70 years
         Birth: 1870   Death: 1940/11/21   Burial: 1940/11/23
         Cause: Heart Disease   TS: Wife of Amos B. Slaymaker

Lot: 841 W   Owner: Miss Mabel Miskell   Purchased: 1928/03/06
Site 2   Rosalie M. Costello   Age: 56 years
         Birth: 1887   Death: 1943/06/03   Burial: 1943/06/05
Site 3   George Robert Costello Cause: H. of throat   Age: 56 years
         Birth: 1880   Death: 1936/06/08   Burial: 1936/06/10
Site 4   Winfield Scott Miskell Cause: Valvular Heart Disease   Age: 90 years
         Birth: 1846   Death: 1938/06/23   Burial: 1938/06/25
Site 5   Lydia Maria Miskell   Age: 64 years
         Birth: 1860/04/08   Death: 1928/03/04   Burial: 1928/03/06
         Cause: Paralysis   TS: Wife of W. Scott Miskell
Site 6   Mabel L. Miskell   Died: Charles Town, VA   Age: 88 years
         Birth: 1890/01/08   Death: 1978/07/03   Burial: 1978/07/06

Lot: 842 Owner: Samuel H. Rogers   Purchased: 1922/12/19
Site 1   Jane Cochran Rogers
         Birth: 1918/07/04   Death: 1991/12/25   Burial: 1991/12/28
         Died: Leesburg, VA   TS: Pre-school educator
Site 2   Miss Elizabeth Megeath Rogers   Age: 83 years
         Birth: 1886/07/10   Death: 1969/09/14   Burial: 1969/09/17
                                Died: Washington, DC
Site 4   Dr. Joseph Decatur Rogers Cause: Atrophy   Age: 52 years
         Birth: 1880/11/23   Death: 1933/01/12   Burial: 1933/01/14
         TS: Son of Samuel E. & Elizabeth C. Rogers
Site 5   Beulah Corbin Rogers   Age: 65 years
         Birth: 1883/02/14   Death: 1948/08/18   Burial: 1948/08/20
Site 8   Howard Cochran Rogers   Age: 72 years
         Birth: 1885/04/13   Death: 1957/05/27

Lot: 843 Owner: Samuel H. Rogers   Purchased: 1922/12/19
Site 3   Lulu Rogers   Cause: Tuberculosis   Age: 62 years
         Birth: 1876/02/19   Death: 1940/02/05   Burial: 1940/02/07
         TS: Daughter of Samuel E. & Elizabeth C. Rogers
Site 5   Samuel E. Rogers   Cause: Grippe   Age: 76 years
         Birth: 1845/06/20   Death: 1921/08/26

Site 6 Elizabeth Cochran Rogers Age: 86 years
Birth: 1846/06/03 Death: 1933/05/10 Burial: 1933/05/12
Cause: Myocarditis

Lot: 844 Owner: Samuel H. Rogers Purchased: 1922/12/19
Site 4 Infant son Rogers Cause: Cerebral Hemorrhage Age: 17 hours
Birth: 1934/09/22 Death: 1934/09/23 Burial: 1934/09/25
TS: Infant son of Samuel H. Rogers & Willa A. Rogers
Site 5 Samuel Hamilton Rogers Age: 77 years
Birth: 1877/09/27 Death: 1954/05/29
Site 6 Willa Ashby Rogers Died: Hamilton, VA Age: 98 years
Birth: 1894/04/18 Death: 1992/09/07 Burial: 1992/09/09

Lot: 846 Owner: Dr. & Mrs. M.C. Freilinger 1928/08/08
Site 6 Corinne W. Freilinger TS: Wife Age: 79 years
Birth: 1878 Death: 1957/07/15
Site 9 Dr. Matthew C. Freilinger Age: 59 years
Birth: 1873 Death: 1933/07/05 Burial: 1933/07/07
Cause: Cancer of Lung TS: Husband
Site 11 Matthew W. Freilinger
Birth: 1902/06/14 Death: 1903/02/16 Burial: 1903/02/18
TS: Son of M.C. & ? Freilinger Stone dates unreadable

Lot: 847 E Owner: Elizabeth M. Bailey Purchased: 1928/06/28
Site 7 William M. Bailey Cause: C. Vansosis Age: 76 years
Birth: 1857/04/03 Death: 1933/08/16 Burial: 1933/08/18
Site 8 Miss Elizabeth M. Bailey Cause: Angina Pectoris
Birth: 1846/10/04 Death: 1935/09/04 Burial: 1935/09/06
Site 9 George T. Bailey Cause: Liver Trouble Age: 71 years
Birth: 1859/12/20 Death: 1931/08/26 Burial: 1931/08/28
Site 10 Mary Elizabeth Bailey Age: 30 years
Birth: 1908/04/19 Death: 1939/04/17 Burial: 1939/04/19
Cause: Auto Accident On stone with Lulu Temple Bailey
Site 10 Lula Temple Bailey Died: Culpeper, VA Age: 93 years
Birth: 1881/02/15 Death: 1974/02/27 Burial: 1974/03/02
Site 11 John T. Bailey Cause: Heart Disease Age: 80 years
Birth: 1851/09/01 Death: 1932/05/18 Burial: 1932/05/20
Site 12 Thomas Bailey Cause: Apoplexy Age: 79 years
Birth: 1848/04/24 Death: 1928/03/13 Burial: 1928/03/14

Lot: 847 W Owner: Miscellaneous
Site 2 Michael Lynn Hammer Died: Leesburg, VA Age: 41 years
Birth: 1946/10/13 Death: 1988/08/22 Burial: 1988/10/01
Site 3 Col. Magnus Stribling Thompson Age: 89 years
Birth: 1846/07/31 Death: 1936/01/04 Burial: 1936/01/06
Cause: Nephritis TS: A Confederate Soldier Co. C 35th
Battl'n VA Cav

Site 4   Mrs. Laura Edmunds Conrad Thompson   Age: 78 years
         Birth: 1871/06/28   Death: 1949/07/31   Burial: 1949/08/03
         Wife of Col. Magnus Stribling Thompson. Daughter of Lt. Benj. F. &
         Elizabeth Stuart Conrad
Site 5   Clinton William Flynn   Cause: S. Carcenoma   Age: 65 years
         Birth: 1869   Death: 1934/11/09   Burial: 1934/11/11
Site 6   Ada K. Flynn   Age: 76 years
         Birth: 1871   Death: 1948/05/26   Burial: 1948/05/28
         On stone with Clinton William Flynn

Lot: 848 E   Owner: Charles E. Newton   Purchased: 1934/07/10
Site 7   John H. Elgin I   Age: 63 years
         Birth: 1905/09/27   Death: 1969/04/11   Burial: 1969/04/14
         Cause: Suicide   Died: Leesburg, VA
Site 9   Charles Edward Newton   Age: 60 years
         Birth: 1892/03/07   Death: 1952/09/11   Burial: 1952/09/14
Site 10 Mrs. Maggie B. Newton   Age: 80 years
         Birth: 1889/11/27   Death: 1970/07/12   Burial: 1970/07/15
         Died: Leesburg, VA   On stone with Charles Edward Newton
Site 11 Jennifer Feezle   Died: Reston, VA   Age: 4 months
         Birth: 1988   Death: 1989/02/05   Burial: 1989/02/08
Site 12 Roy P. Newton   Cause: Drowned   Age: 20 years
         Birth: 1913/08/25   Death: 1934/07/09   Burial: 1934/07/11

Lot: 848 W   Owner: Miscellaneous
Site 1   Milton Hope Brooks Jr.   Died: Arlington, VA
         Birth: 1928/11/10   Death: 1995/03/02   Burial: 1995/03/06
Site 2   John Albert Bushong   Cause: Cancer of Prostate   Age: 74 years
         Birth: 1868   Death: 1942/05/15   Burial: 1942/05/17
Site 3   Pearl Rake Bushong   Age: 77 years
         Birth: 1877   Death: 1955   Burial: 1955/04/19
         Died: Bethesda, MD   On stone with John Albert Bushong

Lot: 849 E   Owner: Miscellaneous
Site 7   Katherine (Katie) A. Jacobs Saffer   Age: 68 years
         Birth: 1871/10/05   Death: 1940/11/27   Burial: 1940/11/29
         Cause: Pulmonary Thrombosis   TS: Wife of Clinton Saffer
Site 11 Nelson A. Loucks   Cause: Brights Disease   Age: 59 years
         Birth: 1873/10/04   Death: 1931/10/06   Burial: 1931/10/18
Site 12 Ruth Saffer Loucks   Age: 80 years
         Birth: 1903/07/25   Death: 1984/06/21   Burial: 1984/06/25
         Died: Washington, DC   On stone with Nelson A. Loucks

Lot: 849 W   Owner: V.S. & E.W. Bushong   Purchased: 1933/12/22
Site 1   Worthington Bowie Houghton   Age: 67 years
         Birth: 1915/05/16   Death: 1982/12/23   Burial: 1982/12/28
         Died: Hagerstown, MD
Site 3   Charles Edward Bushong TS: Uncle Charlie   Age: 82 years
         Birth: 1867/08/14   Death: 1949/10/21   Burial: 1949/10/25

Site 4 Elizabeth W. Bushong   Age: 75 years
        Birth: 1884/06/29   Death: 1960/04/04   Burial: 1960/04/06
        On stone with Virgil S. Bushong
Site 5 Virgil S. Bushong   Age: 64 years
        Birth: 1877/02/03   Death: 1941/04/20   Burial: 1941/04/22
Site 6 Minnie B. Bushong   Age: 68 years
        Birth: 1865/09/15   Death: 1933/12/21   Burial: 1933/12/23
        Cause: Apoplexy   TS: Our beloved sister

Lot: 850 E   Owner: Mrs. Mary A. Williams   Purchased:
Site 8 John H. Williams   Age: 60 years
        Birth: 1919   Death: 1980/06/20   Burial: 1980/06/23
        Died: Middleburg, VA   TS: PFC US Army WWII
Site 9 Charles Ashby Williams Cause: Cerebral Hemorrhage   Age: 72 years
        Birth: 1862   Death: 1935/06/10   Burial: 1935/06/12
Site 10 Mary Augusta Williams Died: Middleburg, VA   Age: 86 years
        Birth: 1876   Death: 1962/07/23   Burial: 1962/07/25
site 11 Charles A. Williams   Died: Peterstown, WV   Age: 66 years
        Birth: 1914/01/16   Death: 1980/07/22   Burial: 1980/07/30

Lot: 850 W   Owner: Miscellaneous
Site 1 Wilber D. Jackson   Cause: Brain Tumor   Age: 42 years
        Birth: 1896/11/15   Death: 1939/10/21   Burial: 1939/10/23
Site 4 Enos Beavers   No stone   Age: 71 years
        Died: Leesburg, VA   Death: 1962/12/16   Burial: 1962/12/18
Site 5 Ernest Benjamin Trittipoe Cause: Cerebral Hemorrhage Age: 69 years
        Birth: 1870   Death: 1939/01/28   Burial: 1939/01/30
Site 6 Gussie Virginia Trittipoe   Age: 88 years
        Birth: 1874   Death: 1962/10/02   Burial: 1962/10/05
        Died: Sterling, VA   On stone with Ernest Benjamin Trittipoe

Lot: 851 E   Owner: Miscellaneous
Site 7 Edwin Spencer Virts   Cause: Coronary Occlusion   Age: 72 years
        Birth: 1867/12/05   Death: 1940/02/17   Burial: 1940/02/19
Site 8 Nina Russell Virts   Age: 83 years
        Birth: 1870/01/05   Death: 1953/10/06   Burial: 1953/10/08
        Died: Arlington, VA   On stone with E. Spencer Virts
Site 9 Thomas Alexander   Age: 78 years
                               Death: Unreadable   Burial: 1960/11/05
        Cause: Heart   Died: Purcelville, VA   Stone Unreadable
Site 9 Edward Alexander   Age: 76 years
                               Death: Unreadable   Burial: 1960/11/05
        Cause: Heart   Died: Purcelville, VA   Stone Unreadable
Site 10 Carrie Alexander   No stone   Age: 67 years
        Died: Leesburg, VA   Death: 1960/08/21   Burial: 1960/08/24
Site 11 Edith M. Jones Bullard Died: Manassas, VA   Age: 64 years
        Birth: 1906/07/29   Death: 1974/07/28   Burial: 1974/08/01
Site 12 Mrs. Kate Jones   Cause: Intestinal Obstruction Age: 73 years
        Birth: 1865/09   Death: 1938/08/16   Burial: 1938/08/18

Lot: 851 W   Owner: Mrs. George E. & Crighton Vogel
Site 1   George E. Vogel   Cause: Angina Pectoris   Age: 68 years
         Birth: 1870   Death: 1937/10/04   Burial: 1937/10/06
Site 2   Mrs. Margaret Miller C. Vogel   Age: 70 years
         Birth: 1867   Death: 1944/03/26   Burial: 1944/03/28
Site 3   Miss Lily B. Crighton   Age: 75 years
         Birth: 1876   Death: 1950/11/26   Burial: 1950/11/29
Site 5   William Crighton   Age: 73 years
         Birth: 1865   Death: 1938/08/03   Burial: 1938/08/05
         TS: Born Dundee, Scotland. Died Herndon, VA
Site 6   Mrs. Elizabeth Crighton   Age: 82 years
         Birth: 1870/06/22   Death: 1952/07/30   Burial: 1952/08/01
         On stone with William Crighton

Lot: 852 E   Owner: B.F. Swart   Purchased: 1944/09/25
Site 8   Benjamin Franklin Swart   Age: 58 years
         Birth: 1891/09/22   Death: 1950/03/02
Site 9   Mrs. Cora Edna Swart   Age: 48 years
         Birth: 1895/08/30   Death: 1944/09/24   Burial: 1944/09/26
         On stone with Benjamin Franklin Swart

Lot: 852 W   Owner: James A. Downs   Purchased: 1956/03/29
Site 1   Percy R. Grimes   Died: Culpeper, VA   Age: 86 years
         Birth: 1889/12/05   Death: 1976/02/06   Burial: 1976/02/08
Site 2   Nettie Grimes   Age: 85 years
         Birth: 1891-07-22   Death: 1976/08/17   Burial: 1976/08/20
         Died: Culpeper, VA   On stone with Percy R. Grimes
Site 5   Mary Darnes Downs   Died: Leesburg, VA   Age: 80 years
         Birth: 1890/07/23   Death: 1970/11/09   Burial: 1970/11/12
Site 6   John Noland Downs   Died: Sykesville, VA   Age: 81 years
         Birth: 1884/03/17   Death: 1961/01/23   Burial: 1961/01/27

Lot: 853   Owner: Mrs. Daisy M. Myers   Purchased: 1947/10/02
Site 3   Harry Myers   Age: 58 years
         Birth: 1877/04/28   Death: 1936/02/09   Burial: 1936/02/12
         Cause: Paralysis   Moved from Lot 620 April 9, 1948
Site 5   Daisy M. Myers   Age: 90 years
         Birth: 1881/05/09   Death: 1972/01/22   Burial: 1972/01/26
         Died: Manassas, VA   On stone with Harry Myers
Site 6   Heyl (Jack) Leighton   Age: 53 years
         Birth: 1903/09/18   Death: 1957/07/23
Site 7   John Donald Athey   Died: Alexandria, VA
         Birth: 1914/02/14   Death: 1971/07/01   Burial: 1971/07/05
Site 8   Myrtle Myers Athey   Died: Manassas, VA   Age: 75 years
         Birth: 1903/10/03   Death: 1979/01/27   Burial: 1979/01/30
         On stone with John Donald Athey
Site 12 Sarah Ellen Kitchen   Age: 1 day
         Birth: 1949/06/27   Death: 1949/06/29   Burial: 1949/06/29

Lot: 854   Owner: Clarence B. James   Purchased: 1939/11/20
Site 1	Child James	Cause: Stillborn	No stone
		Death: 1947/11/15	Burial: 1947/11/17
Site 3	Clarence B. James Sr.	Died: Leesburg, VA	Age: 83 years
	Birth: 1883	Death: 1967/09/19	Burial: 1967/09/22
Site 4	Nettie Rinker James		Age: 63 years
	Birth: 1884	Death: 1947/12/09	Burial: 1947/12/11
Site 5	Oscar C. James		Age: 26 years
	Birth: 1913	Death: 1939/11/14	Burial: 1939/11/21
Site 8	Helen L. James	Died: Leesburg, VA	Age: 75 years
	Birth: 1913	Death: 1989/02/17	Burial: 1989/02/21
Site 9	Elmer E. James Sr.	Died: Leesburg, VA	Age: 82 years
	Birth: 1904	Death: 1986/12/26	Burial: 1986/12/29
Site 10	Mrs. Jessie E. Jackson James		Age: 45 years
	Birth: 1905	Death: 1951/08/20	Burial: 1951/08/23
Site 11	Nettie Mae James		Age: 16 years
	Birth: 1927/05/24	Death: 1943/06/29	Burial: 1943/07/01
	TS: Daughter of Elmer & Jessie James		

Lot: 855 E   Owner: Miscellaneous
Site 9	James Edgar Jones	Died: Leesburg, VA	Age: 49 years
	Birth: 1903/12/23	Death: 1953/12/21	Burial: 1953/12/23
Site 11	George C. Rollison		Age: 53 years
	Birth: 1888	Death: 1941/03/24	Burial: 1941/03/26

Lot: 855 W   Owner: C.R. Marcum   Purchased: 1954/04/13
Site 3	Arthur H. Marcum	Died: Front Royal, VA	
	Birth: 1905/04/17	Death: 1991/03/13	Burial: 1991/03/15
Site 4	Annie Middleton Marcum		Age: 70 years
	Birth: 1881/12/28	Death: 1954/03/18	
Site 5	Charles R. Marcum		Age: 69 years
	Birth: 1880/05/19	Death: 1949/12/29	Burial: 1949/12/31
Site 6	Ida Hawkins Marcum		Age: 26 years
	Birth: 1916/12/23	Death: 1942/04/13	

Lot: 856   Owner: Miscellaneous
Site 1	Lester Aden Scott	Died: Martinsburg, WV	Age: 78 years
	Birth: 1896/02/16	Death: 1974/05/04	Burial: 1974/05/07
Site 2	Ella Keys Scott		Age: 74 years
	Birth: 1904/02/28	Death: 1978/09/01	Burial: 1978/09/04
	Died: Leesburg, VA		On stone with Lester Aden Scott
Site 6	Child of William M. Rutherford		Cause: Stillborn
	Birth: 1947/05/23	Death: 1947/05/23	Burial: 1947/05/25
Site 11	Margaret L. Anderson	Died: Leesburg, VA	Age: 63 years
	Birth: 1922	Death: 1985/12/17	Burial: 1985/12/19
Site 12	Child of Webb Anderson	Cause: Stillborn	No stone
	Birth: 1946/10/20	Death: 1946/10/20	Burial: 1946/10/22

Lot: 857 Owner: Miscellaneous
Site 1   James H. (Jimmy) Tavenner   Age: 57 years
         Birth: 1928/12/31   Death: 1986/11/19   Burial: 1986/11/22
                                Died: Leesburg, VA
Site 3   Doris Ann Tavenner   Died: Washington, DC   Age: 29 years
         Birth: 1952/07/28   Death: 1982/06/10   Burial: 1982/06/13
         TS: Daughter of James H. & Hazel A. Tavenner
Site 7   Stephen Lee Luckett   Age: 56 years
         Birth: 1895   Death: 1951/09/19   Burial: 1951/09/21
Site 8   Anne Luckett Keys Hart Died: Falls Church, VA   Age: 78 years
         Birth: 1897   Death: 1975/06/26   Burial: 1975/06/30

Lot: 858 Owner: Miscellaneous
Site 1   Leonard Charles Markland Sr.
         Birth: 1924/08/04   Death: 1991/01/21   Burial: 1991/01/25
         Died: Lucketts, VA   TS: T Sgt US Army WWII
Site 3   Dorothy Louise Flynn   Died: Leesburg, VA
         Birth: 1918/05/03   Death: 1992/06/08   Burial: 1992/06/11
Site 5   Shirley M. Flynn   Died: Arlington, VA
         Birth: 1939/07/14   Death: 1993/03/14   Burial: 1993/03/18
Site 7   Cecil Vernon Phillips   Age: 66 years
         Birth: 1914/11/24   Death: 1981/02/15   Burial: 1981/02/18
         Died: Silver Spring, MD   TS: Pvt. US Army WWII
Site 10 Ann U. Keyes   Died: Leesburg, VA   Age: 59 years
         Birth: 1928/07/21   Death: 1986/09/01   Burial: 1986/09/05
Site 12 Mrs. Blair Dissette Jamarik   Age: 49 years
         Birth: 1938/05/28   Death: 1987/10/14   Burial: 1987/10/19
         Died: Round Hill, VA   TS: Physician, Mother, Wife

Lot: 859 Owner: Miscellaneous
Site 6   Peggy A. Harkleroad   Died: Leesburg, VA   Age: 55 years
         Birth: 1936/12/08   Death: 1992/10/28   Burial: 1992/10/31
Site 7   Russell B. Harding   Died: Leesburg, VA
         Birth: 1926/09/09   Death: 1993/10/11   Burial: 1993/10/16
Site 8   Dorothy Lee Harding   Died: Leesburg, VA   Age: 60 years
         Birth: 1929   Death: 1989/08/24   Burial: 1989/08/28
Site 10 Marylee Ward Weed   Age: 58 years
         Birth: 1925   Death: 1984/03/15   Burial: 1984/03/21
         Cause: Heart   Died: Tucson, Pima Co., AZ
Site 11 Ray Wilson Hardy   Age: 68 years
         Birth: 1911/12/11   Death: 1980/03/27   Burial: 1980/03/29
         Cause: Cancer   Died: Leesburg, VA
Site 12 Helen J. Hardy
         Birth: 1918/01/30   Death: 1992/02/01   Burial: 1992/02/05
         Died: Berryville, VA   On stone with Ray W. Hardy

Lot: 864 Owner: Miscellaneous
Site 8   Madelyn Sarah Deibel   No stone   Age: 5 days
         Died: Washington, DC   Death: 1988/02/20   Burial: 1988/02/23

Site 9   Morgan Marie Long   Cause: Stillborn   Age: Baby
          Died: Leesburg, VA   Death: 1987/11/21   Burial: 1987/11/27
          TS: Infant daughter of Fred & Joyce Long
Site 10   Patricia Houston   No stone   Age: Baby
          Died: Leesburg, VA   Death: 1987/11/12   Burial: 1987/11/16
Site 10   Shayne William K. Harr   No stone   Age: Baby
          Died: Fairfax, VA   Death: 1987/10/01   Burial: 1987/10/05
Site 11   Richard A. Doman   No stone   Age: 28 years
          Died: Leesburg, VA   Death: 1984/11/20   Burial: 1984/11/24
Site 12   Elizabeth Ashley Kephart   Died: Washington, DC   Age: 3 days
          Birth: 1984/04/06   Death: 1984/04/08   Burial: 1984/04/12

Lot: 865 Owner: Miscellaneous
Site 2   Gary J. Jones   Died: Paeonian Springs, VA   Age: 63 years
          Birth: 1922   Death: 1985/12/18   Burial: 1985/12/20
Site 4   James L. Dawson   Died: Gaithersburg, MD   Age: 58 years
          Birth: 1927   Death: 1985/12/24   Burial: 1985/12/30
Site 6   Norman W. Funk   Died: Leesburg, VA   Age: 72 years
          Birth: 1913/09/16   Death: 1985/12/10   Burial: 1985/12/12
Site 7   Dillard E. Coffey Jr.   Died: Leesburg, VA   Age: 51 years
          Birth: 1934/11/04   Death: 1986/01/28   Burial: 1986/01/31
Site 10   Alice Elder   Died: Alexandria, VA   Age: 63 years
          Birth: 1922/07/11   Death: 1986/01/22   Burial: 1986/01/25
Site 12   Margot H. Mills   Age: 44 years
          Birth: 1941/03/09   Death: 1986/01/19   Burial: 1986/01/22
          Cause: Heart   Died: Lucketts, VA

Lot: 866 Owner: Miscellaneous
Site 1   Donna Louise Carter   Died: Leesburg, VA   Age: 25 years
          Birth: 1958/06/14   Death: 1983/12/31   Burial: 1984/01/03
Site 2   Everett (E.J.) Woodward II   Age: 2 weeks
          Birth: 1978/09/04   Death: 1978/09/20   Burial: 1978/09/23
                                     Died: Washington, DC
Site 5   William Roy Finney   Died: Arlington, VA   Age: 64 years
          Birth: 1915   Death: 1979/08/28   Burial: 1979/08/31
Site 7   Gladys Bell Henderson   Died: Leesburg, VA   Age: 87 years
          Birth: 1902/05/01   Death: 1989/04/04   Burial: 1989/04/07
Site 8   Gilbert O. (Pete) Kaufman   Age: 62 years
          Birth: 1905   Death: 1968/07/14   Burial: 1968/07/16
Site 11   Walter Scott Allensworth   Died: Leesburg, VA   Age: 62 years
          Birth: 1893/05/14   Death: 1955/05/29   Burial: 1955/05/29
Site 12   Nellie Bell Allensworth   Died: Florence, SC   Age: 64 years
          Birth: 1906/10/12   Death: 1971/06/30   Burial: 1971/07/03

Lot: 867 Owner: Miscellaneous
Site 1   Henry C. Bodine   Age: 81 years
          Birth: 1878/08/01   Death: 1960/02/25   Burial: 1960/02/28
Site 2   Harry G. Kerns   Died: Hamilton, VA   Age: 62 years
          Birth: 1909/07/28   Death: 1972/01/02   Burial: 1972/01/07

Site 3	Annabell Kerns	Died: WV	On stone with Harry G. Kerns
	Birth: 1923/01/18	Death: 1994/09/10	Burial: 1994/09/14
Site 5	James Richard Kerns		Age: 73 years
	Birth: 1910/09/19	Death: 1984/06/25	Burial: 1984/06/28
		Died: Prince George's Co., MD	
Site 6	Leona Mae Kerns		Age: 70 years
	Birth: 1913/10/23	Death: 1984/10/02	Burial: 1984/10/04
	Died: Clinton, MD	On stone with James Richard Kerns	
Site 7	Lee Roy Lemert	Died: Washington, DC	Age: 46 years
	Birth: 1941/05/16	Death: 1987/11/19	Burial: 1987/11/23
Site 10	Mary Ella McLeod		Age: 80 years
	Birth: 1907	Death: 1987/12/03	Burial: 1987/12/05
	Died: Leesburg, VA	On stone with Harry R. McLeod	

Lot: 868 Owner: Miscellaneous

Site 1	James R. Kerns Jr.		Age: 2 years
	Birth: 1943/10/31	Death: 1945/11/29	Burial: 1945/12/03
Site 2	Cecil J. Kerns		Age: 8 years
	Birth: 1945/12/21	Death: 1954/06/28	
Site 7	Emory B.W. Lambert	Died: Leesburg, VA	Age: 78 years
	Birth: 1910/11/29	Death: 1989/06/30	Burial: 1989/07/03
Site 8	William Perry Lambert	Died: Warrenton, VA	Age: 89 years
	Birth: 1888/08/20	Death: 1978/07/23	Burial: 1978/07/26
Site 9	Lourie F. Lambert		Age: 77 years
	Birth: 1895/06/15	Death: 1972/12/27	Burial: 1972/12/30
	Died: Philmont, VA	On stone with William Perry Lambert	
Site 12	Gloria J. Cook		Age: 11 months
	Birth: 1944/04/17	Death: 1945/03/20	Burial: 1945/03/22

Lot: 869 Owner: Miscellaneous

Site 5	Bertha Newberry Moxley	Died: Leesburg, VA	Age: 64 years
	Birth: 1923/06/16	Death: 1987/10/23	Burial: 1987/10/26
Site 6	Mary Margaret Moxley		Age: 2 1/2
	Birth: 1958/09/13	Death: 1961/01/22	Burial: 1961/01/24
Site 8	Flavia Baker McIlvain	Died: Leesburg, VA	Age: 85 years
	Birth: 1902	Death: 1988/02/14	Burial: 1988/02/17
Site 9	James Edgar Utterback	Died: Sterling, VA	Age: 87 years
	Birth: 1902/02/21	Death: 1989/09/28	Burial: 1989/09/30
Site 10	Elsie Caylor Utterback		Age: 86 years
	Birth: 1905/02/25	Death: 1991/09/30	Burial: 1991/10/02
	Died: Fairfax, VA	On stone with James Edgar Utterback	
Site 11	John M. Woodruff	Died: Leesburg, VA	Age: 76 years
	Birth: 1911	Death: 1988/01/09	Burial: 1988/01/12

Lot: 870 E   Owner: M.E. Caylor   Purchased: 1951/09/19

Site 7	Edna V. Wright	Died: Washington, DC	Age: 39 years
	Birth: 1913/09/06	Death: 1953/04/18	Burial: 1953/04/20
Site 10	Milton E. Caylor	Died: Warrenton, VA	Age: 85 years
	Birth: 1880	Death: 1966/02/17	Burial: 1966/02/19

Site 11 Mary Caylor   Age: 74 years
        Birth: 1887   Death: 1961/08/13   Burial: 1961/08/15
        Died: Leesburg, VA   On stone with Milton E. Caylor
Site 12 Lawrence E. Caylor   Age: 49 years
        Birth: 1902/08/15   Death: 1951/09/18   Burial: 1951/09/21

Lot: 870 W Owner: Miscellaneous
Site 1 Oney Charles Triplett   Age: 47 years
        Birth: 1907   Death: 1954/10/25
Site 2 Elton McCoy Best   Died: Leesburg, VA
        Birth: 1897/09/08   Death: 1994/10/29   Burial: 1994/11/01
Site 5 Nina Leonard   No stone   Age: 70 years
        Died: Washington, DC   Death: 1960/03/17   Burial: 1960/03/21
Site 6 Montgomery G. Leonard No stone   Age: 72 years
        Died: Washington, DC   Death: 1960/05/12   Burial: 1960/05/14

Lot: 871 Owner: Miscellaneous
Site 2 Mary Ellen Partlow   Died: Leesburg, VA   Age: 55 years
        Birth: 1931/03/14   Death: 1986/03/11   Burial: 1986/03/14
Site 4 Annie E. Espey   Died: Hamilton, VA   Age: 84 years
        Birth: 1905/06/13   Death: 1989/10/26   Burial: 1989/10/28
Site 5 Steven D. Walton   Age: 41 years
        Birth: 1945/02/21   Death: 1986/04/22   Burial: 1986/04/25
        Died: Leesburg, VA   TS: Vietnam Veteran
Site 10 Alice J. Bond   Died: FL   On stone with Paul S. Bond
        Birth: 1913   Death: 1987/09/09   Burial: 1987/10/11
Site 10 Paul S. Bond   Died: FL   Age: 91 years
        Birth: 1898   Death: 1989/11/24   Burial: 1989/12/05

Lot: 872 Owner: Miscellaneous
Site 1 Irving F. Barnhouse   Died: Leesburg, VA   Age: 67 years
        Birth: 1918/03/11   Death: 1986/02/20   Burial: 1986/02/22
Site 5 Harry Edgar Barnhouse Died: Leesburg, VA   Age: 70 years
        Birth: 1921/09/19   Death: 1991/09/28   Burial: 1991/10/01
Site 9 Rebecca Louise Horn   Died: Clearwater, FL   Age: 21 years
        Birth: 1965   Death: 1986/05/30   Burial: 1986/06/02
Site 11 Thomas P. Fleming   Died: Leesburg, VA   Age: 55 years
        Birth: 1931   Death: 1986/03/24   Burial: 1986/03/27

Lot: 873 E   Owner: Mrs. John A. Beaver   Purchased: 1942/07/15
Site 8 Louise Huger Beaver   Age: 73 years
        Birth: 1903/03/03   Death: 1976/04/08   Burial: 1976/06/04
        Died: Williamstown   On stone with John Andrew Beaver
Site 9 John Andrew Beaver   Age: 58 years
        Birth: 1884/04/01   Death: 1942/07/12   Burial: 1942/07/15
Site 10 Louise W. Huger   Died: NY   Age: 87 years
        Birth: 1872/08/13   Death: 1959/12/09   Burial: 1960/05/21
Site 11 Marshall Braxton Pugh   Age: 91 years
        Birth: 1851   Death: 1942/11/07   Burial: 1942/11/09

Site 12 Mrs. Ann Hampton Pugh   Age: 98 years
         Birth: 1859   Death: 1957/05/19
         On stone with Marshall Braxton Pugh

Lot: 873 W   Owner: Charles W. Fry   Purchased: 1942/08/28
Site 2   Melvin C. Fry   Birth: 1902/06/12   Death: 1978/05/24
Site 5   Charles William Fry   Age: 81 years
         Birth: 1871/02/23   Death: 1952/12/01   Burial: 1952/12/04
Site 6   Mrs. Maggie Roberta Fry Cause: Chronic Cardiac   Age: 66 years
         Birth: 1876/05/02   Death: 1942/08/27   Burial: 1942/08/29

Lot: 874   Owner: Miscellaneous
Site 1   Mrs. Lula Catherine P. Rinker   Age: 62 years
         Birth: 1881/09/15   Death: 1943/02/27   Burial: 1943/02/29
         On stone with Thomas S. Rinker
Site 2   Thomas S. Rinker   Died: Alexandria, VA   Age: 85 years
         Birth: 1880/03/13   Death: 1965/11/07   Burial: 1965/11/10
Site 3   Ronnie Lee Marcum   No stone   Age: 3 months
                                 Death: 1946/05/24   Burial: 1946/05/26
Site 4   William B. Smith   No stone   Age: 55 years
                                 Death: 1943/10/08   Burial: 1943/10/10
Site 5   Orville Daniel   No stone   Age: 72 years
         Died: FL   Death: 1964/09/06   Burial: 1964/09/11
Site 6   Mrs. Elizabeth Daniel   Age: 46 years
         Birth: 1896/05/04   Death: 1942/12/22   Burial: 1942/12/24
Site 9   Philip Howell Lightfoot Sr.   Age: 75 years
         Birth: 1880   Death: 1956/04/12   Burial: 1956/04/12
         Died: Suitland, MD   TS: Husband of Bertha Helen Quilliam
Site 12 Bertha Helen Quilliam Lightfoot   Age: 48 years
         Birth: 1888   Death: 1937/06/26   Burial: 1937/06/28
         Cause: C. Seral   TS: Wife of Philip Howell Lightfoot

Lot: 875 E   Owner: Frances E. Oliver   Purchased: 1982/04/12
Site 7   William L. Oliver   Died: Leesburg, VA   Age: 61 years
         Birth: 1920/10/04   Death: 1982/03/23   Burial: 1982/03/25
Site 12 Joseph Nelson Oliver   Age: 70 years
         Birth: 1914/06/27   Death: 1985/02/06   Burial: 1985/02/08
                                 Died: Prince George's Co., MD

Lot: 875 W   Owner: H.R. Stowers   Purchased: 1935/12/02
Site 2   Hiram R. Stowers   Died: L.C.H. Leesburg, VA   Age: 90 years
         Birth: 1868/02/20   Death: 1959/01/07   Burial: 1959/01/09
Site 5   Lena May Stowers   Cause: Heart   Age: 34 years
         Birth: 1901/10/14   Death: 1935/11/30   Burial: 1935/12/01
Site 6   William Vance Stowers   Age: 56 years
         Birth: 1895/07/14   Death: 1952/06/27   Burial: 1952/06/29

Lot: 876 Owner: Horace L. English   Purchased:
Site 2   Horace L. English   Died: Wheaton, MD   Age: 95 years
         Birth: 1875/05/31   Death: 1970/08/08   Burial: 1970/08/12

Site 4   Lelia Steiner English   Cause: Carcinoma   Age: 53 years
         Birth: 1881/12/01   Death: 1934/08/28   Burial: 1934/08/30

Lot: 877   Owner: Robert L. Bentley   Purchased: 1927/05/12
Site 2   Charles Edward Lyon   Died: Savannah, GA   Age: 20 years
         Birth: 1969/11/06   Death: 1990/01/11   Burial: 1990/02/10
         TS:Son of Robert Bentley & Jo Ann Vestal Lyon. Born Baltimore
         County, MD. Died Savannah, GA
Site 4   Moncure Nelson Lyon   Age: 83 years
         Birth: 1883/09/26   Death: 1967/08/14   Burial: 1967/08/16
         Died: Leesburg, VA   Son of James William Lyon & Fanny
         Moncure Nelson. Born "Wester Ogle" Baltimore County, MD. Died
         "Black Oak Ridge", Loudoun County, VA
Site 5   M. Constance Bentley Lyon   Age: 97 years
         Birth: 1890/01/23   Death: 1987/04/09   Burial: 1987/04/11
         Died: Purcellville, VA   TS: Daughter of Robert Longden Bentley &
         Marie Constance Myer. Wife of Moncure Nelson Lyon
Site 6   Robert Longden Bentley Died: Baltimore Co., MD   Age: 70 years
         Birth: 1858/07/25   Death: 1929/07/22   Burial: 1929/07/24
         Cause: Prostate   TS: Son of Richard Mongomery Bentley &
         Ann Catherine Drake. Born Loudoun County, VA
Site 9   Alice Whelan Chatard   Age: 1 year
         Birth: 1944/12/10   Death: 1945/01/31   Burial: 1955/08/03
         Disinterrment from Cathedral-Baltimore, MD. Infant daughter of
         Ferdinand E & Constance Chatard
Site 9   Mary Chatard   Age: 2 hrs
                                       Death: 1949/11/07   Burial: 1955/08/03
         Disinterrment from Cathedral-Baltimore, MD   No stone
Site 11 Ferdinand Edme Chatard   Age: 73 years
         Birth: 1914/04/28   Death: 1987/10/17   Burial: 1987/10/20
         Died: Baltimore, MD   TS: Capt US Navy WWII Medical Corp.

Lot: 878   Owner: Robert L. Bentley   Purchased: 1927/05/12
Site 1   Mrs. Marie Constance Bentley   Age: 76 years
         Birth: 1869/02/04   Death: 1945/03/31   Burial: 1945/04/03
         Died: Baltimore Co., MD   TS: Wife of Robert Longden Bentley.
         Daughter of Thomas Jacob & Elizabeth Shreve Myer of Baltimore Co.,
         MD
Site 2   Robert Longden Bentley Jr.   Age: 79 years
         Birth: 1905/04/16   Death: 1985/04/05   Burial: 1992/06/13
         Died: Englewood, FL   TS: Son of Robert Longden Bentley & Marie
         Constance Myer. Born in Roslyn near Pikesville, MD
Site 3   Anne Leiper Martin Breed Bentley   Died: Winter Park, FL
         Birth: 1905/03/02   Death: 1991/12/20   Burial: 1991/12/28
         TS: Wife of Robert Longden Bentley, Jr. Daughter of Dr. Charles
         Henry Breed & Frances deForest Martin. Born Lawrenceville, NJ
Site 4   Robert Longden Bentley III   Age: 1 year
         Birth: 1927   Death: 1929/02/04   Burial: 1955/08/03
         Disinterrment from Cathedral-Baltimore, MD TS: Son of Robert L.
         Bentley, Jr. & Ann Breed Bentley

Site 7   Dr. Valentine de Balla   Cause: Auto Accident   Died: Austria
         Birth: 1899/10/23   Death: 1957/11/25   Burial: 1957/12/14
Site 7   Ann Katherine Drake Bentley De Balla   Age: 91 years
         Birth: 1892/07/26   Death: 1983/12/19   Burial: 1983/12/21
         Died: Richmond, VA
Site 12 Ambers Robb   Birth: 1881/07/03   Death: 1974/10/08

Lot: 879   Owner: Mrs. N.B. Hawthorne   Purchased: 1934/06/01
Site 3   Henry Malcolm Hay   Died: Silver Spring, MD   Age: 76 years
         Birth: 1902/10/24   Death: 1979/09/10   Burial: 1979/09/13
Site 5   James W. Hawthorne   Died: Falls Church, VA   Age: 66 years
         Birth: 1908/04/10   Death: 1974/09/03   Burial: 1974/09/05
Site 6   Maria Parr Hawthorne   Age: 54 years
         Birth: 1918/04/10   Death: 1972/09/09
Site 8   Elizabeth Hawthorne Lueck   Age: 97 years
         Birth: 1890/02/04   Death: 1987/12/29   Burial: 1988/01/01
Site 9   Noah B. Hawthorn   Cause: Arteriosclerosis   Age: 75 years
         Birth: 1859/02/05   Death: 1934/05/28   Burial: 1934/05/30
Site 11 Mrs. Hettie J. Grant Hawthorne   Age: 81 years
         Birth: 1868/05/19   Death: 1949/08/12   Burial: 1949/08/14
Site 12 Mary Lucretia Hawthorne   Died: Washington, DC   Age: 76 years
         Birth: 1887/06/30   Death: 1965/03/02   Burial: 1965/03/04

Lot: 880 E   Owner: Emma S. Franklin   Purchased: 1929/04/13
Site 10 Benjamin Willard Franklin   Age: 55 years
         Birth: 1874/05/22   Death: 1929/04/12   Burial: 1929/04/14
         Cause: Indigestion
Site 11 Emma Shaffar Franklin   Age: 96 years
         Birth: 1885/05/22   Death: 1981/04/20   Burial: 1981/04/22
         Died: Tazewell, VA   On stone with Benjamin Willard Franklin

Lot: 880 W   Owner: Mrs. J. H. Leslie   Purchased: 1932/08/11
Site 4   John Harrison (Harry) Leslie   Age: 60 years
         Birth: 1871/06/27   Death: 1932/06/13   Burial: 1932/06/15
         Cause: Apoplexy

Lot: 881 E   Owner: John T. Sewell   Purchased: 1934/09/21
Site 7   Walter N. Downs   Age: 58 years
         Birth: 1919/06/20   Death: 1977/08/26   Burial: 1977/08/28
         Died: Leesburg, VA   TS: CPL US Army WWII
Site 8   Charles Franklin Shugars   Age: 53 years
         Birth: 1932   Death: 1985/07/15   Burial: 1985/07/17
         Cause: Cancer   Died: Manassas, VA
         TS: Married Hattie C. Shugars June 9, 1967
Site 10 Michael Burl Whetsell   Died: Leesburg, VA
         Birth: 1937/04/15   Death: 1992/06/18   Burial: 1992/06/22
         TS: Married Bonnie S. Whetsell June 18, 1964
Site 11 John T. Sewell   No stone   Age: 89 years
                                     Death: 1950/01/14   Burial: 1950/01/17

Site 12 Susie B. Sewell   Cause: Cerebral Hemorrhage   Age: 72 years
        No stone   Death: 1940/03/24   Burial: 1940/03/26

Lot: 881 W   Owner: L.E. Sugars   Purchased: 1934/11/23
Site 1 Lewis E. Shugars   Died: Leesburg, VA   Age: 91 years
        Birth: 1871   Death: 1963/07/13   Burial: 1963/07/15
Site 2 Mrs. Annie Virginia Shugars   Age: 63 years
        Birth: 1879   Death: 1942/11/04   Burial: 1942/11/06
        On stone with Lewis E. Shugars
Site 3 Edward Shugars Sr.   Died: Leesburg, VA   Age: 68 years
        Birth: 1898/08/11   Death: 1966/12/23   Burial: 1966/12/26
Site 4 Bertha J. Shugars   Age: 75 years
        Birth: 1896/11/26   Death: 1972/04/30   Burial: 1972/05/03
        Died: Leesburg, VA   On stone with Edward P. Shugars
Site 5 Edward Preston Shugars Jr.   Age: 49 years
        Birth: 1926/01/19   Death: 1975/02/09   Burial: 1975/02/12
        Died: Winchester, VA   TS: PFC US Army
Site 6 Linda K. Shugars   Died: L.C.H. Leesburg, VA   Age: 6 months
                                 Death: 1958/05/17   Burial: 1958/05/18
Site 6 Edward Preston Shugars III   Age: 4 years
        Birth: 1955   Death: 1959/06/17   Burial: 1959/06/20
        Cause: Leukemia   Died: Leesburg, VA

Lot: 882 E   Owner: Miscellaneous
Site 7 Jacob H. Peters   Cause: Senility   Age: 85 years
        Birth: 1855   Death: 1940/11/20   Burial: 1940/11/22
Site 8 Sarah Alice Peters   On stone with J. Henry Peters
        Birth: 1861   Death: 1948/04/22   Burial: 1948/04/24
Site 9 Michael A. Donley   Cause: Valvular Heart Disease Age: 87 years
        No stone   Death: 1941/11/15   Burial: 1941/11/17
Site 11 Alfred F. Mathers   No death date on stone   Age: 90 years
        Birth: 1856   Death: 1947/01/22   Burial: 1947/01/24
Site 12 Sarah Belle Mathers   Cause: Cerebral Hemorrhage   Age: 75 years
        Birth: 1864   Death: 1940/06/07   Burial: 1940/06/09
        On stone with Alfred F. Mathers   TS: Age 76 years

Lot: 882 W   Owner: John S. Simpson   Purchased: 1937/05/20
Site 1 Howard Smoot Simpson Died: Paeonian Springs, VA   Age: 50 years
        Birth: 1907/11/06   Death: 1958/06/25   Burial: 1958/06/27
Site 2 John Smith Simpson   Cause: Coronary Thrombosis   Age: 88 years
        Birth: 1854/08/15   Death: 1941/04/11   Burial: 1941/04/13
Site 4 Mary J. Simpson   Cause: Cerebral Hemorrhage   Age: 67 years
        Birth: 1869/09/28   Death: 1937/05/20   Burial: 1937/05/22
Site 5 J. Lupton Simpson   Died: Paeonian Springs, VA   Age: 65 years
        Birth: 1902/05/24   Death: 1967/06/25   Burial: 1967/06/28

Lot: 883   Owner: Miscellaneous
Site 1 George B. Carson   Age: 80 years
        Birth: 1862   Death: 1943/06/15   Burial: 1943/06/17

Site 2   Mrs. Florence Lillian Carson   Age: 77 years
         Birth: 1866   Death: 1943/11/25   Burial: 1943/11/27
         On stone with George B. Carson
Site 3   Pearl E. Baker   Died: Leesburg, VA   Age: 14 years
         Birth: 1948   Death: 1962/01/26   Burial: 1962/01/29
Site 4   Maphis F. Lunsford   Died: Leesburg, VA
         Birth: 1910/11/06   Death: 1992/09/02   Burial: 1992/09/04
Site 5   Nelly Jane Lunsford   Age: 4 years
         Birth: 1938/08/28   Death: 1943/06/11   Burial: 1943/06/13
         Cause: Perotonitis   TS: Daughter of M.F. & L.L. Lunsford
Site 6   Lydia L. Winks Lunsford Died: Leesburg, VA   Age: 58 years
         Birth: 1912   Death: 1971/07/01   Burial: 1971/07/03
Site 7   Harry C. Adams   Died: Washington, DC   Age: 74 years
         Birth: 1881/12/28   Death: 1956/06/09   Burial: 1956/06/11
Site 9   Mary C. Adams   Age: 82 years
         Birth: 1884/07/18   Death: 1966/08/19   Burial: 1966/08/22
         Died: Fairfax, VA   On stone with Harry C. Adams
Site 11 Daniel F. Kerwin   Died: Leesburg, VA   Age: 86 years
         Birth: 1875/08/31   Death: 1961/11/08   Burial: 1961/11/10
Site 12 Mrs. Susan Bertha Kerwin   Age: 66 years
         Birth: 1879/10/25   Death: 1943/03/09   Burial: 1943/03/11
         On stone with Daniel F. Kerwin

Lot: 884 E   Owner: Mrs. W. W. Waters   Purchased: 1950/08/07
Site 10 William Wright Waters   Age: 65 years
         Birth: 1883/05/10   Death: 1950/08/03   Burial: 1950/08/06
Site 11 Mrs. Susie Daniel Waters Died: Leesburg, VA   Age: 68 years
         Birth: 1891/05/12   Death: 1960/03/03   Burial: 1960/03/07
         On stone with William Wright Waters

Lot: 884 W   Owner: Forest Furr   Purchased: 1955/04/13
Site 1   Earl Rollison   No dates on stone   Age: 68 years
         Died: Hadley Hosp.   Death: 1965/12/01   Burial: 1965/12/03
Site 2   Rose Ella Rollison   Died: Montgomery, MD   Age: 67 years
         Birth: 1898/07/04   Death: 1965/08/23   Burial: 1965/08/26
Site 3   Raymond Keyes   No stone   Age: 62 years
                                  Death: 1965/01/01   Burial: 1965/01/05
Site 4   Lillian Rebecca Fletcher Died: Baltimore, MD   Age: 65 years
         Birth: 1900/07/24   Death: 1965/07/28   Burial: 1965/07/31
Site 6   Mrs. Dorothy Ellen Keyes Furr   Age: 26 years
         Birth: 1928/06/22   Death: 1955/04/12   Burial: 1955/04/13
                                  Died: Leesburg, VA
Site 6   Viola May Keyes   Died: FL   No stone
         Birth: 1909/01/31   Death: 1992/12/20   Burial: 1995/08/07

Lot: 885 E   Owner: Zane G. Lawson   Purchased: 1962/12/28
Site 9   Christopher Zane Lawson   Age: 7 years
         Birth: 1962/04/12   Death: 1969/09/13   Burial: 1969/09/16
         Died: Washington, DC   TS: "Punky"

Lot: 885 W   Owner: William F. Mayer & Dorothy R. Arndt
       Purchased: 1956/06/02
Site 2   William Francis Mayer   Died: Springfield, VA   Age: 47 years
         Birth: 1913/02/28   Death: 1960/12/22   Burial: 1960/12/24
Site 3   Franklin A. Mayer   Died: Washington, DC   Age: 39 years
         Birth: 1917   Death: 1956/05/31   Burial: 1956/06/02
         Cause: Cancer   Wife of William F. Mayer
Site 4   Minnie A. Strickler   Died: Leesburg, VA   Age: 96 years
         Birth: 1888/09/12   Death: 1985/05/05   Burial: 1985/05/08

Lot: 886 E   Owner: Miscellaneous
Site 7   Donald W. (Donnie) Lanham   Died: Nashville, TN
         Birth: 1957/03/01   Death: 1991/08/18   Burial: 1991/08/22
Site 10 Marvin P. White   Died: Leesburg, VA   Age: 94 years
         Birth: 1885/08/11   Death: 1980/08/03   Burial: 1980/08/07
Site 12 Hannah Frances White   Age: 58 years
         Birth: 1889/08/01   Death: 1947/08/01   Burial: 1947/08/03
         On stone with Marvin P. White

Lot: 886 W   Owner: C.J. Lawson   Purchased: 1946/04/09
Site 1   John William Lawson   Age: 82 years
         Birth: 1864   Death: 1946/04/09   Burial: 1946/04/11
Site 2   Ora Belle Lawson   Age: 83 years
         Birth: 1871   Death: 1954/03/22
Site 3   Clarence J. Lawson   Age: 65 years
         Birth: 1894   Death: 1958/04/11   Burial: 1958/04/13
         Cause: Heart Failure   Died: Lucketts, VA
Site 4   Mrs. Annie Ward Lawson   Age: 73 years
         Birth: 1895   Death: 1968/05/09   Burial: 1968/05/11
         Died: Leesburg, VA   On stone with Clarence J. Lawson
Site 5   Harry West (Buck) Lawson   Age: 59 years
         Birth: 1927/10/18   Death: 1986/12/10   Burial: 1986/12/13
         Died: Lucketts, VA   TS: US Army

Lot: 887   Owner: J.F. Ellmore & Mrs. Andrew Crosen
        Purchased: 1946/08/03
Site 1   John Franklin Ellmore   Died: Philadelphia, PA   Age: 88 years
         Birth: 1870   Death: 1958/11/23   Burial: 1958/11/25
Site 2   Amos Ellmore   No stone   Age: 80 years
         Died: Lovettsville, VA Death: 1963/01/08   Burial: 1963/01/11
Site 4   Lucy Edna Adrain   No stone   Age: 83 years
         Died: Lucketts, VA   Death: 1960/01/28   Burial: 1960/01/30
Site 5   Andrew Noland Crosen   Age: 60 years
         Birth: 1890/04/14   Death: 1951/02/25   Burial: 1951/02/28
Site 6   Minnie M. Croson   Age: 73 years
         Birth: 1893/12/16   Death: 1967/04/27   Burial: 1967/04/28
         Died: Fairfax, VA   On stone with Andrew Noland Crosen

Lot: 888   Owner: Miscellaneous
Site 2   Charlcie B. Caylor   Died: Leesburg, VA   Age: 68 years
         Birth: 1923/05/30   Death: 1992/03/16   Burial: 1992/03/19
Site 5   Darrell E. Rodgers   Age: 63 years
         Birth: 1925/10/21   Death: 1989/05/06   Burial: 1989/05/09
         Died: Sterling, VA   TS: SO2 US Navy WWII
Site 7   Patricia Martzell Calef Died: Hamilton, VA   Age: 73 years
         Birth: 1908   Death: 1982/10/23   Burial: 1982/10/26
Site 11 George N. Everhart   Died: MD
         Birth: 1909/10/09   Death: 1993/03/24   Burial: 1993/03/26
Site 12 Mildred Jane Everhart   Age: 62 years
         Birth: 1922/01/15   Death: 1984/02/21   Burial: 1984/02/25
         Died: Bethesda, MD   On stone with George N. Everhart

Lot: 889 E   Owner: Frank Teates   Purchased: 1950/10/15
Site 7   Frank W. Teates Jr.   Age: 15 years
         Birth: 1936/07/15   Death: 1950/10/14   Burial: 1950/10/17
Site 8   Christopher Teates   Died: Arlington, VA   Age: 13 months
         Birth: 1965/01/09   Death: 1966/02/18   Burial: 1966/02/20
Site 9   Frank W. Teates Sr.   Age: 73 years
         Birth: 1905/12/11   Death: 1979/03/16

Lot: 889 W   Owner: Miscellaneous
Site 3   Edward M. Blair   No stone   Age: 79 years
         Died: Staunton, VA   Death: 1978/09/28   Burial: 1978/09/30
Site 4   Marjorie Wood Hutt   Died: Leesburg, VA
         Birth: 1904/09/16   Death: 1992/05/27   Burial: 1992/05/31

Lot: 890   Owner: Miscellaneous
Site 4   Emory C. Crouch   Died: Bethesda, MD   Age: 74 years
         Birth: 1906/02/23   Death: 1980/09/19   Burial: 1980/09/22
Site 5   Otho D. Baker   No stone   Age: 83 years
         Died: Leesburg, VA   Death: 1992/06/16   Burial: 1992/06/19
Site 6   Minnie E. Baker   Died: Leesburg, VA   Age: 63 years
         Birth: 1917   Death: 1980/09/11   Burial: 1980/09/14
Site 11 Carl E. Reynard   Died: Arlington, VA   Age: 84 years
         Birth: 1902   Death: 1987/03/14   Burial: 1987/03/17
Site 12 Alma M. Reynard   Age: 73 years
         Birth: 1906   Death: 1980/10/02   Burial: 1980/10/04
         Died: Leesburg, VA   On stone with Carl E. Reynard

Lot: 891   Owner: Miscellaneous
Site 7   Henry P.D. Mabe   Died: Leesburg, VA   Age: 67 years
         Birth: 1919   Death: 1986/10/18   Burial: 1986/10/22
Site 8   Audrey E. Mabe   Died: Leesburg, VA   Age: 62 years
         Birth: 1918   Death: 1980/09/03   Burial: 1980/09/06
         Cause: Heart   On stone with Henry P.D. Mabe
Site 9   Thomas F. Owens   No stone   Age: 66 years
         Died: Alexandria, VA   Death: 1980/09/11   Burial: 1980/09/15

Site 10 Remains of Potters Field Removed from Leesburg, VA to Union
Cemetery on December 5, 1983
Site 11 Howard Edward Woodward Sr.   Age: 54 years
Birth: 1925   Death: 1980/05/14   Burial: 1980/05/17
Cause: Suicide   Died: Leesburg, VA
TS: MOMM 3 US Navy WWII

Lot: 897 Owner: Miscellaneous
Site 6 Tex Hunter Austin   No stone   Age: Baby 1 day
        Died: Fairfax, VA   Death: 1988/09/19   Burial: 1988/10/03
Site 7 Katryna Anne Hall   Cause: Stillborn   Died: Fair Oaks, VA
        Birth: 1994/07/09   Death: 1994/07/09   Burial: 1994/08/01
Site 7 Oliver S. Bell   Died: Leesburg, VA   Age: 66 years
        Birth: 1913   Death: 1980/07/28   Burial: 1980/07/30
Site 7 Eleanor S. Bell   Died: Mt. Kesco, NY
        Birth: 1914/01/26   Death: 1995/03/21   Burial: 1995/04/12
Site 11 Paul Edward Smith Sr. Died: Leesburg, VA
        Birth: 1936/06/15   Death: 1994/06/26   Burial: 1994/06/29
        TS: US Air Force. Married Gloria Fischer June 21, 1958

Lot: 898 Owner: Miscellaneous
Site 1 Timothy Michael Shafer Died: Washington, DC   Age: 3 months
        Birth: 1978/01/02   Death: 1978/04/06   Burial: 1978/04/07
Site 1 Tabitha C. Mercer   Died: Leesburg, VA   Age: 5 hours
                               Death: 1983/07/12   Burial: 1983/07/14
Site 3 Jeremie Lynwood Brewster Died: Washington, DC   Age: 1 year
        Birth: 1978   Death: 1980/10/08   Burial: 1980/10/11
Site 3 Franz Till   Died: Buenos Aires
        Birth: 1893/07/08   Death: 1972/01/05   Burial: 1985/05/02
Site 4 Larry Randolph Smith   Age: Child
        Birth: 1967/05/01   Death: 1968/01/03   Burial: 1983/04/22
        Removed from PA   TS: Son of Paul & Gloria Smith
Site 5 Katrina E. Claypool   Age: Baby
        Birth: 1984   Death: 1984/03/03   Burial: 1984/03/10
        Cause: Stillborn   Died: Washington, DC
Site 5 Baby Milbourne   Death: 1984/03/14   Burial: 1984/03/17
        Cause: Stillborn   Died: Leesburg, VA   No stone
Site 5 Elizabeth Freehof
        Birth: 1894/12/02   Death: 1984/05/11   Burial: 1984/06/28
Site 5 Joff C. Ginn   Died: Blacksburg, VA   Age: 23 years
        Birth: 1962/09/21   Death: 1985/11/20   Burial: 1985/11/26
Site 5 Mortimer E. Freehof   Died: Leesburg, VA   TS: US Army
        Birth: 1893/05/06   Death: 1986/02/14   Burial: 1986/02/24
Site 5 Mrs. Joffrion M. Ginn Died: Washington, DC   Age: 63 years
        Birth: 1923/06/18   Death: 1987/01/14   Burial: 1987/01/18
Site 6 Elizabeth Flagg Simmons No dates on stone   Age: 44 years
        Died: Arlington, VA   Death: 1984/10/08   Burial: 1984/10/29
Site 6 Virginia Peyton Flagg   Age: 77 years
        Birth: 1908/12/23   Death: 1986/03/02   Burial: 1986/03/05

Site 7	Katie Lynn Applegate	Cause: Stillborn	Died: Leesburg, VA
	Birth: 1980	Death: 1980/07/17	Burial: 1980/07/20
Site 7	Kristian Ann Overfelt	Cause: Stillborn	Died: Fairfax, VA
		Death: 1982/09/12	Burial: 1982/09/18
Site 7	Robert Clay Herndon	Died: Leesburg, VA	Age: 2 minutes
		Death: 1983/03/08	Burial: 1983/03/11
Site 8	Baby Blaylock	No stone	Age: Infant
	Died: Front Royal, VA	Death: 1979/08/21	Burial: 1979/08/23
Site 8	Jessica Anne Stuart	No stone	Age: 16 months
	Died: Leesburg, VA	Death: 1980/05/20	Burial: 1980/05/23
Site 8	Harold A. Reisler	Died: San Diego, CA	Age: 75 years
	Birth: 1905/09/15	Death: 1980/06/14	Burial: 1980/09/04
Site 8	Helen E. Reisler	Died: Leesburg, VA	Age: 75 years
	Birth: 1908/08/28	Death: 1984/02/29	Burial: 1984/03/03
Site 9	Daniel W. Hayes	No stone	Age: Infant
	Died: Washington, DC	Death: 1978/03/12	Burial: 1978/03/15
Site 10	Charles E. Gandee II	No stone	Age: Infant
	Died: Washington, DC	Death: 1976/09/12	Burial: 1976/09/13
Site 10	Jerry Brewster Jr.	Died: Leesburg, VA	Age: 3 months
	Birth: 1976	Death: 1977/02/06	Burial: 1977/02/09
Site 10	Masty L. Heline	No stone	Age: 11 1/2 mo
	Died: Leesburg, VA	Death: 1977/07/07	Burial: 1977/07/09
Site 10	Baby Walko	Died: Leesburg, VA	No stone
	Cause: Stillborn	Death: 1978/06/22	Burial: 1978/06/24
Site 11	Margaret F. Wynn	No stone	Age: 6 days
	Died: Leesburg, VA	Death: 1970/10/30	Burial: 1970/11/01
Site 11	Lorrie Ann Henline	No stone	Age: 2 months
	Died: Washington, DC	Death: 1974/03/09	Burial: 1974/03/12
Site 11	Teresa Lynn Danner	Died: Leesburg, VA	Age: 9 days
	Cause: Heart	Death: 1975/08/09	Burial: 1975/08/12
Site 11	William S. Jackson		Age: 1 day
		Death: 1972/07/31	No stone
Site 11	Kenneth Lee Cooper	Death: 1972/08/04	
Site 12	Mary Lee (Molly) Wynn	Died: Leesburg, VA	Age: 2 years
	Birth: 1965/11/01	Death: 1967/08/14	Burial: 1967/08/17
Site 12	Christopher S. Carpenter	Died: Leesburg, VA	Age: 5 months
	Birth: 1969	Death: 1970/05/14	Burial: 1970/05/16

Lot: 899 Owner: Miscellaneous

Site 2	Ernest Lee Fetzer	Died: Alexandria, VA	Age: 51 years
	Birth: 1913	Death: 1965/06/12	Burial: 1965/06/15
Site 3	Clyde Laws	Died: Washington, DC	Age: 52 years
	Birth: 1910	Death: 1964/06/07	Burial: 1964/06/10
Site 5	Carl W. Langston	Died: Washington, DC	Age: 46 years
	Birth: 1917	Death: 1963/10/02	Burial: 1963/10/04
Site 8	Zelda A. Edwards	Died: Washington, DC	Age: 54 years
	Birth: 1934/02/28	Death: 1988/11/11	Burial: 1988/11/15
Site 9	Orbrey J. Fauver	Died: Leesburg, VA	Age: 51 years
	Birth: 1913/08/13	Death: 1965/01/23	Burial: 1965/01/26

Site 11 Arthur B. Atwell   Died: Leesburg, VA   Age: 84 years
        Birth: 1892/01/29   Death: 1976/07/21   Burial: 1976/07/24
Site 12 Cora Atwell   Age: 65 years
        Birth: 1897/04/27   Death: 1963/04/29   Burial: 1963/04/30
        Died: Leesburg, VA   On stone with Arthur B. Atwell

Lot: 900 Owner: Miscellaneous
Site 1 Gary Eugene Repass   Age: 20 months
        Birth: 1960/03/27   Death: 1961/12/31   Burial: 1962/01/03
        Died: Washington, DC   TS: Son of Betty & Eugene Repass
Site 2 Joseph N. Repass   Age: 24 years
        Birth: 1942/12/04   Death: 1967/07/04   Burial: 1967/07/07
        Cause: Drowned   Died: Round Hill, VA
Site 3 Justin William Maclaine   Died: Fairfax, VA   Age: 3 days
        Birth: 1990/03/25   Death: 1990/03/28   Burial: 1990/03/31
Site 3 Aaron Michael Haynes   Died: Fairfax, VA   TS: Our third angel
        Birth: 1992/07/02   Death: 1992/07/06   Burial: 1992/07/08
Site 4 Miss Jennie White   Died: Washington, DC   Age: 72 years
        Birth: 1890   Death: 1962/10/21   Burial: 1962/10/23
Site 5 Elijah T. Sutphin   Died: Winchester, VA   Age: 82 years
        Birth: 1890   Death: 1973/01/10   Burial: 1973/01/13
Site 6 Nannie M. Sutphin   Age: 83 years
        Birth: 1893   Death: 1979/06/21
        On stone with Elijah T. Sutphin
Site 7 George W. Rollison   Died: Leesburg, VA   Age: 63 years
        Birth: 1901   Death: 1963/03/23   Burial: 1963/03/25
Site 8 Mattie B. Rollison   Age: 79 years
        Birth: 1898   Death: 1978/05/14   Burial: 1978/05/16
        Died: Leesburg, VA   On stone with George W. Rollison
Site 10 Mrs. Lucille Lawson Keyes   Age: 43 years
        Birth: 1921/12/01   Death: 1964/07/21   Burial: 1964/07/24
        Died: Leesburg, VA   TS: Wife of Randolph A. Keyes Jr.

Lot: 901 Owner: Miscellaneous
Site 1 Harry Luther Sutphin   Age: 41 years
        Birth: 1918/01/26   Death: 1959/09/14   Burial: 1959/09/17
                                  Died: Arlington Hospital, Arlington, VA
Site 3 Welby Grey   Died: Leesburg, VA   Age: 74 years
        Birth: 1889   Death: 1963/08/30   Burial: 1963/09/02
Site 4 Mildred Lee Grey   Age: 63 years
        Birth: 1896   Death: 1960/08/16   Burial: 1960/08/19
        Died: L.C.H. Leesburg, VA   On stone with Welby Grey
Site 5 Cyrus Smith Tomlin   Died: Alexandria, VA   Age: 30 years
        Birth: 1929   Death: 1959/10/29   Burial: 1959/11/01
Site 7 Roy Phinis Hagenbuch   Died: Leesburg, VA   Age: 73 years
        Birth: 1887/02/05   Death: 1960/08/20   Burial: 1960/08/22
Site 8 Grace O. Hagenbuch   Age: 88 years
        Birth: 1890/08/12   Death: 1978/10/18   Burial: 1978/10/21
        Died: Leesburg, VA   On stone with Roy Phinis Hagenbuch

Site 9	Ann T. Hall	No stone	Age: 68 years
	Died: Leesburg, VA	Death: 1987/07/14	Burial: 1987/07/17
Site 10	George W. Thomas	Died: Washington, DC	Age: 58 years
	Birth: 1902/07/02	Death: 1960/10/06	Burial: 1960/10/10
Site 11	Verna A. Thomas		Age: 75 years
	Birth: 1905/02/05	Death: 1981/01/31	Burial: 1981/02/03
	Died: FL	On stone with George W. Thomas	
Site 12	James Robert Buchanan	Died: Bethesda, MD	Age: 8 years
	Birth: 1951/08/10	Death: 1960/07/21	Burial: 1960/07/23

Lot: 902 Owner: Miscellaneous

Site 1	Perry M. Wolverton	Died: Leesburg, VA	Age: 59 years
	Birth: 1908	Death: 1968/04/18	Burial: 1968/04/25
Site 2	Mary E. Wolverton		
	Birth: 1913/10/05	Death: 1991/12/05	Burial: 1991/12/08
	Died: Deston, FL	On stone with Perry M. Wolverton	
Site 4	Paul M. Wolverton	Died: Bethesda, MD	Age: 15 years
	Birth: 1945	Death: 1960/11/05	Burial: 1960/11/08
	On stone with Mary E. Wolverton and Perry M. Wolverton		
Site 5	Stanley F. McGaha	Died: Leesburg, VA	Age: 55 years
	Birth: 1905/02/20	Death: 1960/03/20	Burial: 1960/03/23
Site 6	Janie L. McGaha		Age: 71 years
	Birth: 1904/04/01	Death: 1975/10/09	Burial: 1975/10/12
	Died: Leesburg, VA	On stone with Stanley F. McGaha	
Site 9	Raymond B. Barnhouse	Died: Leesburg, VA	Age: 79 years
	Birth: 1898/03/26	Death: 1977/06/06	Burial: 1977/06/08
Site 10	Lovetta C. Barnhouse		Age: 55 years
	Birth: 1902/10/24	Death: 1958/08/26	Burial: 1958/08/28
	Died: L.C.H. Leesburg, VA	On stone with Raymond B. Barnhouse	
Site 11	Edgar Barnhouse		Age: 63 years
	Birth: 1893/05/13	Death: 1957/01/22	
Site 12	Mary Agnes S. Barnhouse		Age: 65 years
	Birth: 1896/12/15	Death: 1962/04/13	Burial: 1965/04/15
	Died: Leesburg, VA	On stone with Edgar Barnhouse	

Lot: 903 Owner: Miscellaneous

Site 1	Samuel Thornton Ish	Died: Leesburg, VA	Age: 73 years
	Birth: 1887/10/23	Death: 1961/01/14	Burial: 1961/01/16
	TS: Virginia CPL Co M 318 Infantry WW I		
Site 2	Anna Goode Ish	Died: Leesburg, VA	Age: 78 years
	Birth: 1889/05/22	Death: 1968/02/26	Burial: 1968/02/28
Site 4	Louis A. Bodmer	Died: Ashburn, VA	Age: 55 years
	Birth: 1907/02/08	Death: 1962/05/15	Burial: 1962/05/18
Site 5	Ruby C. Bodmer	Died: Baltimore, MD	Age: 49 years
	Birth: 1912/09/24	Death: 1961 /12/05	Burial: 1961/12/08
	Cause: Cancer	On stone with Louis A. Bodmer	
Site 6	Ernest David Racz	Died: Prince Georges, MD	Age: 45 years
	Birth: 1916	Death: 1962/01/22	Burial: 1962/01/25

Site 11 William J. Carroll　　　　　　　　　　　　　Age: 71 years
　　　　Birth: 1911/08/10　　Death: 1982/12/14　　Burial: 1982/12/17
　　　　Died: Ranson, WV　　　　　　　　　TS: TEC 5 US Army WWII

Lot: 904 Owner: Miscellaneous
Site 2　Curtis Lanham　　　Died: Fairfax, VA　　　Age: 74 years
　　　　Birth: 1905/08/17　　Death: 1979/11/30　　Burial: 1979/12/03
Site 3　Mrs. Irene Lanham　　Died: Manassas, VA　　Age: 66 years
　　　　Birth: 1904/10/04　　Death: 1971/05/03　　Burial: 1971/05/05
Site 4　Howard T. Johnson　　Died: Leesburg, VA　　Age: 92 years
　　　　Birth: 1876/08/10　　Death: 1968/09/14　　Burial: 1968/09/16
Site 5　Dora K. Johnson　　　　　　　　　　　　　Age: 78 years
　　　　Birth: 1881/07/09　　Death: 1959/08/28　　Burial: 1959/08/31
　　　　Died: Waterford, VA　　On stone with Howard T. Johnson
Site 6　Wilton C. Johnson
　　　　Birth: 1906/12/01　　Death: 1933/08/24　　Burial: 1944/10/24
　　　　Removal from Paris　　On stone with Dora K. & Howard T. Johnson
Site 7　Undred T. Courtney　　No stone　　　　　　Age: 63 years
　　　　　　　　　　　　　　Death: 1944/10/30　　Burial: 1944/11/02
Site 8　John William Kephart　　　　　　　　　　Age: 40 years
　　　　Birth: 1904/08/21　　Death: 1944/10/07　　Burial: 1944/10/09
Site 11 Miss Alice Preston　　　　　　　　　　　　Age: 83 years
　　　　Birth: 1871/01/01　　Death: 1955/11/16　　Burial: 1955/11/17
　　　　Cause: Arteriosclerosis　Died: Islip, NY
Site 12 George Rutledge Preston　　　　　　　　　Age: 73 years
　　　　Birth: 1869/04/03　　Death: 1943/03/26　　Burial: 1943/03/28

Lot: 905 Owner: J. Sherman Hutchison   Purchased: 1942/07/27
Site 1　Baby Girl Hutchison　Death: 1965/07/23　　Burial: 1965/07/24
　　　　Cause: Stillborn　　　Died: Leesburg, VA　　No stone
Site 3　Eligah C. Hutchison　　　　　　　　　　　Age: 79 years
　　　　Birth: 1863/01/03　　Death: 1942/07/26　　Burial: 1942/07/28
Site 4　Harriet T. Hutchison Gibson　　　　　　　Age: 92 years
　　　　Birth: 1866　　　　　Death: 1958/06/12　　Burial: 1958/06/14
　　　　　　　　　　　　　　Died: Waterford, VA
Site 5　John S. Hutchison　　Died: Waterford, VA　　Age: 86 years
　　　　Birth: 1893/12/10　　Death: 1980/07/15　　Burial: 1980/07/17
Site 6　Leila Rankin Hutchison
　　　　Birth: 1899/05/01　　Death: 1995/12/11　　Burial: 1995/12/14
　　　　Died: Leesburg, VA　　On stone with John S. Hutchison
Site 7　William R. Hutchison　Died: Waterford, VA　　Age: 65 years
　　　　Birth: 1926/08/15　　Death: 1991/11/20　　Burial: 1991/11/22

Lot: 906 Owner: Miscellaneous
Site 2　Nelson Partlow　　　Died: Warrenton, VA　　Age: 63 years
　　　　Birth: 1897/03/13　　Death: 1961/01/17　　Burial: 1961/01/19
Site 3　Mrs. Francis Elizabeth Partlow　　　　　　Age: 43 years
　　　　Birth: 1907/04/07　　Death: 1950/06/11　　Burial: 1950/06/13
　　　　On stone with Nelson Partlow

Site 4   John Wesley Hough   Age: 81 years
         Birth: 1861   Death: 1943/10/08   Burial: 1943/10/10
Site 5   Mary V. B. Hough   Age: 95 years
         Birth: 1871   Death: 1967/07/31   Burial: 1967/08/03
         Died: Montgomery, MD   On stone with John Wesley Hough
Site 6   Cora Virginia Hough   Died: Maryland Park, MD   Age: 47 years
         Birth: 1903/05/31   Death: 1955/02/01   Burial: 1955/02/01
Site 7   Arthur S. Hough   Cause: Gun Shot   Age: 55 years
         Birth: 1884/12/13   Death: 1943/02/26   Burial: 1943/02/29
Site 8   Bessie Pearl Hough   Age: 62 years
         Birth: 1894/01/05   Death: 1956/05/07   Burial: 1956/05/08
         Died: Leesburg, VA   TS: Wife of Arthur S. Hough
Site 9   Arthur Lee Hough   Died: Warrenton, VA   Age: 55 years
         Birth: 1931/12/31   Death: 1987/05/23   Burial: 1987/05/26

Lot: 907 Owner: Miscellaneous
Site 2   James F. Harris Died: Leesburg, VA   Age: 72
         Birth: 1916   Death: 1988/10/20   Burial: 1988/10/22
         TS: Married Dorothy J. Harris August 30, 1948
Site 4   John David Kitts   Died: Hamilton, VA   Age: 74 years
         Birth: 1910/08/24   Death: 1984/10/08   Burial: 1984/10/10
Site 6   Grace Virginia (Peggy) Powell   Age: 68 years
         Birth: 1915/07/02   Death: 1983/09/30   Burial: 1983/10/03
         Died: Leesburg, VA

Lot: 908 Owner: Thurman & Hazel G. Nichols   1945/12/26
Site 3   James E. Nichols Sr.   Died: Martinsburg, WV   Age: 83 years
         Birth: 1894   Death: 1978/01/24   Burial: 1978/01/27
Site 4   Hazel G. Nichols   Age: 75 years
         Birth: 1902   Death: 1977/02/16   Burial: 1977/02/19
         Died: Leesburg, VA   On stone with James E. Nichols Sr.
Site 5   Thurman Henry Nichols Jr.   No stone
         Cause: Stillborn   Death: 1947/10/20   Burial: 1947/10/22
Site 5   Baby Nichols   No stone
                                  Death: 1948/10/25   Burial: 1948/10/27
Site 5   Thurman H. Nichols   Died: Falls Church, VA   Age: 49 years
         Birth: 1921/01/21   Death: 1969/11/24   Burial: 1969/11/26
Site 6   Mrs. Dorothy Lillian Nichols   Age: 29 years
         Birth: 1917/09/26   Death: 1945/12/22   Burial: 1945/12/25
Site 12 Eugene E. Nichols   Died: MD   Age: 69 years
         Birth: 1922   Death: 1992/05/28   Burial: 1992/06/04
Site 12 Lillian May Nichols   Age: 35 years
                                  Death: 1957/10/12   No stone

Lot: 909 E   Owner: A. Eugene & Lucy Kitts   1947/01/02
Site 7   Andrew Clinton Kitts   Age: 80 years
         Birth: 1866   Death: 1947/01/01   Burial: 1947/01/03
Site 8   Mrs. Eva Bell Kitts   Age: 83 years
         Birth: 1878   Death: 1961/07/22   Burial: 1961/07/25
         Died: Leesburg, VA   On stone with Andrew Clinton Kitts

Site 9   A. Eugene Kitts   Died: Leesburg, VA
         Birth: 1909/05/24   Death: 1991/09/30   Burial: 1991/10/04
Site 10 Lucy D. Kitts   Age: 80 years
         Birth: 1904/01/15   Death: 1984/05/22   Burial: 1984/05/25
         Died: Leesburg, VA   On stone with A. Eugene Kitts
Site 11 Joseph I. Kitts   Died: Winchester, VA   Age: 76 years
         Birth: 1893   Death: 1970/02/12   Burial: 1970/02/14
Site 12 Lula F. Kitts Moore   CR:Mrs. Scott Moore   Age: 72 years
         Birth: 1881   Death: 1952/10/22   Burial: 1952/10/24

Lot: 909 W   Owner: Miscellaneous
Site 1   Ira Cecil Kitts   Age: 72 years
         Birth: 1915   Death: 1987/10/09   Burial: 1987/10/12
         Died: Southern MD   TS: PFC US Army WWII

Lot: 910 E   Owner: Helen E. O'Reilly   Purchased:
Site 7   Lorne B. O'Reilly   Died: Boston, MA   Age: 56 years
         Birth: 1909/08/28   Death: 1965/08/03   Burial: 1965/08/07
Site 8   Helen E. O'Reilly   Age: 69 years
         Birth: 1915/06/01   Death: 1984/11/30   Burial: 1984/12/03
         Died: Washington, DC   On stone with Lorne B. O'Reilly
Site 10 Eugene G. Caylor   Died: Leesburg, VA   Age: 60 years
         Birth: 1915   Death: 1975/10/25   Burial: 1975/10/28

Lot: 910 W   Owner: Anna Lee Carlisle   Purchased: 1952/02/25
Site 6   Bessie Frances Jenkins   Age: 66 years
         Birth: 1889/04/10   Death: 1954/11/27

Lot: 911   Owner: Miscellaneous
Site 1   Oliver Lee Swart   Died: Leesburg, VA   Age: 50 years
         Birth: 1927/09/11   Death: 1978/04/06   Burial: 1978/04/09
Site 4   Albert N. Carlisle   Age: 51 years
         Birth: 1896/08/18   Death: 1947/11/10   Burial: 1947/11/12
Site 5   Myrtle R. Carlisle   Age: 90 years
         Birth: 1900/12/08   Death: 1990/06/03   Burial: 1990/06/07
         Died: Leesburg, VA   On stone with Albert N. Carlisle
Site 8   Lorenzo Daw Clemens Sr.   Age: 85 years
         Birth: 1875/08/01   Death: 1960/11/25   Burial: 1960/11/28
                                 Died: Staunton, VA
Site 9   Hattie Cambell Clemens   Age: 60 years
         Birth: 1886/10/04   Death: 1946/03/30   Burial: 1946/04/02
         On stone with Lorenzo Daw Clemens Sr.
Site 10 Elmer Augustus Bodmer   Age: 36 years
         No stone   Death: 1946/01/19   Burial: 1946/01/21
Site 11 Harold L. Day   Died: Arlington, VA   Age: 79 years
         Birth: 1888   Death: 1968/09/13   Burial: 1968/09/17
Site 12 Julia D. Day   Age: 73 years
         Birth: 1895   Death: 1969/01/17   Burial: 1969/01/19
         Died: Arlington, VA   On stone with Harold L. Day

Lot: 912 Owner: Miscellaneous
Site 1 James William Elliott Died: Leesburg, VA Age: 81 years
        Birth: 1875 Death: 1956/09/19 Burial: 1956/09/20
Site 2 Marie C. Elliott Age: 68 years
        Birth: 1874 Death: 1947/04/21 Burial: 1947/04/23
        On stone with James William Elliott
Site 3 Mrs. Florida Fling Feagans Age: 90 years
        No stone Death: 1947/04/27 Burial: 1947/04/29
Site 4 John W. Hensley Age: 70 years
        Birth: 1877 Death: 1947/06/17 Burial: 1947/06/19
Site 5 Etta May Hensley Age: 105 years
        Birth: 1884 Death: 1989/08/07 Burial: 1989/08/11
        Died: Arlington, VA On stone with John W. Hensley
Site 7 Irene Blanche Shryock TS: Wife of C.E. Shryock Age: 80 years
        Birth: 1866 Death: 1946/09/25 Burial: 1946/09/27
Site 8 Charles Edward Shryock Age: 75 years
        TS: Aged 75 years Death: 1930/03/01 Removal
Site 10 Norman B. Elgin Age: 79 years
        Birth: 1866/12/15 Death: 1946/06/06 Burial: 1946/06/18
Site 11 William W. Rutter Sr. Age: 54 years
        Birth: 1906/08/08 Death: 1960/07/19 Burial: 1960/07/22
Site 12 Mildred C. Rutter
        Birth: 1912/06/24 Death: 1994/08/07 Burial: 1994/08/11
        Died: Leesburg, VA On stone with William W. Rutter

Lot: 913 Owner: Miscellaneous
Site 1 Baby Lester Middleton Death: No stone Burial: 1957/11/06
        Cause: Stillborn Died: Leesburg, VA No stone
Site 1 Baby Fletcher Died: L.C.H. Leesburg, VA Age: 7 hours
        No stone Death: 1958/07/25 Burial: 1958/07/27
Site 1 Baby Sukler Age: 31 hours
        Death: 1957/09/23 No stone
Site 2 Anders Hanan Davetson Death: 1957/03/18
Site 2 James E. Conrad Died: Leesburg, VA Age: 69 years
        Birth: 1918/11/18 Death: 1988/11/09 Burial: 1988/11/12
Site 4 Loretta Ann Fletcher No stone Age: 18 hours
        Death: 1951/10/21 Burial: 1951/10/22
Site 4 Baby Girl Ellis Death: 1956/09/10 Burial: 1956/09/10
        Cause: Stillborn Died: Leesburg, VA No stone
Site 4 Peggy D. Lee No stone Age: 1 year
        Died: Leesburg, VA Death: 1955/07/01 Burial: 1955/07/02
Site 4 Larry W. Roberts No stone Age: 18 days
        Died: Leesburg, VA Death: 1956/04/21 Burial: 1956/04/21
Site 4 Robert Turner Age: Stillborn
        Death: 1954/12/07 No stone
Site 4 William J. Carroll No stone Age: Baby
        Cause: Stillborn Death: 1956/12/03
Site 5 Larry Allen Dawson No stone Age: 31 hours
        Died: Leesburg, VA Death: 1953/08/03 Burial: 1953/08/07

Site 5	Baby Baker	Died: Leesburg, VA	No stone
	Cause: Stillborn	Death: 1953/09/27	Burial: 1953/09/28
Site 5	Baby Boy Phillips	Death: 1953/12/06	Burial: 1953/12/07
	Cause: Stillborn	Died: Leesburg, VA	No stone
Site 5	James N. Leith Jr.	No stone	Age: 3 months
	Died: Leesburg, VA	Death: 1954/03/29	Burial: 1954/03/31
Site 5	Lois Howard Mayer		Age: 5 hours
		Death: 1957/01/18	No stone
Site 6	Child Fletcher	No stone	Age: 6 hours
	Cause: Stillborn	Death: 1952/12/04	Burial: 1952/12/04
Site 6	Cynthia Jerry	No stone	Age: 4 months
	Died: Leesburg, VA	Death: 1952/12/31	Burial: 1953/01/01
Site 7	Emmett O. Farmer	Died: Berkely Spring, WV	Age: 74 years
	Birth: 1896/09/03	Death: 1970/05/12	Burial: 1970/05/14
Site 8	Mrs. Lucy V. Farmer		Age: 49 years
	Birth: 1903/05/03	Death: 1952/05/21	Burial: 1952/05/23
Site 11	Nellie Johnson Addison	Died: Leesburg, VA	
	Birth: 1908/08/16	Death: 1993/03/09	Burial: 1993/03/12
Site 12	Robert Lawrence Addison		Age: 3 months
	Birth: 1935/06/30	Death: 1935/10/07	Burial: 1951/10/19
	Removed from Paris, VA		

Lot: 914 Owner: Miscellaneous

Site 1	Mrs. Lillie Rufus Campbell		Age: 77 years
	No stone	Death: 1951/12/28	Burial: 1951/12/31
Site 2	Mrs. Edna L. Rollison		Age: 69 years
	Birth: 1893	Death: 1962/10/30	Burial: 1962/11/02
	Died: Leesburg, VA		TS: Mother
Site 3	Stephenson C. Campbell		Age: 87 years
	Birth: 1886	Death: 1973/12/09	Burial: 1973/12/12
	Died: Frederick, MD		TS: Uncle
Site 7	Robert G. Cooper	Died: Leesburg, VA	Age: 80 years
	Birth: 1880/09/03	Death: 1961/01/21	Burial: 1961/01/25
Site 8	Ollie L. Atwell Cooper		Age: 88 years
	Birth: 1890/01/20	Death: 1978/12/05	Burial: 1978/12/08
	Died: Leesburg, VA	On stone with Robert G. Cooper	
Site 9	Lester Neal Kinser		Age: 58 years
	Birth: 1902	Death: 1961/01/02	Burial: 1961/01/05
	Cause: Cancer	Died: L.C.H. Leesburg, VA	TS: Father
Site 10	Ollie Goode Kinser		Age: 71 years
	Birth: 1916/07/27	Death: 1987/09/19	Burial: 1987/09/22
	Died: Leesburg, VA		TS: Mother
Site 11	Wade B. Geiman	Died: Leesburg, VA	Age: 77 years
	Birth: 1905	Death: 1982/12/01	Burial: 1982/12/04
Site 12	Mazie Pearson Geiman		Age: 50 years
	Birth: 1910	Death: 1961/11/28	Burial: 1961/11/30
	Died: Purcellville, VA	On stone with Wade B. Geiman	

Lot: 915 Owner: Miscellaneous
Site 1 James Harrison Russell   Age: 83 years
        Birth: 1888   Death: 1972/09/20
Site 2 Linnie E. Russell   Age: 85 years
        Birth: 1889   Death: 1975/01/07   Burial: 1975/01/10
        Died: Leesburg, VA   On stone with James H. Russell
Site 3 John Henry Furr   Age: 37 years
        Birth: 1920/09/17   Death: 1958/03/27   Burial: 1958/03/30
        Cause: Heart Failure   Died: Waterford, VA
Site 4 Edward S. Dawson   Age: 64 years
        Birth: 1893/07/17   Death: 1957/10/28
Site 5 Larry Franklin Lee   Age: 8 months
                                 Death: 1958/07/30   Burial: 1958/08/01
        Cause: Heart   Died: L.C.H. Leesburg, VA   No stone
Site 6 Dorothy S. Dawson   Age: 28 years
        Birth: 1928   Death: 1957/06/10
Site 7 Samuel E. Thomas   Died: Winchester, VA   Age: 65 years
        Birth: 1915   Death: 1980/04/16   Burial: 1980/04/19
Site 8 Eva Belle Thomas   Cause: Auto Accident   Age: 41 years
        Birth: 1916   Death: 1957/12/11   Burial: 1957/12/14
        Died: Leesburg, VA   On stone with Samuel E. Thomas
Site 9 Carrie Lee Furr   Died: Purcellville, VA Age: 81 years
        Birth: 1884/06/17   Death: 1965/12/22   Burial: 1965/12/26
Site 10 Rita Fox Perfater   Died: Hampton, VA   Age: 31 years
        Birth: 1930   Death: 1961/08/05   Burial: 1961/08/08
Site 11 Cora Hazel Orrison   No dates on stone   Age: 86 years
        Died: Falls Church, VA   Death: 1980/01/05   Burial: 1980/01/08
Site 12 Margaret C. VanSickler   Died: Washington, DC   Age: 94 years
        Birth: 1864/10/19   Death: 1959/02/28   Burial: 1959/03/03

Lot: 916 Owner: Miscellaneous
Site 1 John H. Hanes   No death date on stone Age: 87 years
        Birth: 1879   Death: 1964/05/26   Died: Ashburn, VA
Site 2 Mary Georgia Hanes   Age: 78 years
        Birth: 1879   Death: 1958/02/10   Burial: 1958/02/13
        Died: Leesburg, VA   On stone with John H. Hanes
Site 3 Herbert James McWilliams   Age: 32 years
        Birth: 1925/07/02   Death: 1958/02/17   Burial: 1958/02/21
                                 Died: Leesburg, VA
Site 5 Norman B. Seaton   Age: 57 years
        Birth: 1910/02/07   Death: 1967/10/13   Burial: 1967/10/16
        Died: Leesburg, VA   TS: Son
Site 6 Georgia Elizabeth Seaton   Age: 80 years
        Birth: 1876/11/03   Death: 1960/01/31   Burial: 1960/02/02
        Died: Leesburg, VA   TS: Mother
Site 7 Harry C. Jenkins   Died: L.C.H. Leesburg, VA   Age: 70 years
        Birth: 1888   Death: 1958/06/20   Burial: 1958/06/23

Site 8	Ruby A. Jenkins		Age: 91 years
	Birth: 1889/06/15	Death: 1981/01/21	Burial: 1981/01/24
	Died: PA	On stone with Harry C. Jenkins	
Site 9	Herbert T. Farmer	Died: Staunton, VA	Age: 76 years
	Birth: 1883	Death: 1959/07/03	Burial: 1959/07/05
Site 10	Mrs. Rosie F. Farmer		Age: 80 years
	Birth: 1883	Death: 1965/03/13	Burial: 1965/03/17
	Died: High Point, NC	On stone with Herbert T. Farmer	
Site 11	Charles Preston Fleming	Died: Leesburg, VA	Age: 62 years
	Birth: 1895	Death: 1958/06/17	Burial: 1958/06/19
Site 12	Glennie M. Fleming		Age: 90 years
	Birth: 1901	Death: 1992/11/18	Burial: 1992/11/20
	Died: Leesburg, VA	On stone with Charles Preston Fleming	

Lot: 917 Owner: Miscellaneous

Site 1	George L. Carnes		Age: 58 years
	Birth: 1903/11/02	Death: 1962/10/18	Burial: 1962/10/21
	Cause: Heart	Died: Leesburg, VA	
Site 3	Richard A. Dove	Birth: 1896	Death: 1979/06/23
Site 4	Mrs. Dollie A. Dove		
	Birth: 1894	Death: 1976/03/22	Burial: 1976/03/24
	Died: Fairfax, VA	On stone with Richard A. Dove	
Site 5	John F. Bodine	Died: Ashburn, VA	Age: 88 years
	Birth: 1877/07/07	Death: 1966/05/13	Burial: 1966/05/16
Site 6	Grace May Bodine		Age: 85 years
	Birth: 1886/06/16	Death: 1971/07/25	Burial: 1971/07/28
	Died: Leesburg, VA	On stone with John F. Bodine	
Site 7	George W. Conrad	Died: Leesburg, VA	Age: 77 years
	Birth: 1884/12/20	Death: 1962/08/05	Burial: 1962/08/08
Site 7	Baby Boy Barnette	Death: 1963/02/18	Burial: 1963/02/19
	Cause: Stillborn	Died: Leesburg, VA	No stone
Site 8	Mabel C. Conrad		Age: 90 years
	Birth: 1890/12/18	Death: 1981/12/07	Burial: 1981/12/10
	Died: Leesburg, VA	On stone with George W. Conrad	
Site 9	Roy Preston Gray	Died: Leesburg, VA	Age: 78 years
	Birth: 1884/09/07	Death: 1963/04/10	Burial: 1963/04/12
Site 10	Pearl Kephart Gray	No death date on stone	Age: 89 years
	Birth: 1896/05/17	Death: 1984/09/24	Burial: 1984/09/27
	Died: Winchester, VA	On stone with Roy Preston Gray	
Site 11	Charles S. Newcomb	Died: Leesburg, VA	Age: 71 years
	Birth: 1890/06/24	Death: 1961/08/04	Burial: 1961/08/07
Site 12	Vallie V. Newcomb	Died: Leesburg, VA	Age: 88 years
	Birth: 1895/06/12	Death: 1984/04/10	Burial: 1984/04/13
	TS: Mother to Virginia Adrain	On stone with Charles S. Newcomb	

Lot: 918 Owner: Miscellaneous

Site 3	Richard W. Irwin Jr.	Died: Washington, DC	Age: 22 years
	Birth: 1942/02/17	Death: 1965/06/06	Burial: 1965/06/08
Site 4	Richard W. Irwin Sr.	Died: Phillmont, VA	Age: 85 years
	Birth: 1901/01/12	Death: 1986/08/12	Burial: 1986/08/14

Site 4   Mary K. Irwin
          Birth: 1902/10/17   Death: 1987/05/07   Burial: 1987/05/09
          Died: Leesburg, VA   TS: On stone with Richard W. Irwin Sr.
Site 5   Thomas L. Whetsell   Died: Leesburg, VA   Age: 66 years
          Birth: 1896   Death: 1963/01/30   Burial: 1963/02/01
Site 6   Aletha Whetsell Campbell   Age: 57 years
          Birth: 1916   Death: 1974/01/31   Burial: 1974/02/04
                                     Died: Leesburg, VA
Site 8   Ivan C. Woodward   Died: Waterford, VA   Age: 63 years
          Birth: 1900   Death: 1964/06/10   Burial: 1964/06/13
Site 9   Nannie Woodward   Died: Leesburg, VA   No stone
          Birth: 1910/02/23   Death: 1995/10/21   Burial: 1995/10/24
Site 10   Cadle Hooppaw   Died: Leesburg, VA   Age: 73 years
          Birth: 1890   Death: 1964/08/30   Burial: 1964/09/01
Site 10   Bessie Hooppaw   Died: MD
          Birth: 1883   Death: 1967/12/06   Burial: 1967/12/11
Site 11   Helene Hooppaw   Died: CT
          Birth: 1901/07/22   Death: 1994/01/24   Burial: 1994/05/18
Site 12   Justine Girard   Died: Leesburg, VA   Age: 86 years
          Birth: 1878   Death: 1964/03/13   Burial: 1964/03/19

Lot: 923 Owner: Miscellaneous
Site 12   Mary Jones   No stone   Age: 11 days
          Died: Leesburg, VA   Death: 1967/08/19   Burial: 1967/08/21

Lot: 924 Owner: Baby Sites
Site 3   Baby Smith   Death: 1967/05/22   Burial: 1967/05/22
          Cause: Stillborn   Died: Leesburg, VA   No stone
Site 3   Stephenson Sturgill   No stone   Age: 2 Months
          Died: Leesburg, VA   Death: 1967/06/22   Burial: 1967/06/25
Site 3   Leah Michelle Smith   No stone   Age: 2 days
          Died: NC   Death: 1968/01/13   Burial: 1968/01/17
Site 4   Baby Moore   Death: 1967/04/12   Burial: 1967/04/14
          Cause: Stillborn   Died: Leesburg, VA   No stone
Site 4   Baby Smith   Death: 1966/04/22   Burial: 1966/04/24
          Cause: Stillborn   Died: Leesburg, VA   No stone
Site 5   Ronald Keith Carter   Age: 2 months
          Birth: 1965/10/16   Death: 1965/12/31   Burial: 1966/01/03
          Died: Leesburg, VA   TS: Infant son of Mr. & Mrs. Fred Carter
Site 6   Baby Pirce   Death: 1962/02/15   Burial: 1962/02/16
          Cause: Stillborn   Died: Leesburg, VA   No stone
Site 7   Baby Boy Stillions   Died: L.C.H. Leesburg, VA Age: 1 day
          No stone   Death: 1962/05/13   Burial: 1962/05/14
Site 7   Steven William Adams Jr.   Died: Leesburg, VA   Age: 25 days
          Birth: 1966/06/13   Death: 1966/07/08   Burial: 1966/07/10
Site 7   Barbara Ennis   No stone   Age: 6 weeks
          Died: Leesburg, VA   Death: 1966/11/03   Burial: 1966/11/05
Site 8   Baby Hummer   Death: 1962/01/16   Burial: 1962/01/17
          Cause: Stillborn   Died: Leesburg, VA   No stone

Site 9	Baby Harrison	Death: 1961/03/25	Burial: 1961/03/29
	Cause: Stillborn	Died: Leesburg, VA	
Site 9	Mary M. McGhee	No stone	Age: 3 months
	Died: Leesburg, VA	Death: 1965/04/24	Burial: 1965/04/26
Site 9	William Powell		Age: 1 day
		Death: 1965/07/06	Burial: 1965/07/06
	Cause: 7 month baby	Died: Leesburg, VA	No dates on stone
Site 9	James B. Pumphrey	No stone	Age: Baby
	Died: Leesburg, VA	Death: 1965/10/06	Burial: 1965/10/07
Site 9	Larry Dale Secrest		Age: 6 months
	Birth: 1959/09/27	Death: 1960/04/01	Burial: 1960/04/03
	Died: Leesburg, VA	TS: Son of Robert & Lavaun Secrest	
Site 10	Robert E. Johnson Jr.		Age: 1 day
	Died: Washington, DC	Death: 1963/06/03	Burial: 1963/06/05
Site 10	Tina Marie Taylor	Cause: Stillborn	Died: Washington, DC
	Birth: 1963/07/26	Death: 1963/07/31	Burial: 1963/08/04
Site 10	Jennifer Dawn Dearden	Death: 1970/03/01	Burial: 1970/03/09
	Cause: Stillborn	Died: Manassas, VA	
Site 11	Pattie Downs Bartee	Death: 1959/12/21	Burial: 1959/12/22
	Cause: Stillborn	Died: L.C.H. Leesburg, VA	No stone
Site 11	Cathey Ellen Robinson	Died: L.C.H. Leesburg, VA	Age: 4 months
	No stone	Death: 1959/12/26	Burial: 1959/12/28
Site 11	Rick Owen Lockwood	Died: L.C.H. Leesburg, VA	
	Birth: 1963/02/28	Death: 1963/03/14	Burial: 1963/03/19
Site 11	Baby Girl Mullins	Death: 1960/02/14	Burial: 1960/02/15
	Cause: Stillborn	Died: LCH, Leesburg, VA	
Site 11	Baby Girl Young	Death: 1970/03/01	Burial: 1970/03/02
	Cause: Stillborn	Died: Leesburg, VA	
	TS: Daughter of Ronald & Carole Young		
Site 12	Baby Chastain	Death: 1958/10/07	Burial: 1958/10/09
	Cause: Stillborn	Died: Arlington Hosp. Arlington	No stone
Site 12	Thomas Russell Reed Jr.	Died: Leesburg, VA	Age: 3 months
	Birth: 1962/02/17	Death: 1962/05/17	Burial: 1962/05/18
Site 12	Pamela Sue Lee	No stone	Age: 3 months
	Died: Leesburg, VA	Death: 1963/03/08	Burial: 1963/03/10
Site 12	Infant Boy Betterly	Death: 1965/04/10	Burial: 1965/04/12
	Cause: Stillborn	Died: Leesburg, VA	
Site 12	Baby Girl Holland	Death: 1969/09/14	Burial: 1969/09/15
	Cause: Stillborn	Died: Winchester, VA	
	Removed to Hillsboro, VA Nov. 13, 1972		No stone
Site 12	Vicki Angela Bark		Age: 6 years
	Birth: 1957/05/30	Death: 1963/12/22	Burial: 1963/12/23
	Died: Leesburg, VA	TS: Daughter of Edw. & Eliz. Bark	

Lot: 925 Owner: Miscellaneous

Site 7	Hubert C. Jenkins	Died: Leesburg, VA	Age: 73 years
	Birth: 1908	Death: 1982/02/04	Burial: 1982/02/06

Site 8   Dorothy S. Jenkins   Died: Berryville, VA
         Birth: 1909/02/08   Death: 1995/07/05   Burial: 1995/07/07
         On stone with Hubert C. Jenkins
Site 9   Arthur Wesley Mathews   Died: Frederick, MD   Age: 75 years
         Birth: 1882/07/26   Death: 1958/07/19   Burial: 1958/07/22
Site 10 Mrs. Gracie Carmen Mathews   Age: 76 years
         Birth: 1882/10/13   Death: 1958/11/03   Burial: 1958/11/06
         Died: Frederick, MD   On stone with Arthur Wesley Mathews
Site 11 Azel A. Painter   Died: Leesburg, VA   Age: 88 years
         Birth: 1888   Death: 1976/03/10   Burial: 1976/03/12
Site 12 Maggie Myrtle Painter   On stone with Azel A. Painter   Age: 60 years
         Birth: 1896   Death: 1956/12/21

Lot: 926 Owner: Miscellaneous
Site 1   Shirley Randolph Beach Died: Stanton, VA   Age: 73 years
         Birth: 1884   Death: 1957/11/13   Burial: 1957/11/15
Site 2   Mrs. Bertha W. Beach   Age: 78 years
         Birth: 1882   Death: 1961/09/24   Burial: 1961/09/26
         Died: Paeonian Springs, VA   On stone with Shirley Randolph Beach
Site 3   Mrs. Allie Martin   Age: 72 years
                                 Death: 1957/08/13   No stone
Site 4   Walter Allen Walker   Age: 66 years
         Birth: 1890/07/29   Death: 1956/12/23
Site 7   William Joseph Ball   Died: Leesburg, VA   Age: 68 years
         Birth: 1888/08/14   Death: 1956/09/10   Burial: 1956/09/12
Site 8   Bessie W. Ball   Age: 72 years
         Birth: 1893/10/06   Death: 1966/06/10   Burial: 1966/06/14
         Died: Vienna, VA   On stone with William Joseph Ball
Site 9   Harry McFarland   No stone   Age: 65 years
         Died: Leesburg, VA   Death: 1956/02/03   Burial: 1956/02/05
Site 10 Nathaniel W. Maddox   Age: 75 years
         Birth: 1880   Death: 1955   Burial: 1955/12/28
         Died: Dunn Loring, Fairfax Co.,VA
Site 12 Robert Thrift Fetzer Jr. Died: Leesburg, VA   Age: 56 years
         Birth: 1899   Death: 1955/11/14   Burial: 1955/11/15

Lot: 927 Owner: Miscellaneous
Site 1   John Franklin Rose   Age: 73 years
         Birth: 1878/03/14   Death: 1951/04/27   Burial: 1951/04/29
Site 2   Annie Parsons Rose   Age: 83 years
         Birth: 1884/12/26   Death: 1967/02/26   Burial: 1967/03/01
         Died: Leesburg, VA   On stone with John Franklin Rose
Site 4   Howard H. McNealy   Died: Leesburg, VA   Age: 76 years
         Birth: 1904/01/16   Death: 1980/03/30   Burial: 1980/05/02
Site 5   Maurice Bill McNealy   Age: 78 years
         Birth: 1876   Death: 1954/04/22
Site 6   Mrs. Estella Geneva McNealy   Age: 72 years
         Birth: 1879   Death: 1951/02/09   Burial: 1951/02/11
         IB:Mrs. M.B. McNealy   On stone with Maurice B. McNealy

Site 7 Mervin T. (Pete) Fetzer TS: Husband Age: 51 years
Birth: 1901 Death: 1952/03/05 Burial: 1952/03/08
Site 8 Ivy M. Carlisle Fetzer Age: 44 years
Birth: 1908 Death: 1953/05/23 Burial: 1953/05/28
Died: Jamaica, VA On stone with Mervin T. (Pete) Fetzer
Site 9 Martins Lasdins No stone Age: 80 years
Death: 1952/05/17 Burial: 1952/05/20
Site 11 Doolin Dewitt Ford Age: 68 years
Birth: 1883/03/11 Death: 1951/05/18 Burial: 1951/05/20
Site 12 Winnie D. Ford Age: 67 years
Birth: 1891/05/31 Death: 1959/05/22 Burial: 1959/05/24
Died: Paeonian Springs, VA On stone with Doolin Dewitt Ford

Lot: 928 Owner: Miscellaneous

Site 1 Robert B. Bell Died: Leesburg, VA Age: 81 years
Birth: 1877 Death: 1958/10/08 Burial: 1958/10/11
Site 2 Mrs. Catherine Jane Bell On stone with Robert B. Bell Age: 63 years
Birth: 1887 Death: 1950/09/01 Burial: 1950/09/04
Site 3 Child Green Death: 1951/05/24 Burial: 1951/05/24
No stone
Site 3 Child-Fred Peppin Death: 1951/07/24 Burial: 1951/07/24
Cause: Premature Birth No stone
Site 4 Emmett Hawkins Age: 55 years
Birth: 1891/05 Death: 1951/01/03 Burial: 1951/01/06
Site 5 Walter Elias Castle Died: Paeonian Springs, VA Age: 67 years
Birth: 1886/03/17 Death: 1953/07/16 Burial: 1953/07/19
Site 6 Mrs. Rose Frances Castle Age: 59 years
Birth: 1890/05/12 Death: 1950/07/30 Burial: 1950/08/01
IB:Mrs. W.E. Castle On stone with Walter Elias Castle
Site 7 Cary C. Jones Died: Sterling, VA Age: 82 years
Birth: 1877 Death: 1959/11/09 Burial: 1959/11/12
Site 8 Mrs. Elizabeth Frances Jones Age: 66 years
Birth: 1883 Death: 1950/11/19 Burial: 1950/11/21
On stone with Cary C. Jones
Site 9 Mrs. Mattie Perry Herndon Age: 88 years
Birth: 1863/11/25 Death: 1951/08/28 Burial: 1951/08/30
Site 10 Arbie Harrison Hawkins Died: Leesburg, VA Age: 77 years
Birth: 1911/02/18 Death: 1988/03/27 Burial: 1988/03/30
Site 11 Baby Boy Deans Death: 1959/07/04 Burial: 1959/07/05
Cause: Stillborn Died: L.C.H. Leesburg, VA No stone
Site 11 Henry C. Jewell Died: Manassas, VA Age: 90 years
Birth: 1882/03/15 Death: 1973/03/01 Burial: 1973/03/04
Site 12 Mrs. Lila Virginia Jewell Age: 72 years
Birth: 1878/03/26 Death: 1950/09/05 Burial: 1950/09/07
On stone with Henry C. Jewell

Lot: 929 Owner: Miscellaneous

Site 1 Samuel Peerce Hersperger Age: 85 years
Birth: 1898/02/22 Death: 1984/02/21 Burial: 1984/02/25
Died: Rockville, MD TS: Married Laura V. Gibbons August 7, 1965

Site 2	Samuel Ahalt Hersperger		Age: 86 years
	Birth: 1862/05/18	Death: 1948/01/05	Burial: 1948/01/07
Site 4	Mary L. Hersperger	Died: Round Hill, VA	Age: 90 years
	Birth: 1873/09/26	Death: 1964/03/25	Burial: 1964/03/27
Site 5	Clare Louise Hersperger		Age: 87 years
	Birth: 1899/02/08	Death: 1986/04/24	Burial: 1986/04/27
	Cause: Heart Disease	Died: Berryville, VA	
Site 10	Leo Quackenbush	Died: Washington, DC	Age: 73 years
	Birth: 1895/11/01	Death: 1969/06/01	Burial: 1969/06/11
Site 11	Lucile H. Quackenbush	Died: Santa Clara County, CA	
	Birth: 1901/02/20	Death: 1991/01/01	Burial: 1991/04/08
Site 12	Donald Quackenbush	Died: CA	
	Birth: 1942/12/19	Death: 1991/11/14	Burial: 1991/11/25

Lot: 930   Owner: Miscellaneous

Site 1	John W. Riley		Age: 75 years
	Birth: 1885	Death: 1960/10/28	Burial: 1960/10/31
	Died: L.C.H. Leesburg, VA		No death date on stone
Site 2	Mary E. Riley	On stone with John W. Riley	Age: 63 years
	Birth: 1882	Death: 1947/08/09	Burial: 1947/08/11
Site 3	John W. Legg		Age: 70 years
	Birth: 1878	Death: 1947/10/05	Burial: 1947/10/07
Site 4	Loretta V. Legg		Age: 85 years
	Birth: 1890	Death: 1975/10/09	Burial: 1975/10/11
	Died: Leesburg, VA	On stone with John W. Legg	
Site 5	William E. Virts		
	Birth: 1879/10/05	Death: 1949/09/27	Burial: 1949/09/29
Site 6	Henrietta A. Virts		Age: 72 years
	Birth: 1893/11/13	Death: 1965/09/28	Burial: 1965/10/01
	Died: Washington, DC	On stone with William E. Virts	
Site 7	Margaret Elizabeth Fox		Age: 34 years
	Birth: 1912	Death: 1947/07/08	Burial: 1947/07/10
Site 8	Lula Ellen Legge	Died: L.C.H. Leesburg, VA	Age: 88 years
	Birth: 1869	Death: 1958/04/25	Burial: 1958/04/28
Site 9	Roger Willis Fox	Died: Leesburg, VA	Age: 79 years
	Birth: 1907	Death: 1986/11/24	Burial: 1986/11/28
Site 10	Thelma J. Fox	Died: Leesburg, VA	Age: 71 years
	Birth: 1912	Death: 1983/07/08	Burial: 1983/07/10
	Cause: Heart	On stone with Roger Willis Fox	
Site 11	Raymond L. Hough	Died: Leesburg, VA	Age: 80 years
	Birth: 1898	Death: 1978/06/06	Burial: 1978/06/09
Site 12	Mrs. Louise V. Hough		Age: 62 years
	Birth: 1900	Death: 1962/12/06	Burial: 1962/12/09
	Died: L.C.H. Leesburg, VA	On stone with Raymond L. Hough	

Lot: 931 E   Owner: Norman D. & Nancy K. Greenfield   1955/01/04

Site 10	Norman D. Greenfield	Died: Leesburg, VA	Age: 59 years
	Birth: 1921/07/15	Death: 1980/08/13	Burial: 1980/08/16

Site 11 Nancy K. Greenfield Died: Brunswick, VA
Birth: 1924/01/13 Death: 1994/06/12 Burial: 1994/06/15
TS: Married Norman D. Greenfield May 25, 1942
Site 12 May Virginia Collins Died: Leesburg, VA No stone
Death: 1955/01/04 Burial: 1955/01/06

Lot: 931 W Owner: Miscellaneous
Site 3 Charles A. Stallings Died: Washington, DC Age: 62 years
Birth: 1904/05/20 Death: 1966/06/28 Burial: 1966/07/01
Site 4 Ethel S. Stallings Age: 72 years
Birth: 1911/04/05 Death: 1983/07/21 Burial: 1983/07/24
Died: Leesburg, VA On stone with Charles A. Stallings

Lot: 932 Owner: Miscellaneous
Site 3 Martha Collins Vesey Died: Forest Hills, NY Age: 67 years
Birth: 1910 Death: 1977/01/22 Burial: 1977/01/25
Site 4 Arthur H. Schmidt Age: 91 years
Birth: 1881/01/27 Death: 1972/09/14
Site 5 Marie U. Schmidt Age: 80 years
Birth: 1898/05/29 Death: 1978/06/09 Burial: 1978/06/12
Died: NJ On stone with Arthur H. Schmidt
Site 6 James R. L. Comer Died: Fairfax, VA Age: 18 years
Birth: 1949 Death: 1967/07/23 Burial: 1967/07/26
Cause: Auto Accident TS: Son of Ralph & Hazel Comer
Site 9 Ray N. Campbell Age: 60 years
Birth: 1905 Death: 1965/10/12 Burial: 1965/10/15
Cause: Heart Died: Leesburg, VA
Site 10 Ellen C. Campbell Died: Fairfax, VA Age: 74 years
Birth: 1902 Death: 1974/03/01 Burial: 1077/03/04
Site 11 Henry Lee Sisk Died: Purcellville, VA Age: 65 years
Birth: 1909 Death: 1974/10/30 Burial: 1974/11/02
Site 12 Frances Lee Sisk Died: Purcellville, VA Age: 53 years
Birth: 1912 Death: 1965/08/04 Burial: 1965/08/06

Lot: 933 Owner: Miscellaneous
Site Infant Son Davidson Death: 1957
Site 1 Julian Clark Johnson Died: Washington, DC Age: 60 years
Birth: 1907/01/17 Death: 1967/08/01 Burial: 1967/08/04
Site 2 Vivian H. Johnson
Birth: 1916/10/15 Death: 1977/06/30 Burial: 1977/07/04
Died: Arlington, VA On stone with Julian Clark Johnson
Site 3 Albert A. DeJonghe Age: 40 years
Birth: 1926 Death: 1966/06/05 Burial: 1966/06/08
Cause: Auto Accident Died: Broad Run, VA
Site 5 Robert Fred Herndon Died: Leesburg, VA Age: 49 years
Birth: 1917/03/30 Death: 1966/05/03 Burial: 1966/05/06
Site 7 Raymond A. Cooper Died: Orange Co., VA
Birth: 1910/11/28 Death: 1992/11/15 Burial: 1992/11/18

Site 8   Helen N. Cooper   Age: 58 years
         Birth: 1908/04/25   Death: 1966/04/21   Burial: 1966/04/23
         Died: Washington, DC   TS: Mother
Site 9   Harry Th. Davidson   Age: 70 years
         Birth: 1889   Death: 1960/06/27   Burial: 1960/07/05
         Died: Ashburn, VA   Removed from Lot 913 Apr 11, 1966
Site 10 Peter Hilderbrand Davidson Died: TX   Age: 21 years
         Birth: 1944   Death: 1966/04/06   Burial: 1966/04/11
         On stone with Harry Th. Davidson and Infant son Andrew Davidson
Site 11 Perceval Stanway Gault Died: Leesburg, VA   Age: 73 years
         Birth: 1900   Death: 1973/07/04   Burial: 1973/07/07
Site 12 Marjorie Craik Gault   Died: Washington, DC   Age: 62 years
         Birth: 1904   Death: 1966/03/11   Burial: 1966/03/14

Lot: 934 Owner: Miscellaneous
Site 4   James Franklin Reed   Died: Leesburg, VA   Age: 60 years
         Birth: 1907/12/02   Death: 1967/10/09   Burial: 1967/10/18
Site 6   Dorothy K. Cowne   Age: 79 years
         Birth: 1901/04/24   Death: 1980/07/05   Burial: 1980/07/07
         Died: Harrisonburg, VA   TS: Wife of Leroy J. Cowne
Site 6   Leroy J. Cowne   TS: 1st Sgt US Army WWI   Age: 85 years
         Birth: 1885   Death: 1979/02/28
Site 9   L. Kinard Martin   Died: Leesburg, VA   Age: 60 years
         Birth: 1905   Death: 1966/01/24   Burial: 1966/01/26
Site 10 Kathleen Armentrout Martin   Age: 82 years
         Birth: 1902   Death: 1985/04/14   Burial: 1985/04/17
                                 Died: Richmond, VA
Site 11 Harry S. Sommers   Died: Paeonian Springs, VA   Age: 80 years
         Birth: 1905/01/31   Death: 1985/05/30   Burial: 1985/06/01
Site 12 Alice McC. Sommers   Age: 61 years
         Birth: 1910/02/22   Death: 1966/03/03   Burial: 1966/03/05
         Died: Leesburg, VA   On stone with Harry S. Sommers

Lot: 935 Owner: Miscellaneous
Site 1   Mrs. Grace G. Ball   Age: 79 years
         Birth: 1885   Death: 1964/08/07   Burial: 1964/08/09
         Died: Leesburg, VA   On stone with Harvey Hamilton Ball
Site 2   Harvey Hamilton Ball   Age: 63 years
         Birth: 1884   Death: 1947/12/09   Burial: 1947/12/11
Site 3   Mattie May Harper   Age: 70 years
         Birth: 1880/01/16   Death: 1950/05/19   Burial: 1950/05/21
Site 8   Clinton Henry Harris Sr.   Age: 71 years
         Birth: 1881   Death: 1951/11/20   Burial: 1951/11/22
Site 9   Clinton H. Harris Jr.
         Birth: 1919/12/06   Death: 1944/07/31   Burial: 1949/01/05
         Cause: Veteran   TS: Virginia PFC 16 INF WWII
Site 10 Mary Elizabeth Ramsey Harris   Age: 70 years
         Birth: 1883   Death: 1954/04/12
Site 11 Joseph Willard Robey   Age: 69 years
         Birth: 1878   Death: 1947/12/21   Burial: 1947/12/23

Site 12 Mrs. Anna S. Robey Cause: Peritonitis Age: 74 years
Birth: 1880 Death: 1955/04/11 Burial: 1955/04/12
Died: Washington, DC On stone with Joseph Willard Robey

Lot: 936 Owner: Miscellaneous
Site 1 Eugene E. Williams Died: Leesburg, VA Age: 83 years
Birth: 1903/03/11 Death: 1986/08/15 Burial: 1986/08/19
Site 2 Alice M. Williams Age: 79 years
Birth: 1909/06/05 Death: 1988/10/19 Burial: 1988/10/22
Died: Clinton, MD On stone with Eugene E. Williams
Site 3 Child of James Morgan Death: 1947/10/16 Burial: 1947/10/17
Moved to Floyd, VA on May 8, 1953 No stone
Site 3 Earl E. Williams Died: Leesburg, VA Age: 29 years
Birth: 1929/11/15 Death: 1959/04/11 Burial: 1959/04/14
On stone with Eugene E. & Alice M. Williams
Site 4 Walter Henry Kitts Age: 69 years
Birth: 1878 Death: 1948/07/11 Burial: 1948/07/13
Site 5 Laura E. Kitts Died: Leesburg, VA Age: 94 years
Birth: 1881 Death: 1975/11/27 Burial: 1975/11/30
Site 6 Robert Lee Orrison TS: Age 80 years Age: 80 years
 Death: 1947/12/20 Burial: 1947/12/22
Site 8 Child Martin No stone Age: 1 day
 Death: 1949/08/14 Burial: 1949/08/15
Site 9 Velvet C. Ogburn IB: Child of Henry Ogburn Age: 2 days
Birth: 1950/01/26 Death: 1950/01/28 Burial: 1950/01/30
Site 10 Polly Belle Hawkins Age: 33 years
Birth: 1915/08/27 Death: 1949/04/09 Burial: 1949/04/11
Site 11 Thomas Richard Keyes Age: 57 years
Birth: 1892/10/22 Death: 1949/03/12 Burial: 1949/03/14
Site 12 Sarah E. Keyes Age: 92 years
Birth: 1888/07/09 Death: 1981/04/29 Burial: 1981/05/02
Died: Arlington, VA On stone with Thomas Richard Keyes

Lot: 937 Owner: Miscellaneous
Site 1-12 Capital Airlines Inc. Cause: Plane Crash 6/13/47
10 bodies, 12 sites Death: 1947/06/13 Burial: 1947/06/16
Harry C. Crogham Death: 1947/06/13
Dorothea Peters DeCray Death: 1947/06/13
Mrs. John H. Dewar Death: 1947/06/13
Robert K. Garretson Death: 1947/06/13
Walter D. Hodson Death: 1947/06/13
Chevalier H. Ludlow Death: 1947/06/13
Charles Haylett McCafferty Death: 1947/06/13
Percy John Ness Death: 1947/06/13
Marjorie Louise Southerland Death: 1947/06/13
Mrs. Logan A. Webster Death: 1947/06/13

Lot: 938 Owner: Miscellaneous
Site 2 Herbert Lee Wortman Died: Leesburg, VA Age: 60 years
Birth: 1895 Death: 1956/02/03 Burial: 1956/02/03

Site 3   Annie R. Ball Wortman   Birth: 1892   Death: 1954/05/20
         On stone with Herbert Lee Wortman
Site 4   Marguerite L. Thompson   No stone   Age: 69 years
         Died: Leesburg, VA   Death: 1953/12/19
Site 5   Bernard Minor   Age: 72 years
         Birth: 1880   Death: 1952/12/02   Burial: 1952/12/04
Site 6   Mrs. Rhua E. Minor   Age: 77 years
         Birth: 1882   Death: 1959/11/17   Burial: 1959/11/19
         Died: Leesburg, VA   On stone with Bernard Minor
Site 9   W. Luck Fletcher   Died: Leesburg, VA   Age: 84 years
         Birth: 1872   Death: 1955/07/14   Burial: 1955/07/16
Site 12 Anna Lazenby Burdick   Died: Lucketts, VA   Age: 75 years
         Birth: 1881/05/30   Death: 1956/03/11   Burial: 1956/03/11

Lot: 939   Owner: Miscellaneous
Site 1   Mrs. Goldie May Thompson   Age: 71 years
         Birth: 1897/05/05   Death: 1969/04/18   Burial: 1969/04/21
         Died: Manassas, VA
Site 3   Mary L. Arnett   Died: Staunton, VA   Age: 61 years
         Birth: 1908   Death: 1969/10/20   Burial: 1969/10/23
Site 4   Frances G. Arnett   Died: Loudoun Co., VA   Age: 70 years
         Birth: 1890   Death: 1961/05/05   Burial: 1961/05/08
Site 5   William T. Kitts   Died: Hamilton, VA   Age: 87 years
         Birth: 1875/11/18   Death: 1965/04/16   Burial: 1965/04/19
Site 6   Carrie L. Moore Kitts   Died: L.C.H. Leesburg, VA   Age: 63 years
         Birth: 1895   Death: 1958/04/26   Burial: 1958/04/29
Site 7   Thomas Donovan Thompson   Age: 77 years
         Birth: 1883/03/03   Death: 1957/12/01   Burial: 1957/12/04
         Died: Leesburg, VA
Site 8   Charles J. Maxcy   Died: Fairfax, VA   Age: 53 years
         Birth: 1910   Death: 1964/09/17   Burial: 1964/09/19
Site 10 Garnie Craven Virts   Age: 54 years
         Birth: 1903/10/01   Death: 1957/10/16
Site 12 Coleman Aaron Maxcy   Age: 83 years
         Birth: 1873   Death: 1957/02/08

Lot: 940   Owner: Miscellaneous
Site 10 George F. Danner   Died: Leesburg, VA   TS: US Army WWII
         Birth: 1923/04/30   Death: 1991/07/15   Burial: 1991/07/18
Site 12 Mrs. Lily Williams Ryon   Age: 66 years
         Birth: 1891/03/21   Death: 1958/01/19   Burial: 1958/01/22
         Died: Arlington Hosp., Arlington, VA

Lot: 945   Owner: Evelyn B. Caylor   Purchased: 1970/10/05
Site 9   Ralph H. (Tommy) Caylor   Age: 81 years
         Birth: 1909/12/04   Death: 1991/11/03   Burial: 1991/11/06
         Died: Leesburg, VA
Site 10 Evelyn B. (Puddin) Caylor
         Birth: 1908/11/29   Death: 1991/11/08   Burial: 1991/11/10
         Died: Leesburg, VA   On stone with Ralph H. (Tommy) Caylor

Site 11 Thomas E. Bodmer　　　Died: Leesburg, VA　　　Age: 70 years
　　　　Birth: 1910/02/01　　　　Death: 1980/10/17　　　Burial: 1980/10/19
Site 12 Susie Virginia Bodmer　Died: Ashburn, VA　　　　Age: 58 years
　　　　Birth: 1912/01/18　　　　Death: 1970/09/30　　　Burial: 1970/10/03
　　　　Cause: Heart　　　　　　　　　　　　On stone with Thomas E. Bodmer

Lot: 946 Owner: Miscellaneous
Site 1　Arville Hawkins　　　　Died: Leesburg, VA　　　Age: 53 years
　　　　Birth: 1937/03/10　　　　Death: 1990/06/02　　　Burial: 1990/06/06
Site 4　Marietta S. Mathews　　Died: Fairfax, VA　　　　Age: 56 years
　　　　Birth: 1924　　　　　　　 Death: 1981/04/11　　　Burial: 1981/04/15
Site 5　William E. Burgess　　　Died: MD　　　　　　　 Age: 76 years
　　　　Birth: 1909/05/28　　　　Death: 1986/01/23　　　Burial: 1986/01/27

Lot: 947 Owner: Miscellaneous
Site 3　Carroll T. Jones　　　　 Died: Fairfax, VA　　　　Age: 72 years
　　　　Birth: 1906/05/28　　　　Death: 1978/12/19　　　Burial: 1978/12/22
Site 4　Della E. Jones　　　　　　　　　　　　　　　　　Age: 66 years
　　　　Birth: 1911/02/10　　　　Death: 1977/05/17　　　Burial: 1977/05/20
　　　　Died: Storm Lake, IA　　　　　　　On stone with Carroll T. Jones
Site 5　Roger William Harmon　 No stone　　　　　　　 Age: 69 years
　　　　Died: Leesburg, VA　　　 Death: 1977/07/19　　　Burial: 1977/07/21
Site 5　Elizabeth S. Harman　　 Died: Leesburg, VA
　　　　Birth: 1920/09/19　　　　Death: 1991/08/01　　　Burial: 1991/08/05

Lot: 948 Owner: Miscellaneous
Site 4　Hrefna Sobol　　　　　　Birth: 1925/06/11　　　　Death: 1979/06/27
Site 5　Frederick Lee Donaldson Died: Leesburg, VA　　　Age: 62 years
　　　　Birth: 1923　　　　　　　Death: 1986/08/09　　　Burial: 1986/08/12
Site 10 Amy Louise Sloyan　　　　　　　　　　　　　　　Age: 15 years
　　　　Birth: 1964/05/14　　　　Death: 1979/06/02
Site 12 Sonny Julian Clark Johnson　Died: NY　　　　　 Age: 42 years
　　　　Birth: 1939/10/06　　　　Death: 1981/12/05　　　Burial: 1981/12/09

Lot: 949 Owner: Miscellaneous
Site 1　Eulogia L. DeSilva　　　No stone　　　　　　　　Age: 81 years
　　　　Died: Winchester, VA　　Death: 1974/05/13　　　Burial: 1974/05/16
Site 6　Reginald Bifield Cocroft Jr.　　　　　　　　　　Age: 65 years
　　　　Birth: 1921/10/17　　　　Death: 1987/04/24　　　Burial: 1987/04/28
　　　　Died: Washington, DC　　　　　　　　　　　　 TS: USMA June, 1943

Lot: 950 Owner: Miscellaneous
Site 1　Robert W. Frye Sr.　　　Died: Leesburg, VA　　　Age: 79 years
　　　　Birth: 1907/04/07　　　　Death: 1984/11/29　　　Burial: 1984/12/01
Site 3　Melissa Proctor　　　　 No stone　　　　　　　　Age: Infant
　　　　Died: Washington, DC　　Death: 1974/09/27　　　Burial: 1974/10/02
Site 4　Terry Lee Frye　　　　　　　　　　　　　　　　Age: 23 years
　　　　Birth: 1953/07/07　　　　Death: 1977/04/11　　　Burial: 1977/04/14
　　　　Died: Leesburg, VA　　　　　　　　　　　　TS: SP 4 US Army Vietnam

Site 6   Maude K. Rollison   No stone   Age: 67 years
         Died: MD   Death: 1977/02/07   Burial: 1977/02/09
Site 6   Lawrence E. Rollison   No stone   Age: 70 years
         Died: Leland, MD   Death: 1981/09/18   Burial: 1981/09/24
Site 7   Dr. Thomas Gualtieri   Age: 72 years
         Birth: 1904   Death: 1976/10/09   Burial: 1976/10/11
         Died: Leesburg, VA   TS: MD

Lot: 951 Owner: Miscellaneous
Site 5   Florence Elizabeth Marcus Kiley   Age: 35 years
         Birth: 1950   Death: 1985/06/14   Burial: 1985/06/15
         Cause: Cancer   Died: Baltimore, MD
Site 12 Dirk Handley Hinkle   Age: 21 years
         Birth: 1964/07/16   Death: 1985/07/03   Burial: 1985/07/06
         Cause: Suicide   Died: Fairfax, VA

Lot: 952 Owner: Miscellaneous
Site 4   Jennifer E. McMorran   Died: Washington, DC   Age: 13 months
         Birth: 1979/12/28   Death: 1981/02/11   Burial: 1981/02/14
Site 8   Wanda R. Eamich   Died: Leesburg, VA   Age: 58 years
         Birth: 1923/01/09   Death: 1981/08/02   Burial: 1981/08/06
Site 9   Charles H. Leete   Died: Knoxville, TN   Age: 61 years
         Birth: 1923/08/05   Death: 1984/12/13   Burial: 1984/12/19

Lot: 957 Owner: Robert E. & Agnes Marcum   1969/05/12
Site 11 John Marcum   No stone   Age: 90 years
         Died: Hagerstown, MD   Death: 1973/09/02   Burial: 1973/09/04
Site 12 Hessie Marcum   No stone   Age: 87 years
         Died: Hagerstown, MD   Death: 1975/01/04   Burial: 1975/01/07

Lot: 959 E Owner: Morton Riddle III   Purchased: 1977/03/03
Site 7   Morton Riddle III   Died: Leesburg, VA   TS: MAJ US Army
         Birth: 1913/02/16   Death: 1990/06/29   Burial: 1990/07/02
Site 8   Mrs. Frances B. Riddle   Died: Leesburg, VA   Age: 59 years
         Birth: 1917/07/24   Death: 1977/02/20   Burial: 1977/02/23
Site 9   Dr. A. Lacy Tynes   Age: 75 years
         Birth: 1905/11/03   Death: 1981/04/07   Burial: 1981/04/10
         Died: Leesburg, VA   TS: MAJ GEN US Army
Site 10 Bessie Meade Tynes   Died: Leesburg, VA
         Birth: 1906/01/09   Death: 1992/09/23   Burial: 1992/09/25
Site 11 Catharine B. Riddle   Died: Leesburg, VA   Age: 74 years
         Birth: 1898/02/15   Death: 1982/07/13   Burial: 1982/07/16

Lot: 961 Owner: Miscellaneous
Site 4   Peggy Ray Cook   Died: Leesburg, VA   Age: 46 years
         Birth: 1942   Death: 1988/05/18   Burial: 1988/05/19
Site 5   Dr. James Thomas Jackson   Age: 79 years
         Birth: 1901/03/15   Death: 1980/04/12   Burial: 1980/04/15
         Cause: Cancer   Died: Leesburg, VA

Site 7	Thomas Joshua Hatcher	Died: Leesburg, VA	Age: 85 years
	Birth: 1899	Death: 1985/10/21	Burial: 1985/10/24
Site 8	Naomi Pierce Hatcher		Age: 76 years
	Birth: 1901	Death: 1977/09/10	Burial: 1977/09/12
	Died: Purcellville, VA	On stone with Thomas Joshua Hatcher	
Site 12	Harry H. Huntley		Age: 85 years
	Birth: 1895	Death: 1980/08/31	Burial: 1980/09/05
	Died: Leesburg, VA		TS: SGT US Army WWI
Site 12	Mabel F. Huntley	No stone	Age: 92 years
	Died: Leesburg, VA	Death: 1988/01/22	Burial: 1988/01/30

UNION CEMETERY
LEESBURG, LOUDOUN CO., VA

PLAT D

Lot: 952 Owner: Miscellaneous
Site 11 Barry A. Marks   Place: RI   Age: 57 years
        Birth: 1926/02/01   Death: 1983/07/18   Burial: 1983/07/21
        TS: Husband of Patricia Jackson

Lot: 953 Owner: Miscellaneous
Site 7   Russell L. Minard   Place: FL   Age: 87 years
       Birth: 1901   Death: 1989/08/10   Burial: 1989/08/31

Lot: 955 Owner: Tony Duncan & Sons   Purchase date:
Site 1   Edward Lee Duncan   Place: Washington, DC   Age: 54 years
       Birth: 1932/02/27   Death: 1986/06/27   Burial: 1986/06/30
Site 4   Grace M. Duncan   Place: Leesburg, VA   Age: 86 years
       Birth: 1910/07/25   Death: 1988/10/16   Burial: 1988/10/19
Site 12 Timothy Allen Duncan   Cause: Stillborn   Place: Leesburg, VA
       Birth: 1959/04/25   Death: 1959/04/25   Burial: 1959/04/25

Lot: 956 Owner: Miscellaneous
Site 1   Robert Henry Bentley   Place: Fairfax, VA   Age: 62 years
       Birth: 1924   Death: 1986/07/18   Burial: 1986/07/22
Site 2   Rozit A. Hashemizadeh   Place: Vienna, VA   Age: 26 years
       Birth: 1959/10/16   Death: 1986/09/20   Burial: 1986/09/24
Site 3   Marvin F. Smith   Place: Leesburg, VA   Age: 65 years
       Birth: 1911/12/16   Death: 1977/06/24   Burial: 1977/06/26
Site 6   Ross L. Wagar   Place: Leesburg, VA   Age: 59 years
       Birth: 1928/02/29   Death: 1987/06/03   Burial: 1987/06/06
Site 9   James Terrence McCracken Sr.   Place: Sterling, VA
       Birth: 1912/12/13   Death: 1994/10/12   Burial: 1994/10/17
Site 10 Anne Walker McCracken   Place: Leesburg, VA
       Birth: 1915/06/30   Death: 1994/11/03   Burial: 1994/11/05
       On stone with James Terrence McCracken, Sr.
Site 11 Gene Wayne Barnes   Place: Newport News, VA   Age: 32 years
       Birth: 1950/01/21   Death: 1982/05/27   Burial: 1982/06/02

Lot: 958 Owner: Miscellaneous
Site 1   Charles Theodore Rinker   Place: Chantilly, VA   TS: US Army WWII
       Birth: 1914/11/14   Death: 1994/04/17   Burial: 1994/04/19

Lot: 964 Owner: Miscellaneous
Site 9   Joe B. Wilson   Place: Fairfax, VA   Age: 53 years
       Birth: 1922   Death: 1975/10/11   Burial: 1975/10/14
Site 11 Charles H. Seale   Place: Leesburg, VA   Age: 65 years
       Birth: 1909   Death: 1975/09/27   Burial: 1975/10/01

Site 12 Allie M. Seale   Place: Leesburg, VA   Age: 84 years
Birth: 1893   Death: 1977/12/10   Burial: 1977/12/13

Lot: 965 Owner: Miscellaneous
Site 8 Elizabeth F. Provost   Place: Arlington, VA   Age: 88 years
Birth: 1902/11/05   Death: 1991/10/18   Burial: 1991/10/21
Site 9 Clarence William Hall   Place: Leesburg, VA   Age: 68 years
Birth: 1910   Death: 1978/07/06   Burial: 1978/07/08
Site 12 Harry Franklin Tribby Sr.   Age: 73 years
Birth: 1902   Death: 1975/06/23   Burial: 1975/06/25
    Place: Leesburg, VA

Lot: 967 Owner: Miscellaneous
Site 8 Walter G. Gardner   Place: Leesburg, VA   Age: 70 years
Birth: 1907/06/03   Death: 1977/08/05   Burial: 1977/08/08
TS: CMOMM US Navy WWII
Site 9 Sylvester Glenn Cross   Place: Leesburg, VA   Age: 55 years
Birth: 1921   Death: 1977/08/17   Burial: 1977/08/19
TS: PFC US Army WWII
Site 9 Martin Cross   Place: Winchester, VA   Age: 69 years
No stone   Death: 1989/03/15   Burial: 1989/03/27
Site 10 Lawrence S. Rutherford   Place: Fairfax, VA   Age: 58 years
Birth: 1931/03/01   Death: 1988/03/01   Burial: 1988/03/04
Site 11 James B. Repass   Place: Leesburg, VA   Age: 79 years
Birth: 1905/07/20   Death: 1984/09/06   Burial: 1984/09/08
Site 12 Nannie R. Repass   Place: Leesburg, VA   Age: 79 years
Birth: 1908/03/01   Death: 1987/11/21   Burial: 1987/11/24
On stone with James B. Repass

Lot: 968 Owner: Miscellaneous
Site 3 Kenneth I. Lee   Place: Washington, DC   Age: 61 years
Birth: 1925   Death: 1986/12/19   Burial: 1986/12/22
TS: Married Mary M. Lee September 22, 1946
Site 7 Sylvester John Weiskircher   Age: 64 years
Birth: 1911   Death: 1975/03/08   Burial: 1975/03/11
    Place: Leesburg, VA

Lot: 969 Owner: Miscellaneous
Site 4 Michael Eugene Taylor   Place: Leesburg, VA   Age: 19 years
Birth: 1957   Death: 1976/09/11   Burial: 1976/09/16
Cause: Auto Accident   TS: Pvt US Army Vietnam

Lot: 970 E   Owner: Dorothy Beaver Sutphin   1968/09/11
Site 7 Everett W. Sutphin   Age: 47 years
Birth: 1921/09/22   Death: 1968/08/31   Burial: 1968/09/03
Cause: Suicide   Place: Leesburg, VA
TS: Virginia TEC5 Co B 288 ENGR CMBT BN WWII
Site 8 Roy Arnold Sutphin   IB: Child of Everett Sutphin   Age: 1 month
Birth: 1955/09/16   Death: 1955/09/17   Burial: 1955/09/18
    Place: Leesburg, VA

Site 8   Dorothy B. Sutphin   Place: Leesburg, VA
         Birth: 1926/04/15   Death: 1993/12/20   Burial: 1993/12/24
Site 11 Annie Sutphin Lorenz   Place: Washington, DC   Age: 42 years
         No stone   Death: 1973/01/26   Burial: 1973/01/31
Site 12 Jesse W. Sutphin   Place: Bronx, NY   Age: 55 years
         Birth: 1915/09/22   Death: 1970/07/25   Burial: 1970/07/28
         TS: Virginia SGT Army Air Forces WWII

Lot: 970 W   Owner: Marie R. Gray   Purchase date: 1968/07/16
Site 1   William M. Gray   Place: Lexington, KY   Age: 40 years
         Birth: 1927/10/01   Death: 1968/07/02   Burial: 1968/07/05
Site 4   Dexter C. Gray   Place: Leesburg, VA   Age: 85 years
         Birth: 1899   Death: 1985/03/01   Burial: 1985/03/04
Site 5   Sally Josephine Gray   On stone with Dexter C. Gray   Age: 72 years
         Birth: 1900   Death: 1972/05/22   TS: Aunt Josie

Lot: 971   Owner: Mrs. Eileen Fry   Purchase date: 1964/06/30
Site 1   Delia Theresa Frye   Place: Leesburg, VA   Age: 78 years
         Birth: 1886   Death: 1964/06/07   Burial: 1964/06/10
Site 2   Clarence J. Frye   Place: Leesburg, VA   Age: 50 years
         Birth: 1921/05/24   Death: 1972/10/05   Burial: 1972/10/08
         TS: T-5, Co D 543rd ENGR Reg WWII
Site 3   Leo Fry   Place: Leesburg, VA   Age: 64 years
         Birth: 1919/10/23   Death: 1984/09/30   Burial: 1984/10/03
         TS: US Navy WWII
Site 4   Mary Paver Fry   Place: Leesburg, VA   Age: 63 years
         Birth: 1915/09/05   Death: 1979/01/08   Burial: 1979/01/10
         On stone with Leo Fry   TS: US Navy WWII
Site 5   Kathy Loretta Fry   Place: Leesburg, VA
         Birth: 1955/02/27   Death: 1992/04/21   Burial: 1992/04/24
Site 7   Viola Mary Frye   Place: Cheverly, MD   Age: 60 years
         Birth: 1914/11/12   Death: 1974/12/12   Burial: 1974/12/15

Lot: 972 E   Owner: Miscellaneous
Site 7   Bernard A. Norfolk   Place: Leesburg, VA   Age: 85 years
         Birth: 1905/03/16   Death: 1990/05/07   Burial: 1990/05/09
         On stone with Ira M. Norfolk
Site 8   Ira M. Norfolk   Place: Loudoun Co, VA
         Birth: 1906/09/05   Death: 1993/02/15   Burial: 1993/02/18
         On stone with Bernard A. Norfolk
Site 10 Pauline Wilson   Place: Rockville, MD   Age: 74 years
         Birth: 1915/09/13   Death: 1990/05/17   Burial: 1990/05/20

Lot: 972 W   Owner: Walter & Marian Rubel   1974/04/25
Site 1   Roy F. Pinner   Place: Leesburg, VA   Age: 76 years
         Birth: 1905   Death: 1981/12/13   Burial: 1981/12/16
Site 2   Suzanner Rubel Pinner   Place: Fairfax, VA   Age: 56 years
         Birth: 1932   Death: 1988/08/30   Burial: 1988/09/01
Site 3   Walter Louis Rubel   Place: Leesburg, VA   Age: 89 years
         Birth: 1897   Death: 1986/02/12   Burial: 1986/02/15

Site 4   Marian Richardson Rubel   Place: Leesburg, VA   Age: 89 years
         Birth: 1901   Death: 1990/03/09   Burial: 1990/03/13
Site 5   Gordon Richardson Rubel   Birth: 1929   Death: 1987

Lot: 973   Owner: Miscellaneous
Site 1   James Edwin Arnold Jr.   Place: Leesburg, VA
         Birth: 1928/06/03   Death: 1993/02/12   Burial: 1993/02/16

Lot: 974E   Owner: Miscellaneous
Site 7   Betty J. (Bonnie) Grubbs   Place: Winchester, VA   Age: 62 years
         Birth: 1930   Death: 1992/10/31   Burial: 1992/11/03
Site 11 Philip Ashlin May   Place: Washington, DC
         Birth: 1967/05/24   Death: 1994/05/21   Burial: 1994/10/21

Lot: 974W   Owner: Samuel L. Marcum   Purchased: 1968/10/26
Site 1   Roy Fred Marcum   Place: Leesburg, VA   Age: 32 years
         Birth: 1936/08/18   Death: 1968/10/16   Burial: 1968/10/19
Site 5   Samuel L. Marcum   Place: Winchester, VA   Age: 62 years
         Birth: 1906/06/01   Death: 1969/01/20   Burial: 1969/01/23

Lot: 976   Owner: Miscellaneous
Site 4   Mary Chase Lawrence   Place: New Haven, CT   Age: 63 years
         Birth: 1924/11/24   Death: 1988/08/21   Burial: 1988/08/27
Site 6   Peter Y. Goetz   Place: MD
         Birth: 1958/06/16   Death: 1993/06/18   Burial: 1993/06/24

Lot: 977 E   Owner: Miscellaneous
Site 7   Robert Lee Barker   Place: Leesburg, VA   Age: 80 years
         Birth: 1905/01/27   Death: 1985/02/02   Burial: 1985/02/05

Lot: 977 W   Owner: Philip E. Hilbert   Purchase date:
Site 3   Philip Fox Hilbert   Place: Leesburg, VA   Age: 80 years
         Birth: 1902/09/21   Death: 1983/08/30   Burial: 1983/09/02
Site 4   Dorothy Rinda Coe Hilbert   Age: 68 years
         Birth: 1903/01/22   Death: 1971/03/01   Burial: 1971/03/04
         Place: Leesburg, VA   TS: Wife of Philip Fox Hilbert

Lot: 978   Owner: Miscellaneous
Site 8   Annie I. Bell   Place: Leesburg, VA   Age: 82 years
         Birth: 1903/01/18   Death: 1985/09/17   Burial: 1985/09/20

Lot: 979   Owner: Miscellaneous
Site 7   Robert Bruce Cotton   Age: 25 years
         Birth: 1950/03/17   Death: 1975/06/09   Burial: 1975/06/12
         Place: Middletown Township, PA   TS: VMD
Site 8   George Bruce Cotton
         Birth: 1918/07/30   Death: 1995/03/23   Burial: 1995/04/14
         Place: Inverness, FL   TS: SGT US Marine Corps WWII
Site 10 Jack Walsh   Age: 64 years
         Birth: 1911/03/25   Death: 1975/06/13   Burial: 1975/06/16
         Place: Leesburg, VA   TS: 1st Lt. US Army WWII

Lot: 980 Owner: Miscellaneous
Site 1   John D. Alderman   Place: Leesburg, VA   Age: 61 years
         Birth: 1913/07/03   Death: 1975/06/07   Burial: 1975/06/10
Site 5   Joseph Patrick Gaines   Place: Washington, DC   Age: 49 years
         Birth: 1925/04/16   Death: 1975/04/04   Burial: 1975/04/07
Site 6   Elenita Charlotte Gaines   Place: Leesburg, VA
         Birth: 1905/08/11   Death: 1993/11/05   Burial: 1993/11/08
Site 7   Joseph S. Petersen Jr.   Place: Woodbridge, VA
         Birth: 1914/09/30   Death: 1992/04/17   Burial: 1992/04/23
Site 8   Imogene Colburn Petersen   Place: Alexandria, VA
         Birth: 1919/09/21   Death: 1987/02/25   Burial: 1987/02/28
         TS: Married Joseph S. Petersen, Jr. July 14, 1953
Site 12 Christopher Eugene Fletcher   Age: 20 years
         No stone   Death: 1976/12/25   Burial: 1976/12/30
         Cause: Auto Accident   Place: Leesburg, VA

Lot: 981 Owner: Miscellaneous
Site 1   Leonard W. Parker   Place: Winchester, VA   Age: 74 years
         Birth: 1899   Death: 1974/11/08   Burial: 1974/11/11
Site 2   Claude H. Hopkins   Place: Winchester, VA   TSDeath: 1977
         Birth: 1905   IBDeath: 1978/01/02   Burial: 1978/01/06
Site 3   Nancy Jane S. Hopkins   Age: 69 years
         Birth: 1905   Death: 1974/10/05   Burial: 1974/10/09
         Place: Leesburg, VA   On stone with Claude H. Hopkins
Site 10 Dale Lee Bishel   Place: Fairfax, VA   Age: 21 years
         Birth: 1953/02/26   Death: 1974/10/01   Burial: 1974/10/04
Site 11 Van Iden Zeiler   Place: Winchester, VA   Age: 71 years
         Birth: 1902   Death: 1974/04/11   Burial: 1974/04/13

Lot: 982 Owner: Miscellaneous
Site 1   Calvin C. Grimes   Place: Taylorstown, VA   Age: 51 years
         Birth: 1928   Death: 1979/12/31   Burial: 1980/01/13
Site 4   James Scott Marshall   Place: Herndon, VA   Age: 15 years
         Birth: 1959/08/09   Death: 1975/06/12   Burial: 1975/06/16
Site 6   Louis Promos   Place: Leesburg, VA   Age: 82 years
         Birth: 1893/05/10   Death: 1975/05/10   Burial: 1975/05/13
         TS: "Elias Promponas". Born Noxos, Greece
Site 7   Arthur S. Fry   Place: Leesburg, VA   Age: 89 years
         Birth: 1887/12/02   Death: 1977/08/12   Burial: 1977/08/15
Site 8   Gracie M. Fry   Age: 89 years
         Birth: 1888/02/04   Death: 1977/10/10   Burial: 1977/10/13
         Place: Leesburg, VA   On stone with Arthur S. Fry
Site 9   Clifford N. Fry   Place: Hyattsville, MD   Age: 53 years
         Birth: 1921   Death: 1975/04/18   Burial: 1975/04/22
Site 10 Paul S. Frye   Place: Leesburg, VA   Age: 81 years
         Birth: 1909   Death: 1991/06/03   Burial: 1991/06/05

Lot: 983 Owner: Mrs. Martha DeHart
Site 1 Claude William DeHart　　　　　　　　　　　　Age: 48 years
　　　　Birth: 1928/03/13　　Death: 1976/04/13　　Burial: 1976/04/16
　　　　Place: Reston, VA　　　　　　　　　TS: PFC US Army WWII
Site 6 Gerald C. DeHart　　　Place: PA　　　　　　Age: 53 years
　　　　Birth: 1936/01/30　　Death: 1990/06/16　　Burial: 1990/06/19

Lot: 984 Owner: Miscellaneous
Site 5 Tyler Eugene Bell　　　　　　　　　　　　　Age: 57 years
　　　　Birth: 1932/09/24　　Death: 1990/03/15　　Burial: 1990/03/18
　　　　Place: Martinsburg, WV　　　　　　　TS: M Sgt US Army
Site 8 Shannon Dale Warf Firestone　　　　　　　Age: 24 years
　　　　Birth: 1965/05/20　　Death: 1989/10/30　　Burial: 1989/11/02
　　　　　　　　　　　　　　　Place: Leesburg, VA
Site 11 Clarence Duke Bell　　Place: Ashburn, VA　　Age: 84 years
　　　　Birth: 1894　　　　　Death: 1978/11/08　　Burial: 1978/11/11
Site 12 Susie L. Kitts Bell　　No death date on stone
　　　　Birth: 1900/03/22　　Death: 1991/12/27　　Burial: 1991/12/30
　　　　Place: Leesburg, VA　　On stone with Clarence Duke Bell

Lot: 985 Owner: Miscellaneous
Site 6 Nellie May Fisher　　　　　　　　　　　　Age: 44 years
　　　　Birth: 1932/09/10　　Death: 1976/12/28　　Burial: 1976/12/30
　　　　Cause: Heart　　　　Place: Leesburg, VA
Site 7 Emmitt Farmer　　　　Place: Leesburg, VA　　Age: 77 years
　　　　Birth: 1907　　　　　Death: 1984/04/15　　Burial: 1984/04/18

Lot: 986 Owner: Miscellaneous
Site 2 Shirley Ann Cockrell　Place: Leesburg, VA
　　　　Birth: 1938/03/16　　Death: 1992/07/04　　Burial: 1992/07/07
Site 8 Elva M. Davis　　　　Place: Woodbridge, VA　Age: 49 years
　　　　Birth: 1928/04/26　　Death: 1977/06/07　　Burial: 1977/06/09

Lot: 987 Owner: Miscellaneous
Site　　Ann Hubbard Allen　　Birth: 1885　　　　　Death: 1990
Site　　Robert H. Allen　　　Birth: 1908　　　　　Death: 1957
Site 1 Randolph A. Keyes Sr.　Place: Harrisonburg, VA　Age: 77 years
　　　　Birth: 1900/01/27　　Death: 1977/04/21　　Burial: 1977/04/23
Site 2 Mrs. Janet H. Keyes　Place: Leesburg, VA　　Age: 79 years
　　　　Birth: 1900/09/18　　Death: 1980/09/12　　Burial: 1980/09/15
Site 3 Elizabeth M. (Betty) Keyes　　　　　　　　　Age: 62 years
　　　　Birth: 1922/11/06　　Death: 1985/06/22　　Burial: 1985/06/24
　　　　　　　　　　　　　　　Place: Leesburg, VA
Site 4 David Dawson　　　　Place: Fairfax, VA　　Age: 54 years
　　　　Birth: 1922/06/15　　Death: 1977/05/26　　Burial: 1977/05/28
Site 8 Marjorie M. Mersinger　Place: Leesburg, VA　Age: 56 years
　　　　Birth: 1919　　　　　Death: 1976/01/13　　Burial: 1976/01/15
Site 9 William B. Ridgeway　Place: Leesburg, VA
　　　　Birth: 1904/11/21　　Death: 1994　　　　　Burial: 1994/09/23

Site 10 Willie Ann Ridgeway   Place: Leesburg, VA   Age: 84 years
         Birth: 1905   Death: 1989/12/07   Burial: 1989/12/09
         TS: Married William B. Ridgeway November 4, 1936
Site 11 James W. Newcomb   Place: Leesburg, VA   Age: 60 years
         Birth: 1924   Death: 1985/05/02   Burial: 1985/05/04

Lot: 988 Owner: Miscellaneous
Site 1   John D. Mercer   Place: Washington, DC   Age: 33 years
         Birth: 1942/02/02   Death: 1975/09/30   Burial: 1975/10/02
Site 3   Eugene H. Fleenor   Place: Charlottesville, VA Age: 87 years
         Birth: 1902   Death: 1989/06/05   Burial: 1989/06/08
Site 6   John Nathaniel Mercer Place: Leesburg, VA   TS: S2 US Navy
         Birth: 1909/02/26   Death: 1995/04/26   Burial: 1995/04/29
Site 8   Robert W. Jackson   Age: 66 years
         Birth: 1916/04/01   Death: 1984/06/19   Burial: 1984/06/23
         Place: Santa Clara   TS: US Coast Guard WWII
Site 9   Owen L. Hough   Place: Leesburg, VA   Age: 72 years
         Birth: 1914   Death: 1986/01/16   Burial: 1986/01/20
Site 10 Sylvia C. Hough   Age: 63 years
         Birth: 1912   Death: 1975/11/14   Burial: 1975/11/17
         Place: Leesburg, VA   On stone with Owen L. Hough
Site 11 Reginald C. Groff   Place: Leesburg, VA
         Birth: 1921/01/26   Death: 1992/09/03   Burial: 1992/09/05

Lot: 989 Owner: Miscellaneous
Site 1   Clarence Michael Bussinger   Age: 81 years
         Birth: 1903/02/03   Death: 1985/02/13   Burial: 1985/02/17
                                 Place: Clearwater, FL
Site 4   Frederick G. LeGrys   Age: 57 years
         Birth: 1927/11/03   Death: 1985/03/09   Burial: 1985/03/13
         Cause: Heart   Place: Leesburg, VA
Site 5   Robert Elmore Seaton   Place: Leesburg, VA   Age: 66 years
         Birth: 1906   Death: 1975/11/26   Burial: 1975/11/29
Site 6   Bertha V. Seaton   Age: 62 years
         Birth: 1914   Death: 1976/08/17   Burial: 1976/08/20
         Place: Leesburg, VA   On stone with Robert Elmore Seaton
Site 8   Verner Lee Simpson   Place: Leesburg, VA
         Birth: 1934/07/10   Death: 1995/07/15   Burial: 1995/07/19
Site 9   Thomas B. Sweeney   Place: Leesburg, VA   Age: 80 years
         Birth: 1904   Death: 1984/10/07   Burial: 1984/10/10
Site 10 Lorna S. Sweeney   Age: 70 years
         Birth: 1905   Death: 1975/08/23   Burial: 1975/08/26
         Place: Leesburg, VA   On stone with Thomas B. Sweeney

Lot: 990 Owner: Miscellaneous
Site 3   Jesse Anthony (Tony) Hawkins   Age: 29 years
         No stone   Death: 1976/11/19   Burial: 1976/11/23
         Cause: Motorcycle accident   Place: Leesburg, VA

Site 5　Richard A. Zimmerly　　Place: Arcola, VA　　Age: 34 years
　　　　Birth: 1954/12/20　　　 Death: 1989/09/18　　Burial: 1989/09/21
　　　　TS: Married Barbara L. Zimmerly June 20, 1981
Site 7　Herman F. Moran　　　 Place: Leesburg, VA　Age: 73 years
　　　　Birth: 1903　　　　　　 Death: 1976/05/17　　Burial: 1976/05/20
Site 8　Lizzie E. Moran　　　　 Place: Leesburg, VA　Age: 81 years
　　　　Birth: 1900　　　　　　 Death: 1981/11/25　　Burial: 1981/11/26
Site 12 Pamela Marie Murphy　　 Place: Leesburg, VA　Age: 14 years
　　　　Birth: 1961/09/04　　　 Death: 1976/05/27　　Burial: 1976/06/01

Lot: 991 Owner: Miscellaneous
Site 1　William O. (Billy) Hensley　　　　　　　　　 Age: 19 years
　　　　Birth: 1958　　　　　　 Death: 1977/08/29　　Burial: 1977/09/01
　　　　Cause: Gun Shot　　　　 Place: Leesburg, VA
Site 2　William O. Hensley　　　　　　　　　　　　　 Age: 66 years
　　　　Birth: 1912/02/16　　　 Death: 1979/01/12　　Burial: 1979/01/15
　　　　Cause: Heart　　　　　　Place: Leesburg, VA
Site 3　Della M. Hensley
　　　　Birth: 1919/07/20　　　 Death: 1992/03/18　　Burial: 1992/03/21
　　　　Place: Leesburg, VA　　 　　 On stone with William O. Hensley
Site 5　Milton B. Milburn　　　 Place: Sykesville, MD　Age: 70 years
　　　　Birth: 1907/07/11　　　 Death: 1977/12/20　　Burial: 1977/12/22
Site 7　Philip Brian Raflo　　　　　　　　　　　　　 Age: 23 years
　　　　Birth: 1954/07/28　　　 Death: 1977/09/01　　Burial: 1977/09/05
　　　　Cause: Auto Accident　　Place: CA
Site 8　Josephine Raflo Fagan　　　　　　　　　　　 Age: 36 years
　　　　Birth: 1949/01/16　　　 Death: 1985/11/26　　Burial: 1985/11/30
　　　　Cause: Auto Accident　　Place: Bluemont, VA　　　　　TS: Jo

Lot: 992 Owner: Miscellaneous
Site 1　Alfred H. Jewell　　　　Place: Leesburg, VA　Age: 73 years
　　　　Birth: 1914/11/21　　　 Death: 1988/04/09　　Burial: 1988/04/11
　　　　TS: Married R. Genevieve Jewell January 19, 1937
Site 3　Walter Scott Holland　　Place: Warrenton, VA
　　　　Birth: 1950/06/16　　　 Death: 1994/08/06　　Burial: 1994/08/10

Lot: 993 Owner: Miscellaneous
Site 1　Patricia Ann Miller Murphy　　　　　　　　　 Age: 46 years
　　　　Birth: 1940/07/08　　　 Death: 1986/08/19　　Burial: 1986/08/22
　　　　　　　　　　　　　　　　Place: Frederick, MD
Site 4　Shirley L. Lowe　　　　 Place: Manassas, VA　Age: 46 years
　　　　No stone　　　　　　　　Death: 1986/12/05　　Burial: 1986/12/08
Site 5　Margaret E. Scott　　　　　　　　　　　　　　 Age: 83 years
　　　　Birth: 1902/01/06　　　 Death: 1987/01/21　　Burial: 1987/01/31
　　　　Place: NC　　　　　　　　On stone with William James Scott
Site 5　William James Scott
　　　　Birth: 1900/12/25　　　 Death: 1982/09/21　　Burial: 1987/01/31

Lot: 994 Owner: Miscellaneous
Site 4 John William (Bill) Titus Jr.   Age: 31 years
        Birth: 1951/01/03   Death: 1982/04/02   Burial: 1982/04/07
        Place: Fairfax, VA   TS: First born son & brother
Site 7 Robert Amos Dawson   Place: Frederick, MD   Age: 47 years
        Birth: 1937/11/12   Death: 1985/04/27   Burial: 1985/05/01
Site 9 Robert Lee Peltonen   Place: Leesburg, VA   Age: 45 years
        No stone   Death: 1987/07/30   Burial: 1987/08/03
        Removed to Jackson Center, PA 1988/07/11
Site 10 Frank A. Herczyk Jr.   Place: Leesburg, VA   Age: 46 years
        Birth: 1938/05/26   Death: 1985/05/05   Burial: 1985/05/09

Lot: 995 Owner: Miscellaneous
Site 1 Harry F. Baker   Place: Manassas, VA   Age: 88 years
        Birth: 1897   Death: 1986/03/30   Burial: 1986/04/02
Site 2 Mattie May Baker   Place: Warrenton, VA   Age: 88 years
        Birth: 1899   Death: 1987/10/13   Burial: 1987/10/16
        TS: Married Harry F. Baker November 5, 1921
Site 3 Joseph E. Monaco Sr.   Place: Baltimore, MD   Age: 61 years
        Birth: 1912   Death: 1973/12/04   Burial: 1973/12/07
Site 5 Stephen Clapp   Place: Radford, VA   Age: 18 years
        Birth: 1956   Death: 1975/01/11   Burial: 1975/01/15
Site 8 Blanch A. Underwood   Age: 98 years
        Birth: 1890   Death: 1989/03/07   Burial: 1989/03/11
        Place: FL   On stone with George Y. Underwood
Site 9 George Y. Underwood   Place: FL   Age: 70 years
        Birth: 1902   Death: 1973/09/30   Burial: 1973/10/03
Site 10 Edward H. Blankenship Place: Leesburg, VA   Age: 77 years
        Birth: 1897   Death: 1973/10/25   Burial: 1973/10/27
Site 11 Bacil F. Blankenship   Age: 89 years
        Birth: 1898   Death: 1987/05/24   Burial: 1987/05/27
        On stone with Edward H. Blankenship

Lot: 996 Owner: Miscellaneous
Site 9 Madge Venable Barclay Place: Leesburg, VA   Age: 46 years
        Birth: 1927/03/23   Death: 1973/12/21   Burial: 1973/12/23
Site 10 Robert L. Dulaney   Place: Charlottesville, VA   Age: 82 years
        Birth: 1902/03/04   Death: 1984/11/07   Burial: 1984/11/09
        TS: MAJ GEN US Army WWII Korea
Site 11 Polly Venable Dulaney Place: Charlottesville, VA   Age: 86 years
        Birth: 1901/06/21   Death: 1988/03/30   Burial: 1988/04/02

Lot: 997 Owner: Miscellaneous
Site 1 Vivian Ann Fletcher   Place: Richmond, VA   Age: 20 years
        Birth: 1952   Death: 1972/12/01   Burial: 1972/12/04
Site 2 Frank Robert Fletcher TS: 73 years 3 months 9 days Age: 73 years
        Place: Leesburg, VA   Death: 1987/10/27   Burial: 1987/10/30
Site 7 William Henry Gamble Jr. Removed from Culpeper National Cemetery
        Birth: 1908/04/20   Death: 1967/12/16   Burial: 1971/08/26
        TS: Virginia LCDR USNR WWII

Site 9　Andrew King　　　　　　　　　　　　　　　　　　　Age: 87 years
　　　　Birth: 1888/07/10　　Death: 1976/02/26　　Burial: 1976/02/29
　　　　Place: Leesburg, VA　　　　　　　　　　　TS: Father, IOOF
Site 10　Wesley A. King　　　Place: Fairfax, VA　　　Age: 55 years
　　　　Birth: 1928　　　　　Death: 1983/11/03　　Burial: 1983/11/10
Site 10　John Andrew Madigan　Place: Washington, DC　　　Infant
　　　　　　　　　　　　　　　Death: 1985/10/23　　Burial: 1985/10/29
Site 12　James B. Madigan　　Place: Lucketts, VA
　　　　Birth: 1917/12/15　　Death: 1990/12/02　　Burial: 1990/12/05

Lot: 998　Owner: Miscellaneous
Site 1　Franklin Perry Miller　　　　　　　　　　　　　Age: 53 years
　　　　Birth: 1919/12/27　　Death: 1973/04/21　　Burial: 1973/04/25
　　　　Place: Puerto Rico　　　　　　TS: Virginia Sgt US Army WWII
Site 6　John P. Vinoski　　　　Place: Alexandria, VA　　　Age: 64 years
　　　　Birth: 1909　　　　　　Death: 1974/01/06　　Burial: 1974/01/09
Site 7　Theresa Kitts Tribby　　　　　　　　　　　　　Age: 67 years
　　　　Birth: 1913　　　　　　Death: 1980/01/21　　Burial: 1980/01/24
　　　　Cause: Heart　　　　　Place: Washington, DC

Lot: 999　Owner: Miscellaneous
Site 1　Francis (Frank) Marr　Place: Leesburg, VA　　　Age: 72 years
　　　　Birth: 1908/09/05　　Death: 1981/06/12　　Burial: 1981/06/15
Site 2　Helen Cockrill Marr　　　　　　　　　　　　　Age: 59 years
　　　　Birth: 1907/10/01　　Death: 1967/08/25　　Burial: 1967/08/27
　　　　Place: Leesburg, VA　　　　　　　　On stone with Francis Marr
Site 3　Walter Gibson Smith　Place: Leesburg, VA　　　Age: 64 years
　　　　Birth: 1903/07/24　　Death: 1968/03/31　　Burial: 1968/04/02
Site 4　Joseph Lee Smith　　Place: Round Hill, VA　　　Age: 79 years
　　　　Birth: 1908/10/03　　Death: 1988/06/20　　Burial: 1988/06/22
Site 5　Annie Ward Smith　　Place: Leesburg, VA　　　Age: 73 years
　　　　Birth: 1910/03/26　　Death: 1984/02/25　　Burial: 1984/02/28
　　　　On stone with Joseph Lee Smith
Site 7　John G. Atwell Sr.　　Place: Glen Burnie, MD　　Age: 59 years
　　　　Birth: 1907/10/13　　Death: 1966/10/17　　Burial: 1966/10/20
Site 8　Kathleen P. Atwell　Place: MD　On stone with John G. Atwell
　　　　Birth: 1920/02/18　　Death: 1992/07/22　　Burial: 1992/07/24
Site 9　Aldridge Y. Hitt　　　Place: Arlington, VA　　　Age: 65 years
　　　　Birth: 1901　　　　　Death: 1966/12/01　　Burial: 1966/12/04
Site 10　Flossie L. Hitt　　Place: East Brunswick, NJ　　Age: 86 years
　　　　Birth: 1904　　　　　Death: 1990/12/03　　Burial: 1990/12/05
Site 12　Florance May Woodyard　Place: Martinsburg, WV　Age: 79 years
　　　　Birth: 1899/12/20　　Death: 1979/01/03　　Burial: 1979/01/06

Lot: 1000　Owner: Miscellaneous
Site 1　Sean Patrick Hawley　　　　　　　　　　　　　Age: 27 years
　　　　Birth: 1955/11/19　　Death: 1983/07/02　　Burial: 1983/07/05
　　　　Cause: Cancer　　　　Place: Leesburg, VA
Site 3　Albert Clogan Bilson　Died: Leesburg, VA　　　Age: 77 years
　　　　Birth: 1891/10/17　　Death: 1968/10/17　　Burial: 1968/10/21

Site 4 William Brackett   Died: Winchester, VA   Age: 62 years
        No stone   Death: 1968/09/19   Burial: 1968/09/21
Site 5 Charles Edward Merchant   Died: Washington, DC   Age: 77 years
        Birth: 1908/07/01   Death: 1986/06/07   Burial: 1986/06/12
Site 7 Gerold Edward Luebben   Died: Washington, DC   Age: 74 years
        Birth: 1894/08/16   Death: 1967/11/12   Burial: 1968/01/01
Site 8 Ingeborg Wiener Luebben   Age: 93 years
        Birth: 1895/02/17   Death: 1989/04/17   Burial: 1989/04/20
        Died: Leesburg, VA   On stone with Gerold Edward Luebben
Site 10 Mrs. Velma Patricia Farmer   Age: 32 years
        Birth: 1935/12/23   Death: 1968/09/17   Burial: 1968/09/19
                                   Died: Harpers Ferry, MD
Site 11 Mr. Vivian Ruth Smith Rollins   Age: 87 years
        Birth: 1888/09/27   Death: 1975/12/17   Burial: 1975/12/20
                                   Died: Leesburg, VA
Site 12 Esther Marshall Rollins   Died: Leesburg, VA   Age: 81 years
        Birth: 1894/05/08   Death: 1975/08/24   Burial: 1975/08/26

Lot: 1001   Owner: Miscellaneous
Site 1 George S. Wagner   Died: Leesburg, VA
        Birth: 1913/11/10   Death: 1995/11/27   Burial: 1995/11/30
Site 2 Francis M. Wagner   Died: Leesburg, VA
        Birth: 1910/02/24   Death: 1995/09/15   Burial: 1995/09/18
Site 3 Edgar Stunkle   Died: Point of Rocks, MD   Age: 83 years
        Birth: 1885   Death: 1968/04/23   Burial: 1968/04/25
Site 4 Bessie S. Stunkle   Age: 91 years
        Birth: 1893   Death: 1984/05/12   Burial: 1984/05/15
        Died: Frederick, MD   On stone with Edgar Stunkle
Site 5 John William Tavenner   Died: Fairfax, VA   Age: 52 years
        Birth: 1919/10/09   Death: 1971/01/10   Burial: 1971/01/13
        TS: Virginia S Sgt 1874 Engr AVN BN WWII
Site 6 Edgar J. Herndon   Died: Staunton, VA   Age: 66 years
        Birth: 1904   Death: 1971/01/18   Burial: 1971/01/21
Site 7 Norman Lee Burton   Died: Atlanta, GA   Age: 85 years
        Birth: 1890/08/30   Death: 1976/01/02   Burial: 1976/01/06
Site 8 Ruth Van Waters Burton   Age: 73 years
        Birth: 1893/07/07   Death: 1967/07/20   Burial: 1967/07/24
        Died: Leesburg, VA   On stone with Norman Lee Burton
Site 9 Humphrey L. Ainsworth   Age: 56 years
        Birth: 1910   Death: 1967/07/16   Burial: 1967/07/19
        Cause: Heart   Died: Leesburg, VA
Site 11 Thomas Lewis Kent   Died: Manassas, VA
        Birth: 1911/07/16   Death: 1993/03/06   Burial: 1993/03/10
Site 12 Nellie Alberta Kent   Age: 42 years
        Birth: 1924/12/30   Death: 1967/05/07   Burial: 1967/05/10
        Died: Fairfax, VA   On stone with Thomas Lewis Kent

Lot: 1002   Owner: Miscellaneous
Site 1 Richard Lee Russell Sr.   Age: 73 years
        Birth: 1917/11/30   Death: 1991/07/13   Burial: 1991/07/16
        Died: FL   TS: US Army WWII
Site 2 Mrs. Catherine Elizabeth Russell   Age: 50 years
        Birth: 1917   Death: 1968/10/12   Burial: 1968/10/16
                                   Died: Manassas, VA
Site 4 Ada V. Detrick   Died: Charlottesville, VA
        Birth: 1897/07/30   Death: 1976/01/19   Burial: 1976/01/22
Site 5 Thomas W. Briggs   Died: Leesburg, VA   Age: 56 years
        Birth: 1911/04/06   Death: 1967/10/25   Burial: 1967/10/27
Site 7 Summerfield B. Tillett Jr. Died: Leesburg, VA   Age: 58 years
        Birth: 1909/11/01   Death: 1967/11/30   Burial: 1967/12/03
Site 8 Evelyn May Tillett   Died: Winchester, VA
        Birth: 1911/10/13   Death: 1993/12/18   Burial: 1993/12/20
Site 10 Benjamin F. Swart   Age: 50 years
        Birth: 1917/07/25   Death: 1968/01/27   Burial: 1968/01/29

Lot: 1003   Owner: Miscellaneous
Site   Frank Gordon Orrison Sr.
        Birth: 1917/03/06   Death: 1983/04/12
Site 1 Paul Bliss Baker   Died: Leesburg, VA   Age: 58 years
        Birth: 1911/03/23   Death: 1969/08/18   Burial: 1969/08/20
Site 2 Nellie Hellen Baker   Age: 56 years
        Birth: 1916/08/06   Death: 1973/09/24   Burial: 1973/09/27
        Died: Leesburg, VA   On stone with Paul Bliss Baker
Site 3 Jeffrey Gordon Orrison   Age: 18 years
        Birth: 1969/01/29   Death: 1987/12/19   Burial: 1987/12/23
        Died: Purcellville, VA   TS: "Cheify"
Site 4 Lynne Johnson Orrison   Died: Leesburg, VA
        Birth: 1942/03/09   Death: 1990/02/14   Burial: 1990/12/04
Site 5 Harry Garth Barnes   Died: Arlington, VA   Age: 56 years
        Birth: 1913   Death: 1969/08/25   Burial: 1969/08/27
Site 9 Wilbert Ezra Akers   Died: Leesburg, VA   Age: 68 years
        Birth: 1900/02/03   Death: 1969/06/27   Burial: 1969/06/29
Site 10 Ida Hedge Akers   Age: 72 years
        Birth: 1902/12/13   Death: 1975/11/09   Burial: 1975/11/12
        Died: Leesburg, VA   On stone with Wilbert Ezra Akers
Site 11 Johnny C. Rorrer   Age: 28 years
        Birth: 1941/03/01   Death: 1969/07/22   Burial: 1969/07/25
        Died: Warrenton, VA   TS: Virginia S Sgt. US Air Force

Lot: 1004   Owner: Miscellaneous
Site 1 Lorenzo D. Clemens Jr.   Died: Leesburg, VA
        Birth: 1909/06/28   Death: 1995/04/11   Burial: 1995/04/14
Site 3 David Carton Muncy   Cause: Auto Accident   Age: 42 years
        Birth: 1940/04/14   Death: 1987/09/21   Burial: 1987/09/24
        Died: Leesburg, VA TS: Married Joann P. Muncy December 22, 1962

Site 6 Mary Lee Hammes Wittman　　　　　　　　Age: 32 years
　　　　Birth: 1947/05/27　　　Death: 1979/07/29　　　Burial: 1979/08/01
　　　　　　　　　　　　　　　Died: Drakes Branch, VA
Site 7 John C. Frizzell　　　　Died: Baltimore, MD　　　Age: 51 years
　　　　Birth: 1917/03/15　　　Death: 1968/11/14　　　Burial: 1968/11/17
　　　　TS: North Carolina TEC 5 1 PRCHT TNG REGT WWII
Site 9 Samuel Irwin　　　　　　Died: Phoenixville, PA　　Age: 81 years
　　　　Birth: 1903/04/18　　　Death: 1984/10/17　　　Burial: 1984/10/20
Site 11 George H. Grimsley Jr.　Died: Paeonian Springs, VA　Age: 26 years
　　　　Birth: 1942/03/01　　　Death: 1968/12/16　　　Burial: 1968/12/19
Site 11 George H. (Tex) Grimsley　No stone　　　　　Age: 63 years
　　　　Died: Leesburg, VA　　Death: 1984/02/18　　　Burial: 1984/03/16
Site 11 Evelyn B. (Dorothy) Grimsley　No stone　　　　Age: 67 years
　　　　Died: Leesburg, VA　　Death: 1991/11/06　　　Burial: 1991/11/12
Site 12 Theodore Ashton Lunsford　Died: RI　　　　　Age: 58 years
　　　　Birth: 1911　　　　　　Death: 1970/03/20　　　Burial: 1970/03/23

Lot: 1005　　Owner: Miscellaneous
Site 1　Paul Snyder　　　　　　Died: Leesburg, VA　　　Age: 56 years
　　　　Birth: 1912/12/13　　　Death: 1969/04/24　　　Burial: 1969/04/27
Site 3　Elmer Stanley Orrison　Died: Fairfax, VA　　　　Age: 53 years
　　　　Birth: 1919/07/29　　　Death: 1973/01/25　　　Burial: 1973/01/27
Site 4　James C. Hammes　　　　　　　　　　　　　　　Age: 26 years
　　　　Birth: 1942　　　　　　Death: 1969/02/17　　　Burial: 1969/02/21
　　　　Died: Lakeland, FL　　　　On stone with George K. Hammes
Site 6　George K. Hammes　　　Died: Winchester, VA　　Age: 68 years
　　　　Birth: 1905　　　　　　Death: 1973/09/27　　　Burial: 1973/10/01
Site 7　Orville M. Muncy　　　Died: Leesburg, VA
　　　　Birth: 1901/09/28　　　Death: 1991/12/14　　　Burial: 1991/12/17
Site 8　Maude Agnes Muncy　　　Died: Leesburg, VA　　　Age: 61 years
　　　　Birth: 1907/10/01　　　Death: 1969/02/06　　　Burial: 1969/02/09
　　　　On stone with Orville M. Muncy
Site 11 George Thomas Brown　　Died: Leesburg, VA　　　Age: 69 years
　　　　Birth: 1899　　　　　　Death: 1968/12/18　　　Burial: 1968/12/20
Site 12 Della A. Brown　　　　　　　　　　　　　　　Age: 84 years
　　　　Birth: 1898　　　　　　Death: 1983/01/25　　　Burial: 1983/01/28
　　　　Died: Leesburg, VA　　　On stone with George Thomas Brown

Lot: 1006　　Owner: Miscellaneous
Site　　Anthony John Lomax　　Birth: 1943/05/05　　　Death: 1953/01/09
Site　　Christine Ann Lomax　　Birth: 1946/05/01　　　Death: 1982/11/17
Site 1　Bobby Jordan　　　　　No stone　　　　　　　Age: 19 years
　　　　Cause: Killed on farm　Death: 1969/10/11　　　Burial: 1969/10/13
Site 2　Raymond F. McKimmey　No stone　　　　　　　Age: 74 years
　　　　Died: Waterford, VA　　Death: 1990/06/03　　　Burial: 1990/06/07
Site 4　Raymond F. McKinney　Died: Lynchburg, VA　　Age: 12 years
　　　　Birth: 1956/08/11　　　Death: 1969/08/10　　　Burial: 1969/08/12
Site 5　Charles Adron Saunders　Died: Leesburg, VA　　Age: 60 years
　　　　Birth: 1908/09/26　　　Death: 1969/07/31　　　Burial: 1969/08/02

Site 6   Rebecca E. Bell Saunders   Age: 67 years
         Birth: 1911/06/26   Death: 1979/06/09
         On stone with Charles Adron Saunders
Site 7   Kenneth D. McCool   Died: Leesburg, VA   Age: 48 years
         Birth: 1940/01/08   Death: 1988/12/15   Burial: 1988/12/17
Site 9   John W. Minick   Died: Winchester, VA   Age: 44 years
         Birth: 1930   Death: 1974/09/19   Burial: 1974/09/21
Site 10 Mrs. Alice R. Minick   Age: 38 years
         Birth: 1931   Death: 1970/01/17   Burial: 1970/01/22
         Died: Ketron, VA   On stone with John W. Minick
Site 11 Sydney Evans Lomax   Died: Leesburg, VA   Age: 54 years
         Birth: 1915   Death: 1970/01/25   Burial: 1970/01/28

Lot: 1007   Owner: Miscellaneous
Site 1   Irvin V.D. Foote   Died: Leesburg, VA   Age: 69 years
         Birth: 1901   Death: 1970/06/13   Burial: 1970/06/16
         Michel Foote removed and buried with his Daddy.
Site 5   Ada M. Judd   Age: 68 years
         Birth: 1910/11/15   Death: 1979/01/14   Burial: 1979/01/17
         Died: Ashburn, VA   On stone with John R. Judd
Site 5   John R. Judd   Died: Ashburn, VA   Age: 77 years
         Birth: 1908/03/03   Death: 1985/05/07   Burial: 1985/05/10
Site 6   Thomas Moriarty   Died: Washington, DC   Age: 91 years
         Birth: 1896   Death: 1988/07/27   Burial: 1988/07/29
Site 7   Louis E. Beach   Age: 52 years
         Birth: 1917/10/14   Death: 1970/04/19   Burial: 1970/04/22
         Died: Washington, DC   TS: Virginia PFC US Army WWII
Site 10 George W. Gates   Age: 69 years
         Birth: 1905/11/11   Death: 1975/04/22   Burial: 1975/04/24
         Cause: Cancer   Died: Sterling Park, VA
Site 11 Kathryn D. Gates
         Birth: 1908/06/16   Death: 1994/12/23   Burial: 1994/12/27
         Died: Warsaw, VA   On stone with George W. Gates
Site 12 Katie E. Spann   Died: Bethesda, MD   Age: 83 years
         Birth: 1886   Death: 1970/04/02   Burial: 1970/04/06

Lot: 1008   Owner: Miscellaneous
Site 4   Gloria Lee Hinckle   Died: Leesburg, VA
         Birth: 1927/11/03   Death: 1991/04/23   Burial: 1991/04/26
         TS: Married Franklin M. Hinckle Sr. September 25, 1948
Site 7   Sylvan J. Crooker   Died: Leesburg, VA   Age: 81 years
         Birth: 1893/07/03   Death: 1974/11/24   Burial: 1974/11/27
Site 8   Arleigh T. Crooker   Age: 83 years
         Birth: 1895/03/23   Death: 1979/01/10   Burial: 1979/01/13
         Died: Leesburg, VA   On stone with Sylvan J. Crooker
Site 9   Barbara Crooker Talmadge Died: Leesburg, VA   Age: 46 years
         Birth: 1923   Death: 1970/03/12   Burial: 1970/03/14
         On stone with Sylvan J. Crooker and Arleigh T. Crocker
Site 10 John Oscar Boone   Died: Leesburg, VA   Age: 61 years
         Birth: 1912   Death: 1973/08/18   Burial: 1973/08/20

Site 12 Samuel Messina Beach Died: Leesburg, VA Age: 65 years
Birth: 1906 Death: 1971/07/15 Burial: 1971/07/17

Lot: 1009 Owner: Miscellaneous

Site 1 Clarence F. Flynn Died: Fairfax, VA Age: 79 years
Birth: 1900 Death: 1979/11/21 Burial: 1979/11/24

Site 2 Edith M. Flynn Age: 84 years
Birth: 1903 Death: 1987/04/30 Burial: 1987/05/04
Died: Front Royal, VA On stone with Clarence F. Flynn

Site 3 Elbert Hough Died: Leesburg, VA Age: 83 years
Birth: 1905 Death: 1989/06/07 Burial: 1989/06/10

Site 4 Mrs. Elizabeth C. Hough Age: 60 years
Birth: 1910 Death: 1970/11/20 Burial: 1970/11/24
Died: Leesburg, VA On stone with Elbert Hough

Site 5 Lester A. McClellan Age: 76 years
Birth: 1902 Death: 1979/03/30

Site 7 Theodore A. Schulz Died: Fairfax, VA Age: 69 years
Birth: 1903 Death: 1973/03/23 Burial: 1973/03/26

Site 8 Helen Charlotte Schulz Age: 63 years
Birth: 1906 Death: 1970/07/01 Burial: 1970/07/04
Died: Leesburg, VA On stone with Theodore A. Schulz

Site 9 Vernon L. Beggs Died: Burlington, WI Age: 95 years
Birth: 1894 Death: 1989/10/23 Burial: 1989/10/28

Site 10 Bessie Mae D. Beggs Age: 89 years
Birth: 1892 Death: 1981/11/03 Burial: 1981/11/06
Died: Leesburg, VA On stone with Vernon L. Beggs

Site 11 Bertha Pearce Age: 82 years
Birth: 1895/10/27 Death: 1977/12/06 Burial: 1977/12/09
Died: Arlington, VA On stone with Claude Pearce

Site 12 Claude Pearce Died: Arlington, VA Age: 74 years
Birth: 1894/01/09 Death: 1976/05/25 Burial: 1976/05/28

Lot: 1010 Owner: Miscellaneous

Site 1 John Smith Age: 63 years
Birth: 1907/01/08 Death: 1970/11/30 Burial: 1970/12/02
Died: Washington, DC TS: Born in England

Site 2 Dr. Lincoln Paul Ellis Died: Leesburg, VA Age: 83 years
Birth: 1887 Death: 1971/03/23 Burial: 1971/03/26

Site 3 Rhonda Joy Smith Died: Winchester, VA Age: 17 years
Birth: 1957 Death: 1974/01/26 Burial: 1974/01/29

Site 7 Clarence Ashby Fling Died: Leesburg, VA Age: 83 years
Birth: 1887 Death: 1971/01/09 Burial: 1971/01/11

Site 8 Clifford Ashby Fling Age: 50 years
Birth: 1933/05/31 Death: 1989/08/31 Burial: 1989/09/05
Died: Leesburg, VA On stone with Clarence Ashby Fling

Site 9 William U. Ashton Died: Round Hill, VA Age: 61 years
Birth: 1909 Death: 1971/02/20 Burial: 1971/02/23

Site 11 George Bryant Wertz Died: Clearwater, FL Age: 72 years
Birth: 1898 Death: 1971/04/10 Burial: 1971/04/14

Site 12 Ruth E. Wertz   Died: Leesburg, VA   Age: 87 years
Birth: 1901   Death: 1988/12/19   Burial: 1988/12/21

Lot: 1011   Owner: Miscellaneous
Site 3 Thomas Franklin Jackson   Died: Leesburg, VA   Age: 58 years
Birth: 1926/09/02   Death: 1984/11/18   Burial: 1984/11/23
Site 5 Thomas Edward Welsh   Age: 59 years
Birth: 1925/03/01   Death: 1984/11/13   Burial: 1984/11/16
Died: Washington, DC   TS: US Army
Site 6 Floyd L. Gooden III   Age: 21 years
Birth: 1961/12/28   Death: 1983/08/01   Burial: 1983/08/05
Died: Leesburg, VA   TS: "Dutch"
Site 11 Helen Veronica Kelly   Died: Sterling, VA   Age: 82 years
Birth: 1903   Death: 1985/09/12   Burial: 1985/09/16
Site 12 William A. Kelly Jr.   Age: 82 years
Birth: 1902/12/10   Death: 1985/06/30   Burial: 1985/07/04
Died: Sterling, VA   TS: Sgt. US Army WWII

Lot: 1012   Owner: Miscellaneous
Site 10 Ann Davies Rieley   Age: 64 years
Birth: 1930/12/21   Death: 1995/02/25   Burial: 1995/03/01
Died: PA   TS: "Chickie"
Site 11 E. David Seekford Jr.   Died: Chesapeake, VA
Birth: 1939/06/17   Death: 1993/01/01   Burial: 1993/06/05

Lot: 1013   Owner: Miscellaneous
Site   William Garrett Owen   TS: Lieutenant Commander
Birth: 1947/09/03   Death: 1993/04/15
Site 1 Garry Grant Owen   Died: Leesburg, VA   Age: 69 years
Birth: 1902/01/31   Death: 1971/03/07   Burial: 1971/03/10
Site 10 Richard Henry (Dick) Beales
Birth: 1925/02/23   Death: 1993/05/01   Burial: 1993/05/05
Died: Virginia Beach, VA   TS: US Army
Site 11 Mattie K. Ellis   Died: Beltsville, MD   Age: 52 years
Birth: 1923   Death: 1975/07/12   Burial: 1975/07/19
Site 12 Dale Beales   Died: Washington, DC   Age: 19 years
Birth: 1953   Death: 1973/11/26   Burial: 1973/11/29

Lot: 1014   Owner: Miscellaneous
Site 3 Alice Tyler Mills   Died: Leesburg, VA   Age: 82 years
Birth: 1903/01/15   Death: 1985/05/08   Burial: 1985/05/10
Site 7 Michael Phaethon Perinis   Age: 52 years
Birth: 1933/01/29   Death: 1985/06/05   Burial: 1985/06/10
Died: Washington, DC   TS: IMS 3 US Navy
Site 9 Roman Frank Yerovsek   Died: Leesburg, VA   Age: 63 years
Birth: 1922/03/22   Death: 1985/05/14   Burial: 1985/05/17
Site 11 Angela Nicole Yerovsek   Died: Richmond, VA
Birth: 1965/08/10   Death: 1994/05/29   Burial: 1994/06/02

Lot: 1015   Owner: Miscellaneous

Site 1   William T. Greenwade   Died: Leesburg, VA   Age: 71 years
         Birth: 1900   Death: 1971/10/04   Burial: 1971/10/07
Site 2   William G. Ballenger   Died: Leesburg, VA   Age: 70 years
         Birth: 1914   Death: 1985/07/07   Burial: 1985/07/10
Site 3   Alfred Leith Megeath   Died: Leesburg, VA   Age: 67 years
         Birth: 1909   Death: 1976/05/20   Burial: 1976/05/22
Site 4   Mary Hardesty Megeath   Age: 71 years
         Birth: 1910   Death: 1981/04/12   Burial: 1981/04/15
         Died: Leesburg, VA   On stone with Alfred Leith Megeath
Site 5   James B. Jennings   Died: Leesburg, VA   Age: 80 years
         Birth: 1891/01/19   Death: 1971/10/05   Burial: 1971/10/07
Site 6   Hattie E. Jennings   Age: 88 years
         Birth: 1889/05/30   Death: 1978/04/21   Burial: 1978/04/28
         Died: Leesburg, VA   On stone with James B. Jennings
Site 7   Louis Bartel   Died: Leesburg, VA   Age: 83 years
         Birth: 1899   Death: 1982/10/05   Burial: 1982/10/09
Site 8   Hannah E. Bartel   Age: 78 years
         Birth: 1893   Death: 1971/12/07   Burial: 1971/12/10
         Died: Fairfax, VA   On stone with Louis Bartel
Site 9   Harry Lucius Ritenour   Age: 57 years
         Birth: 1914/12/13   Death: 1972/08/10
Site 11 Robert W. Spence   Died: Fairfax, VA   Age: 71 years
         No stone   Death: 1971/12/11   Burial: 1971/12/14
Site 12 Ethel Altie Spence   Died: Fairfax, VA   Age: 73 years
         Birth: 1909   Death: 1983/01/30   Burial: 1983/02/03

Lot: 1017   Owner: Miscellaneous

Site 1   Leroy Wallace Thorpe   Age: 52 years
         Birth: 1920/04/17   Death: 1972/09/04
         TS: Virginia PFC 272 MIL Police Co. WWII
Site 2   Daniel Leroy Thorpe   Died: Martinsburg, WV
         Birth: 1948/02/02   Death: 1992/10/09   Burial: 1992/10/12
         TS: CPL US Marine Corps Vietnam
Site 3   Charles Henry Brady   Died: Leesburg, VA   Age: 69 years
         Birth: 1921/08/21   Death: 1991/03/19   Burial: 1991/03/22
Site 6   Mary Anne Newman   Died: Leesburg, VA
         Birth: 1924/03/10   Death: 1995/01/19   Burial: 1995/01/23
         TS: Married Stanley Newman November 27, 1965
Site 11 Raymond A. Jewell   Died: Leesburg, VA   Age: 75 years
         Birth: 1907/02/08   Death: 1982/07/21   Burial: 1982/07/23

Lot: 1018   Owner: Miscellaneous

Site 1   Jean Charles Chatel   Died: Washington, DC   Age: 66 years
         Birth: 1905   Death: 1971/12/29   Burial: 1972/01/03
Site 3   Clarence E. Hardy   Died: Leesburg, VA   Age: 80 years
         Birth: 1904   Death: 1985/04/22   Burial: 1985/04/25

Site 4 Mrs. Lena P. Hardy   Died: Leesburg, VA   Age: 63 years
        Birth: 1908   Death: 1972/02/24   Burial: 1972/02/26
        IB:Mrs. Clarence Hardy   On stone with Clarence E. Hardy
Site 6 Mary Lucille Cheney   Died: Annandale, VA   Age: 61 years
        Birth: 1910   Death: 1972/03/08   Burial: 1972/03/10
Site 7 John S. Howser   Died: Paeonian Springs, VA   Age: 74 years
        Birth: 1897/12/31   Death: 1972/03/30   Burial: 1972/04/01
Site 8 Ethel Virginia Howser   Age: 68 years
        Birth: 1911/03/29   Death: 1980/03/15   Burial: 1980/03/17
        Died: Leesburg, VA   On stone with John S. Howser
Site 9 Frank S. Howser   Died: Leesburg, VA   Age: 66 years
        Birth: 1924/09/29   Death: 1991/06/25   Burial: 1991/06/28

Lot: 1019   Owner: Miscellaneous
Site 3 Heidi Theresa Billy   Age: 34 years
        Birth: 1938/07/28   Death: 1973/11/03   Burial: 1973/11/06
        Died: Fairfax, VA   On stone with Joel John Billy
Site 3 Joel John Billy   Died: Reston, VA
        Birth: 1936/07/21   Death: 1987/12/10   Burial: 1987/12/12
Site 5 Brenda Sue Woodward   Died: Winchester, VA   Age: 20 years
        Birth: 1952/03/25   Death: 1972/10/23   Burial: 1972/10/25
Site 10 Albert C. Cooper   Age: 59 years
        Birth: 1913   Death: 1972/09/16
        TS: Married Evelyn M. Cooper 1944

Lot: 1020   Owner: Miscellaneous
Site 1 Richard John Klyn   Died: Leesburg, VA   Age: 90 years
        Birth: 1894   Death: 1986/05/12   Burial: 1986/05/15
Site 2 Dorothy Darroch Klyn
        Birth: 1904/09/26   Death: 1994/06/28   Burial: 1994/07/01
        Died: Watson. VA   On stone with Richard John Klyn
Site 3 Amos H. Brady
        Birth: 1918/07/29   Death: 1995/07/31   Burial: 1995/08/02
        Died: MD   On stone with Norris W. Brady
Site 4 Norris W. Brady   Age: 58 years
        Birth: 1924   Death: 1982/02/09   Burial: 1982/02/11
        Died: Front Royal, VA   On stone with Amos H. Brady
Site 9 C. Browning Walter
        Birth: 1911   Death: 1986/04/21   Burial: 1986/04/24

Lot: 1022   Owner: Miscellaneous
Site 1 Towney R. Grimes Sr.   Died: Leesburg, VA   Age: 72 years
        Birth: 1919   Death: 1991/08/27   Burial: 1991/08/30
Site 2 Mary Ellen Grimes   Age: 47 years
        Birth: 1925   Death: 1972/09/29
        On stone with Towney R. Grimes Sr.
Site 7 Charles C. Shugars   Died: Winchester, VA   Age: 74 years
        Birth: 1910   Death: 1985/03/30   Burial: 1985/04/02
Site 9 John Freed Scheetz   Died: Leesburg, VA   Age: 77 years
        Birth: 1895/03/13   Death: 1973/01/29   Burial: 1973/01/31

Site 11 Gladys A. Allen   Age: 80 years
         Birth: 1892   Death: 1973/08/17   Burial: 1973/08/20
         Died: Fairfax, VA   On stone with G. Dudley Allen
Site 11 G. Dudley Allen   Age: 90 years
         Birth: 1890   Death: 1981/11/30   Burial: 1981/12/03
Site 12 Wilma E. Moatz   Died: LaGrange Park, IL   Age: 52 years
         Birth: 1921/12/18   Death: 1974/04/03   Burial: 1974/04/06

Lot: 1023   Owner: Miscellaneous
Site 1   Larry D. Simpson   Died: Fairfax, VA   Age: 18 years
         Birth: 1965/07/01   Death: 1984/02/28   Burial: 1984/03/02
Site 2   Lonie John Phillips Died: Leesburg, VA   Age: 82 years
         Birth: 1905   Death: 1988/07/25   Burial: 1988/07/27
Site 7   Lloyd McCord   Died: Arlington, VA   Age: 84 years
         Birth: 1896   Death: 1980/10/10   Burial: 1980/10/13
Site 8   Hilda O. McCord   Age: 84 years
         Birth: 1898   Death: 1983/07/01   Burial: 1983/07/05
         Died: IN   On stone with Lloyd McCord
Site 9   Esther Perry Stewart Died: Leesburg, VA
         Birth: 1899/10/26   Death: 1990/12/30   Burial: 1991/01/03
         TS: Mother of Barbara Stewart Fred
Site 10 William Thomas Clagett Rogers   Age: 70 years
         Birth: 1875/05/10   Death: 1930/12/11   Burial: 1985/09/03
                              Died: Leesburg, VA
Site 11 Mrs. Anna Ferguson Rogers   Age: 89 years
         Birth: 1883/10/16   Death: 1973/02/17   Burial: 1973/02/20
         Died: Leesburg, VA   TS: Daughter of J.S. & N.G. Ferguson.
         Wife of William Thomas Clagett Rogers

Lot: 1024   Owner: Miscellaneous
Site 2   Mary Catherine Schreiner Died: Leesburg, VA   Age: 68 years
         Birth: 1919/07/18   Death: 1988/06/28   Burial: 1988/07/02
Site 3   Elizabeth A. Harvich Died: Leesburg, VA   Age: 79 years
         Birth: 1909   Death: 1988/12/19   Burial: 1988/12/22
Site 4   Robert F. Lynn   Died: Leesburg, VA
         Birth: 1929/06/03   Death: 1993/04/11   Burial: 1993/04/15
Site 6   Florence Carlson Carper Died: Leesburg, VA   Age: 77 years
         Birth: 1917/05/13   Death: 1988/05/24   Burial: 1988/05/28

Lot: 1025   Owner: Miscellaneous
Site 1   Samuel Aston Wallace Died: Leesburg, VA   Age: 78 years
         Birth: 1899/02/02   Death: 1977/09/10   Burial: 1977/09/12
Site 2   Ruby Maffett Wallace   Age: 83 years
         Birth: 1903/05/21   Death: 1987/01/29   Burial: 1987/02/02
         Died: Berryville, VA   On stone with Samuel Aston Wallace

Lot: 1026   Owner: Miscellaneous
Site 1   Betty H. Benford   Age: 63 years
         Birth: 1923   Death: 1986/04/26   Burial: 1986/05/03
         Cause: Cancer   Died: Washington, DC

Site 2	Ethel G. Honicon	Died: Washington, DC	Age: 90 years
	Birth: 1898	Death: 1988/12/24	Burial: 1988/12/31
Site 3	Claude Honicon	Died: Leesburg, VA	Age: 84 years
	Birth: 1890	Death: 1975/04/10	Burial: 1975/04/16
Site 4	Mervin Francis Calhoun	Died: Manassass, VA	Age: 35 years
	Birth: 1946/10/13	Death: 1982/06/14	Burial: 1982/06/19
	Cause: Suicide		TS: Sgt. US Air Force Vietnam
Site 5	Hencil M. Calhoun	Died: Winchester, VA	Age: 74 years
	Birth: 1915/08/12	Death: 1989/10/18	Burial: 1989/10/20
Site 9	Arthur W. Allison	Died: Leesburg, VA	Age: 63 years
	Birth: 1912	Death: 1976/05/02	Burial: 1976/05/05
Site 10	Olive M. Allison		Age: 77 years
	Birth: 1910	Death: 1987/10/27	Burial: 1987/10/30
	Died: Leesburg, VA		On stone with Arthur W. Allison

Lot: 1027   Owner: Miscellaneous

Site 4	Ethyl Valerie Focer	Cause: Run over by truck	Age: 19 years
	Birth: 1966	Death: 1985/08/16	Burial: 1985/08/20
Site 6	Donald F. Holliday	Died: Alexandria, VA	Age: 51 years
	Birth: 1934	Death: 1985/08/14	Burial: 1985/08/16

Lot: 1028   Owner: Miscellaneous

Site 3	Margaret M. Lynn	Died: Leesburg, VA	
	Birth: 1907/10/04	Death: 1992/01/04	Burial: 1992/01/07
Site 6	Charles W. Lynn	Died: Leesburg, VA	Age: 48 years
	Birth: 1927/02/15	Death: 1975/03/20	Burial: 1975/03/24
Site 7	Eugene Lee Warner	Died: Leesburg, VA	Age: 48 years
	Birth: 1924/04/23	Death: 1973/02/12	Burial: 1973/02/14
Site 7	Patricia Ann Tillett Warner Malloy		Age: 63 years
	Birth: 1928/02/14	Death: 1991/12/01	Burial: 1991/12/07
		Died: SC	

Lot: 1029   Owner: Miscellaneous

Site 1	Col. Lowell Meeker Riley		Age: 78 years
	Birth: 1892/06/14	Death: 1971/01/22	Burial: 1971/01/25
	Died: Washington, DC		TS: Colonel, USA
Site 2	Elizabeth Brooks Riley	Died: Leesburg, VA	Age: 81 years
	Birth: 1902/02/22	Death: 1983/07/03	Burial: 1983/07/05
Site 3	Olive Brooks	Died: Berryville, VA	No stone
		Death: 1985/01/22	Burial: 1985/01/26

Lot: 1030   Owner: Miscellaneous

Site 9	Theodore R. Heskett Sr.	Died: Leesburg, VA	Age: 79 years
	Birth: 1905/11/29	Death: 1985/11/24	Burial: 1985/11/27
Site 10	Grace M. Heskett	Died: Leesburg, VA	Age: 52 years
	Birth: 1914/09/23	Death: 1967/04/15	Burial: 1967/04/18
Site 11	Florence H. Welch	Died: Winchester, VA	
	Birth: 1932/01/20	Death: 1993/11/16	Burial: 1993/11/19

Lot: 1031   Owner: Miscellaneous
Site 3   Roland B. Flint   Died: Leesburg, VA   Age: 76 years
         Birth: 1910/04/14   Death: 1986/04/21   Burial: 1986/04/24
Site 4   Margie D. Flint
         Birth: 1912/11/16   Death: 1975/12/22   Burial: 1995/12/27
         Died: Herndon, VA   On stone with Roland B. Flint
Site 10 Katherine N. Costello   Died: Leesburg, VA   Age: 68 years
         Birth: 1921/11/11   Death: 1990/01/05   Burial: 1990/01/08

Lot: 1032 E Owner: H.M. Bradshaw   Purchased: 1954/10/09
Site 7   Hugh M. Bradshaw   Age: 2 years
         Birth: 1918/10/19   Death: 1920/09/06   Burial: 1920/09/09
         Cause: Deocolitis   TS: Son of H.M. & S.I. Bradshaw
Site 7   Hugh M. Bradshaw   Died: Venice, FL   Age: 76 years
         Birth: 1891/07/09   Death: 1965/01/09   Burial: 1965/01/14
Site 8   Infant Helen Margaret Bradshaw   Age: 1 day
         Birth: 1923/03/08   Death: 1923/03/09   Burial: 1923/03/11
         TS: Daughter of H.M. & L.J. Bradshaw
Site 8   Mrs. Lydia J. Bradshaw   Age: 87 years
         Birth: 1881/04/23   Death: 1968/07/12   Burial: 1968/07/17
         Died: Fort Dodge, IA   On stone with Hugh M. Bradshaw

Lot: 1032 W Owner: William Thomas Williams   1953/06/04
Site 1   William Thomas Lamar Williams   Age: 52 years
         Birth: 1906   Death: 1958/02/06   Burial: 1958/02/08
         Cause: Cancer   Died: Leesburg, VA
Site 2   Mary Virginia Williams Died: Leesburg, VA   Age: 77 years
         Birth: 1880   Death: 1958/03/08   Burial: 1958/03/11
Site 3   Elizabeth Glasscock   Died: Leesburg, VA   Age: 81 years
         Birth: 1909   Death: 1990/10/15   Burial: 1990/10/18
         No stone
Site 5   John T. Quesenberry   Died: Richmond, VA   Age: 81 years
         Birth: 1893   Death: 1974/12/13   Burial: 1974/12/16
Site 6   Ethel Howell   Died: Leesburg, VA   Age: 85 years
         Birth: 1883   Death: 1970/03/12   Burial: 1970/03/14

Lot: 1033 E Owner: Anita F. Daniel & John Orr Daniel   1955/09/12
Site 10 John William Daniel   Died: Leesburg, VA   Age: 60 years
         Birth: 1894/12/08   Death: 1955/09/10   Burial: 1955/09/10
Site 10 Mary A. Daniel   Died: Washington, DC   Age: 7 days
         Birth: 1977   Death: 1977/12/31   Burial: 1977/12/31
Site 12 Anita Frasier Daniel   Age: 82 years
         Birth: 1892/03/31   Death: 1974/05/08   Burial: 1974/05/10
         Died: Catonsville, MD   On stone with John William Daniel

Lot: 1033 W Owner: Myron Jewell   Purchased: 1957/10/16
Site 1   Janet Virginia Jewell   Age: 17 years
         Birth: 1939/11/07   Death: 1957/10/22
Site 2   Myron R. Jewell   No stone   Age: 75 years
         Died: Leesburg, VA   Death: 1979/06/29   Burial: 1979/07/03

Site 3   Rosabell G. Jewell   Died: Leesburg, VA   Age: 82 years
         Birth: 1909/04/06   Death: 1992/03/09   Burial: 1992/03/11
Site 5   James Randolph Jewell   Age: 61 years
         Birth: 1930/04/24   Death: 1992/02/12   Burial: 1992/02/15
         Died: Baltimore, MD   TS: PFC US Army Korea

Lot: 1034   Owner: Clarence G. & Gilbert H. Jewell   1959
Site 6   Peggy Anne Sasser   Died: Sterling, VA
         Birth: 1941/07/17   Death: 1993/09/13   Burial: 1993/09/16
Site 7   Gilbert Hunter Jewell   Died: Fairfax, VA   Age: 73 years
         Birth: 1901   Death: 1974/09/15   Burial: 1974/09/17
Site 8   Lina Lillian Jewell   Died: Washington, DC   Age: 62 years
         Birth: 1897   Death: 1959/01/03   Burial: 1959/01/05
         Cause: Brain Tumor   On stone with Gilbert Hunter Jewell
Site 9   Bartie C. Peyton   Died: Leesburg, VA
         Birth: 1916   Death: 1972/12/21   Burial: 1972/12/24

Lot: 1035 E   Owner: Mrs. Melvie H. Savopoulos   1966/11/05
Site 7   Steve Savopoulos   Died: Leesburg, VA   Age: 72 years
         Birth: 1894/04/18   Death: 1966/11/06   Burial: 1966/11/08
Site 9   William S. Savopoulos   Died: Rochester, MN   Age: 54 years
         Birth: 1929/07/09   Death: 1983/10/06   Burial: 1983/10/09

Lot: 1035 W Owner: Mr. & Mrs. James H. Symington   1963/11/14
Site 1   Powers Symington   Age: 21 years
         Birth: 1942/07/31   Death: 1963/11/03   Burial: 1963/11/05
         Cause: Suicide   Died: Leesburg, VA   TS: "Jim"
Site 2   Miss Diedre Huntington Symington   Age: 21 years
         Birth: 1945/09/27   Death: 1967/06/11   Burial: 1967/06/13
         Cause: Jump from plane   Died: Stormville, NY   TS: "Dee Dee"
Site 3   James Huntington Symington   Age: 60 years
         Birth: 1913/04/27   Death: 1974/06/26   Burial: 1974/09/23
                                   Died: Leesburg, VA

Lot: 1036   Owner: Miscellaneous
Site 1   Donald F. Larson   Died: Leesburg, VA   Age: 53 years
         Birth: 1928   Death: 1981/03/25   Burial: 1981/03/28
Site 3   Berle Margaret Rush   Died: Huntington Beach, CA Age: 72 years
         Birth: 1909   Death: 1981/10/28   Burial: 1981/11/07
Site 4   William B. Douglas   Died: Arlington, VA   Age: 81 years
         Birth: 1900   Death: 1982/05/05   Burial: 1982/05/08
Site 5   Charles Roland Atwell   Age: 78 years
         Birth: 1901/09/17   Death: 1980/05/29   Burial: 1980/06/01
         Died: Leesburg, VA   TS: USAAF No. 14140063 WWII
Site 6   Virginia Wilson Atwell   Died: Leesburg, VA   Age: 83 years
         Birth: 1904/01/30   Death: 1987/04/29   Burial: 1987/05/01
         On stone with Carles Roland Atwell

Lot: 1037   Owner: Mrs. Betty Chamblin Smoot
**   & Ernestine F. Chamblin   Purchased: 1965/09/08**
Site 4   Ernestine Fox Chamblin   Died: Leesburg, VA
         Birth: 1909/02/08   Death: 1994/11/05   Burial: 1994/11/08
Site 5   Frank Purcell Smoot III Died: Leesburg, VA   Age: 7 hours
         Birth: 1961/08/29   Death: 1961/08/30   Burial: 1961/08/31
         TS: Son of Betty C. & Frank P. Smoot Jr.

Lot: 1038 E Owner: Anne J. Moore
Site 10 John W. Moore Jr.   Age: 57 years
         Birth: 1918/08/18   Death: 1975/12/11   Burial: 1975/12/15
         Died: Woodbury, NJ   TS: Sgt. US Army WWII

Lot: 1038 W Owner: Robert L. Galleher   Purchased: 1970/10/29
Site 3   Robert Lee Galleher   Died: Falls Church, VA   Age: 72 years
         Birth: 1906/07/13   Death: 1978/10/29   Burial: 1978/10/31

Lot: 1039   Owner: John William Fiske   Purchased: 1978/10/17
Site 1   Charles W. Fiske   Died: Leesburg, VA   Age: 85 years
         Birth: 1904/02/24   Death: 1989/10/21   Burial: 1989/10/24
Site 2   Elizabeth May Fiske   Age: 71 years
         Birth: 1906/06/29   Death: 1978/02/18   Burial: 1978/02/21
         Died: Winchester, VA   On stone with Charles W. Fiske

Lot: 1040 E Owner: Mrs. John J. Payette   Purchased: 1970/09/08
Site 7   Richard C. Payette   Age: 1 year
         Birth: 1934/02/08   Death: 1936/02/06   Burial: 1970/10/02
         Died: Washington, DC   Removed from Mt. Olivet Cemetery
Site 8   John Jay Payette
         Birth: 1892/08/24   Death: 1948/08/01   Burial: 1970/10/02
         Died: Washington, DC   Removed from Mt. Olivet Cemetery
Site 9   Dorothy Crandall Payette Died: Leesburg, VA   Age: 74 years
         Birth: 1909/04/06   Death: 1983/06/23   Burial: 1983/06/27
Site 10 Robert C. Payette   Died: Fairfax, VA   Age: 44 years
         Birth: 1936/06/01   Death: 1980/02/24   Burial: 1980/02/26

Lot: 1040 W Owner: Mrs. Charles Newton   Purchased: 1982/03/08
Site 1   Charles E. Newton Jr.   Died: Leesburg, VA   Age: 49 years
         Birth: 1924/07/01   Death: 1973/10/16   Burial: 1973/10/19
         TS: "Shag", Anzio '44, TEC 5 US Army

Lot: 1041   Owner: Mrs. Melcinia H. Burbank
**   & Richard W. Burbank   Purchased: 1967/08/26**
Site 1   Richard Willoughby Burbank Sr.   Age: 61 years
         Birth: 1905/09/20   Death: 1967/08/22   Burial: 1967/08/26
                                  Died: Leesburg, VA
Site 2   Melcinia Burbank Heffelfinger   Age: 67 years
         Birth: 1908   Death: 1975/12/07   Burial: 1977/05/23
Site 12 William Lawson Cowart   Died: Hamilton, VA   Age: 70 years
         Birth: 1906/11/26   Death: 1973/08/29   Burial: 1973/09/01

Lot: 1042 E Owner: Mrs. Clellie Campbel Daniel   1969/02/17
Site 8   Harry Camel Daniel   Died: Leesburg, VA   Age: 40 years
         Birth: 1931/11/14   Death: 1972/02/12   Burial: 1972/02/15
Site 9   Harry C. Daniel   Age: 72 years
         Birth: 1897/01/07   Death: 1969/02/11   Burial: 1969/02/13
         Cause: Heart Attack   Died: Leesburg, VA
Site 10 Clellie C. Daniel   Age: 89 years
         Birth: 1899/06/14   Death: 1988/12/10   Burial: 1988/12/14
         Died: Leesburg, VA   On stone with Harry C. Daniel

Lot: 1042 W Owner: Marion F. Havener   Purchased:
Site 1   John R. Havener   Died: Warrenton, VA   Age: 66 years
         Birth: 1911/08/09   Death: 1978/06/09   Burial: 1978/06/12
Site 2   Marion F. Havener   Died: Leesburg, VA
         Birth: 1921/01/04   Death: 1991/06/19   Burial: 1991/06/22
         TS: Married John R. Havener September 11, 1938

Lot: 1043 E Owner: Miscellaneous
Site 9   Rev. Emory Staley Ellmore   Died: Piney River, VA
         Birth: 1915/03/11   Death: 1994/04/13   Burial: 1994/04/16

Lot: 1043 W Owner: Mrs. Naomi F. Bell   Purchased: 1969/03/03
Site 1   William T. Bell   Age: 50 years
         Birth: 1919/01/31   Death: 1969/04/02   Burial: 1969/04/05
         Cause: Cancer of Head   Died: Leesburg, VA
Site 2   Naomi F. Bell Edelen   Died: Prince Frederick, MD   Age: 56 years
         Birth: 1923/05/17   Death: 1980/05/13   Burial: 1980/05/15
         TS: Married William T. Bell April 26, 1941; Edelen not on tombstone
Site 3   William Thomas Bell II   Age: 23 years
         Birth: 1957/04/07   Death: 1980/09/05   Burial: 1980/09/10
         Cause: Auto Accident   Died: Hagerstown, MD

Lot: 1044 E Owner: G.B. Wolford   Purchased: 1965/03/07
Site 9   Virginia B. Wolford   Died: Winchester, VA   Age: 46 years
         Birth: 1918/05/23   Death: 1965/04/30   Burial: 1965/05/03
Site 11 Gillespie Blaine Wolford Died: Round Hill, VA   Age: 93 years
         Birth: 1892/09/04   Death: 1986/01/16   Burial: 1986/01/20
Site 12 Elsie P. Wolford   Birth: 1897/12/10   Death: 1979/06/10

Lot: 1044 W Owner: Miscellaneous
Site 2   Alexander D. Marriott   Died: GA   Age: 76 years
         Birth: 1886/02/13   Death: 1962/09/10   Burial: 1973/11/03
Site 2   Lillian L. Marriott   Age: 86 years
         Birth: 1887/07/12   Death: 1973/07/08   Burial: 1973/11/03
         On stone with Alexander D. Marriott
Site 3   Kalil D. Ackad   Died: Leesburg, VA   Age: 65 years
         Birth: 1907   Death: 1973/02/22   Burial: 1973/02/26
Site 4   Rose G. Ackad   Died: Leesburg, VA   No dates on stone
         Birth: 1905/06/04   Death: 1992/12/22   Burial: 1992/12/31

Site 5 Harold L. Lowry Died: Hamilton, VA Age: 75 years
Birth: 1913 Death: 1989/01/26 Burial: 1989/01/29
Site 6 Mrs. Beatrice M. Cortez Lowry Age: 56 years
Birth: 1912 Death: 1971/10/14 Burial: 1971/10/17
Died: Leesburg, VA On stone with Harold L. Lowry

Lot: 1045   Owner: Miscellaneous
Site 1 Donald E. Womeldorph Died: Wilmington, DE
Birth: 1918/05/24 Death: 1994/08/23 Burial: 1994/08/29

Lot: 1046 E Owner: Mrs. Edmund Noyes   Purchased: 1968/07/22
Site 11 Catherine L. Noyes Age: 81 years
Birth: 1908/10/18 Death: 1974/05/14 Burial: 1974/05/16
Died: Leesburg, VA On stone with Maj. Edmund Noyes
Site 12 Maj. Edmund Noyes Died: Leesburg, VA Age: 62 years
Birth: 1905/10/13 Death: 1968/05/18 Burial: 1968/05/21

Lot: 1046 W Owner: Elizabeth V. Stub & Ellen B. Spelman
                            Purchased: 1968/02/12
Site 2 Joseph Quayle Bristow Age: 85 years
Birth: 1884/03/05 Death: 1969/11/01 Burial: 1969/11/03
Died: Arlington, VA TS: Father
Site 3 Rosamond Ingalls Bristow Age: 84 years
Birth: 1887/12/08 Death: 1972/05/28 TS: Mother
Site 4 Rose Belknap Ingalls
Birth: 1872 Death: 1948/09/12 Burial: 1991/11/21
Disinterment from Oakwood Cemetery, Falls Church, VA
Site 5 Elizabeth V. Stub Died: Williamsburg, VA
Birth: 1918/10/19 Death: 1991/11/02 Burial: 1991/11/06
Site 6 Ione Ingalls Stub TS: Mother Age: 78 years
Birth: 1889/01/04 Death: 1967/12/02 Burial: 1968/02/22
Removed from Oakwood Cemetery, Falls Church

Lot: 1047   Owner: Richard A. Rogers   Purchased: 1957/06/22
Site 1 Child of Rogers Age: 20 hours
Birth: 1957/06/20 Death: 1957/06/21
TS: Infant son of Richard A. Rogers & Sally T. Rogers

Lot: 1048   Owner: Ernest W. Smith   Purchased: 1949/04/05
Site 5 Mary B. Smith Age: 82 years
Birth: 1903/09/27 Death: 1987/11/12 Burial: 1987/11/14
Died: Sterling, VA On stone with Ernest W. Smith Sr.
Site 6 Ernest W. Smith Sr. Died: Sterling, VA Age: 86 years
Birth: 1899/07/22 Death: 1985/10/28 Burial: 1985/10/30
Site 11 Gladys M. Smith Age: 22 years
Birth: 1926/05/20 Death: 1949/04/05 Burial: 1949/04/07

Lot: 1049 E Owner: Louis B. Saunders   Purchased: 1952/03/06
Site 7 John Robert Grimes Age: 72 years
Birth: 1879/04/07 Death: 1952/03/06 Burial: 1952/03/08

Site 8 Lena L. Grimes   Age: 92 years
        Birth: 1888/02/27   Death: 1980/03/28   Burial: 1980/03/31
        Died: Leesburg, VA   On stone with John R. Grimes
Site 10 Louise B. Saunders   Died: Leesburg, VA   Age: 81 years
        Birth: 1901/04/27   Death: 1982/12/11   Burial: 1982/12/14
Site 11 Margaret N. Saunders   Age: 71 years
        Birth: 1907/11/25   Death: 1979/04/24
        TS: Married Louis B. Saunders February 14, 1925
Site 12 Infant Saunders   Death: 1957/06/30
        TS: Infant son of D.L. & B.L. Saunders

Lot: 1049 W Owner: Miscellaneous
Site 3 Frank B. Williams   Died: Leesburg, VA   Age: 95 years
        Birth: 1882/02/05   Death: 1977/12/20   Burial: 1977/12/22
Site 4 Mary Ellen Williams   Age: 74 years
        Birth: 1887/05/05   Death: 1961/12/14   Burial: 1961/12/16
        Died: Leesburg, VA   On stone with Frank B. Williams
Site 5 Carl Pack Peters
        Birth: 1903/01/19   Death: 1949/08/10   Burial: 1949/08/13
        TS: Ohio CPL 312 AAF Bomb Squadron WWII
Site 5 Anna Peters Bobbitt Died: Akron, OH   Age: 74 years
        Birth: 1889/12/22   Death: 1966/07/31   Burial: 1966/08/04
Site 5 Harold Bobbitt   Age: 76 years
                             Death: 1990/02/22   Burial: 1990/03/23
        Cause: Pneumonia   Died: Cleveland, OH   No stone

Lot: 1050   Owner: Alfred W. Williams   Purchased: 1964/09/10
Site 2 Lottie P. Williams   Died: Aldie, VA   Age: 71 years
        Birth: 1915/03/07   Death: 1987/03/04   Burial: 1987/03/07
        TS: Married Alfred W. Williams April 15, 1936
Site 7 Ted Byron Williams   Died: Fairfax, VA   Age: 22 years
        Birth: 1941/12/06   Death: 1964/09/06   Burial: 1964/09/10
        TS: Virginia L. CPL US Marine Corps
Site 8 James Pack Peters   Died: Manassas, VA   Age: 77 years
        Birth: 1894/01/19   Death: 1971/02/19   Burial: 1971/02/21
        TS: West Virginia PVT US Army WW I

Lot: 1051   Owner: Fulton Want   Purchased: 1962/01/25
Site 1 Fulton Want Sr.   Died: Leesburg, VA   Age: 77 years
        Birth: 1902/02/04   Death: 1980/01/20   Burial: 1980/01/22
Site 3 Dorothy Elliotte Want Died: Leesburg, VA   Age: 85 years
        Birth: 1904/01/13   Death: 1989/12/30   Burial: 1990/01/03
Site 4 Elliotte Cullen Want Died: Arlington, VA   Age: 50 years
        Birth: 1928/06/11   Death: 1979/02/01   Burial: 1979/02/04

Lot: 1054   Owner: Rogers Fred   Purchased: 1956/05/18
Site 1 Hugh Wharton Fred   Age: 67 years
        Birth: 1878   Death: 1946   Burial: 1947/06/27
Site 2 Mrs. Ruby W. Fred   Age: 91 years
        Birth: 1876/11/16   Death: 1968/01/26

Site 8   Barbara S. Fred   Died: Leesburg, VA   Age: 49 years
         Birth: 1933/03/11   Death: 1982/06/07   Burial: 1982/06/10

Lot: 1055   Owner: William T. & Edgar F. Burch   Purchased:
Site 6   Edgar Francis Burch   Died: Chicago, IL
         Birth: 1899/05/07   Death: 1968/07/06   Burial: 1972/10

Lot: 1058   Owner: William T. & Edgar F. Burch   1952/08/04
Site 7   Dr. William Thompson Burch   Age: 75 years
         Birth: 1899/05/07   Death: 1975/04/23   Burial: 1975/04/26
                                     Died: Leesburg, VA
Site 8   Olga Crandall Burch   Died: Leesburg, VA   Age: 66 years
         Birth: 1907/12/07   Death: 1974/03/17   Burial: 1974/03/19

Lot: 1059   Owner: Arthur M. & Mary B. Godfrey   1964/07/01
Site 2   Margaret B. Mason   Died: CA   No stone
         Birth: 1911/09/29   Death: 1994/12/29   Burial: 1995/01/03
Site 3   Josephine Ott Bourke   Died: L.C.H. Leesburg, VA   Age: 79 years
         Birth: 1884   Death: 1964/ 07/02   Burial: 1964/07/04
Site 4   Anne Rosaleen Bourke   Died: Fairfax Co., VA   Age: 77 years
         Birth: 1914   Death: 1991/11/05   Burial: 1991/11/07

Lot: 1060   Owner: Dr. Robert A. Orr   Purchased: 1981/01/12
Site 3   Mary Frances Orr   Age: 54 years
         Birth: 1926/03/09   Death: 1980/11/15   Burial: 1980/11/18
         Cause: Cancer   Died: Leesburg, VA

Lot: 1062   Owner: Arthur M. & Mary B. Godfrey   1964/07/01
Site 11 Arthur Morton Godfrey   Died: NY
         Birth: 1903   Death: 1983   Burial: 1984/11/20

Lot: 1063   Owner: Beverly Marshall Norris   1967/03/09
Site 7   Roland S. Marshall   Died: Washington, DC   Age: 82 years
         Birth: 1888/04/02   Death: 1970/08/09   Burial: 1970/08/12
Site 8   Katharine Tennent Marshall   Age: 90 years
         Birth: 1884/03/14   Death: 1974/10/25   Burial: 1974/10/28
                                     Died: McLean, VA
Site 11 Raymond Alan Norris   Died: McLean, VA   Age: 70 years
         Birth: 1897/03/16   Death: 1967/06/25   Burial: 1967/06/27
         TS: New Hampshire Major Army Air Force WWII

Lot: 1064   Owner: M. Louise Connelly   Purchased: 1956/06/15
Site 4   James Carrington Foster   Age: 53 years
         Birth: 1902   Death: 1956/06/15   Burial: 1956/06/15
         Cause: Cancer   Died: Washington, DC
Site 5   Katherine E. Foster   Died: FL   Age: 70 years
         Birth: 1901   Death: 1981/09/18   Burial: 1981/09/21
         On stone with James Carrington Foster
Site 10 Marie Louise Connelly   Age: 75 years
         Birth: 1899   Death: 1975/07/22   Burial: 1975/07/24
         Cause: Cancer   Died: Leesburg, VA

Lot: 1065 E Owner: Clinton Ballenger   Purchased: 1954/07/24
Site 8 Clinton Ballenger   Died: Leesburg, VA   Age: 85 years
        Birth: 1880   Death: 1966/01/15   Burial: 1966/01/18
Site 9 India G. Ballenger   On stone with Clinton Ballenger Age: 69 years
        Birth: 1885   Death: 1954/07/22
Site 11 Mrs. Mildred J. Payne Died: Leesburg, VA   Age: 84 years
        Birth: 1903   Death: 1988/01/05   Burial: 1988/01/07
        On stone with Ewell J. Payne Sr.
Site 12 Ewell J. Payne Sr.   Died: Leesburg, VA   Age: 68 years
        Birth: 1897   Death: 1966/08/12   Burial: 1966/08/15

Lot: 1065 W Owner: Robert Gray   Purchased: 1955/12/31
Site 6 Robert Edward Lee Gray Jr.   Age: 11 years
        Birth: 1944   Death: 1955/12/20   Burial: 1955/12/21
                               Died: Leesburg, VA

Lot: 1066   Owner: Dr. John D. Wynkoop   Purchased: 1955/08/04
Site 1 Mrs. Nancy Wynkoop Warner   Age: 66 years
        Birth: 1901/02/22   Death: 1967/04/07   Burial: 1967/04/09
        Died: Leesburg, VA
Site 2 James C. Wynkoop Jr.   Age: 57 years
        Birth: 1899/10/17   Death: 1956/12/15
Site 3 Dr. James Cartwright Wynkoop Sr.   Age: 88 years
        Birth: 1867/01/09   Death: 1955/08/03   Burial: 1955/08/04
        Died: Leesburg, VA   TS: MD
Site 4 Bessie deButts Wynkoop Died: Leesburg, VA   Age: 94 years
        Birth: 1872/10/04   Death: 1967/06/25   Burial: 1967/06/27
Site 6 Harold B. Walker   Age: 75 years
        Birth: 1906/04/02   Death: 1976/03/06   Burial: 1976/03/11
        Died: Martinsburg, WV   TS: Sgt. US Army WWII
Site 7 Thomas Kelley Wynkoop Sr.   Age: 50 years
        Birth: 1908/04/13   Death: 1958/06/02   Burial: 1958/06/04
                               Died: Washington, DC
Site 9 Dr. John deB. Wynkoop   Age: 77 years
        Birth: 1905/07/13   Death: 1981/11/15   Burial: 1981/11/18
        Cause: Heart   Died: Leesburg, VA

Lot: 1067 E Owner: Mrs. Geneva Phillips   Purchased: 1954/12/14
Site   Geneva A. Phillips   On stone with Arnold I. Phillips
        Birth: 1919/05/31   Death: 1990/03/30
Site 7 Silas D. Phillips   Age: 86 years
        Birth: 1897   Death: 1983/05/08   Burial: 1983/05/10
        Cause: Cancer   Died: Leesburg, VA
Site 11 Arnold I. Phillips   Birth: 1907/06/24   Death: 1954/12/12

Lot: 1067 W Owner: Silas D. Phillips   Purchased: 1954/12/14
Site 1 Odie Phillips Yowell   Died: Winchester, VA
        Birth: 1927/04/07   Death: 1994/04/19   Burial: 1994/04/22

141

Lot: 1068   Owner: Charles M. Graham   Purchased: 1968/06/28
Site 1   Earl David Updegrove   Died: Arlington, VA   Age: 69 years
         Birth: 1919/10/31   Death: 1989/09/30   Burial: 1989/10/03
Site 3   Charles M. Graham Sr. Died: Purcellville, VA
         Birth: 1897/11/21   Death: 1993/07/31   Burial: 1993/08/03
Site 4   Kathleen A. Graham   Died: Leesburg, VA
         Birth: 1902/02/24   Death: 1995/09/12   Burial: 1995/09/15
         On stone with Charles M. Graham Sr.

Lot: 1069 E Owner: Lawrence S.
           & Elizabeth Howard Hutchinson, Jr.   **1965/09/29**
Site 12 Baby Hutchison   No stone   Age: 3 hours
         Died: Leesburg, VA   Death: 1968/09/17   Burial: 1968/09/19

Lot: 1069 W Owner: Arthur J. Abell   Purchased:
Site 1   William Dennis Abell   Died: Arlington, VA   Age: 29 years
         Birth: 1951/11/09   Death: 1976/11/21   Burial: 1976/11/24
Site 3   Dixie M. Abell   Age: 75 years
         Birth: 1918   Death: 1993/11/02   Burial: 1993/11/05
         Died: Fairfax, VA   On stone with Arthur J. Abell
Site 5   Arthur J. Abell Sr.   Died: Arlington, VA   Age: 63 years
         Birth: 1922   Death: 1985/01/19   Burial: 1985/01/23
Site 6   Holly Sue Abell   No stone   Age: 8 days
         Died: Arlington, VA   Death: 1966/03/22   Burial: 1966/03/24

Lot: 1070   Owner: Miscellaneous
Site 6   Velora Smith   No stone   Age: 73 years
         Died: Leesburg, VA   Death: 1976/03/07   Burial: 1976/03/10
Site 7   Joseph O. Gandolph   Died: Martnsburg, WV   Age: 56 years
         Birth: 1913/08/31   Death: 1970/07/27   Burial: 1970/07/29
         TS: Maryland TEC 4 Co A 3186 SIG SVC BN WWII
Site 8   Stanley D. Herrell   Died: Somerset, PA
         Birth: 1932/10/03   Death: 1993/12/29   Burial: 1993/12/31
Site 11 Pauline Willson Gunn   Died: Leesburg, VA   Age: 58 years
         Birth: 1921/09/30   Death: 1980/05/04   Burial: 1980/05/07

Lot: 1071   Owner: Miscellaneous
Site 3   John W. Shetter   Died: Sterling, VA   Age: 93 years
         Birth: 1894/09/14   Death: 1987/10/04   Burial: 1987/10/07
Site 4   Viola B. Shetter
         Birth: 1903/11/03   Death: 1995/05/25   Burial: 1995/05/28
         Died: Sterling, VA   On stone with John W. Shetter

Lot: 1072   Owner: Miscellaneous
Site 2   Marjorie A. Feeney   Died: Fairfax, VA   Age: 65 years
         Birth: 1922/03/12   Death: 1987/03/30   Burial: 1987/04/02
Site 4   Eugene Douglas Goff   Died: Leesburg, VA   Age: 49 years
         Birth: 1937/08/29   Death: 1987/04/05   Burial: 1987/04/08

Site 6 Joseph O. Pepin   Age: 75 years
        Birth: 1914/08/15   Death: 1990/05/04   Burial: 1991/05/15
        Died: Sterling, VA   TS: CPL US Army WWII
Site 7 Irene Virginia (Moore) Lay   Age: 81 years
        Birth: 1898/05/29   Death: 1979/12/09   Burial: 1979/12/12
        Died: Leesburg, VA   TS: Born in TN
Site 9 Rudolph F. Keyes   Age: 64 years
        Birth: 1922/03/19   Death: 1986/09/29   Burial: 1986/10/03
        Died: Martinsburg, WV   TS: US Army WWII; POW; Purple Heart
Site 10 Thomas L. Keyes   Age: 42 years
        Birth: 1939/10/08   Death: 1982/08/23   Burial: 1982/08/27
        Cause: Cancer   Died: Leesburg, VA
Site 11 Lee Thomas Keyes
        Birth: 1919/03/31   Death: 1992/03/07   Burial: 1992/03/11
        TS: Constitutional Officer State of VA, Loudoun Co.; TEC 5 US
        Army WWII

Lot: 1073   Owner: Miscellaneous
Site 11 Jack Ellis Grant   Age: 74 years
        Birth: 1915/03/07   Death: 1989/10/25   Burial: 1989/10/29
        Died: Mannassas, VA   TS: Born Cincinnati, OH

Lot: 1074   Owner: Miscellaneous
Site 1 Donald C. Steadman   Died: Leesburg, VA   Age: 50 years
        Birth: 1927/05/15   Death: 1976/06/15   Burial: 1976/06/17

Lot: 1075   Owner: Frederick McLean Bugher   1962/10/03
Site 3 Henry Treat Chittenden   Age: 50 years
        Birth: 1893/07/27   Death: 1944/03/31   Burial: 1944/04/05
Site 9 John Young Bassell   Cause: Heart Failure   Age: 75 years
        Birth: 1847/06/23   Death: 1922/07/08   Burial: 1922/07/10
Site 10 Mrs. Rebecca Gray Benedict Bassell   Age: 72 years
        Birth: 1850/09/26   Death: 1922/09/30   Burial: 1922/10/01
        Cause: Apoplexy

Lot: 1077   Owner: Frederick McLean Bugher   1962/10/03
Site 5 Henrietta Benedict Bassell Bugher   Age: 86 years
        Birth: 1874/04/11   Death: 1960/11/28   Burial: 1960/12/01
                               Died: FL
Site 6 Frederick McLean Bugher   Age: 83 years
        Birth: 1901/11/15   Death: 1984/03/27   Burial: 1984/04/09
                               Died: Miami, Dade Co., FL

Lot: 1079   Owner: Mr. & Mrs. James B. Anderson   1954/08/09
Site 3 Bessie Roberta McCarthy   Age: 72 years
        Birth: 1885/07/03   Death: 1957/10/24   TS: Mother
Site 4 Peggy McCarthy   Age: 41 years
        Birth: 1913/03/03   Death: 1954/08/05   TS: Sister

Site 6　Charles Raymond McCarthy　　　　　　　　　Age: 56 years
　　　　Birth: 1904/11/22　　Death: 1961/04/20　　Burial: 1961/04/23
　　　　Died: New York　　　　　　　　　　　　　　TS: Brother
Site 8　James B. Anderson　　Died: Leesburg, VA
　　　　Birth: 1905/06/06　　Death: 1993/02/05　　Burial: 1993/02/08
Site 9　Edythe E. Anderson　　　　　　　　　　　　Age: 66 years
　　　　Birth: 1907/04/02　　Death: 1973/11/15　　Burial: 1973/11/17
　　　　Died: Leesburg, VA　　　　On stone with James B. Anderson

Lot: 1080　Owner: Miscellaneous
Site 1　Clifton Register Kirby　　　　　　　　　　　Age: 37 years
　　　　Birth: 1912/04/06　　Death: 1949/12/25　　Burial: 1949/12/28
Site 6　Anna Mae Simon　　　Died: Falls Church, VA　Age: 70 years
　　　　Birth: 1914　　　　　Death: 1985/05/16　　Burial: 1985/05/20
Site 7　Henry R. Bishop Sr.　Died: Waterford, VA　　Age: 73 years
　　　　Birth: 1903　　　　　Death: 1976/08　　　　Burial: 1976/08/09
Site 8　Genevieve K. Bishop　　　　　　　　　　　　Age: 80 years
　　　　Birth: 1908　　　　　Death: 1988　　　　　Burial: 1988/09
　　　　Died: Leesburg, VA　　　　On stone with Henry R. Bishop Sr.

Lot: 1081　Owner: Miscellaneous
Site 3　Mary E. Davis　　　　Died: Winchester, VA　Age: 80 years
　　　　No stone　　　　　　Death: 1972/01/01　　Burial: 1972/01/04
Site 4　Roger I. Moffett　　　Died: Arlington, VA　　Age: 78 years
　　　　Birth: 1891/11/08　　Death: 1970/08/14　　Burial: 1970/08/18
Site 5　Margaret C. Moffett　　　　　　　　　　　　Age: 75 years
　　　　Birth: 1885/08/07　　Death: 1962/02/04　　Burial: 1962/02/06
　　　　Died: Arlington, VA　　　　On stone with Roger I. Moffett
Site 6　Roger P. Moffett　　　Died: Arlington, VA　　Age: 70 years
　　　　Birth: 1918/08/31　　Death: 1989/01/15　　Burial: 1989/01/18
　　　　On stone with Roger I. Moffett and Margaret C. Moffett
Site 10 Eileen Hogan Mahoney　Died: Washington, DC　Age: 61 years
　　　　Birth: 1918　　　　　Death: 1980/03/24　　Burial: 1980/03/29
　　　　TS: Married Bernard J. Mahoney May 18, 1940
Site 10 Bernard J. Mahoney　Died: Leesburg, VA
　　　　Birth: 1918/10/31　　Death: 1994/10/16　　Burial: 1994/10/19
Site 11 Eva Hogan Turner　　　　　　　　　　　　　Age: 77 years
　　　　Birth: 1893/12/24　　Death: 1971/11/02　　Burial: 1971/11/04
　　　　Died: Hyattsville, MD　　　On stone with Righter Turner
Site 12 Righter Turner　　　　Died: Arlington, VA　　Age: 50 years
　　　　Birth: 1905/10/14　　Death: 1956/02/04　　Burial: 1956/02/05

Lot: 1082 E Owner: Estate of George H. Musgrave　　1954/04/21
Site 7　Bess D. Ridley Musgrave　　　　　　　　　　Age: 90 years
　　　　Birth: 1894/08/23　　Death: 1984/11/30　　Burial: 1984/12/03
　　　　Died: Leesburg, VA　　　TS: Born Southhampton Co, VA
Site 8　George Harrison Musgrave　　　　　　　　　Age: 69 years
　　　　Birth: 1884/07/12　　Death: 1954/04/21　　Burial: 1954/04/23
　　　　Died: Leesburg, VA　　TS: MD. Major US Army Medical Corps
　　　　Born in Southhampton Co., VA

Site 11 Nancy Musgrave Phillips
Birth: 1929/02/07   Death: 1993/07/02   Burial: 1993/07/06
Died: Leesburg, VA   TS: Born in Leesburg, Loudoun Co., VA

Lot: 1083   Owner: Miscellaneous
Site 2 Helen Moore Williams
Birth: 1918/09/03   Death: 1991/09/10   Burial: 1991/09/12
Died: Leesburg, VA   On stone with Winslow Williams
Site 2 Winslow Williams   Died: Leesburg, VA
Birth: 1913/01/10   Death: 1993/02/19   Burial: 1993/02/23
Site 8 Edouard J. Fath   Age: 59 years
Birth: 1926   Death: 1985/10/29   Burial: 1985/11/01
Died: Bluemont, VA   TS: US Navy WWII
Site 10 Stanley Hinman   Died: Leesburg, VA   Age: 93 years
Birth: 1889   Death: 1982/09/08   Burial: 1982/09/10
Site 11 Annie V. Hinman   Age: 74 years
Birth: 1891   Death: 1966/03/22   Burial: 1966/03/27
Died: Ditchley, VA   On stone with Stanley Hinman

Lot: 1084 E   Owner: Mr. & Mrs. Lloyd B. Wilson   1960/12/01
Site 7 William Harrison Triplett   Died: Washington, DC
Birth: 1912/06/13   Death: 1993/07/02   Burial: 1993/07/11
Site 8 Martha Wilson Triplett
Birth: 1917/09/18   Death: 1994/04/05   Burial: 1994/04/12
Died: MD   On stone with William Harrison Triplett
Site 9 Karl Haus Michelet   Age: 83 years
Birth: 1904/04/03   Death: 1987/09/03   Burial: 1987/09/05
Site 11 Bruce F. Johnston   Age: 73 years
Birth: 1912   Death: 1986/07/21   Burial: 1986/07/28
Site 12 Madge W. Johnston   Died: Washington, DC   77 years
Birth: 1885   Death: 1962/09/22   Burial: 1962/09/26

Lot: 1084 W   Owner: Miscellaneous
Site 2 Rev. Frank Hazlett Moss Jr.   Age: 54 years
Birth: 1909/02/08   Death: 1963/12/19   Burial: 1963/12/21
Died: Leesburg, VA
Site 4 Frances Elizabeth Hutchison   Age: 91 years
Birth: 1886/08/27   Death: 1978/02/03   Burial: 1978/02/07
Died: Bethesda, MD
Site 5 Mary Ellen Hutchison   Died: Bethesda, MD   Age: 89 years
Birth: 1884/09/15   Death: 1973/10/03   Burial: 1973/11/06
Site 6 James Walter Hutchison   Died: Montgomery Co., MD   Age: 88 years
Birth: 1899/08/28   Death: 1987/10/04   Burial: 1987/10/07

Lot: 1085 E   Owner: Louis F. & Mary W. Atwell   1954/02/27
Site 7 Louis F. Atwell   Died: Leesburg, VA   Age: 79 years
Birth: 1888   Death: 1968/05/08   Burial: 1968/05/11
Site 8 Mary Waters Atwell   Age: 77 years
Birth: 1912/10/04   Death: 1989/10/10   Burial: 1989/10/13
Died: Leesburg, VA   On stone with Louis F. Atwell

Lot: 1085 WOwner: L.S. Hutchison   Purchased: 1954/05/07
Site 3   Lawrence S. Hutchison Sr.   Age: 76 years
         Birth: 1900/01/26   Death: 1976/06/08   Burial: 1976/06/10
                                  Died: Leesburg, VA
Site 4   Elizabeth Howser Hutchison   Age: 66 years
         Birth: 1909/07/10   Death: 1975/12/27   Burial: 1975/12/29
                                  Died: Leesburg, VA
Site 5   Nell Cabell Hutchison   Died: Berryville, VA   Age: 102 years
         Birth: 1888/07/07   Death: 1990/02/25   Burial: 1990/02/27
Site 6   Granville Randolph Hutchison   Age: 59 years
         Birth: 1903/02/06   Death: 1962/12/25   Burial: 1962/12/28
                                  Died: Leesburg, VA

Lot: 1086   Owner: Coleman C. Gore & Robert R. Smith
Site 4   Robert Rumley Smith   Age: 60 years
         Birth: 1920/01/09   Death: 1980/09/30   Burial: 1980/10/01
         Cause: Suicide   Died: Leesburg, VA
Site 5   Elizabeth Gore Smith   Died: Leesburg, VA   Age: 52 years
         Birth: 1924/01/15   Death: 1976/11/27   Burial: 1976/11/29
         TS: Married Robert Rumley Smith September 25, 1942
         Parents of Betti, Bob
Site 6   Mabel Rumley Smith   Died: Annapolis, MD   Age: 77 years
         Birth: 1901/11/24   Death: 1979/02/04   Burial: 1979/02/06
         TS: Mother of Robert Rumley Smith & William Clyde Smith Jr.
Site 10 Coleman C. Gore   Age: 79 years
         Birth: 1899/10/19   Death: 1979/03/07
Site 11 Lucy Jackson Gore   Age: 72 years
         Birth: 1900/03/18   Death: 1972/07/07
         TS: Wife of Coleman C. Gore; Mother of John Coleman, Elizabeth
         Payne & Raymond Earl
Site 12 John Coleman Gore   Removed from Lebon, TN   Age: 2 years
         Birth: 1922/02/09   Death: 1924/02/02   Burial: 1977/12/22

Lot: 1087   Owner: Miscellaneous
Site 2   Audrey Beatty   Died: Reston, VA   Age: 62 years
         Birth: 1927/01/14   Death: 1989/03/19   Burial: 1989/03/22
Site 7   Aileen Beatty Willoughby Died: Arlington, VA   Age: 66 years
         Birth: 1898   Death: 1966/01/17   Burial: 1966/01/19
Site 8   Jessica Corrine Lowe   Age: 78 years
         Birth: 1900/10/02   Death: 1990/03/16   Burial: 1990/03/19
         Died: Alexandria, VA   On stone with Preston Hamilton Lowe
Site 9   Preston Hamilton Lowe   Died: Arlington, VA   Age: 80 years
         Birth: 1904/02/17   Death: 1984/05/12   Burial: 1984/05/16
Site 12 Agnes H. Carlson   Died: Leesburg, VA   Age: 75 years
         Birth: 1890/07/28   Death: 1966/03/08   Burial: 1966/03/11

Lot: 1088   Owner: Miscellaneous
Site 1   Michael A. Cooper   Died: Bethesda, MD   Age: 20 years
         Birth: 1966/09/23   Death: 1987/09/14   Burial: 1987/09/19

Site 2　Edwin E. Beaver　　　　　　　　　　　　　　　　Age: 69 years
　　　　Birth: 1917/06/19　　Death: 1987/06/09　　Burial: 1987/06/13
　　　　Cause: Heart　　　　Died: Fairfax, VA
Site 3　Anna G. Beaver
　　　　Birth: 1923/03/28　　Death: 1994/09/15　　Burial: 1994/09/19
　　　　Died: Leesburg, VA　　　　On stone with Edwin H. Beaver
Site 4　Carroll F. Schaub　　Died: FL　　　　　　Age: 75 years
　　　　Birth: 1900/06/15　　Death: 1975/07/20　　Burial: 1975/07/25
Site 5　Lilian H. Schaub　　Died: FL　　　　　　Age: 67 years
　　　　Birth: 1903/09/25　　Death: 1973/01/05　　Burial: 1973/01/09
Site 6　John Lacey Harvey　　　　　　　　　　　　Age: 30 years
　　　　　　　　　　　　　　Death: 1954/07/24　　No stone
Site 7　Louis Morgan Wharton　　　　　　　　　　Age: 58 years
　　　　Birth: 1902/08/02　　Death: 1961/06/07　　Burial: 1961/06/09
　　　　Died: Leesburg, VA　　　TS: Virginia HA 2 US Navy WW I
Site 9　Charles H. Jenkins　　Died: Leesburg, VA
　　　　Birth: 1906/08/19　　Death: 1995/04/10　　Burial: 1995/04/13
Site 10 Edith V. Jenkins　　Died: Winchester, VA　　No stone
　　　　Birth: 1911/04/18　　Death: 1993/01/01　　Burial: 1993/01/04
Site 11 Edward S. Rakes　　Died: Hamilton, VA　　Age: 90 years
　　　　Birth: 1897　　　　　Death: 1988/12/04　　Burial: 1988/12/06
Site 12 Cathrine M. Rakes　　　　　　　　　　　　Age: 51 years
　　　　Birth: 1910　　　　　Death: 1961/05/28　　Burial: 1961/05/31
　　　　Died: Washington, DC　　　On stone with Edward S. Rakes

Lot: 1089　Owner: Miscellaneous
Site 9　Ruth Fowler Johnston Dickson　　　　　　Age: 37 years
　　　　Birth: 1923/06/01　　Death: 1960/07/13　　Burial: 1960/07/16
　　　　Cause: Cancer　　　　Died: LCH, Leesburg, VA
　　　　TS: Mother of Elizabeth, Ann & Jane

Lot: 1090 E Owner: George G. & Geraldine Fairall
Site 8　Geraldine Fairall　　　　　　　　　　　　Age: 70 years
　　　　Birth: 1906/10/28　　Death: 1979/08/14　　Burial: 1979/08/16
　　　　Died: Leesburg, VA　　　TS: Daughter of Frances Rhea
Site 9　Frances Hooper Shelby Rhea　　　　　　　Age: 89 years
　　　　Birth: 1881/11/04　　Death: 1971/08/22　　Burial: 1971/08/23
　　　　Died: Leesburg, VA　　TS: Born at "East Lake" Jackson Co NC
　　　　Daughter of Thomas Hillman Hooper & Luzenia Adeline Randolph
　　　　Stevens. Mother of Geraldine Hooper Holcombe Fairall. Grandmother
　　　　of Joan Hooper Holcombe Polen.
Site 12 Virginia Fairall　　Died: Leesburg, VA　　Age: 81 years
　　　　Birth: 1909/03/11　　Death: 1990/08/27　　Burial: 1990/08/30

Lot: 1090 W Owner: Mrs. George R. Galleher　　Purchased:
Site 1　George Raymond Galleher
　　　　Birth: 1914/08/08　　Death: 1957/01/30

Lot: 1091 E   Owner: Mr. & Mrs. Elmer C. Myers   1963/01/16
Site 7   Michael Allen Jenkins   Died: Baltimore, MD
         Birth: 1971/11/04   Death: 1992/08/25   Burial: 1992/08/28
Site 8   Michelle Lee Jenkins   Cause: Stillborn   Died: Silver Spring, MD
                                 Death: 1976/04/21   Burial: 1976/04/23
Site 9   Elmer C. Myers   Died: Montgomery, MD   Age: 69 years
         Birth: 1905/06/18   Death: 1975/05/06   Burial: 1975/05/09

Lot: 1091 W Owner: Robert M. Harris   Purchased: 1964/01/09
Site 1   Robert M. Harris   Died: Leesburg, VA   Age: 60 years
         Birth: 1904/07/02   Death: 1964/07/13   Burial: 1964/07/16
Site 3   Eliza V. Harris   On stone with Robert M. Harris   63 years
         Birth: 1913/10/02   Death: 1917/02/20

Lot: 1092   Owner: Miscellaneous
Site   John Franklin Kincaid Jr., MD
         Birth: 1917/05/09   Death: 1945/04/12
         Memorial TS: Lt. U.S.N.; Lost in the Pacific
Site 1   Infant of J. F. Kincaid   Death: 1919/08/18
         TS: Infant child of J.F. & N.L. Kincaid
Site 1   John Franklin Kincaid   Died: Woodstock, VA   Age: 85 years
         Birth: 1894/06/15   Death: 1979/07/10   Burial: 1979/07/12
Site 2-3 Mrs. Nan Lin Anderson Kincaid   Age: 70 years
         Birth: 1894/08/04   Death: 1965/07/29   Burial: 1965/08/01
         Died: Leesburg, VA   BP:Mrs. John Kincaid
Site 12 Katherine Hawthorne   No stone   Age: 72 years
         Died: Leesburg, VA   Death: 1964/09/10   Burial: 1964/09/12

Lot: 1093 E   Owner: Hampton E. Burton   Purchased:
Site 11 William R. Burton   Died: Frederick, MD   Age: 54 years
         Birth: 1936/01/05   Death: 1990/06/12   Burial: 1990/06/15
Site 12 Hampton E. Burton Jr.   Age: 19 years
         Birth: 1943/11/02   Death: 1962/11/06   Burial: 1962/11/08
         Cause: Auto Accident   Died: Arlington Hosp. Arlington, VA

Lot: 1093 W Owner: Mrs. Ruth Reed Grimes   Purchased:
Site 1   Samuel Houston Grimes Jr.   Age: 62 years
         Birth: 1896/10/28   Death: 1958/05/20   Burial: 1959/05/23
                                 Died: Washington, DC
Site 3   Ruth S. Grimes   Age: 85 years
         Birth: 1898/04/20   Death: 1984/01/10   Burial: 1984/01/12
         Died: Leesburg, VA   On stone with Samuel H. Grimes
Site 4   Peggy L. Wallace   Died: Leesburg, VA   Age: 67 years
         Birth: 1914/11/28   Death: 1984/07/24

Lot: 1094   Owner: Miscellaneous
Site 1   Robert Graham Steadman Died: Leesburg, VA   Age: 68 years
         Birth: 1901/08/18   Death: 1969/09/16   Burial: 1969/09/18
Site 2   Dixie D. Steadman   Died: Leesburg, VA   Age: 74 years
         Birth: 1903/07/11   Death: 1978/01/19   Burial: 1978/01/22

Site 9 Ruth Virginia Mason   Died: Hamilton, VA   Age: 16 years
        Birth: 1948/08/02   Death: 1965/06/28   Burial: 1965/07/01

Lot: 1095 E Owner: Robert W. & Odie M. Ryan   1949/10/04
Site 8   Millicent P. Ryan   Died: Arlington, VA   Age: 62 years
         Birth: 1921   Death: 1984/02/17   Burial: 1984/02/20
Site 10 Robert William Ryan   Died: Arlington, VA   Age: 75 years
         Birth: 1877   Death: 1953/02/08   Burial: 1953/02/09
Site 11 Odie Margaret Ryan   Died: Alexandria, VA   Age: 77 years
         Birth: 1887   Death: 1964/10/12   Burial: 1964/10/14
         On stone with Robert William Ryan
Site 12 Henry Preston Ryan   Age: 39 years
         Birth: 1914   Death: 1954/04/18

Lot: 1095 W Owner: Miscellaneous
Site 1 Kenneth Brady Rollins Died: Fairfax, VA   Age: 52 years
        Birth: 1936/01/16   Death: 1988/08/28   Burial: 1988/08/31
Site 4 Mary B. Rollins   Died: Leesburg, VA   Age: 77 years
        Birth: 1909/03/03   Death: 1987/01/07   Burial: 1987/01/10
Site 5 Charles H. Brady   Died: Leesburg, VA   Age: 94 years
        Birth: 1884/08/31   Death: 1978/12/17   Burial: 1978/12/20
Site 6 Lovie Newton Brady   Age: 89 years
        Birth: 1890/10/22   Death: 1980/06/13   Burial: 1980/06/15
        Died: Leesburg, VA   On stone with Charles H. Brady

Lot: 1096 E Owner: Mrs. Louis T. Titus   Purchased: 1948/10/01
Site 8 Louis Templar Titus   Age: 38 years
        Birth: 1910/02/13   Death: 1948/09/05   Burial: 1948/09/07
Site 9 Margaret Titus Dudley Died: Leesburg, VA
        Birth: 1908/06/21   Death: 1994/07/23   Burial: 1994/07/28

Lot: 1096 W Owner: Louise R. & William W. Fetzer   1948/10/01
Site 2 Robert William Fetzer Died: Leesburg, VA   Age: 45 years
        Birth: 1943/02/02   Death: 1988/10/22   Burial: 1988/10/27
Site 3 William W. Fetzer   Died: Leesburg, VA
        Birth: 1907/09/25   Death: 1992/04/10   Burial: 1992/04/14
Site 4 Louise R. Fetzer   Age: 74 years
        Birth: 1910/04/22   Death: 1984/05/03   Burial: 1984/05/07
        Died: Leesburg, VA   On stone with William W. Fetzer
Site 5 Robert T. Fetzer   Died: Lincoln, VA   Age: 85 years
        Birth: 1873   Death: 1959/03/01   Burial: 1959/03/03
Site 6 Leslie G. Fetzer   Age: 78 years
        Birth: 1879   Death: 1958/07/12   Burial: 1958/07/15
        Died: Lincoln, VA   On stone with Robert T. Fetzer

Lot: 1097 E Owner: Mrs. Liela H. Galleher   Purchased:
Site 9 Edmund Randolph Galleher   Age: 70 years
        Birth: 1890/02/18   Death: 1960/04/24   Burial: 1960
                               Died: Leesburg, VA

Site 10 Leila Hickman Galleher Age: 80 years
Birth: 1893/01/20 Death: 1973/07/21 Burial: 1973/07/23
Died: Leesburg, VA On stone with Edmund Randolph Galleher

Lot: 1097 W Owner: Mrs. Charles D. Prather   1950/06/30
Site 3 Dr. Charles DeVault Prather Jr.   Age: 28 years
Birth: 1921/08/07 Death: 1950/06/29 Burial: 1950/07/01
TS: MD

Lot: 1098 E Owner: Bruce Timms   Purchased: 1955/01/24
Site 7 Benjamin Franklin Timms No stone   Age: 81 years
Died: Lucketts, VA Death: 1965/02/04 Burial: 1965/02/07
Site 8 Bruce F. Timms   Died: Richmond, VA   Age: 62 years
Birth: 1911/01/05 Death: 1973/06/04 Burial: 1973/06/07
Site 11 James Robert Newton Died: Washington, DC   Age: 62 years
Birth: 1905/01/26 Death: 1967/01/30 Burial: 1967/02/02
Site 12 Ronald L. Fox   Age: 3 months
Death: 1964/11/01 Burial: 1964/11/03
TS: Son of Robert & Katherine Fox

Lot: 1098 W Owner: Mrs. Harry Newton   Purchased: 1955/01/24
Site 3 Harry Franklin Newton Died: Leesburg, VA
Birth: 1895/08/12 Death: 1955/01/24 Burial: 1955/01/24
Site 5 Mrs. Clara Best Newton Died: Leesburg, VA   Age: 65 years
Birth: 1900/04/17 Death: 1965/10/18 Burial: 1965/10/20
Cause: Cancer   On stone with Harry Franklin Newton

Lot: 1099   Owner:Mr. & Mrs. Lloyd B. Wilson   Purchased:
Site 0 Frank H. Wilson Jr. Died: Fremont, NE   Age: 22 years
Birth: 1896/05/19 Death: 1918/06/17 Burial: 1959/03/09
Site   Willard E. Stewart   Birth: 1853   Death: 1935
Memorial TS: Father. Interred Tecumseh, NE
Site   Mattie Benton Stewart Birth: 1859   Death: 1942
Memorial TS: Mother. Interred Tecumseh, NE
Site   Frank H. Wilson   Birth: 1844   Death: 1900
Memorial TS: Father. Interred Plattsmouth, NE
Site   Lloyd Bennett Wilson Jr. Birth: 1909/04/29   Death: 1988/06/07
Memorial TS: Interred Arlington National Cemetery
Site 3 Mrs. Silence Stewart Wilson   Age: 82 years
Birth: 1887/09/22 Death: 1970/07/22 Burial: 1970/07/25
Died: Leesburg, VA   TS: Wife, Mother, Friend
Site 4 Lloyd Bennett Wilson Died: Silver Spring, MD   Age: 94 years
Birth: 1885/05/27 Death: 1977/11/16 Burial: 1977/11/19
Site 6 Carrie Louise Bennett Wilson   Age: 93 years
Birth: 1860/03/07 Death: 1953/04/21 Burial: 1953/08/01
Died: Leesburg, VA   TS: Mother

Lot: 1100 E   Owner: W.H. Trittipoe   Purchased: 1944/06/07
Site 8   William H. Trittipoe   Age: 66 years
         Birth: 1897   Death: 1964/05/31   Burial: 1964/06/03
         Died: Leesburg, VA   TS: Father
Site 9   Lucy Ella Trittipoe   TS: Mother   Age: 46 years
         Birth: 1898   Death: 1944/10/21   Burial: 1944/10/23
Site 12 Child Trittipoe   No stone   Age: 5 hours
                                  Death: 1946/05/10   Burial: 1946/05/12

Lot: 1100 W Owner: Miscellaneous
Site 5   James Sterling Adams   Died: Leesburg, VA   Age: 74 years
         Birth: 1894/12/20   Death: 1969/05/09   Burial: 1969/05/12
Site 6   Mrs. Mae Trittipoe Adams   Age: 82 years
         Birth: 1904/07/23   Death: 1986/10/09   Burial: 1986/10/13
                                  Died: Leesburg, VA

Lot: 1101   Owner: Miscellaneous
Site 2   Charles H. Hibbs   Age: 50 years
         Birth: 1926   Death: 1977/02/09   Burial: 1977/02/11
         Died: Herndon, VA   TS: COX US Navy WWII
Site 3   Charles B. Hibbs   Died: Fairfax, VA   Age: 89 years
         Birth: 1891/06/22   Death: 1981/02/28   Burial: 1981/03/03
Site 4   Elsie G. Hibbs   Age: 80 years
         Birth: 1892/08/21   Death: 1973/03/10   Burial: 1973/03/13
         Died: Fairfax, VA   On stone with Charles B. Hibbs
Site 5   Anna Miles   Died: Alexandria, VA   No stone
         Birth: 1918/12/17   Death: 1995/12/02   Burial: 1995/12/05
Site 9   Floyd W. Worley   Died: Brevard Cocoa Beach, FL
         Birth: 1921   Death: 1985/10/16   Burial: 1985/10/20
Site 11 Roy C. Stowers   Age: 69 years
         Birth: 1909   Death: 1979/03/12

Lot: 1102   Owner: Theodore S. Hill & Gene Hill   1954/01/04
Site 6   Wilbur L. Isenberg Sr.   Age: 73 years
         Birth: 1903/02/16   Death: 1968/05/10   Burial: 1968/10/02
Site 6   Helen Goldstrohm Isenberg   Age: 73 years
         Birth: 1905/11/09   Death: 1978/03/22   Burial: 1978/03/24
                                  Died: Leesburg, VA
Site 9   Arthur J. Thompson   No stone   Age: 66 years
         Died: Alexandria, VA   Death: 1970/09/12   Burial: 1970/09/15
Site 10 Mrs. Marguerite L. Thompson   Age: 69 years
         Birth: 1884/09/22   Death: 1953/12/16   Burial: 1954/01/04
         Disinterment   TS: Mother
Site 11 Theodore S. Hill   Age: 70 years
         Birth: 1892/09/22   Death: 1962/10/14   Burial: 1962/10/16
         Cause: Suicide   Died: Leesburg, VA
Site 12 Gene Hill   Died: Arlington, VA   Age: 85 years
         Birth: 1894/07/31   Death: 1978/08/29   Burial: 1978/09/01

Lot: 1103   Owner: Miscellaneous

Site 1   Douglas Ray Collins   TS: Son   Age: 31 years
          Birth: 1952/09/05   Death: 1984/05/28   Burial: 1984/05/31
          Cause: Cancer   Died: Leesburg, VA
Site 3   Eva W. Gaines   Age: 76 years
          Birth: 1908/01/16   Death: 1984/11/11   Burial: 1984/11/14
          Died: Leesburg, VA   TS: Only daughter of T.W. & L.V. Gaines
Site 4   Eleanor A. Simcox   Died: Jacksonville   Age: 84 years
          Birth: 1914/05/02   Death: 1984/08/27   Burial: 1984/08/30
Site 6   Michael Shane Williams   Age: 16 years
          Birth: 1968/03/06   Death: 1984/07/13   Burial: 1984/07/16
          Cause: Auto Accident   Died: Leesburg, VA
Site 7   Devillo W. Neish   Died: Leesburg, VA   Age: 86 years
          Birth: 1881   Death: 1968/01/30   Burial: 1968/02/01
Site 8   Myrtle O. Neish   Age: 95 years
          Birth: 1889   Death: 1985/01/05   Burial: 1985/01/08
          Died: Berryville, VA   On stone with Devillo W. Neish
Site 9   Luther D. Kirby Jr.   Died: Alexandria, VA   Age: 48 years
          Birth: 1914   Death: 1962/04/17   Burial: 1962/04/19
Site 11   George E. Ward   Age: 71 years
          Birth: 1900/06/19   Death: 1971/11/03   Burial: 1971/11/05
          Cause: Heart   Died: Leesburg, VA   TS: WWII
Site 12   Della K. Ward   Age: 85 years
          Birth: 1903/08/16   Death: 1989/03/15   Burial: 1989/03/17
          Died: Leesburg, VA   On stone with George E. Ward

Lot: 1104   Owner: Miscellaneous

Site 1   Fred Smerheim   Died: FL
          Birth: 1899   Death: 1981/01/27   Burial: 1981/01/31
Site 2   Quintin H. Lacey   Died: Montgomery, MD   Age: 61 years
          Birth: 1903   Death: 1964/10/26   Burial: 1964/10/28
Site 3   James Mason Melton   66 years
          Birth: 1903   Death: 1969/10/20   Burial: 1969/10/24
          Cause: Auto Accident   Died: Blossburg, PA
Site 4   Mrs. Pearl Hughes Melton   Age: 70 years
          Birth: 1899   Death: 1969/10/20   Burial: 1969/10/24
          Cause: Auto Accident   Died: Blossburg, PA
          BP:Mrs. Mason Melton   On stone with James Mason Melton
Site 9   Edward Neville Bradfield   Died: Leesburg, VA   Age: 80 years
          Birth: 1901/03/07   Death: 1981/07/31   Burial: 1981/08/03
Site 10   Ruth Crim Bradfield   Died: Leesburg, VA   Age: 80 years
          Birth: 1904/11/15   Death: 1985/03/08   Burial: 1985/03/11

Lot: 1105 E Owner: Mary L. & A.C. Moffett   Purchased:

Site 7   Augustus Courtney Moffett   Age: 71 years
          Birth: 1877/08/13   Death: 1949/02/12   Burial: 1949/02/14
Site 9   Mary Lee Moffett   Age: 86 years
          Birth: 1880/03/05   Death: 1967/01/17   Burial: 1967/01/20
          Died: Leesburg, VA   On stone with Augustus Courtney Moffett

Site 10 George T. Moffett   Died: Martinsburg, WV   Age: 67 years
        Birth: 1907/03/04   Death: 1973/08/09   Burial: 1973/08/12
Site 11 Augustus Courtney Moffett Jr.   Died: Stanton, VA
        Birth: 1915/09/26   Death: 1992/06/04   Burial: 1992/06/06

Lot: 1105 W Owner: Mrs. Mary Payne & Mrs. Wade Lynn
                                                Purchased: 1944/09/22
Site 1 Harry S. Payne   Age: 58 years
        Birth: 1866   Death: 1944/09/21   Burial: 1944/09/23
Site 3 Mary C. Payne   Age: 85 years
        Birth: 1887   Death: 1972/09/27   Burial: 1972/09/29
        Died: Winchester, VA   On stone with Harry S. Payne
Site 4 Bessie F. Lynn   Age: 81 years
        Birth: 1891/08/03   Death: 1972/12/09   Burial: 1972/12/12
        Died: Winchester, VA   On stone with Wade Hampton Lynn
Site 5 Wade Hampton Lynn   Died: Warrenton, VA   Age: 79 years
        Birth: 1883/07/20   Death: 1963/01/31   Burial: 1963/02/03

Lot: 1106   Owner: Lloyd E. Frye   Purchased: 1959/09/24
Site 2 Blanche W. Frye   Age: 48 years
        Birth: 1911/01/20   Death: 1959/09/21   Burial: 1959/09/24
        Cause: Cancer   Died: L.C.H. Leesburg, VA
Site 7 Charles T. Sensabaugh   Age: 23 years
        Birth: 1937/04/22   Death: 1960/10/27   Burial: 1960/10/30
        Cause: Auto Accident   Died: Fairfax, VA
Site 9 Evelyn Frye Neff   Died: Lucketts, VA
        Birth: 1941/03/15   Death: 1992/11/04   Burial: 1992/11/07

Lot: 1107   Owner: Miscellaneous
Site 1 James F. Peebles Sr.   Died: L.C.H. Leesburg, VA
        Birth: 1899/04/13   Death: 1960/09/20   Burial: 1960/09/22
Site 4 John S. Witul   Died: Leesburg, VA   TS: US Navy WWII
        Birth: 1916/07/29   Death: 1993/06/02   Burial: 1993/06/05
Site 7 Modestino J. Frasca   Died: Leesburg, VA   Age: 82 years
        Birth: 1904   Death: 1987/05/22   Burial: 1987/08/11
Site 8 Dr. Huai Chin Sun   Died: Sterling, VA
        Birth: 1904/07/26   Death: 1994/04/22   Burial: 1994/04/27
Site 9 John Edwin Muncaster Jr.   Died: Hamilton, VA   Age: 86 years
        Birth: 1902   Death: 1988/10/15   Burial: 1988/10/18
Site 11 George B. Kehr Jr.   Died: Leesburg, VA   Age: 75 years
        Birth: 1912/05/31   Death: 1987/07/21   Burial: 1987/07/25
Site 12 Margaret L. Kehr   Died: Sterling, VA   Age: 72 years
        Birth: 1911/08/18   Death: 1984/02/28   Burial: 1984/03/02

Lot: 1108   Owner: Miscellaneous
Site 1 James E. George   Died: Loudoun Co., VA   Age: 48 years
        Birth: 1917/12/04   Death: 1963/06/11   Burial: 1963/06/14
Site 2 Thelma T. George   Died: Leesburg, VA   Age: 54 years
        Birth: 1920/12/22   Death: 1975/06/29   Burial: 1975/07/01

Site 7   Stacy R. Collins Sr.   Age: 68 years
         Birth: 1907   Death: 1976/01/19   Burial: 1976/01/21
         Died: Leesburg, VA   TS: Army Air Force WWII
Site 11 Warren Wentworth Matthew   Age: 45 years
         Birth: 1927/02/05   Death: 1972/08/16   Burial: 1973/08/01
         TS: Son of Walton & Carrie Matthew. Virginia, Sgt HQ HQCo 27
         Infantry WWII, Korea.   Removed from Culpeper, VA
Site 12 Kathryn Griffin Walsh   Died: Leesburg, VA   Age: 82 years
         Birth: 1882/04/20   Death: 1965/04/08   Burial: 1965/04/10

Lot: 1109   Owner: Miscellaneous
Site 1   James B. Light   Died: Leesburg, VA   Age: 72 years
         Birth: 1911/05/08   Death: 1983/08/17   Burial: 1983/08/19
Site 6   Vicki Wenner   No stone   Age: 37 years
         Died: Leesburg, VA   Death: 1992/01/22   Burial: 1991/01/27
Site 8   Walton Janney Matthew   Died: Fairfax, VA
         Birth: 1901/10/28   Death: 1982/09/04   Burial: 1982/09/08
Site 9   Frederick F. Day   Died: Leesburg, VA   Age: 60 years
         Birth: 1904/09/19   Death: 1964/07/11   Burial: 1964/07/13
Site 10 Jewell Jane Day   Age: 68 years
         Birth: 1910/10/25   Death: 1978/08/01   Burial: 1978/08/04
         Died: Fairfax, VA   On stone with Frederick F. Day
Site 11 Carroll W. Spring   Died: Fairfax, VA   Age: 61 years
         Birth: 1904/01/31   Death: 1965/04/03   Burial: 1965/04/06
Site 12 Helen R. Spring   Age: 72 years
         Birth: 1908/04/02   Death: 1979/10/18   Burial: 1979/10/20
         Died: Arlington, VA   On stone with Carroll W. Spring

Lot: 1110   Owner: Miscellaneous
Site 2   Margory Brown   Age: 66 years
         Birth: 1924/08/01   Death: 1990/08/24   Burial: 1990/08/27
         Died: Lovettsville, VA   TS: Married Harry E. Brown June 8, 1945
Site 3   Dennis P. Miller   Age: 26 years
         Birth: 1961/04/04   Death: 1987/11/02   Burial: 1988/04/01
Site 4   Katherine Marcum   Died: Washington, DC   TS: Mother
         Birth: 1918/04/02   Death: 1994/09/29   Burial: 1994/10/02
Site 6   Donna Singleton   Died: Washington, DC   Age: 44 years
         Birth: 1943   Death: 1987/11/09   Burial: 1987/11/13
Site 7   William Edward Bishop   Age: 73 years
         Birth: 1905   Death: 1978/11/05   Burial: 1978/11/08
         Died: Leesburg, VA   TS: PFC US Army WWII
Site 9   Troy M. Fitzgerald   Died: Leesburg, VA   Age: 71 years
         Birth: 1905   Death: 1976/02/02   Burial: 1976/02/04
Site 11 Delores C. Hass   Age: 72 years
         Birth: 1911   Death: 1983/11/21   Burial: 1983/11/26
         Died: Knoxville, TN   On stone with Loysciel V. Hass
Site 12 Loysciel V. Hass   Died: TN
         Birth: 1897   Death: 1989/12/17   Burial: 1989/12/20

Lot: 1111 E Owner: W. H. & George M. Martin   1938/02/21
Site 7   Wm. H. Martin   Cause: Cerebral Embolism   Age: 63 years
         Birth: 1874   Death: 1938/02/19   Burial: 1938/02/21
Site 8   Mrs. Norita S. Martin   IB:Mrs. William Martin
         Birth: 1874   Death: 1932   Burial: 1938/08/22
         Removal.   On stone with William H. Martin
Site 9   Marie V. Martin   Died: Arlington, VA   Age: 62 years
         Birth: 1916/01/06   Death: 1979/01/04   Burial: 1979/01/06
Site 11 William H. Martin II   Died: Leesburg, VA   Age: 76 years
         Birth: 1912/07/25   Death: 1989/01/22   Burial: 1989/01/24

Lot: 1111 W Owner: John T. Phillips   Purchased: 1939/02/11
Site 1   John T. Phillips   Age: 76 years
         Birth: 1871/01/27   Death: 1947/07/27   Burial: 1947/07/29
Site 2   Carrie Jane C. Phillips   Age: 84 years
         Birth: 1873/06/01   Death: 1957/09/27
Site 3   Thomas Oxley Phillips   TS: Born VA. Died Washington, DC
         Birth: 1847/12/23   Death: 1895/05/14   Burial: 1939/02/15
Site 4   Mrs. Mary Sanderson Phillips   Age: 80 years
         Birth: 1850/10/03   Death: 1940/12/20   Burial: 1940/12/22
         Cause: Bronchial Pneumonia   TS: Wife of Thomas Oxley Phillips
Site 5   Mary Phillips Sager   Age: 90 years
         Birth: 1874/02/18   Death: 1964/10/05   Burial: 1964/10/07
Site 6   Lawrence Kinsley Sager   Age: 77 years
         Birth: 1873/09/09   Death: 1951/01/28   Burial: 1951/01/31

Lot: 1112 E Owner: Lee Campbell   Purchased: 1969/08/26
Site 8   Lona Russell Rusmiselle No stone   Age: 81 years
         Died: Roanoke, VA   Death: 1974/05/26   Burial: 1974/05/29
Site 12 Ruth Lee Campbell   No stone   Age: 53 years
         Died: Fairfax, VA   Death: 1971/11/22   Burial: 1971/11/26

Lot: 1112 W Owner: Mrs. Mollie C. Russell   Purchased: 1937/08/21
Site 1   Dr. Clift P. Berger   TS: MD   Age: 59 years
         Birth: 1902   Death: 1961/09/29   Burial: 1961/10/02
         Cause: Rt. Coronary Artery   Died: Washington, DC
Site 2   Dorothy R. Berger   Age: 73 years
         Birth: 1905   Death: 1979/09/04   Burial: 1979/09/07
         Died: WV   On stone with Clift P. Berger
Site 3   William O. Russell   Cause: Cancer   Age: 72 years
         Birth: 1864   Death: 1937/03/10   Burial: 1937/03/12
Site 4   Mollie Compher Russell   Age: 89 years
         Birth: 1868   Death: 1957/07/30

Lot: 1113 E Owner: Mrs. E.B. Rusk   Purchased: 1938/02/05
Site 7   Edgar B. Rusk   Cause: Myocarditis
         Birth: 1861   Death: 1938/02/03   Burial: 1938/02/05
Site 8   Mrs. May Ernestine Rusk   Age: 76 years
         Birth: 1868   Death: 1945/04/13   Burial: 1945/04/15
         On stone with Edgar B. Rusk

Site 10 Roger Edgar Rusk   Died: Aldie, VA   Age: 65 years
         Birth: 1895/09/29   Death: 1961/05/15   Burial: 1961/05/17
Site 10 Mrs. Ruth Elizabeth Rusk   Age: 72 years
         Birth: 1901/08/27   Death: 1973/11/29   Burial: 1973/12/02
         Died: Leesburg, VA   On stone with Roger Edgar Rusk

Lot: 1113 W Owner: Mrs. Gibson S. Payne   Purchased: 1938/02/15
Site 3   Gibson S. Payne   Cause: Suicide   Age: 57 years
         Birth: 1881/01/25   Death: 1938/02/14   Burial: 1938/02/16
Site 4   Martha Ann Payne   Died: Herndon, VA   Age: 89 years
         Birth: 1873/12/25   Death: 1963/05/23   Burial: 1963/05/26

Lot: 1114   Owner: Mrs. Bessie M. Laughlin   1938/11/05
Site 9   John Page Laughlin   Cause: Pneumonia   Age: 63 years
         Birth: 1875/08/29   Death: 1938/11/05   Burial: 1938/11/08
Site 9   Mrs. Bessie Merritt Laughlin   Age: 73 years
         Birth: 1876/04/03   Death: 1950/10/12   Burial: 1950/10/20

Lot: 1115 E Owner: Elliott L. Ward & Rosalie S. Blackwell
Site 7   Elliot Lee Ward   Died: Leesburg, VA   Age: 75 years
         Birth: 1902/08/01   Death: 1978/03/03   Burial: 1978/03/06
Site 8   Virginia Steadman Ward   Age: 60 years
         Birth: 1908/04/26   Death: 1968/08/19   Burial: 1968/08/22
         Died: Leesburg, VA   On stone with Elliot Lee Ward
Site 9   Rosalie Steadman Blackwell   Age: 66 years
         Birth: 1917/11/24   Death: 1983/12/23   Burial: 1983/12/27
         Cause: Cancer   Died: Leesburg, VA

Lot: 1115 W Owner: Mrs. Mary Nixon   Purchased: 1940/04/24
Site 1   Lewis Nixon   Cause: Hypostatic Pneumonia Age: 79 years
         Birth: 1861/04/07   Death: 1940/09/23   Burial: 1940/09/25
Site 2   Mary Doran Nixon   No stone   Age: 87 years
         Died: NY   Death: 1987/07/24   Burial: 1987/07/28

Lot: 1116   Owner: Matthew Farris   Purchased: 1938/02/09
Site 1   Donald Lee Farris   Died: Leesburg, VA   Age: 1 month
         Birth: 1953/10/16   Death: 1953/11/22   Burial: 1953/11/24
Site 3   Myrtle Elizabeth Farris   Age: 35 years
         Birth: 1902/04/07   Death: 1938/02/07   Burial: 1938/02/09
         Cause: Tuberculosis   On stone with Matthew E. Farris Sr.
Site 4   Matthew E. Farris Sr.   Died: Leesburg, VA   Age: 63 years
         Birth: 1902/06/21   Death: 1969/11/09   Burial: 1969/11/12

Lot: 1117 E Owner: Mrs. W. Emory Plaster   1941/03/07
Site 7   Hugh Ashby Thompson   Age: 78 years
         Birth: 1861/09/27   Death: 1941/03/07   Burial: 1941/03/09
Site 8   Hannah Elizabeth Norris Thompson   Age: 79 years
         Birth: 1862/05/30   Death: 1941/11/23   Burial: 1941/11/26
         On stone with Hugh Ashby Thompson

Site 9   Helen Thompson Plaster   Age: 73 years
         Birth: 1889/07/01   Death: 1961/01/19   Burial: 1961/01/21
         Died: Leesburg, VA   On stone with William Emory Plaster
Site 9   William Emory Plaster
         Birth: 1887/01/27   Death: 1936/06/19   Burial: 1962/06/27

Lot: 1117 W Owner: Lucas D. & Elizabeth L. Phillips   1971/05/10
Site 2   Lucas Dallam Phillips   Died: Leesburg, VA
         Birth: 1903/12/07   Death: 1994/03/24   Burial: 1994/03/26
Site 3   Elizabeth Littlejohn Phillips   Age: 64 years
         Birth: 1913/06/14   Death: 1978/04/13   Burial: 1978/04/15
         Cause: Cancer   Died: Jackson, MS
         On stone with Lucas Dallam Phillips
Site 4   Mrs. Helen Elizabeth Phillips Chamblin   Age: 24 years
         Birth: 1946/06/08   Death: 1971/04/25   Burial: 1971/04/27
                                Died: Richmond, VA

Lot: 1118   Owner: Mrs. George Ward Loveless   1941/11/25
Site 3   George Ward Loveless   Cause: Murdered   Age: 51 years
         Birth: 1890   Death: 1941/11/24   Burial: 1941/11/26
Site 5   Irene Loveless   Age: 95 years
         Birth: 1888   Death: 1984/07/28   Burial: 1984/08/01
         Died: Warrenton, VA   On stone with George Ward Loveless
Site 6   Evelyn Loveless Carr   Died: Waterford, VA   Age: 72 years
         Birth: 1917/12/02   Death: 1990/10/11   Burial: 1990/10/15

Lot: 1119   Owner: H. Clinton Stowers   Purchased: 1943/05/10
Site 3   Henry Clinton Stowers   Age: 76 years
         Birth: 1879/12/01   Death: 1956/10/26   Burial: 1956/10/29
         Died: Leesburg, VA   TS: Father
Site 4   Ella Jane Stowers   TS: Mother   Age: 61 years
         Birth: 1882/03/02   Death: 1943/05/10   Burial: 1943/05/12
Site 5   William S. Stowers   Age: 60 years
         Birth: 1918/04/13   Death: 1979/05/28   TS: Pvt US Army WWII
Site 6   Terry Franklin Stowers   Age: 82 years
         Birth: 1907/09/12   Death: 1989/12/05   Burial: 1989/12/08
         Died: Winchester, VA   TS: US Army WWII
Site 9   Doak Clinton Stowers   Died: Alexandria, VA   Age: 70 years
         Birth: 1906/11/29   Death: 1976/06/07   Burial: 1976/06/10
Site 10 Theresa R. Kirkpatrick Stowers   Age: 53 years
         Birth: 1916/08/15   Death: 1969/12/13   Burial: 1969/12/15
         Died: Manassas, VA   On stone with Doak Clinton Stowers

Lot: 1120   Owner: W.C. Whitmore   Purchased: 1941/08/18
Site 3   William C. Whitmore   Died: Leesburg, VA   Age: 85 years
         Birth: 1881/03/22   Death: 1966/05/01   Burial: 1966/05/03
Site 4   Mrs. Marguerite Fadeley Whitmore   Age: 59 years
         Birth: 1891/05/12   Death: 1951/03/29   Burial: 1951/03/31

Lot: 1121   Owner: Tunis H. Plaster   Purchased: 1944/02/18
Site 1   Oden K. Semones   Age: 71 years
         Birth: 1915/10/08   Death: 1987/09/17   Burial: 1987/09/20
         Died: Leesburg, VA   TS: Father
Site 2   Tunis Henry Plaster   TS: Father   Age: 60 years
         Birth: 1888/05/30   Death: 1948/04/26   Burial: 1948/04/28
Site 4   Marie F. Plaster   Died: Leesburg, VA   Age: 94 years
         Birth: 1889/03/26   Death: 1984/02/11   Burial: 1984/02/13
         On stone with Tunis Henry Plaster   TS: Mother

Lot: 1122   Owner: Dyer Gum   Purchased: 1944/02/15
Site 1   Leroy Dyer Gum   Died: Leesburg, VA
         Birth: 1913/04/16   Death: 1992/05/18   Burial: 1992/05/21
Site 2   Isaac Dyer Gum   Age: 89 years
         Birth: 1878/04/02   Death: 1967/11/01   Burial: 1967/11/04
         Died: Leesburg, VA   TS: Father
Site 3   Mrs. Gertie E. Gum   Age: 71 years
         Birth: 1872/04/11   Death: 1944/02/15   Burial: 1944/02/17
         On stone with Isaac Dyer Gum   TS: Mother
Site 7   J. Nelson Titus   Died: Leesburg, VA   Age: 61 years
         Birth: 1905/07/22   Death: 1966/11/30   Burial: 1966/12/02
Site 8   Marie G. Titus
         Birth: 1907/05/26   Death: 1995/11/20   Burial: 1995/11/25
         Died: Leesburg, VA   On stone with J. Nelson Titus

Lot: 1123 E   Owner: Miscellaneous
Site 9   David E. Hawthorne Sr. Died: Leesburg, VA   Age: 62 years
         Birth: 1898   Death: 1974/03/31   Burial: 1974/04/03
Site 10 Dorothy I. Hawthorne   Died: Purcellville, VA   Age: 84 years
         Birth: 1900   Death: 1985/06/21   Burial: 1985/06/24
         On stone with David E. Hawthorne
Site 11 Carl L. Pearson   Died: Leesburg, VA   Age: 57 years
         Birth: 1904   Death: 1962/11/21   Burial: 1962/11/24
Site 12 Mary J. Pearson   Age: 82 years
         Birth: 1905   Death: 1988/01/07   Burial: 1988/01/09
         Died: Manassas, VA   On stone with Carl L. Pearson

Lot: 1123 W Owner: Archie L. & Cora O. Fry   1956/08/15
Site 3   Archie Linwood Fry   Died: Winchester, VA   Age: 71 years
         Birth: 1910/01/05   Death: 1982/05/06   Burial: 1982/05/09
Site 4   Cora Osborn Fry   Died: Winchester, VA   Age: 73 years
         Birth: 1911/09/23   Death: 1985/03/14   Burial: 1985/03/16
         TS: Married Archie Linwood Fry June 21, 1935

Lot: 1124 E   Owner: Edward R. Carr   Purchased:
Site 9   Dr. William B. Carr   Age: 72 years
         Birth: 1884   Death: 1956/10/27   Burial: 1956/10/29
         Cause: Heart Attack   Died: NY
Site 11 Edward R. Carr   Died: Sarasoto, FL   Age: 77 years
         Birth: 1897   Death: 1974/05/15   Burial: 1974/05/18

Site 12 Emma B. Carr   Died: Barnstable, MA   Age: 66 years
        Birth: 1906   Death: 1973/08/20   Burial: 1973/08/24

Lot: 1124 W Owner: Thomas & Hilda U. Donohoe   Purchased:
Site 1 Harry Stanley Utterback   Age: 65 years
        Birth: 1893   Death: 1958/08/03   Burial: 1958/08/05
        Cause: Suicide   Died: Leesburg, VA
Site 2 Josephine Atwell Utterback   Age: 79 years
        Birth: 1896   Death: 1975/12/09   Burial: 1975/12/12
        Died: Leesburg, VA   On stone with Harry S. Utterback
Site 3 Hilda G. Donohoe   Died: Leesburg, VA
        Birth: 1917/03/05   Death: 1995/05/26   Burial: 1995/05/31

Lot: 1125 E Owner: Daniel M. & Betty Hyatt   1962/05/10
Site 11 Lori Jean Hyatt   Died: Washington, DC   Age: 6 months
        Birth: 1962/06/14   Death: 1962/12/31   Burial: 1963/01/03
Site 12 David Wayne Hyatt   Died: L.C.H. Leesburg, VA   Age: 3 days
        Birth: 1961   Death: 1961/02/03   Burial: 1961/02/08

Lot: 1125 W Owner: Jack W. & Edith K. Fleming   Purchased:
Site 1 Edith K. Fleming   Age: 59 years
        Birth: 1906/09/15   Death: 1967/09/01   Burial: 1967/09/03
        Died: Leesburg, VA   On stone with Jack W. Fleming Sr.
Site 1 Jack W. Fleming Sr.   Died: Leesburg, VA   Age: 82 years
        Birth: 1902/08/09   Death: 1984/11/27   Burial: 1984/11/29
Site 3 Jack West Fleming   Died: Winchester, VA   TS: US Navy WWII
        Birth: 1928/01/16   Death: 1992/09/13   Burial: 1992/09/16

Lot: 1126   Owner: Miscellaneous
Site 1 Roy Thomas Trail   Died: Leesburg, VA   Age: 72 years
        Birth: 1898/03/23   Death: 1970/12/09   Burial: 1970/12/12
Site 2 Dorothy S. Trail   Age: 83 years
        Birth: 1898/11/07   Death: 1982/05/19   Burial: 1982/05/22
        Died: Purcellville, VA   On stone with Roy Thomas Trail
Site 3 Carroll H. Howard   Died: Leesburg, VA   Age: 42 years
        Birth: 1921   Death: 1964/03/26   Burial: 1964/03/29
Site 4 Ethel V. Howard
        Birth: 1919/10/20   Death: 1994/10/10   Burial: 1994/10/13
        Died: Leesburg, VA   On stone with Carroll H. Howard
Site 9 Charles Lochte Allison   Died: Bethesda, MD   Age: 63 years
        Birth: 1911/11/21   Death: 1975/05/31   Burial: 1975/06/03
Site 11 Cecil G. Daymude   Age: 0 years
        Birth: 1911/06/07   Death: 1972/04/06   Burial: 1972/04/10

Lot: 1127   Owner: S. M. Rust   Purchased: 1938/01/15
Site 3 Stirling Murray Rust   Age: 72 years
        Birth: 1881/10/19   Death: 1954/01/29   Burial: 1954/01/31
        Died: Homestead, PA   Cause: Acute Coronary Occlusion
        Born at Rockland near Leesburg. Died at Pittsburgh, PA. Son of
        Armistead T.M. & Ida Lee Rust.

Site 4   Mary Hilton Coburn Rust   Age: 100 years
         Birth: 1878/09/15   Death: 1979/01/30   Burial: 1979/02/03
         Died: Naples, FL   Wife of Stirling Murray Rust. Daughter of
         Harry W. Coburn & Alice Hilton Coburn. Born at Tewksbury, MA.
         Died Naples, FL

Lot: 1128   Owner: Mrs. Henry B. Rust   Purchased: 1937/08/21
Site 1   Elizabeth Fitzhugh Rust Brown   Died: Leesburg, VA
         Birth: 1902/08/02   Death: 1972/12/20   Burial: 1972/12/22
         TS: Wife of Stanley Noel Brown. Daughter of Henry Bedinger Rust &
         Elizabeth Watkins Rust. Born Pueblo, CO.
Site 1   Stanley Noel Brown   Died: Leesburg, VA
         Birth: 1901/12/25   Death: 1982/04/23   Burial: 1982/04/24
         TS: Son of Addison Brown & Helen Carpenter Gaskin Brown. Born
         NY, NY. Died Leesburg, VA
Site 3   Henry Bedinger Rust   Cause: Arteriosclerosis   Age: 63 years
         Birth: 1872/12/13   Death: 1936/01/17   Burial: 1936/01/19
         TS: Son of Armistead T.M. & Ida Lee Rust. Born at Rockland. Died
         Pittsburgh, PA
Site 4   Elizabeth Watkins Rust   Died: Leesburg, VA   91 years
         Birth: 1879/10/01   Death: 1970/11/09   Burial: 1970/11/11
         TS: Wife of Henry Bedinger Rust. Daughter of Hezekiah & Elizabeth
         Fitzhugh Watkins. Born Arlington, NJ

Lot: 1129   Owner: William F. Rust   Purchased: 1938/01/29
Site   William Junkin Cox   TS: Born Portland, OR. Died Leesburg
         Birth: 1896/09/16   Death: 1989/03/30
Site 1   Robert Vernier Brundage Died: Raphine, VA   Age: 64 years
         Birth: 1919/05/26   Death: 1983/12/06   Burial: 1983/12/10
Site 2   Jane Rust Cox   Died: Leesburg, VA   Age: 59 years
         Birth: 1918/01/15   Death: 1977/05/28   Burial: 1977/05/31
         TS: Wife of William Junkin Cox. Daughter of William Fitzhugh &
         Mary Fleming Rust. Born Pittsburgh, PA
Site 3   William Fitzhugh Rust   Cause: Cancer of Stomach   Age: 66 years
         Birth: 1874/08/11   Death: 1940/10/29   Burial: 1940/11/02
         TS: Son of Armistead T.M. & Ida Lee Rust. Born at Rockland. Died
         at Yeocomico
Site 5   Mary E.L. Fleming Rust   Died: Leesburg, VA   Age: 81 years
         Birth: 1886/10/14   Death: 1967/12/25   Burial: 1967/12/28
         TS: Wife of William Fitzhugh Rust. Born at Greenmont.
Site 6   William Fitzhugh Rust Jr.   Died: Leesburg, VA   Age: 77 years
         Birth: 1914/01/27   Death: 1991/06/07   Burial: 1991/06/11
         TS: Son of William Fitzhugh & Mary Fleming Rust.
         Born Cleveland, OH. Died at Yeocomco
Site 6   Margaret D. Rust   Died: Washington, DC
         Birth: 1918/07/17   Death: 1995/09/22   Burial: 1995/09/30

Lot: 1130   Owner: E. Marshall Rust   Purchased: 1937/12/07
Site 3   Ellsworth Marshall Rust   Age: 67 years
         Birth: 1879/06/22   Death: 1946/07/24   Burial: 1946/07/26
         TS: Son of Armistead T.M. & Ida Lee Rust. Born at Rockland. Died
         at Leesburg
Site 5   Eva Thompson Rust   Age: 69 years
         Birth: 1876/03/11   Death: 1945/07/30   Burial: 1945/08/01
         TS: Wife of Ellsworth Marshall Rust. Daughter of Sidney Augustus
         Hillman & Emily Rivers Thompson. Born near Louisville, GA. Died
         Washington, DC

Lot: 1131   Owner: Robert W. & Carolyn E. Ector   1968/04/24
Site 11 Robert Warren Ector   Died: Leesburg, VA
         Birth: 1924/01/17   Death: 1993/01/29   Burial: 1993/02/03
Site 12 Hannah A. Ector   Died: Leesburg, VA   Age: 75 years
         Birth: 1893/05/02   Death: 1970/04/13   Burial: 1970/04/16

Lot: 1132   Owner: Miscellaneous
Site 1   Frederick Louis Grammer   Age: 54 years
         Birth: 1906   Death: 1960/06/18   Burial: 1960/06/21
         Died: LCH, Leesburg, VA   TS: USAF 1942-1945
Site 3   Elizabeth Grammer   Age: 74 years
         Birth: 1898/03/15   Death: 1972/07/14
Site 4   Harriet McK. Grammer   Age: 80 years
         Birth: 1899/04/30   Death: 1979/05/13
Site 9   Sarah E. Cole   Age: 81 years
         Cause: Pneumonia   Death: 1938/04/07   Burial: 1938/04/09
         Removed Aug. 23, 1949 to Ebenezer;   No stone
Site 10 Howard Eeton Cole   No stone   Age: 67 years
                                  Death: 1947/06/06   Burial: 1947/06/08

Lot: 1133   Owner: Herbert Howard   Purchased: 1941/07/24
Site 1   Dr. Herbert H. Howard Sr.   Age: 70 years
         Birth: 1890   Death: 1960/11/27   Burial: 1960/11/29
         Died: Leesburg, VA   TS: D.V.M.
Site 2   Lillian M. Howard   Died: Fairfax, VA   Age: 79 years
         Birth: 1895   Death: 1974/04/05   Burial: 1974/04/07
         On stone with Herbert H. Howard Sr. D.V.M.
Site 3   Margaret Ellen Howard   Cause: Auto Accident   Age: 19 years
         Birth: 1922/03/15   Death: 1941/07/23   Burial: 1941/07/26
Site 7   Mary E. Howard Hopkins   Age: 48 years
         Birth: 1931/09/26   Death: 1980/09/13   Burial: 1980/09/16
         Cause: Cancer   Died: Fairfax, VA

Lot: 1134 E   Owner: James C. Fleming   Purchased: 1942/03/21
Site 7   Margaret Craig Fleming   Age: 31 years
         Birth: 1911/09/13   Death: 1943/06/04   Burial: 1943/06/07
         TS: Wife of James C. Fleming
Site 7   James Clayton Fleming   Died: Leesburg, VA   Age: 67 years
         Birth: 1905/08/03   Death: 1973/01/24   Burial: 1973/01/27

Site 11 Robert William Edmondson Age: 53 years
Birth: 1900   Death: 1953/09/05   Burial: 1953/09/07
Died: Leesburg, VA
Site 12 Marie T. Edmondson Age: 72 years
Birth: 1902   Death: 1975/09/20   Burial: 1975/09/23
Died: Leesburg, VA   On stone with Robert W. Edmondson

Lot: 1134 WOwner: Carrie E. Lowenbach Hanger   1942/03/21
Site 1 Andrew Davis Edmondson   Age: 85 years
Birth: 1864/05/08   Death: 1950/03/08   Burial: 1950/03/10
Site 2 Carrie Jane Preston Edmondson   Age: 74 years
Birth: 1868/01/28   Death: 1942/03/20   Burial: 1942/03/22
On stone with Andrew D. Edmondson
Site 3 John T. Hanger   Age: 52 years
Birth: 1896/06/09   Death: 1948/09/27   Burial: 1948/09/29
Site 4 Carrie E. Hanger
Birth: 1902/12/08   Death: 1993/11/30   Burial: 1993/12/03
Died: Harrisonburg, VA   On stone with John T. Hanger

Lot: 1135   Owner: Leroy J. Myers   Purchased: 1943/11/08
Site 2 Clara B. Myers   Age: 65 years
Birth: 1896   Death: 1961/05/11   Burial: 1961/05/15
Died: G.W.U. Hospital, Washington, DC
Site 4 Leroy J. Myers   Died: Washington, DC
Birth: 1895/10/25   Death: 1994/10/06   Burial: 1994/10/12
Site 5 Grace Gum Myers   Died: Washington, DC
Birth: 1899   Death: 1978/04/29   Age: 78 years
Burial: 1978/05/03
Site 8 Kate Lee Myers   Died: Arlington, VA
Birth: 1915   Death: 1975/01/15   Burial: 1975/01/17

Lot: 1136   Owner: Mrs. M.D. Arnold   Purchased:
Site 1 Mahlon David Arnold   Age: 89 years
Birth: 1855   Death: 1944/02/18   Burial: 1944/02/20
Site 2 Etta Leola Arnold   Age: 81 years
Birth: 1888   Death: 1969/10/15   Burial: 1969/10/17
Died: Leesburg, VA   On stone with Mahlon D. Arnold

Lot: 1137   Owner: Leonard Kip Sparrow   1944/10/06
Site 1 Leonard Kip Sparrow   Age: 62 years
Birth: 1881/10/09   Death: 1944/10/06   Burial: 1944/10/08
Site 3 Mary E. Williams Sparrow   Age: 93 years
Birth: 1878/12/09   Death: 1972/06/09
On stone with William Edward Sparrow Jr.
Site 4 William Edward Sparrow Jr.   Age: 84 years
Birth: 1877/12/09   Death: 1961/12/06   Burial: 1961/12/08
Died: Winchester, VA
Site 8 William Clinton Saffer   Age: 69 years
Birth: 1876   Death: 1946/01/12   Burial: 1946/01/14

Site 10 Mrs. Sadie A. Saffer Age: 76 years
Birth: 1890 Death: 1967/09/09 Burial: 1967/09/11
Died: Leesburg, VA On stone with W. Clinton Saffer

Lot: 1138 Owner: John G. Dodd Purchased:
Site 1 Cammie Louise Peters Died: McLean, VA Age: 83 years
Birth: 1878/08/01 Death: 1961/10/17 Burial: 1961/10/19
Site 2 Alma Estell Peters Age: 58 years
Birth: 1910/02/23 Death: 1968/04/29 Burial: 1968/05/02
Died: Woodstock, VA On stone with Charles W. Peters
Site 4 Charles W. Peters Died: Charlestown, WV Age: 72 years
Birth: 1903/10/07 Death: 1976/08/07 Burial: 1976/08/11
Site 5 James Walker Peters Sr. Died: Washington, DC Age: 80 years
Birth: 1901/02/03 Death: 1981/12/31 Burial: 1982/01/02
Site 7 John G. Dodd Died: Leesburg, VA Age: 85 years
Birth: 1879/04/27 Death: 1965/04/22 Burial: 1965/04/24
Site 8 Laura V. Dodd Age: 83 years
Birth: 1881/08/25 Death: 1964/01/25 Burial: 1964/01/27
Died: Leesburg, VA On stone with John G. Dodd
Site 9 James W. Hutchison Died: Leesburg, VA Age: 64 years
Birth: 1913/05/23 Death: 1978/01/23 Burial: 1978/01/25

Lot: 1139 E Owner: Wesley Dodd Purchased: 1947/08/25
Site 7 Joseph Foster Dodd Died: Leesburg, VA Age: 44 years
Birth: 1928 Death: 1973/06/14 Burial: 1973/06/16
Site 11 Wesley F. Dodd Died: Leesburg, VA Age: 74 years
Birth: 1906/10/22 Death: 1981/06/22 Burial: 1981/06/25
Site 12 Mae W. Dodd Age: 81 years
Birth: 1908/10/03 Death: 1989/12/18 Burial: 1989/12/21
Died: Leesburg, VA On stone with Wesley F. Dodd

Lot: 1139 W Owner: C. Grey & Paul Dodd Purchased: 1947/08/25
Site 3 Charles Grey Dodd Died: Leesburg, VA Age: 71 years
Birth: 1903/03/22 Death: 1974/06/21 Burial: 1974/06/23
Site 4 Ada Bridges Dodd Age: 81 years
Birth: 1895/12/04 Death: 1977/10/25 Burial: 1977/10/27
Died: Leesburg, VA On stone with Charles Grey Dodd

Lot: 1140 Owner: Miscellaneous
Site 2 Joseph C. Titus Sr. Age: 63 years
Birth: 1925 Death: 1988/09/10 Burial: 1988/09/15
Died: Danville, PA TS: TEC5 US Army
Site 3 James Eugene Titus Age: 58 years
Birth: 1886/05/23 Death: 1944/05/07 Buriel: 1944/05/07
Site 4 Hattie Blanche Fadeley Titus Age: 71 years
Birth: 1887/08/03 Death: 1958/06/05 Burial: 1958/06/09
Died: Arlington, VA On stone with James Eugene Titus
Site 5 James Eugene Titus Jr. Died: Upper Marlboro, MD Age: 66 years
Birth: 1911/03/04 Death: 1977/12/25 Burial: 1977/12/28

Site 7   Elizabeth Hopper Hopkins   Age: 80 years
         Birth: 1899/06/21   Death: 1979/10/27   Burial: 1979/10/30
                                  Died: Leesburg, VA
Site 8   Fred L. Ball Jr.   Died: Martinsburg, WV   Age: 62 years
         Birth: 1917/05/14   Death: 1979/12/27   Burial: 1979/12/31
Site 9   Edna Irene Ball
         Birth: 1913/12/31   Death: 1994/11/21   Burial: 1994/11/25
         Died: Leesburg, VA   On stone with Fred L. Ball Jr.
Site 10 Harvey Brown Titus
         Birth: 1913/01/02   Death: 1995/04/07   Burial: 1995/04/10
         Died: Arlington, VA   TS: EM2 US Navy WWII

Lot: 1141 W Owner: Mrs. Inez Jenkins   Purchased: 1956/07/18
Site 1   Clinton Columbus Jenkins   Age: 19 years
         Birth: 1936/08/04   Death: 1956/07/16   Burial: 1956/07/18
                                  Died: White's Ferry, VA
Site 2   Rebecca Lew Jenkins   Age: 8 years
         Birth: 1951   Death: 1959/12/01   Burial: 1959/12/04
         Cause: Auto Accident   Died: Lewisburg, PA
Site 3   Lewis Edgar Jenkins   Age: 50 years
         Birth: 1926/06/02   Death: 1976/06/23   Burial: 1976/06/26
         Died: Martinsburg, WV   TS: MSG US Army WWII Korea Vietnam
Site 4   Inez Ashby Howser Jenkins   Died: Leesburg, VA
         Birth: 1898/11/25   Death: 1994/09/13   Burial: 1994/09/17

Lot: 1142 E Owner: John R. & Hazel M. McWilliams
Site 9   John Robert McWilliams   Age: 78 years
         Birth: 1894/09/18   Death: 1972/06/14
Site 10 Hazel Margaret McWilliams   Age: 58 years
         Birth: 1901/09/05   Death: 1960/01/31   Burial: 1960/02/03
         Died: L.C.H. Leesburg, VA   On stone with John Robert McWilliams

Lot: 1142 W Owner: Inola Downs   Purchased: 1962/01/26
Site 1   Grover H. Downs   Died: Washington, DC   Age: 36 years
         Birth: 1926/06/13   Death: 1962/01/24   Burial: 1962/01/26

UNION CEMETERY
LEESBURG, LOUDOUN CO., VA

PLAT E

Lot: 1143   Owner: Dr. Frank P. Smoot   Purchased: 1941/05/01
Site 7   Frank P. Smoot   Place: Elkins, WV   Age: 80 years
         Birth: 1896/06/20   Death: 1976/07/29   Burial: 1976/07/31
         TS: 2nd Lt. US Army WW I   DDS
Site 8   Thelma J. Smoot   Place: Leesburg, VA   Age: 90 years
         Birth: 1900/01/07   Death: 1990/02/26   Burial: 1990/03/01
Site 9   Florence Anne Smoot Coster
         Birth: 1924/09/25   Death: 1994/12/23   Burial: 1994/12/28
         Place: Berryville, VA   Stone reads Florence Anne Smoot

Lot: 1144 E   Owner: W.S. Jenkins   Purchased: 1940/03/14
Site 9   William Herndon Jenkins, MD
         Birth: 1890/12/29   Death: 1967/11/20   Burial: 1968/05/06
Site 10 Gene Montgomery Jenkins   Age: 77 years
         Birth: 1893/01/24   Death: 1970/06/01   Burial: 1970/06/13
                                 Place: Seattle, WA
Site 11 William Smith Jenkins   Age: 90 years
         Birth: 1856/10/20   Death: 1947/08/15   Burial: 1947/08/17
Site 12 Orra Lee Jenkins   TS: Wife of W.S. Jenkins   Age: 63 years
         Birth: 1858/09/12   Death: 1921/09/12   Cause: Cancer

Lot: 1144 W Owner: E.L. Munday & Maude P. Wortman
                                                            1940/02/07
Site 1   Arthur T. Wortman   Cause: Coronary Occlusion Age: 59 years
         Birth: 1880   Death: 1940/02/06   Burial: 1940/02/08
Site 2   Maude P. Wortman   Age: 82 years
         Birth: 1879   Death: 1960/03/11   Burial: 1960/03/13
         Place: Leesburg, VA   On stone with Arthur T. Wortman
Site 3   Ernest L. Munday Sr.   Place: Martinsville, WV   Age: 86 years
         Birth: 1877   Death: 1963/03/02   Burial: 1963/03/04
Site 4   Mrs. Lula A. Munday   Age: 70 years
         Birth: 1888   Death: 1958/09/02   Burial: 1958/09/04
         Place: L.C.H. Leesburg, VA   On stone with Ernest L. Munday

Lot: 1145 E   Owner: Mrs. Daisey K. Myers   Purchased: 1941/03/20
Site 7   Daisy May Myers   No stone   Age: 69 years
                                 Death: 1945/05/30   Burial: 1945/06/01
Site 8   Edward Bruce Myers   Cause: Coronary Occlusion Age: 76 years
         Birth: 1865/02/28   Death: 1941/03/19   Burial: 1941/03/21
Site 9   Edward Bruce Myers Jr.   Removal
         Birth: 1901/06/19   Death: 1925/12/08   Burial: 1941/03/27

Site 11 Douglas Nelson Myers Place: Leesburg, VA Age: 85 years
Birth: 1896/07/19 Death: 1982/01/18 Burial: 1982/01/20
Site 12 Winifrede E. Myers Place: Waterford, VA Age: 71 years
Birth: 1895/01/15 Death: 1966/05/11 Burial: 1966/05/13

Lot: 1145 W Owner: Mrs. M.D. Atwell   Purchased: 1944/02/18
Site 1 Maurice D. Atwell Place: Leesburg, VA Age: 68 years
Birth: 1894/07/14 Death: 1962/08/02 Burial: 1962/08/04
Site 2 Sara Arnold Atwell   Age: 72 years
Birth: 1900/05/03 Death: 1973/02/02 Burial: 1973/02/05
Place: Leesburg, VA   On stone with Maurice D. Atwell

Lot: 1146   Owner: James E. Arnold   Purchased: 1940/07/29
Site 1 John William Arnold Cause: Cerebral Hemorrhage Age: 69 years
Birth: 1871/02/18 Death: 1940/08/02 Burial: 1940/08/04
Site 3 Ella M. Arnold Place: L.C.H. Leesburg, VA Age: 85 years
Birth: 1878/12/03 Death: 1963/03/15 Burial: 1963/03/15
Site 5 Forest Anne Arnold   Age: 14 years
Birth: 1955/01/18 Death: 1969/03/12 Burial: 1969/03/14
Place: Leesburg, VA TS: Daughter of John S. & Janet Lee Arnold
Site 6 Richard Wayne Arnold   Age: 7 months
Birth: 1953/06/24 Death: 1954/02/13
TS: Son of John S. & Janet Lee Arnold
Site 7 Patricia Ann Arnold   Age: 1day
Birth: 1940/07/25 Death: 1940/07/26 Burial: 1940/07/30
Cause: Alelephases Asph. TS: Daughter of James E. & Forest I. Arnold
Site 9 Forest Inez Arnold   Age: 52 years
Birth: 1902/05/22 Death: 1954/03/06
Site 10 James E. Arnold Sr. Place: Waterford, VA Age: 78 years
Birth: 1902/10/14 Death: 1981/03/22 Burial: 1981/03/25

Lot: 1147 E Owner: Harry Trussell   Purchased: 1940/09/14
Site 7 Baby Girl Trussell TS: Infant daughter of R.B. & H.E. Trussell
Cause: Stillborn Death: 1941/02/07 Burial: 1941/02/07
Site 9 Harry Harper Trussell Place: Leesburg, VA Age: 88 years
Birth: 1893/08/30 Death: 1981/01/24 Burial: 1981/01/28
Site 10 Minnie Belle Arnold Trussell   Age: 85 years
Birth: 1903/07/16 Death: 1988/10/13 Burial: 1988/10/15
Place: Leesburg, VA

Lot: 1147 W Owner: Richard Y. Arnold   Purchased: 1941/09/14
Site 2 Richard Yakey Arnold Place: Leesburg, VA Age: 76 years
Birth: 1904/11/26 Death: 1981/06/22 Burial: 1981/06/25
Site 3 Jason Arnold Cause: Bronchial Pneumonia Age: 64 years
Birth: 1876/02/29 Death: 1940/09/14 Burial: 1940/09/16
Site 5 Katherine Bondeena Arnold   Age: 92 years
Birth: 1878/05/22 Death: 1972/11/11 Burial: 1972/11/14
Place: Charles Town, WV

Lot: 1148 E Owner: Ella Lee McFarland   Purchased: 1942/11/14
Site 8   Eppa Lee McFarland   Age: 64 years
         Birth: 1878   Death: 1942/11/13   Burial: 1942/11/15
Site 8   Mrs. Ella Lee McFarland   Age: 69 years
         Birth: 1887   Death: 1956/08/23   Burial: 1956/08/23
         Cause: Heart   Place: Leesburg, VA
         On stone with Eppa Lee McFarland

Lot: 1148 W Owner: Miscellaneous
Site 1   Mary Gertrude Cullen   Age: 44 years
         Birth: 1898/11/14   Death: 1942/12/23   Burial: 1942/12/26
Site 2   Goldie Catherine Lusby   Age: 80 years
         Birth: 1890/02/07   Death: 1969/12/09   Burial: 1969/12/12
         Place: Essex Co., VA   On stone with Charles I. Lusby
Site 3   Charles I. Lusby   Place: Arlington, VA   Age: 81 years
         Birth: 1889/10/09   Death: 1971/07/27   Burial: 1971/07/29
Site 4   George Franklin Cullen   Place: Denver, CO   Age: 87 years
         Birth: 1888   Death: 1976/06/20   Burial: 1976/06/24
Site 5   Ruth Howser Cullen   Place: Arvado, CO   Age: 82 years
         Birth: 1894   Death: 1976/09/12   Burial: 1976/09/16
         On stone with George Franklin Cullen
Site 6   Walter Franklin Cullen   Place: Richmond, VA   TS: US Navy WW II
         Birth: 1915/08/29   Death: 1995/08/22   Burial: 1995/08/25

Lot: 1149 E Owner: Everett Phillips   Purchased: 1944/03/12
Site 7   Everett Phillips   Age: 48 years
         Birth: 1896/01/21   Death: 1944/03/11   Burial: 1944/03/13
Site 8   Lucy Turman Phillips   Age: 81 years
         Birth: 1897/07/31   Death: 1978/11/06   Burial: 1978/11/08
         Place: Akron, OH   On stone with Everett Phillips

Lot: 1149 W Owner: Arthur Holliday   Purchased: 1943/10/21
Site 2   Pearl E. Holliday   Place: Fairfax, VA   No stone
         Birth: 1906/05/14   Death: 1995/12/04   Burial: 1995/12/08
Site 3   Edward M. Holliday   Place: Fairfax, VA   Age: 75 years
         Birth: 1904   Death: 1979/08/21   Burial: 1979/08/24
Site 4   Arthur Henry Holliday   Age: 75 years
         Birth: 1861   Death: 1945/06/24   Burial: 1945/06/26
Site 5   Mrs. Mary S. Molly Holliday   Age: 74 years
         Birth: 1869   Death: 1950/09/26   Burial: 1950/09/28

Lot: 1150 E Owner: Miscellaneous
Site 7   Reed Johnson   Age: 61 years
         Birth: 1916/09/13   Death: 1977/11/26   Burial: 1977/11/29
         Cause: Heart   Place: Leesburg, VA
Site 9   Victor Leon Myers   Age: 60 years
         Birth: 1891/03/10   Death: 1951/04/15   Burial: 1951/04/17
Site 9   Capt. Harold E. Palmer   Place: Glade Hill, VA   Age: 70 years
         Birth: 1916/05/24   Death: 1987/03/27   Burial: 1987/03/31
         TS: Captain U.S.M.M.   Married Louise L. Palmer September 4, 1940

Site 11 Georgia L. Myers   Age: 86 years
         Birth: 1893/10/21   Death: 1980/01/30   Burial: 1980/02/01
         Place: Leesburg, VA   On stone with Victor L. Myers
Site 12 Marian V. Miller   Place: Arlington, VA
         Birth: 1899   Death: 1973/03/28   Burial: 1973/03/31

Lot: 1150 W Owner: V. B. Harding   Purchased: 1942/03/31
Site 3 Victor Buford Harding   Age: 67 years
         Birth: 1878   Death: 1945/06/15   Burial: 1945/06/17
Site 5 Emma Lee Harding   Age: 74 years
         Birth: 1891   Death: 1965/07/08   Burial: 1965/07/10
         Place: Leesburg, VA   On stone with Victor B. Harding
Site 6 L.I. Pearce   Place: FL
         Birth: 1916/01/04   Death: 1991/05/19   Burial: 1991/07/20

Lot: 1151   Owner: Miscellaneous
Site 7 Samuel W. Slusser   Place: Dayton, OH   Age: 86 years
         Birth: 1871   Death: 1958/03/31   Burial: 1958/04/05
Site 9 Della Maude Slusser   Age: 73 years
         Birth: 1876   Death: 1949/12/06   Burial: 1949/12/09
         On stone with Samuel W. Slusser
Site 10 Charlie R. Embrey   Place: Jefferson Memorial Hosp Age: 75 years
         Birth: 1907   Death: 1983/04/21   Burial: 1983/04/25
Site 11 Robert J. Wilson   Place: Miami, FL   Age: 89 years
         Birth: 1902   Death: 1983/02/25   Burial: 1983/03/04

Lot: 1152 E Owner: Mrs. Ralph A. Clark   Purchased: 1946/12/03
Site 7 Ralph A. Clark
         Birth: 1893   Death: 1946/12/03   Burial: 1946/12/05
Site 8 Anna T. Clark   Age: 77 years
         Birth: 1896   Death: 1973/03/21   Burial: 1973/03/23
         Place: Leesburg, VA   On stone with Ralph A. Clark
Site 9 Lillian A. Tracy   Place: Leesburg, VA   Age: 95 years
         Birth: 1884   Death: 1979/10/17   Burial: 1979/10/20
Site 10 Richard T. Clark   Place: Arlington, VA   Age: 57 years
         Birth: 1924   Death: 1982/02/19   Burial: 1982/02/24

Lot: 1152 W Owner: Mrs. Mary Gibson   Purchased: 1946/09/02
Site 1 Robert William Gibson Place: Leesburg, VA   Age: 35 years
         Birth: 1922/02/26   Death: 1958/01/01   Burial: 1958/01/03
         Cause: Poison   TS: Virginia PFC US Army WW II
Site 3 Milton R. Gibson   Place: Fairfax, VA   Age: 76 years
         Birth: 1893   Death: 1969/10/31   Burial: 1969/11/03
Site 4 Mary R. Gibson   Place: Leesburg, VA   Age: 91 years
         Birth: 1896   Death: 1987/12/03   Burial: 1987/12/07
         On stone with Milton R. Gibson

Lot: 1153 E Owner: Miscellaneous
Site 7 Warren D. Ashby   Age: 62 years
         Birth: 1910   Death: 1972/07/04

Site 10 Albert Fox Follin   Birth: 1915/10/16   Death: 1979/04/21

Lot: 1153 W Owner: Herbert Kirkpatrick   Purchased: 1947/01/08
Site 2   Herbert Nelson Kirkpatrick Jr.   Age: 59 years
         Birth: 1929/12/23   Death: 1989/11/19   Burial: 1989/11/22
         Place: Leesburg, VA   TS: Son
Site 3   Herbert N. Kirkpatrick   Place: Leesburg, VA   Age: 80 years
         Birth: 1895/10/30   Death: 1976/06/13   Burial: 1976/06/15
Site 4   Annie E. Kirkpatrick
         Birth: 1905/05/17   Death: 1993/01/16   Burial: 1993/01/19
         Place: Leesburg, VA   On stone with Herbert N. Kirkpatrick Sr.

Lot: 1154   Owner: C. Fenton Connor   Purchased: 1946/02/14
Site 3   Cecil Connor   Cause: Cerebral Hemorrhage   Age: 67 years
         Birth: 1871/02/04   Death: 1938/02/18   Burial: 1938/02/20
         Removal from Lot 506 site 7 April 17, 1946
Site 4   Edna Fadeley Connor   Age: 60 years
         Birth: 1884/03/22   Death: 1946/02/12   Burial: 1946/02/14
Site 5   C. Fenton Connor   Place: FL   Age: 61 years
         Birth: 1907/05/06   Death: 1969/01/03   Burial: 1969/01/08

Lot: 1155   Owner: Francis E. & Ethel L. Bishop   1950/02/13
Site 3   Francis E. Bishop   Place: Leesburg, VA   Age: 64 years
         Birth: 1899/10/16   Death: 1964/07/14   Burial: 1964/07/17
Site 4   Ethel L. Bishop   No death date on stone
         Birth: 1904/09/04   Death: 1994/12/28   Burial: 1994/12/31
         Place: Leesburg, VA   On stone with Francis E. Bishop
Site 9   Francis Bishop   Place: Arlington, VA   No stone
         Birth: 1934/08/05   Death: 1993/09/05   Burial: 1993/09/08

Lot: 1156   Owner: Paul R. Pearson   Purchased: 1950/02/14
Site 3   Joseph Samuel Pearson   Age: 75 years
         Birth: 1874/08/15   Death: 1950/02/14   Burial: 1950/02/17
Site 5   Edith Royston (Minna) Pearson   Age: 82 years
         Birth: 1880/03/21   Death: 1962/07/08   Burial: 1962/07/11
         Place: Montgomery, MD   On stone with Joseph Samuel Pearson
Site 10 Aubrey Linwood Pearson   Place: Winchester, VA   Age: 60 years
         Birth: 1927/12/28   Death: 1988/05/03   Burial: 1988/05/06
Site 11 Paul R. Pearson   Place: Leesburg, VA   Age: 87 years
         Birth: 1900/07/28   Death: 1987/11/23   Burial: 1987/11/27
Site 12 Hattie L. Pearson   Age: 79 years
         Birth: 1907/06/11   Death: 1986/10/29   Burial: 1986/11/02
         Place: Leesburg, VA   On stone with Paul R. Pearson

Lot: 1157   Owner: Miscellaneous
Site 1   John N. Campbell   Age: 60 years
         Birth: 1898/10/07   Death: 1958/11/07   Burial: 1958/11/10
         Cause: Heart Attack   Place: L.C.H. Leesburg, VA

Site 4   John M. Campbell Jr.   Age: 36 years
         Birth: 1942/02/23   Death: 1978/05/26   Burial: 1978/06/01
         Cause: Plane crash   Place: Louisa Co., VA
Site 10 Viola H. Smallwood   Age: 68 years
         Birth: 1914/02/11   Death: 1982/02/13   Burial: 1982/02/16
         Place: Leesburg, VA
Site 12 Baby Boy Smallwood   Cause: Stillborn   Place: Winchester, VA
                                  Death: 1958/11/04   Burial: 1958/11/05

Lot: 1158   Owner: Wilbur R. & Kathleen A. Frye   1956/05/18
Site 1   Elbert H. Frye   Place: Leesburg, VA   Age: 83 years
         Birth: 1874   Death: 1960/01/23   Burial: 1960/01/26
Site 2   Lovie R. Frye   Age: 86 years
         Birth: 1880   Death: 1966/11/15   Burial: 1966/11/18
         Place: Leesburg, VA   On stone with Elbert H. Frye
Site 3   Wilbur R. Frye   Place: Leesburg, VA   Age: 65 years
         Birth: 1905   Death: 1971/01/30   Burial: 1971/02/01
Site 4   Kathleen Athey Frye   Place: Leesburg, VA   Age: 67 years
         Birth: 1909   Death: 1976/11/23   Burial: 1976/11/26
         Cause: Cancer   On stone with Wilbur R. Frye
Site 5   Two Baby Boys Graham   Cause: Stillborn   Place: Leesburg, VA
                                  Death: 1965/06/01   Burial: 1965/06/02
Site 6   Marie S. Atchley   Place: Leesburg, VA   Age: 78 years
         Birth: 1905/01/17   Death: 1983/07/14   Burial: 1983/07/16
Site 9   John Blakely Simpson   Place: Leesburg, VA   Age: 83 years
         Birth: 1905   Death: 1989/04/08   Burial: 1989/04/11
Site 10 Eva R. Simpson   Age: 73 years
         Birth: 1911   Death: 1985/11/04   Burial: 1985/11/06
         Place: Leesburg, VA   On stone with John Blakely Simpson
Site 12 Mrs. Kathleen R. Athey   Place: Leesburg, VA   Age: 43 years
         Birth: 1924/07/07   Death: 1967/03/31   Burial: 1967/04/02

Lot: 1159 E Owner: J. Sterling Moran   Purchased: 1941/05/10
Site 7   James Sterling Moran   Place: Arlington, VA   Age: 80 years
         Birth: 1879   Death: 1960/01/15   Burial: 1960/01/18
Site 9   Nellie Bryant Moran   Age: 78 years
         Birth: 1882   Death: 1961/03/10   Burial: 1961/03/13
         Place: Arlington, VA   On stone with James Sterling Moran
Site 9   Elbert M. Moran Sr.   Age: 70 years
         Birth: 1910/06/10   Death: 1980/07/28   Burial: 1980/07/30
         Place: Prince George, MD

Lot: 1159 W Owner: R. T. Corbell   Purchased: 1940/04/15
Site 4   Robert Thruston Corbell   Age: 65 years
         Birth: 1887/04/04   Death: 1952/06/13   Burial: 1952/06/15
         TS: Husband of Edna Wright Corbell
Site 6   Edna Wright Corbell   Age: 56 years
         Birth: 1883/08/20   Death: 1940/04/15   Burial: 1940/04/17
         Cause: Generalized Carcinomaton

Lot: 1160 E Owner: E.H. Norris   Purchased: 1941/12/27
Site 7 Catherine Ann Norris   Age: 71 years
        Birth: 1911/09/21   Death: 1983/02/08   Burial: 1983/02/11
        Cause: Big snow   Place: Leesburg, VA
Site 8 Elizabeth Newton Norris Place: Leesburg, VA   Age: 77 years
        Birth: 1908/11/01   Death: 1985/06/26   Burial: 1985/06/28
Site 9 Edward Hammet Norris   Age: 71 years
        Birth: 1874   Death: 1945/08/25   Burial: 1945/08/27
Site 10 Essie May Newton Norris   Age: 68 years
        Birth: 1873   Death: 1941/12/27   Burial: 1941/12/29
        Cause: Cirrhosis of Liver   On stone with Edward Hammat Norris
Site 11 Miss Mary F. Norris   Place: Leesburg, VA   Age: 77 years
        Birth: 1901/06/14   Death: 1978/09/09   Burial: 1978/09/12

Lot: 1160 W Owner: Harry G. Anderson   Purchased: 1941/01/13
Site 1 Justin E. Martindale   Removal
        Birth: 1881   Death: 1940   Burial: 1941/01/14ü
Site 3 Harry Gilmore Anderson Place: Loudoun Co., VA   Age: 89 years
        Birth: 1871   Death: 1961/05/05   Burial: 1961/05/07
Site 4 Mary Louise Anderson   Place: Philomont, VA   Age: 84 years
        Birth: 1874   Death: 1958/11/06   Burial: 1958/11/08

Lot: 1161   Owner: Mrs. Augusta Lea Macdonald   1942/01/05
Site 1 Robert Macdonald   Age: 87 years
        Birth: 1854/08/01   Death: 1942/01/05   Burial: 1942/01/07
        TS: Born at Mudale The Highlands of Scotland. Died at Leesburg, VA
Site 2 Mrs. Augusta Lea Macdonald   TS: Wife of Robert Macdonald
        Birth: 1866/10/01   Death: 1950/01/15   Burial: 1950/01/18
        TS: Born at Fulton on the Mississippi in TN.   Died Baird, TX
Site 3 Alastair S. Macdonald   Age: 56 years
        Birth: 1895/07/26   Death: 1951/08/29   Burial: 1951/08/31
        TS: Virginia 1st Lt. 155 Depot Brigade WW I
Site 7 George Peyton Craighill   Age: 70 years
        Birth: 1878   Death: 1950/01/04   Burial: 1950/01/06
Site 8 Anne Macdonald Craighill   Age: 56 years
        Birth: 1881   Death: 1948/03/07   Burial: 1948/03/09
        TS: Wife of Rev. G. Peyton Craighill
Site 9 Children of Payton & Anne Craighill
        Birth: 1934/11/17   Death: 1934/11/18
        TS: Infants of Rev. G.P. & Anna Craighill
Site 10 Robert Macdonald Craighill   Age: 28 years
        Birth: 1926   Death: 1954/12/31   Burial: 1955/01/01
        Place: Charlottesville, VA

Lot: 1162 E Owner: E.S. Adrian   Purchased: 1942/09/28
Site 7 Allen Mercer Adrian   Age: 39 years
        Birth: 1904   Death: 1943/12/06   Burial: 1943/12/08
Site 9 Eugene S. Adrian   Place: Leesburg, VA   Age: 88 years
        Birth: 1877   Death: 1966/03/21   Burial: 1966/03/23

Site 10 Mrs. Lillian H. Adrian Age: 81 years
Birth: 1885 Death: 1966/09/28 Burial: 1966/09/30
Place: Leesburg, VA On stone with Eugene S. Adrian
Site 10 Alice Suits No stone Age: 69 years
Place: Greensboro, NC Death: 1992/03/05 Burial: 1992/03/16
Site 11 Eugene Howard Adrian Place: Leesburg, VA Age: 52 years
Birth: 1916 Death: 1968/08/18 Burial: 1968/08/20

Lot: 1162 W Owner: Miscellaneous
Site 1 Edward H. (Beans) Norris Place: Leesburg, VA Age: 77 years
Birth: 1906/03/23 Death: 1984/01/20 Burial: 1984/01/23
Site 6 Ellen Gaines Norris Age: 69 years
Birth: 1908/03/09 Death: 1977/10/09 Burial: 1977/10/12
Place: Leesburg, VA On stone with Edward H. Norris, Jr.

Lot: 1163 E Owner: John Thomas & William C. Wright 1941/03/31
Site 1 John Thomas Wright Age: 78 years
Birth: 1875 Death: 1952/01/31 Burial: 1952/02/02
Site 2 Katoria Rollins Wright Age: 91 years
Birth: 1870 Death: 1962/03/29 Burial: 1962.03/31
Place: Paeonian Springs, VA
Site 4 William Chester Wright Cause: Carcinoma of Lung Age: 37 years
Birth: 1904 Death: 1942/07/10 Burial: 1942/07/12

Lot: 1164 Owner: Mrs. Gray W. Hume Purchased: 1943/03/27
Site 2 Gray Walton Hume III Age: 43 years
Birth: 1938/11/08 Death: 1982/03/15 Burial: 1982/03/17
Place: Warrenton, VA TS: SP4 US Army
Site 3 Gray Walton Hume Age: 67 years
Birth: 1875 Death: 1943/03/25 Burial: 1943/03/27
Site 4 Mrs. Elsie Payne Hume TS: Wife of Gray Walton Hume
Birth: 1875 Death: 1937 Burial: 1946/05/07
Removal from Orange, VA on May 7, 1946.
Site 5 Elizabeth Hume Carr Place: Winchester, VA Age: 83 years
Birth: 1906/09/19 Death: 1990/04/26 Burial: 1990/04/28
Site 6 Gray Walton Hume Jr. Place: Sarasota, FL TS: Lt. US Navy WW II
Birth: 1910/06/29 Death: 1993/06/16 Burial: 1993/06/29
Site 7 Lillian Lawson Hume Place: Richmond, VA Age: 80 years
Birth: 1886 Death: 1975/04/12 Burial: 1975/04/14
Site 8 Jones Moore Lawson Age: 60 years
Birth: 1917 Death: 1977/12/13 Burial: 1977/12/15
Place: Richmond, VA TS: Sgt. US Marine Corps WW II
Site 9 Elise Gray Hume Lawson Age: 80 years
Birth: No date on stone Death: 1986/02/18 Burial: 1986/02/20
Place: Richmond, VA TS: Wife of Jones M. Lawson

Lot: 1165 Owner: Miscellaneous
Site 4 Jesse Woodrow Frye Place: Leesburg, VA Age: 66 years
Birth: 1915 Death: 1982/06/03 Burial: 1982/06/06

Site 5   Eugene D. Frye   Place: Frederick, MD   Age: 93 years
         Birth: 1880   Death: 1974/11/12   Burial: 1974/11/15
Site 6   Daisy S. Frye   Age: 88 years
         Birth: 1885   Death: 1974/02/01   Burial: 1974/02/03
         Place: Leesburg, VA   On stone with Eugene D. Frye

Lot: 1166   Owner: Scott B. Jenkins   Purchased: 1946/05/04
Site 1   Scott B. Jenkins   Age: 86 years
         Birth: 1859   Death: 1946/05/03   Burial: 1946/05/05
Site 2   Fannie Mae L. Jenkins   Place: Leesburg, VA   Age: 91 years
         Birth: 1869   Death: 1960/03/18   Burial: 1960/03/20
Site 3   Miss Mary Anne Jenkins Place: Leesburg, VA   Age: 75 years
         Birth: 1892   Death: 1970/02/18   Burial: 1970/02/21
Site 7   Arthur S. Jenkins   Place: Leesburg, VA   Age: 88 years
         Birth: 1891   Death: 1980/05/17   Burial: 1980/05/20
Site 8   Pearl Shreve Jenkins   Place: Leesburg, VA   Age: 86 years
         Birth: 1891   Death: 1978/07/14   Burial: 1978/07/17
Site 9   Harry M. Jenkins   Place: Leesburg, VA   Age: 74 years
         Birth: 1907   Death: 1982/01/21   Burial: 1982/01/24
Site 10 Ruby T. Jenkins   Place: Leesburg, VA   Age: 84 years
         Birth: 1909   Death: 1993/04/01   Burial: 1993/04/04

Lot: 1167   Owner: John W. Fouche Jr.   Purchased: 1947/05/02
Site 1   John W. Fouche   Place: Fairfax, VA   Age: 95 years
         Birth: 1873   Death: 1969/02/04   Burial: 1969/02/06
Site 2   Elva Lee Fouche   On stone with John W. Fouche   Age: 67 years
         Birth: 1879   Death: 1947/05/02   Burial: 1947/05/04

Lot: 1168   Owner: Charles R. Hope   Purchased: 1948/01/21
Site 3   Capt. Charles W. Blue   Age: 53 years
         Birth: 1908/07/18   Death: 1962/06/27   Burial: 1962/06/29
         Place: L.C.H. Leesburg, VA   State trooper TS: Father
Site 7   Charles Randolph Hope Jr.   Place: Leesburg, VA   Age: 74 years
         Birth: 1913/11/12   Death: 1988/08/14   Burial: 1988/08/17
Site 8   Miriam L. Lampe Hope
         Birth: 1923/01/07   Death: 1994/01/07   Burial: 1994/01/10
         Place: Leesburg, VA   On stone with Charles Randolph Hope Jr.
Site 9   Charles R. Hope Sr.   TS: Father   Age: 75 years
         Birth: 1885/03/16   Death: 1960/07/04   Burial: 1960/07/07
Site 10 Nora Howser Hope   Age: 85 years
         Birth: 1889/01/01   Death: 1974/08/30   Burial: 1974/09/01
         Place: Leesburg, VA   TS: Mother

Lot: 1169   Owner: Blair S. & Virginia S. Titus   1947/12/29
Site 3   Susan Virginia Wenner Titus
         Birth: 1909/10/13   Death: 1994/10/19   Burial: 1994/10/21
         Place: Cadiz, OH   On stone with Blair Sumner Titus
Site 4   Blair Sumner Titus   Place: Frederick, MD   Age: 73 years
         Birth: 1906/07/08   Death: 1979/08/04   Burial: 1979/08/07

Site 5 William Richard Titus   Age: 72 years
        Birth: 1875   Death: 1947/12/28   Burial: 1947/12/30

Lot: 1170   Owner: Roy F. Titus   Purchased: 1947/11/11
Site 1 George Tunis Titus   Age: 64 years
        Birth: 1883/02/22   Death: 1947/11/11   Burial: 1947/11/13
Site 2 Virginia Ella (Virgie) Titus   Age: 62 years
        Birth: 1885/08/23   Death: 1948/01/20   Burial: 1948/01/22
        On stone with George Tunis Titus
Site 3 Roy F. Titus   Place: Leesburg, VA   Age: 75 years
        Birth: 1909/01/27   Death: 1984/12/25   Burial: 1984/12/28
        TS: Married Helen Ann Titus October 21, 1931
Site 4 Helen Ann Titus   Place: Lucketts, VA
        Birth: 1910/04/29   Death: 1994/02/24   Burial: 1994/02/26

Lot: 1171   Owner: Mr. & Mrs. William M. Filler   1954/06/23
Site 3 Drucella H. Filler   Place: Leesburg, VA   Age: 87 years
        Birth: 1903/01/30   Death: 1990/08/23   Burial: 1990/08/25
Site 4 William Michael Filler   Place: Leesburg, VA   Age: 81 years
        Birth: 1873/05/29   Death: 1955/02/19   Burial: 1955/02/19
Site 5 Mrs. Lula A. Filler Fairfax   Place: Leesburg, VA   Age: 90 years
        Birth: 1877/10/03   Death: 1968/01/28   Burial: 1968/01/31
Site 6 John Holtz   Birth: 1941   Death: 1989
Site 11 James Robert Filler   Place: Hagerstown, MD   Age: 76 years
        Birth: 1899/09/14   Death: 1979/11/04   Burial: 1979/11/06
Site 12 Nina E. Filler   Place: Leesburg, VA   Age: 62 years
        Birth: 1912/12/17   Death: 1975/05/15   Burial: 1975/05/17

Lot: 1172 E Owner: Miscellaneous
Site 7 Kenneth T. Rollison
        Birth: 1923/06/11   Death: 1992/09/17   Burial: 1992/09/19
        Place: WV   TS: PFC US Army Air Corps WW II
Site 8 Neva M. Rollison   Place: Hamilton, VA
        Birth: 1923/09/18   Death: 1995/03/18   Burial: 1995/03/21
        On stone with Kenneth T. Rollison
Site 9 George E. Rollison   Place: Leesburg, VA   Age: 87 years
        Birth: 1894/12/18   Death: 1982/10/05   Burial: 1982/10/08
Site 10 Mazie T. Rollison   Place: Hamilton, VA   Age: 89 years
        Birth: 1895/07/20   Death: 1984/10/21   Burial: 1984/10/24
Site 11 Henry M. Thompson   Place: Winchester, VA   Age: 67 years
        Birth: 1891/03/21   Death: 1955/05/13   Burial: 1955/05/13
Site 12 Annie U. Thompson   Place: Leesburg, VA   Age: 64 years
        Birth: 1908/04/15   Death: 1972/10/08   Burial: 1972/10/10

Lot: 1172 W Owner: Thomas B. & Helen M. Hutchison   1951/06/26
Site 4 Thomas B. Hutchison   Place: Leesburg, VA   Age: 83 years
        Birth: 1901/01/30   Death: 1984/09/03   Burial: 1984/09/06
Site 5 Helen Megeath Hutchison   Place: Leesburg, VA   Age: 60 years
        Birth: 1901/11/13   Death: 1961/01/14   Burial: 1961/01/16

Site 6   Alfred Owens Hutchison   Soldier killed in Korea, reinterred
         Birth: 1927/01/29   Death: 1950/09/05   Burial: 1951/07/24
         TS:Virginia 2D Lt. 21 INF 24 INF DIV Korea PH

Lot: 1173   Owner: Mrs. Mary Johnson   Purchased: 1955/10/03
Site 1   Esker Carl Johnson   Place: Lovettsville, VA   Age: 77 years
         Birth: 1912/09/10   Death: 1989/12/19   Burial: 1989/12/22
Site 3   John W. Johnson   Removed from Mt. Middleton
         Birth: 1875   Death: 1949   Burial: 1955/10/05
Site 5   Mary Elizabeth Johnson   Age: 92 years
         Birth: 1878   Death: 1971/07/07   Burial: 1971/07/09
         Place: Leesburg, VA   On stone with John W. Johnson
Site 6   Wanda Johnson   Place: Round Hill, VA   Age: 68 years
         Birth: 1915/06/05   Death: 1983/08/29   Burial: 1983/09/01
Site 7   Gillis E. LeMarr   Place: Leesburg, VA   Age: 58 years
         Birth: 1907/10/19   Death: 1965/10/31   Burial: 1965/11/03
Site 8   Nancy Arlene J. LeMarr Place: Winchester, VA   Age: 72 years
         Birth: 1909/06/29   Death: 1981/09/30   Burial: 1981/10/03
Site 10 Dorothy J. Lemarr   Removed from Mt. Middleton
         Birth: 1899/06/04   Death: 1941/11/20   Burial: 1955/10/05
         TS: Daughter of John & Mary Johnson
Site 11 Bessie Johnson Lemarr   Removed from Mt. Middleton
         Birth: 1901/11/17   Death: 1938/05/28   Burial: 1955/10/05
         TS: Daughter of John & Mary Johnson
Site 12 James Lemarr   Removed from Mt. Middleton
         Birth: 1936   Death: 1941   Burial: 1955/10/05

Lot: 1174   Owner: J.C. Johnson   Purchased: 1955/06/13
Site 1   Bedford Lee Johnson   Place: Lovettsville, VA   Age: 51 years
         Birth: 1935   Death: 1986/09/22   Burial: 1986/09/24
Site 3   James Chott Johnson   Place: Leesburg, VA   Age: 51 years
         Birth: 1903   Death: 1955/07/03   Burial: 1955/07/03
Site 9   James M. Johnson   Place: Lovettsville, VA   Age: 28 years
         Birth: 1960/05/02   Death: 1988/06/30   Burial: 1988/07/04
         TS: Married Deborah J. Johnson August 1, 1982

Lot: 1175 E Owner: George W. Allison   Purchased: 1970/12/04
Site   Thomas Ryan Allison   TS: Loving son & brother
         Birth: 1962/09/07   Death: 1995/03/06
Site 9   George W. Allison Jr. Place: Salisbury, MD   Age: 44 years
         Birth: 1932/07/28   Death: 1976/12/31   Burial: 1977/01/04
         TS: Married Barbara A. Allison January 17, 1953 BT2 US Navy Korea

Lot: 1175 W Owner: Stanley Gaines   Purchased: 1943/04/14
Site 1   Stanley Newlon Gaines Place: Leesburg, VA   Age: 52 years
         Birth: 1926/03/27   Death: 1978/04/06   Burial: 1978/04/08
Site 2   Stanley Tyler Gaines Place: Leesburg, VA   Age: 68 years
         Birth: 1900/03/24   Death: 1968/11/11   Burial: 1968/11/14

Site 3   Alice Newlon Gaines   Age: 74 years
         Birth: 1895/06/17   Death: 1969/07/06   Burial: 1969/07/08
         Place: Fairfax, VA   On stone with Stanley Tyler Gaines
Site 4   Nannie Florence Newlon Cockerell   Age: 44 years
         Birth: 1899/04/01   Death: 1943/04/12   Burial: 1943/04/14
         Cause: Carcinoma of Cervix
         TS: Daughter of W.R. & F.L. Newlon   Cockerell not on stone

Lot: 1176 E   Owner: Mrs. Clagett Myers   Purchased: 1945/05/22
Site 8   Claggett O. Myers   Age: 58 years
         Birth: 1887   Death: 1945/05/21   Burial: 1945/05/23
Site 9   Nellie M. Myers   Age: 86 years
         Birth: 1892   Death: 1978/12/09   Burial: 1978/12/12
         Place: Leesburg, VA   On stone with Clagett O. Myers
Site 10 Maurice A. Cooper   Place: Leesburg, VA Age: 67 years
         Birth: 1908/09/23   Death: 1976/03/08   Burial: 1976/03/11
Site 12 Melanie Jean Kitzmiller Place: Leesburg, VA   Age: Infant
                              Death: 1977/04/29   Burial: 1977/05/02

Lot: 1176 W Owner: Mr. & Mrs. Daniel Dunn   1945/07/12
Site 4   John Daniel Dunn   Place: Prince Georges Co., MD Age: 72 years
         Birth: 1893/10/20   Death: 1966/09/08   Burial: 1966/09/10
Site 6   Julia L. Dunn   Age: 78 years
         Birth: 1894/10/21   Death: 1973/07/09   Burial: 1973/07/12
         Place: Prince Georges Co., MD   On stone with John Daniel Dunn

Lot: 1177 E   Owner: Mrs. Carrie Myers   Purchased: 1943/04/08
Site 9   Leslie Emerson Myers   Age: 48 years
         Birth: 1894/06/26   Death: 1943/04/07   Burial: 1943/04/10
Site 10 Carrie L. Myers   No stone   Age: 86 years
         Place: Leesburg, VA Death: 1973/04/21   Burial: 1973/04/24

Lot: 1177 W Owner: Rensler E. & Lillie Mae Darnes   1945/10/22
Site 1   Joseph A. Darnes   Age: 6 years
         Birth: 1939   Death: 1945/10/27   Burial: 1945/10/29
Site 2   Stilson Wendell Darnes On stone with Joseph A. Darnes Age: 8 years
         Birth: 1937   Death: 1945/11/19   Burial: 1945/11/21
Site 4   Rensler E. Darnes   Place: Ashburn, VA   Age: 75 years
         Birth: 1899/06/30   Death: 1974/06/26   Burial: 1974/06/28

Lot: 1178   Owner: Andrew F. Athey   Purchased: 1943/08/16
Site 2   Mrs. Mary Estell Athey   Age: 83 years
         Birth: 1882/12/24   Death: 1966/06/06   Burial: 1966/06/09
         Place: Leesburg, VA   On stone with Andrew Fillmore Athey
Site 3   Andrew Fillmore Athey   Age: 67 years
         Birth: 1880/12/11   Death: 1947/12/15   Burial: 1947/12/17
Site 4   Norman Andrew Athey   Age: 27 years
         Birth: 1916/05/14   Death: 1943/08/15   Burial: 1943/08/17
Site 7   Charles F. Athey   Place: Leesburg, VA   Age: 58 years
         Birth: 1906/01/03   Death: 1964/07/05   Burial: 1964/07/08

Site 8   Mildred F. Athey   Age: 58 years
         Birth: 1914/02/21   Death: 1972/10/20   Burial: 1972/10/23
         Place: Lucketts, VA   On stone with Charles F. Athey
Site 9   Henry Lee Carnes   Place: Leesburg, VA   Age: 75 years
         Birth: 1915/11/18   Death: 1991/05/23   Burial: 1991/05/28
Site 11 Leonard W. Jacobs   Place: Leesburg, VA
         Birth: 1921/10/06   Death: 1994/11/13   Burial: 1994/11/17

Lot: 1179 E   Owner: Mrs. William E. Hamilton   1946/03/06
Site 7   William E. Hamilton   Age: 48 years
         Birth: 1898   Death: 1946/03/06   Burial: 1946/03/08
Site 8   Louise A. Hamilton   Age: 93 years
         Birth: 1897   Death: 1988/01/29   Burial: 1988/02/01
         Place: Leesburg, VA   On stone with William E. Hamilton
Site 11 William Hall Hamilton   Age: 35 years
         Birth: 1948/08/31   Death: 1984/02/26   Burial: 1984/03/01
         Cause: Gun Shot   Place: Fairfax, VA   TS: Son
Site 12 David Wayne Hamilton   Place: Loudoun Co., VA   Age: 3
         Birth: 1958/02/09   Death: 1961/05/02   Burial: 1961/05/04

Lot: 1179 W Owner: William W. Craun   Purchased: 1946/01/08
Site 1   William W. Craun   Age: 69 years
         Birth: 1882   Death: 1952/03/24   Burial: 1052/03/26
Site 2   Stella Q. Craun   Age: 59 years
         Birth: 1886   Death: 1946/01/07   Burial: 1946/01/09
         On stone with William W. Craun

Lot: 1180 E   Owner: Samuel C. & Monnie E. Bell   1945/12/26
Site 8   Rufus R. Bell   Age: 75 years
         Birth: 1904   Death: 1979/06/12
Site 9   Arch Samuel Bell   Age: 84 years
         Birth: 1861   Death: 1945/12/28   Burial: 1945/12/30
Site 10 Mary Alice M. Bell   On stone with Arch S. Bell   Age: 78 years
         Birth: 1869   Death: 1947/04/22   Burial: 1947/04/24
Site 11 Samuel C. Bell   Place: Leesburg, VA   Age: 73 years
         Birth: 1892   Death: 1966/06/22   Burial: 1966/06/25
Site 12 Monnie P. Bell   Age: 76 years
         Birth: 1896   Death: 1973/05/19   Burial: 1973/05/22
         Place: Leesburg, VA   On stone with Samuel C. Bell

Lot: 1180 W Owner: Horace E. & Rosa L. Darnes   1945/11/03
Site 1   Horace E. Darnes   Age: 66 years
         Birth: 1896/09/09   Death: 1963/05/15   Burial: 1963/05/18
Site 2   Rosa Lucille U. Darnes
         Birth: 1898/11/27   Death: 1978/01/20   Burial: 1978/01/24
         Place: Vienna, VA   On stone with Horace E. Darnes

Lot: 1181 Owner: Ernest T. Harding Purchased: 1947/04/26
Site 1 Paul Palmer Harding   Age: 68 years
        Birth: 1913/11/23   Death: 1982/04/30   Burial: 1982/05/03
        Place: Washington, DC   TS: US Army
Site 2 Ernest T. Harding   Place: L.C.H. Leesburg, VA   Age: 81 years
        Birth: 1876   Death: 1958/04/04   Burial: 1958/04/06
Site 3 Pauline Ethel Harding   Age: 50 years
        Birth: 1897   Death: 1947/04/25   Burial: 1947/04/27
        On stone with Ernest T. Harding

Lot: 1182 E Owner: Mrs. H. B. Long Purchased:
Site 7 Henry Bowen Long   Age: 58 years
        Birth: 1888/06/24   Death: 1947/01/14   Burial: 1947/01/16
Site 9 Ruth C. Long   Age: 79 years
        Birth: 1888/09/27   Death: 1967/11/02   Burial: 1967/11/06
        Place: Leesburg, VA   On stone with Henry Bowen Long

Lot: 1182 W Owner: C. Lee Franklin Purchased: 1946/05/31
Site 1 C. Lee Franklin   Place: Leesburg, VA Age: 55 years
        Birth: 1909/01/19   Death: 1964/04/09   Burial: 1964/04/12
Site 6 Corbin Hunter Franklin   Age: 77 years
        Birth: 1877/06/06   Death: 1947/11/29   Burial: 1947/12/02

Lot: 1183 Owner: Ronald Hope Purchased: 1948/01/21
Site 1 Ronald A. Hope   Place: Leesburg, VA Age: 75 years
        Birth: 1915/07/19   Death: 1990/11/06   Burial: 1990/11/09
Site 2 Alice Marjorie B. Hope Place: Leesburg, VA Age: 67 years
        Birth: 1919/12/10   Death: 1984/01/06   Burial: 1984/01/09

Lot: 1184 E Owner: Ray Benjamin Purchased: 1948/04/15
Site 7 Ray Benjamin   Place: Leesburg, VA Age: 84 years
        Birth: 1886   Death: 1971/05/11   Burial: 1971/05/13
Site 8 Steven A. Sutphin   Place: Washington, DC Age: 29 years
        Birth: 1955/10/09   Death: 1984/11/14   Burial: 1984/11/17
Site 10 Donald Eugene Reno Sr.   Age: 33 years
        Birth: 1953/10/30   Death: 1987/04/02   Burial: 1987/04/06
        Cause: Suicide   Place: Leesburg, VA

Lot: 1184 W Owner: John T. Thayer Purchased: 1948/04/17
Site 1 Jack Thomas Thayer   Age: 29 years
        Birth: 1918/08/31   Death: 1948/04/17   Burial: 1948/04/19
Site 2 John Thomas Thayer   Place: Leesburg, VA Age: 70 years
        Birth: 1884/09/04   Death: 1955/05/16   Burial: 1955/05/18
Site 3 Gracy P.Y. Thayer   Place: Warrenton, VA Age: 74 years
        Birth: 1889/06/18   Death: 1963/09/13   Burial: 1963/09/16
Site 4 William F. Thayer   Place: Leesburg, VA Age: 61 years
        Birth: 1923/09/16   Death: 1985/04/06   Burial: 1985/04/08
Site 5 James W. Thayer   Age: 83 years
        Birth: 1878   Death: 1962/09/19   Burial: 1962/09/21
        Cause: Old Age   Place: Leesburg, VA

Site 6   Mrs. Sara Holden Thayer   Age: 64 years
          Birth: 1892/01/21   Death: 1952/07/25   Burial: 1952/07/28

Lot: 1185   Owner: Charles G. Epps   Purchased: 1948/03/29
Site 2   Frank Gibson Eppes   No stone   Age: 64 years
          Place: Columbia, MO   Death: 1991/01/08   Burial: 1991/01/12
Site 3   Charles Gibson Eppes   Age: 73 years
          Birth: 1887   Death: 1960/04/27   Burial: 1960/04/29
          Place: Leesburg, VA   TS: Father
Site 4   Sally Joe Eppes   TS: Mother   Age: 58 years
          Birth: 1889   Death: 1948/03/28   Burial: 1948/03/30
Site 6   Jane Eppes Brunner   Place: Washington, DC   Age: 71 years
          Birth: 1913   Death: 1985/01/17   Burial: 1985/01/22
Site 11   Robert Lewis Harper   Age: 64 years
          Birth: 1921/12/30   Death: 1986/03/10   Burial: 1986/03/22
          Place: FL   TS: CPL US Marine Corps WW II

Lot: 1186   Owner: O.T. Tincher   Purchased: 1948/05/14
Site 1   Irol Truman Tincher   Age: 61 years
          Birth: 1887   Death: 1948/05/13   Burial: 1948/05/15
Site 3   Mary Brown Tincher   Place: Roncenerte WV
          Birth: 1887   Death: 1959/12/04   Burial: 1959/12/07
Site 4   John Truman Tincher   Place: Fairfax, VA   Age: 35 years
          Birth: 1938/09/14   Death: 1974/03/09   Burial: 1974/03/11
Site 5   Garland V. Tincher Sr.   Place: Leesburg, VA   Age: 63 years
          Birth: 1916/03/28   Death: 1979/07/14   Burial: 1979/07/17
Site 7   Orville T. Tincher   Place: Leesburg, VA   Age: 72 years
          Birth: 1911/03/01   Death: 1983/10/18   Burial: 1983/10/20
Site 9   William Clay Tincher   Age: 29 years
          Birth: 1960/11/25   Death: 1990/05/27   Burial: 1990/06/02
          Place: San Antonio, TX   TS: Son

Lot: 1187 E Owner: J. Hanson & Dorothy Umbaugh   1964/05/30
Site 8   Dorothy Thayer Umbaugh   Place: Leesburg, VA   Age: 49 years
          Birth: 1915   Death: 1964/12/09   Burial: 1964/12/11
Site 12   Ethel Virginia Thayer   Place: Washington, DC   Age: 51 years
          Birth: 1911   Death: 1964/05/18   Burial: 1964/05/21

Lot: 1187 W Owner: Mrs. John A. Ross   Purchased: 1955/05/30
Site 3   John Anthony Ross   Place: Leesburg, VA   Age: 38 years
          Birth: 1917/01/05   Death: 1955/05/29   Burial: 1955/05/30
Site 5   Marguerite Jenkins Ross Place: Leesburg, VA   Age: 67 years
          Birth: 1915/08/29   Death: 1984/06/02   Burial: 1984/06/05

Lot: 1188   Owner: Miscellaneous
Site 4   Fannie M. Russell   Age: 82 years
          Birth: 1889   Death: 1971/10/07   Burial: 1971/10/10
          Place: Alexandria, VA   On stone with Clifton H. Russell
Site 5   Clifton Herbert Russell Place: Waterford, VA   Age: 72 years
          Birth: 1884   Death: 1956/06/13   Burial: 1956/06/15

Site 6   William Ellmore Russell   Place: Falls Church, VA   Age: 70 years
         Birth: 1915/05/09   Death: 1985/06/22   TS: Son

Lot: 1189   Owner: Miscellaneous
Site 2   Pauline V. Furr   Age: 64 years
         Birth: 1903   Death: 1967/10/13   Burial: 1967/10/15
         Place: Leesburg, VA   On stone with Milton H. Furr
Site 3   Milton H. Furr   Place: Leesburg, VA   Age: 73 years
         Birth: 1901   Death: 1974/10/08   Burial: 1974/10/11
Site 4   Odessie M. Holsinger   Age: 80 years
         Birth: 1897   Death: 1977/02/28   Burial: 1977/03/02
         Place: Fairfax, VA   TS: Mother
Site 8   Spitler A. Legge   Place: Culpepper, VA   Age: 50 years
         Birth: 1915/07/15   Death: 1965/09/28   Burial: 1965/10/01
Site 9   Henry Murt Legg   Place: Aldie, VA   Age: 63 years
         Birth: 1882/06/29   Death: 1955/07/26   Burial: 1955/07/26
Site 10 Dixie Bertha Legg   Age: 75 years
         Birth: 1896/12/12   Death: 1972/11/16   Burial: 1972/11/19
         Place: Leesburg, VA   On stone with Henry Murt Legg

Lot: 1190   Owner: Miscellaneous
Site 1   Paul A. Carter   Place: Leesburg, VA   Age: 56 years
         Birth: 1924/11/27   Death: 1981/11/11   Burial: 1981/11/14
         TS: Married Helen G. Carter September 6, 1963
Site 3   Maurice L. Carnes   Place: Leesburg, VA   Age: 78 years
         Birth: 1910/11/07   Death: 1989/06/21   Burial: 1989/06/24
Site 4   Ruby V. Carnes   Age: 72 years
         Birth: 1914/06/04   Death: 1987/02/27   Burial: 1987/03/01
         Place: Leesburg, VA   On stone with Maurice L. Carnes
Site 5   Leonard O. Warner   Place: Marshall, VA
         Birth: 1916/05/22   Death: 1995/02/20   Burial: 1995/02/25
Site 6   Mildred M. Warner   Age: 65 years
         Birth: 1916/04/21   Death: 1981/11/09   Burial: 1981/11/12
         Place: Leesburg, VA   On stone with Leonard O. Warner
Site 7   Jesse Wogan Jr.   Place: Fairfax, VA   Age: 52 years
         Birth: 1929/01/22   Death: 1981/12/06   Burial: 1981/12/09
Site 9   James Aubrey Athey   Age: 64yers
         Birth: 1924/05/06   Death: 1988/09/03   Burial: 1988/09/07
         Place: Arlington, VA   TS: PFC US Army WW II
Site 10 John Michael Boyd   Place: Purcellville, VA
         Birth: 1944/03/25   Death: 1992/02/03   Burial: 1992/02/06
Site 12 Stephen Michael Ours   Place: Leesburg, VA   Age: 34 years
         Birth: 1947/11/24   Death: 1981/12/31   Burial: 1982/01/03

Lot: 1191   Owner: W.E. Fletcher   Purchased: 1945/12/05
Site 1   Lester Ely Fletcher   Place: Ashburn, VA   Age: 50 years
         Birth: 1918/02/27   Death: 1968/04/24   Burial: 1968/04/26
Site 3   William Essie Fletcher   Age: 63 years
         Birth: 1889   Death: 1952/06/08   Burial: 1952/06/10

Site 5 Geneva M. (Eva) Fletcher   Age: 73 years
        Birth: 1892   Death: 1965/06/17   Burial: 1965/06/20
        Place: Ashburn, VA   On stone with William E. Fletcher
Site 6 James M. Fletcher   Place: Lynchburg, VA   Age: 4 years
        Birth: 1962/08/31   Death: 1966/12/04   Burial: 1966/12/06
Site 7 Carlie James Fletcher Place: Louisville, KY   Age: 77 years
        Birth: 1910   Death: 1988/01/15   Burial: 1988/01/18
Site 8 Albertha D. Fletcher   Age: 66 years
        Birth: 1914   Death: 1980/07/06   Burial: 1980/07/09
        Place: Louisville, KY   On stone with Carlie James Fletcher
Site 9 Terry Lee Fletcher   Place: Leesburg, VA
        Birth: 1959/10/25   Death: 1992/07/23   Burial: 1992/07/27
Site 10 Robert Lee Fletcher   Place: Fairfax, VA   Age: 61 years
        Birth: 1920/04/03   Death: 1982/03/25   Burial: 1982/03/28
Site 11 Dorothy Russell Fletcher   Age: 45 years
        Birth: 1927/09/16   Death: 1972/07/08
Site 12 Deborah Lee Fletcher   Cause: Stillborn   Age: 1day
        Birth: 1952/07/23   Death: 1952/07/24   Burial: 1952/07/25

Lot: 1192 E   Owner: Fred Dove   Purchased: 1946/12/02
Site 9 Frederick M. Dove   Place: Ashburn, VA   Age: 88 years
        Birth: 1874/04/03   Death: 1962/02/12   Burial: 1962/02/14
Site 10 Cleopatra Dove   Age: 83 years
        Birth: 1872/12/13   Death: 1955/02/08   Burial: 1955/02/09
        Place: Leesburg, VA   On stone with Frederick M. Dove
Site 12 John A. Dove   Place: Leesburg, VA   Age: 89 years
        Birth: 1866/09/25   Death: 1955/12/03   Burial: 1955/12/03

Lot: 1192 W Owner: B. Frank Nalle   Purchased: 1941/07/26
Site 1 Robert Lee Preston   Age: 77 years
        Birth: 1863   Death: 1941/07/25   Burial: 1941/07/27
Site 2 Mrs. Leonora Johnston Preston   Age: 87 years
        Birth: 1864   Death: 1952/02/23   Burial: 1952/02/25
        IB:Mrs. Robert Preston
Site 3 Julia Johnston Gerndt Place: Leesburg, VA   Age: 98 years
        Birth: 1866   Death: 1965/02/19   Burial: 1965/02/22
Site 4 Leonora Preston Nalle Place: Leesburg, VA   Age: 72 years
        Birth: 1896   Death: 1968/12/09   Burial: 1968/12/11
Site 5 Bernard Franklin Nalle Place: Winchester, VA   Age: 83 years
        Birth: 1888   Death: 1971/10/29   Burial: 1971/11/01

Lot: 1193   John M. Douglass   Purchased:1947/01/15
Site 3 John Moore Douglass   Age: 58 years
        Birth: 1888/11/30   Death: 1947/01/14   Burial: 1947/01/16
Site 5 Martha Strother Douglass Place: Manassas, VA   Age: 77 years
        Birth: 1892/01/17   Death: 1969/11/13   Burial: 1969/11/15
Site 6 John M. Douglass   Place: Alexandria, VA   Age: 71 years
        No dates on stone   Death: 1990/01/01   Burial: 1990/01/05
Site 7 James Edwards Douglass Place: Aldie, VA   Age: 64 years
        Birth: 1920/06/15   Death: 1985/01/29   Burial: 1985/02/02

Lot: 1194   Owner: Mr. & Mrs. Monroe Flippo   1947/05/26
Site 1 Nina Elizabeth Flippo   Place: Winchester, VA   Age: 80 years
        Birth: 1892/04/20   Death: 1972/11/22   Burial: 1972/11/25
Site 2 Monroe Flippo   Age: 91 years
        Birth: 1860/11/27   Death: 1952/06/26   Burial: 1952/06/29
Site 3 Martha C. (Mattie) Flippo   Age: 85 years
        Birth: 1866/08/01   Death: 1952/03/23   Burial: 1952/03/25
Site 4 William Clifton Flippo   Age: 64 years
        Birth: 1888/08/31   Death: 1952/12/22   Burial: 1952/12/24
Site 6 Margurette Rebecca Flippo Jessee   Age: 67 years
        Birth: 1909/05/09   Death: 1977/01/14   Burial: 1977/01/18
        Place: Leesburg, VA
Site 8 Frank B. Flippo Sr.   Age: 84 years
        Birth: 1900   Death: 1985/02/16   Burial: 1985/02/19
        Place: Leesburg, VA   TS: Married Hilda G. Flippo June 18, 1929
Site 12 Christopher Burton Flippo   Age: 4 days
        Birth: 1984/05/15   Death: 1984/05/19   Burial: 1984/05/21
        Place: Washington, DC

Lot: 1195 E Owner: Mrs. Rebecca Hindman   1948/08/30
Site 7 Raymond Olsen Hindman, Sr.   Age: 41 years
        Birth: 1907/02/16   Death: 1948/08/29   Burial: 1948/08/31
Site 8 Rebecca Smale Hindman   Age: 80 years
        Birth: 1910/02/26   Death: 1991/02/13   Burial: 1991/02/16
        Place: Leesburg, VA   On stone with Raymond Olsen Hindman Sr.
Site 9 Raymond Olsen Hindman Jr.   Age: 51 years
        Birth: 1929/04/25   Death: 1980/09/11   Burial: 1980/09/15
        Place: Leesburg, VA

Lot: 1195 W Owner: J.E. Sowers   Purchased: 1948/08/16
Site 1 John Monroe Marshall   Age: 54 years
        Birth: 1894/05/06   Death: 1948/10/06   Burial: 1948/10/08
Site 2 Susannah R. Marshall   Place: Charlottesville, VA Age: 101 years
        Birth: 1880/05/06   Death: 1981/11/01   Burial: 1981/11/04
Site 3 James Egbert Sowers   Place: Culpeper, VA   Age: 44 years
        Birth: 1916/09/10   Death: 1961/03/20   Burial: 1961/03/24
        TS: Virginia TEC5 Co E 385 Infantry WW II BSM
Site 5 Becky Ann McGrady   Place: Arlington, VA   Age: 36 years
        Birth: 1947/10/24   Death: 1983/11/17   Burial: 1983/11/21
Site 6 Kay E. Sowers   Age: 3 years
        Birth: 1945/03/13   Death: 1948/08/13   Burial: 1948/08/15

Lot: 1196 E Owner: Leon & Mildred K. Smith   1951/06/08
Site 8 Myrtle A. Kidwell
        Birth: 1897/04/26   Death: 1992/01/14   Burial: 1992/01/17
        Place: Sterling, VA   TS: Daughter of Gertrude & Richard Kidwell
Site 9 Leon Smith   Place: Leesburg, VA   Age: 82 years
        Birth: 1904/09/21   Death: 1987/04/07   Burial: 1987/04/09

Site 10 Mildred K. Smith
    Birth: 1904/09/26   Death: 1993/07/22   Burial: 1993/07/26
    Place: Leesburg, VA   On stone with Leon Smith
Site 11 James Emanuel Adrian   Age: 85 years
    Birth: 1872/05/23   Death: 1958/08/26   Burial: 1958/08/29
    Cause: Auto Accident   Place: L.C.H. Leesburg, VA

Lot: 1197   Owner: Miscellaneous

Site 1 Carl Henry Schooley   Age: 67 years
    Birth: 1885   Death: 1952/12/18   Burial: 1952/12/20
Site 2 Francis B. Schooley   Age: 53 years
    Birth: 1917/09/02   Death: 1974/01/16   Burial: 1974/01/19
    Place: Washington, DC   TS: Virginia PFC US Army WW II
Site 2 Audrey B. Schooley   Place: Warrenton, VA   Age: 92 years
    Birth: 1895   Death: 1988/03/30   Burial: 1988/04/02
Site 3 Clifton H. McDonough   Place: Leesburg, VA   Age: 74 years
    Birth: 1900   Death: 1974/09/15   Burial: 1974/09/17
Site 4 Margaret T. McDonough   Place: Leesburg, VA   Age: 77 years
    Birth: 1904   Death: 1982/04/16   Burial: 1982/04/18
Site 11 George E. Humphreys   Place: Leesburg, VA   Age: 66 years
    Birth: 1896/09/27   Death: 1964/04/19   Burial: 1964/04/22

Lot: 1198   Owner: J.M. Sutphin   Purchased: 1948/10/02

Site 6 Margaret R. Sutphin
    Birth: 1932/08/10   Death: 1933/06/10   Burial: 1948/11/24
    Reburial TS: Daughter of J.M. & Cora L. Sutphin
Site 6 Clinton Moore Sutphin   Death: 1931/03/02   Burial: 1948/11/24
    TS: Son of J.M. & Cora L. Sutphin.   Age 4 months 11 days
Site 6 Verley Hazel Sutphin   Age 8 years 4 months 26 days
    Birth: 1920/02/04   Death: 1928/06/03   Burial: 1948/11/24
    TS: Daughter of J.M. & Cora L. Sutphin
Site 6 Willie Sutphin   Death: 1927/04/24   Burial: 1948/11/24
    Reburial   TS: Son of J.M. & Cora L. Sutphin
Site 6 Phillie C. Sutphin   Reburial TS: Son of J.M. & Cora L. Sutphin
    Birth: 1922/01/06   Death: 1925/03/08   Burial: 1948/11/24
Site 7 Marvin M. Sutphin   Age: 65 years
    Birth: 1917/11/29   Death: 1983/03/06   Burial: 1983/03/09
    Cause: Suicide   Place: Leesburg, VA
Site 9 Joshua Mintron Sutphin   Age: 71 years
    Birth: 1883/07/14   Death: 1954/12/06
Site 10 Cora Lee Sutphin   Age: 92 years
    Birth: 1885/05/13   Death: 1978/02/13   Burial: 1978/02/16
    Place: Warrenton, VA   On stone with Joshua Mintron Sutphin

Lot: 1199   Owner: John W. Pumphry   Purchased: 1948/10/03

Site 2 Ruth Hannah Pumphrey   Age: 23 years
    Birth: 1925/01/04   Death: 1948/10/03   Burial: 1948/10/05
Site 7 John W. Pumphrey Sr.   Age: 69 years
    Birth: 1867/12/29   Death: 1936/12/29   Burial: 1937/01/01
    Cause: Myocarditis   Moved from Lot 703, Site 12 March 22, 1971

Site 8 Mary Herndon Pumphrey Place: Leesburg, VA Age: 96 years
        Birth: 1887/01/10   Death: 1983/07/02   Burial: 1983/07/04
Site 9 Dorothy Barbara Pumphrey   Age: 53 minutes
        Birth: 1991/04/14   Death: 1991/04/15   Burial: 1991/04/17
        Place: Richmond, VA
Site 9 Christopher Lawrence Pumphrey   Age: 3 hours
        Birth: 1991/12/06   Death: 1991/12/07   Burial: 1991/12/13
        Place: Richmond, VA

Lot: 1200 E Owner: Edgar Wright   Purchased: 1950/09/14
Site 7 Eleanor L. Wright
        Birth: 1949/11/30   Death: 1950/09/13   Burial: 1950/09/15
Site 8 Tersa L. Wright   No stone
        Place: Leesburg, VA   Death: 1966/03/06   Burial: 1966/03/08
Site 9 David Edgar Wright   Place: Leesburg, VA Age: 23 years
        Birth: 1947/10/04   Death: 1970/10/24   Burial: 1970/10/26
        TS: Virginia SP4 Co A 809 ENGR BN Vietnam

Lot: 1200 W Owner: Alfred Dulin   Purchased: 1950/08/22
Site 1 Alfred Dulin   Place: Leesburg, VA Age: 75 years
        Birth: 1888/11/06   Death: 1964/02/10   Burial: 1964/02/12
Site 2 Mary Alice Dulin   Age: 87 years
        Birth: 1891/01/27   Death: 1979/01/07   Burial: 1979/01/10
        Place: Leesburg, VA   On stone with Alfred Dulin
Site 3 Hugh Brown Pierpoint   Place: FL   Age: 59 years
        Birth: 1915/08/21   Death: 1975/03/11   Burial: 1975/03/15

Lot: 1201 E Owner: Edgar C. Loy   Purchased: 1951/04/30
Site 7 Mary Ellen Champion   Age: 54 years
        Birth: 1902/07/16   Death: 1957/01/03
Site 10 Edgar Calvin Loy   Place: Lucketts, VA Age: 85 years
        Birth: 1873   Death: 1958/03/12   Burial: 1958/03/15
Site 11 Della T. Loy   Age: 78 years
        Birth: 1885   Death: 1963/09/16   Burial: 1963/09/18
        Place: Leesburg, VA   On stone with Edgar Calvin Loy
Site 12 Mrs. Sadie A. Tillett
        Birth: 1885/01/24   Death: 1951/10/04   Burial: 1951/10/06

Lot: 1201 W Owner: Vernon L. Clagett   Purchased: 1950/09/25
Site 1 Vernon Lee Clagett   Place: Leesburg, VA Age: 67 years
        Birth: 1907/08/12   Death: 1974/02/08   Burial: 1974/02/11
Site 2 Sarah Ellen Clagett   Death: 1950/09/25   Burial: 1950/09/27
        No stone

Lot: 1202 E Owner: T.E. Titus   Purchased: 1948/10/26
Site 9 Thomas Edward Titus   Place: Fairfax, VA Age: 53 years
        Birth: 1917/01/28   Death: 1970/09/23   Burial: 1970/09/26
Site 11 Elizabeth Gay Titus   Age: 1 year
        Birth: 1948/03/23   Death: 1949/05/01   Burial: 1949/05/03

Lot: 1202 W Owner: H.C.T. Ewing   Purchased: 1953/04/20
Site 1   Henry Charles T. Ewing   Age: 82 years
         Birth: 1872   Death: 1954/10/01
Site 2   Lucy Litton Ewing   Age: 73 years
         Birth: 1879   Death: 1953/04/19   Burial: 1953/04/21
         Place: Leesburg, VA   On stone with Henry Charles T. Ewing

Lot: 1203 E Owner: Dr. Roger Baker   Purchased:
Site 12 Mark Peter Baker   TS: Infant son of Roger & Genevieve Baker
         Birth: 1958/12/01   Death: 1958/12/03   Burial: 1958/12/03
                                    Place: Washington, DC
Site 12 Christopher Brandenburg Baker   Place: Washington, DC
         Birth: 1964/04/01   Death: 1964/04/02   Burial: 1964/04/03
         TS: Infant son of Roger & Genevieve Baker

Lot: 1204 E Owner: Miscellaneous
Site 7   Annie Carson Grubbs   Place: Leesburg, VA   Age: 84 years
         Birth: 1903/09/26   Death: 1987/10/06   Burial: 1987/10/09
Site 9   Milam Earl Livesay   Age: 59 years
         Birth: 1923/02/16   Death: 1982/05/10   Burial: 1982/05/13
         Cause: Cancer   Place: Leesburg, VA
Site 11 Robert H. Corley   Place: Leesburg, VA   Age: 75 years
         Birth: 1907/04/21   Death: 1983/02/13   Burial: 1983/02/17

Lot: 1204 W Owner: J.H. Sutphin   Purchased: 1963/07/10
Site 4   James H. (Dock) Sutphin   Place: Hamilton, VA   Age: 75 years
         Birth: 1911/03/29   Death: 1987/01/15   Burial: 1987/01/17
Site 6   Orville S. Christian   Place: Leesburg, VA   Age: 51 years
         Birth: 1912/06/04   Death: 1963/07/02   Burial: 1963/07/05

Lot: 1205   Owner: Miscellaneous
Site 1   James Hubert Johnson   Place: Arlington, VA   Age: 91 years
         Birth: 1899/05/09   Death: 1991/03/04   Burial: 1991/03/07
Site 2   Jeannette Harding Johnson   Age: 81 years
         Birth: 1909/06/28   Death: 1990/11/02   Burial: 1990/11/06
         Place: Fairfax, VA   On stone with James Hubert Johnson
Site 4   Jane Heath Johnson   Place: Arlington, DC   Age: 72 years
         Birth: 1935/02/25   Death: 1987/04/28   Burial: 1987/05/02
         TS: Wife of Richard Hubert Johnson. Wife, Mother, Friend

Lot: 1206   Owner: Miscellaneous
Site 3   Lincoln V. Sutphin   Place: Leesburg, VA   Age: 81 years
         Birth: 1907/02/25   Death: 1988/05/19   Burial: 1988/05/22
Site 4   Maudie A. Sutphin   Place: Leesburg, VA   Age: 75 years
         Birth: 1908/10/28   Death: 1984/01/04   Burial: 1984/01/07
         TS: Married Lincoln V. Sutphin June 28, 1928
Site 12 Brian Keith Gardner   Age: 3 days
         Birth: 1958/08/19   Death: 1958/08/22   Burial: 1958/08/24
         Place: L.C.H. Leesburg, VA   Son of Keith & Shirley Gardner

Lot: 1207   Owner: Miscellaneous
Site 1 Harrison Williams   TS: Lawyer, Farmer, Author   Age: 73 years
        Birth: 1873   Death: 1946/06/08   Burial: 1946/06/10
Site 6 Ashley Michelle Fleming   Place: Leesburg, VA
        Birth: 1992/12/14   Death: 1992/12/23   Burial: 1992/12/27

Lot: 1208   Owner: Miscellaneous
Site 6 Mildred Lee Chamblin   Age: 15 years
        Birth: 1932/05/16   Death: 1947/09/01   Burial: 1947/09/03
        TS: Daughter of Daniel S. & Ernestine F. Chamblin
Site 10 Kathryn H. Chamblin   Place: Leesburg, VA   Age: 41 years
        Birth: 1924/07/24   Death: 1965/08/28   Burial: 1965/08/30

Lot: 1209 E Owner: Mrs. Henry J. Beales   Purchased:
Site 7 Mabel Carlisle Pierce Beals   Age: 84 years
        Birth: 1894   Death: 1978/10/20   Burial: 1978/10/24
        Place: Leesburg, VA   TS: Wife of James W. Pierce & Henry Beales
Site 8 Raymond R. Pierce   TS: Virginia PFC 145 INF WWII PH
        Birth: 1920/01/20   Death: 1943/07/31   Burial: 1948/03/06
Site 9 Joseph William Pierce Place: Winchester, VA   Age: 56 years
        Birth: 1915/12/26   Death: 1971/10/21   Burial: 1971/10/23
Site 10 Leon C. Harper   Place: Hillsville   Age: 74 years
        Birth: 1911   Death: 1986/02/25   Burial: 1986/02/28
Site 11 Janet Virginia Harper Place: Hillsville, VA
        Birth: 1917   Death: 1991/01/15   Burial: 1991/01/18
        TS: Married Leon C. Harper December 24, 1935

Lot: 1209 W Owner: Smith & May Powell Blair   1949/12/20
Site 1 Smith Blair   Place: Leesburg, VA   Age: 87 years
        Birth: 1882/10/04   Death: 1970/03/09   Burial: 1970/03/12
Site 2 May Powell Blair   Place: Purcellville, VA   Age: 87 years
        Birth: 1883/01/20   Death: 1970/04/29   Burial: 1970/05/01
Site 4 Marian T. Powell   Place: Fairfax, VA   Age: 99 years
        Birth: 1881/01/26   Death: 1980/07/18   Burial: 1980/07/22
Site 5 Stanley H. Powell   Place: Bethesda, MD   Age: 82 years
        Birth: 1889/06/17   Death: 1971/12/04   Burial: 1971/12/08
Site 6 Nell M. Powell   Age: 84 years
        Birth: 1887/08/16   Death: 1971/09/21   Burial: 1971/09/23
        Place: Bethesda, MD   On stone with Stanley H. Powell

Lot: 1210   Owner: J.C. Rust, Jr.   Purchased: 1947/08/25
Site 2 Myrtle Peacock Rust   On stone with John C. Rust, Jr. Age: 69 years
        Birth: 1887   Death: 1957
Site 3 John C. Rust Jr.   Place: Leesburg, VA   Age: 83 years
        Birth: 1884   Death: 1968/01/06   Burial: 1968/01/06

**Lot: 1211 Owner: James & Martin Kidwell
& Mrs. Louise K. Tavenner Purchased: 1948/12/15**
Site 1 Henry Ashton Tavenner   Age: 81 years
        Birth: 1907/08/07   Death: 1989/08/03   Burial: 1989/08/08
        Cause: Heart Attack   Place: Leesburg, VA
Site 2 Mary Louise Kidwell Tavenner   Age: 76 years
        Birth: 1909/05/13   Death: 1986/05/07   Burial: 1986/05/10
        Place: Leesburg, VA
Site 4 James Israel Kidwell   Age: 71 years
        Birth: 1877/12/19   Death: 1948/12/14   Burial: 1948/12/16
Site 4 Katie Ellen Arnette Kidwell   Age: 27 years
        Birth: 1887/07/20   Death: 1914/12/20   Burial: 1949/09/15
        Removal from Ebenezer Sept. 15, 1949
Site 7 Paul Martin Kidwell
        TSBirth: 1913   Death: 1992/01/13   Burial: 1992/01/16
Site 8 Catherine Gill Kidwell Place: Leesburg, VA   Age: 56 years
        Birth: 1916   Death: 1972/11/22   Burial: 1972/11/24
Site 12 Baby Boy Kidwell   Place: Leesburg, VA   Age: 6 months
        Birth: 1966/09/20   Death: 1966/09/21   Burial: 1966/09/22

Lot: 1212 E Owner: Mrs. Clifton R. Titus Purchased: 1953/11/23
Site   Mildred M. Titus   Birth: 1908   Death: 1993
Site 9 Clifton Ross Titus   Place: Bradford, VA   Age: 53 years
        Birth: 1900   Death: 1953/11/21   Burial: 1953/11/23
Site 12 Lori Lynn Titus   Place: Washington, DC   Age: 10 years
        Birth: 1969   Death: 1979/12/05   Burial: 1979/12/07

Lot: 1212 W Owner: James P. Lindquist Purchased: 1951/12/10
Site 3 James Peter Lindquist   Age: 75 years
        Birth: 1877   Death: 1952/09/29   Burial: 1952/10/01
Site 4 Mrs. Zoe Roblin E. Lindquist   Age: 68 years
        Birth: 1882   Death: 1951/12/13   Burial: 1951/12/15
        On stone with James Peter Lindquist
Site 5 Clarence A.R. Lindquist Place: Newport News, VA
        Birth: 1904/05/17   Death: 1995/08/08   Burial: 1995/08/11

Lot: 1213 E Owner: James C. & Sylvia L. Carnes 1961/07/27
Site 7 Kenneth Wayne Carnes   Place: Childrens' Washington,   Age: 3
        Birth: 1957/11/04   Death: 1961/07/25   Burial: 1961/07/28

Lot: 1213 W Owner: George P. & Esther R. Hammerly 1965/09/09
Site 2 George Preston Hammerly   Age: 63 years
        Birth: 1921/06/16   Death: 1984/10/04   Burial: 1984/10/07
        Place: Perry Point, MD
Site 3 Esther Rhodes Hammerly Cause: Cancer   Age: 49 years
        Birth: 1924/02/08   Death: 1973/11/23   Burial: 1973/11/27
        Place: Fairfax, VA   On stone with George Preston Hammerly
Site 4 George P. Hammerly Jr.   Age: 21 years
        Birth: 1946/12/29   Death: 1968/02/18   Burial: 1968/02/20
        Cause: Auto Accident   Place: Fairfax Co., VA

Site 6 John W. Cooke III   Place: Richmond, VA   Age: 2 years
        Birth: 1964/09/07   Death: 1967/04/08   Burial: 1967/04/12
        TS: Grandson of John W. & Betty L. Cooke
        & George P. & Esther R. Hammerly

Lot: 1214   Owner: Miscellaneous
Site 5   Lester L. Loy   Place: Lucketts, VA   Age: 84 years
         Birth: 1899/03/07   Death: 1983/10/12   Burial: 1983/10/15
Site 6   Geneva L. Loy   Age: 47 years
         Birth: 1915/03/23   Death: 1962/02/15   Burial: 1962/02/18
         Place: Washington, DC   On stone with Lester L. Loy
Site 7   R. Tweed Howser   Place: Leesburg, VA   Age: 78 years
         Birth: 1907/08/25   Death: 1985/11/07   Burial: 1985/11/09
Site 8   Helen A. Howser   Age: 76 years
         Birth: 1906/10/12   Death: 1983/09/03   Burial: 1983/09/06
         Place: Leesburg, VA   On stone with R. Tweed Howser
Site 10 Harry I. Tiffany   Age: 71 years
         Birth: 1888/03/11   Death: 1960/01/17   Burial: 1960/01/19
         Place: Leesburg, VA   TS: Born Middleburg, VA
Site 11 Virginia Alsip Tiffany   Age: 68 years
         Birth: 1893/05/16   Death: 1961/06/20   Burial: 1961/06/24
         Place: Leesburg, VA   TS: Born Chicago, IL

Lot: 1215 E   Owner: Miscellaneous
Site 7   Martha L. Grey   Age: 19 years
         Birth: 1933   Death: 1953/02/11   Burial: 1953/02/14
         Cause: Brain Tumor   Place: Washington, DC
Site 8   Flossie M. Cooper   Place: Leesburg, VA
         Birth: 1907/01/23   Death: 1991/07/14   Burial: 1991/07/17
Site 9   Irving Thomas Cooper   Nothing on stone   Age: 57 years
         Place: Leesburg, VA   Death: 1953/01/19   Burial: 1953/01/19
Site 12 Shirley P. Grey Sr.   Age: 55 years
         Birth: 1926/10/09   Death: 1981/12/25   Burial: 1981/12/28
         Place: Winchester, VA   TS: F1 US Navy
Site 12 Francis Grey   Place: Purcellville, VA   No stone
         Birth: 1930/11/27   Death: 1995/06/07   Burial: 1995/06/11

Lot: 1215 W Owner: Mrs. Lela Grace Beall
           & Mrs. Blanche C. Dunn   Purchased: 1952/11/18
Site 1   Carroll Edwin Dunn   Place: Arlington, VA   Age: 52 years
         Birth: 1898/11/11   Death: 1953/10/22   Burial: 1953/10/25
Site 2   William Dunn   Place: Washington, DC   Age: 82 years
         Birth: 1891   Death: 1974/08/29   Burial: 1974/09/02
Site 3   Blanche C. Dunn   Age: 88 years
         Birth: 1892   Death: 1980/07/31   Burial: 1980/08/02
         Place: Prince George, MD   On stone with William Dunn
Site 4   Ernest M. Beall   Place: Leesburg, VA   Age: 80 years
         Birth: 1878   Death: 1959/02/09   Burial: 1959/02/12

Site 5 Lela Grace Beall
Birth: 1888	Death: 1960/03/06	Burial: 1960/03/09
Place: Leesburg, VA	On stone with Ernest M. Beall
Site 6 Ernest Ellsworth Beall	Age: 41 years
Birth: 1911	Death: 1952/11/18	Burial: 1952/11/20

Lot: 1216   Owner: F.F. Moffett   Purchased: 1955/04/02
Site 2 Ella J. Moffett	Place: Oxen Hill, MD	Age: 62 years
Birth: 1919/08/07	Death: 1981/09/25	Burial: 1981/09/29
Site 3 Harvey Hartgrove Moffett Place: Takoma Park, MD	Age: 71 years
Birth: 1883/04/19	Death: 1955/04/01	Burial: 1955/04/02
Site 5 Margaret F. Moffett	Age: 91 years
Birth: 1885/10/11	Death: 1979/10/31	Burial: 1979/11/03
Place: Alexandria, VA	On stone with Harvey H. Moffett
Site 6 John H. Blincoe	Place: Alexandria, VA	Age: 80 years
Birth: 1890/05/02	Death: 1971/03/25	Burial: 1971/03/27

Lot: 1217   Owner: Miscellaneous
Site 1 Elizabeth Dora Lawson Place: Leesburg, VA	Age: 71 years
Birth: 1916/02/10	Death: 1987/04/30	Burial: 1987/05/01
Site 2 Edwin T. Harrison Jr.
Birth: 1891	Death: 1952/07/13	Burial: 1952/07/15
Site 3 Frances Dora Harrison	Age: 67 years
Birth: 1891	Death: 1956/01/20
Place: Hamilton, VA	On stone with Edwin T. Harrison Jr.
Site 4 Nicholas Johnson	Place: Leesburg, VA
Birth: 1911/12/23	Death: 1994/03/28	Burial: 1994/03/31
Site 5 Mildred H. Johnson
Birth: 1921/02/04	Death: 1995/07/26	Burial: 1995/07/29
Place: Leesburg, VA	On stone with Nicholas Johnson

Lot: 1218   Owner: Mrs. Augustus di Zerega   1951/03/09
Site 1 Louis Augustus di Zerega	Age: 60 years
Birth: 1910/09/27	Death: 1971/02/14	Burial: 1971/02/17
Place: Alexandria, VA
Site 1 Olivia Tyler di Zerega	Age: 80 years
Birth: 1909/08/02	Death: 1990/03/11	Burial: 1990/03/15
Place: Fairfax, VA	On stone with Louis Augustus de Zerega
Site 2 Emile A. di Zerega	Age: 29 years
Birth: 1905/08/25	Death: 1935/02/10	Burial: 1935/02/14
Cause: Gun Shot	Moved from Lot 800 Site 12 on Sept 11,
1951
Site 3 Augustus di Zerega	Age: 82 years
Birth: 1868/09/08	Death: 1951/03/07	Burial: 1951/03/09
Site 4 Agnes Green di Zerega	Place: Leesburg, VA	Age: 82 years
Birth: 1870/10/24	Death: 1953/01/10	Burial: 1953/01/10
Site 5 John P. H. di Zerega	Place: Leesburg, VA	Age: 66 years
Birth: 1897/03/21	Death: 1964/02/11	Burial: 1964/02/14
Site 6 Elizabeth J. Di Zerega	Place: Farifax, VA	Age: 56 years
Birth: 1908/11/22	Death: 1966/10/15	Burial: 1966/10/17

Site 6 William Luck Di Zerega R. PH Age: 82 years
Birth: 1903/11/23 Death: 1986/08/05 Burial: 1986/08/09
Place: Woodstock, VA

Lot: 1219 Owner: Miscellaneous
Site 1 Arthur Lloyd Holtzclaw Age: 27 years
Birth: 1939/05/04 Death: 1966/06/17 Burial: 1966/06/20
Cause: Electrocuted Place: Alexandria, VA TS: Son
Site 3 Carolyn Lee Holtzclaw Age: 15 years
Birth: 1950/09/23 Death: 1966/07/03 Burial: 1966/07/06
Place: MD TS: Daughter
Site 5 Austin M. Holtzclaw Place: Riverdale, MD Age: 66 years
Birth: 1901 Death: 1967/10/17 Burial: 1967/10/20
Site 8 Norman C. Frye Sr. Place: Leesburg, VA Age: 81 years
Birth: 1902/03/12 Death: 1983/10/28 Burial: 1983/10/31
Site 9 Harold Wesley Spargo Place: Leesburg, VA Age: 78 years
Birth: 1907/02/25 Death: 1985/04/23 Burial: 1985/04/26

Lot: 1220 Owner: Miscellaneous
Site 7 William I.H. McCaughey Age: 54 years
Birth: 1925 Death: 1979/11/10 Burial: 1979/11/13
Place: Fairfax, VA TS: TEC4 US Army WWII
Site 9 Lois Walker Gilbertz Age: 51 years
Birth: 1928/04/19 Death: 1980/02/11 Burial: 1980/02/15
Cause: Cancer Place: Fairfax, VA
Site 12 Richard Clark Wagner Age: 18 years
Birth: 1961/04/02 Death: 1979/12/28 Burial: 1980/01/05
Cause: Drowned Place: Leesburg, VA

Lot: 1221 E Owner: Emma Jane French Purchased:
Site 9 Bruce A. French Place: MD No stone
Birth: 1928/09/28 Death: 1992/01/04 Burial: 1992/01/08
Site 10 Emma Jane French Age: 78 years
Birth: 1911/09/19 Death: 1990/05/04 Burial: 1990/05/07
Place: Olney, MD On stone with Alexander B. French
Site 11 Alexander B. French Age: 74 years
Birth: 1904/06/29 Death: 1979/05/29

Lot: 1221 W Owner: George B. Bozel Purchased:
Site 1 George B. Bozel Age: 81 years
Birth: 1897 Death: 1978/03/02 Burial: 1978/03/04
Cause: Heart Attack Place: Leesburg, VA

Lot: 1222E Owner: Roy L. Fry Purchased:
Site 7 Roy L. Fry Place: Lucketts, VA Age: 66 years
Birth: 1909/09/30 Death: 1976/04/08 Burial: 1976/04/11

Lot: 1222 W Owner: Mrs. Mildred Edmondson Purchased:
Site 1 John B. Edmondson Place: Leesburg, VA Age: 85 years
Birth: 1898 Death: 1983/11/19 Burial: 1983/11/22

Site 2 Mildred M. Edmondson   Age: 81 years
        Birth: 1905   Death: 1987/02/16   Burial: 1987/02/18
        Place: Leesburg, VA   On stone with John B. Edmondson
Site 3 Margaret E. Gill
        Birth: 1927   Death: 1994/03/02   Burial: 1994/03/06
        Place: NC   TS: Married Joseph W. Gill March 1, 1946
Site 4 Joseph W. Gill   Place: Winchester, VA   Age: 59 years
        Birth: 1919   Death: 1979/01/09   Burial: 1979/01/12
Site 5 John E. Colbert   Cause: Cancer   Age: 52 years
        Birth: 1930/07/27   Death: 1983/01/02   Burial: 1983/01/04
        Place: Leesburg, VA   TS: SSGT US Air Force Korea
Site 5 Brian Allen Hipkins   Age: 6 days
        Birth: 1987/11/26   Death: 1987/12/02   Burial: 1987/12/08
        Place: Iceland   TS: Son of Mark & Kathy Hipkins
Site 6 Ellen Colbert   Place: Leesburg, VA   No stone
        Birth: 1930/09/04   Death: 1995/11/18   Burial: 1995/11/21

Lot: 1223   Owner: Estate of Charles F. Harrison   1947/09/26
Site 1 Stirling Murray Harrison   Place: Winchester, VA   Age: 55 years
        Birth: 1913/04/19   Death: 1968/08/13   Burial: 1968/08/16
Site 1 Hester Ann LeFevre Harrison Bratney   Age: 70 years
        Birth: 1909/11/16   Death: 1980/11/04   Burial: 1980/11/08
        Place: Virginia Beach, VA
Site 2 Charles F. Harrison Jr.   TS: Major US Army
        Birth: 1910/09/27   Death: 1944/05   Burial: 1944/05
        TS: Murdered by Japanese while Prisoner of War in Phillippines
Site 3 Charles Fauntleroy Harrison   Age: 70 years
        Birth: 1877/07/10   Death: 1947/09/26   Burial: 1947/09/29
Site 4 Mary Arthur Fendall Harrison   Age: 83 years
        Birth: 1877/11/29   Death: 1961/01/05   Burial: 1961/01/07
        Place: Leesburg, VA   TS: Wife of Charles F. Harrison Sr.

Lot: 1224   Owner: Estate of William A. Metzger   1948/06/05
Site 1 William Baylor Metzger   Place: Leesburg, VA   Age: 56 years
        Birth: 1911   Death: 1968/06/21   Burial: 1968/06/22
Site 2 Mary Tyson Metzger   Place: Leesburg, VA   Age: 79 years
        Birth: 1908   Death: 1987/02/15   Burial: 1987/02/18
Site 3 William Albert Metzger   Age: 72 years
        Birth: 1874/01/05   Death: 1948/06/03   Burial: 1948/06/07
Site 4 Fanny Dawson Metzger   Place: Leesburg, VA   Age: 89 years
        Birth: 1873/03/24   Death: 1962/07/30   Burial: 1962/08/03
Site 5 Clare Briggs Metzger   No stone   Age: 67 years
        Place: Richmond, VA   Death: 1985/04/27   Burial: 1985/04/30
Site 5 Sarah Briggs Lewis   Place: Richmond, VA   Age: 90 years
        Birth: 1901   Death: 1992/04/20   Burial: 1992/04/24
Site 6 William (Billy) Metzger Place: Washington, DC   Age: 14 years
        Birth: 1945   Death: 1960/02/18   Burial: 1960/02/20

Lot: 1225 E   Owner: William T. Thomas   Purchased: 1948/11/02
Site 7   Mrs. Eugenia Cullimore Thomas
         Birth: 1883/08/31   Death: 1923/10/12   Burial: 1949/03/30
         TS:Wife of Wm.T. Thomas   Removal from 730W
Site 8   William T. Thomas   Age: 65 years
         Birth: 1885/08/25   Death: 1950/11/10   Burial: 1950/11/12
Site 9   Madeline Compher Thomas   Age: 84 years
         Birth: 1898/11/11   Death: 1983/03/29   Burial: 1983/03/31
         Place: Leesburg, VA   TS: Wife of William T. Thomas
Site 12 William Compher Thomas   Age: 20 years
         Birth: 1928/10/22   Death: 1948/11/01   Burial: 1948/11/03
         TS: Son of William T. & Madeline C. Thomas

Lot: 1225 W Owner: Belle & J. Millard Wynkoop   1951/03/19
Site 1   James Millard Wynkoop Place: Leesburg, VA   Age: 82 years
         Birth: 1888   Death: 1970/05/26   Burial: 1970/05/29
Site 2   Belle C. Wynkoop   Age: 88 years
         Birth: 1900   Death: 1989/06/25   Burial: 1989/06/28
         Place: Fairfax, VA   On stone with James Millard Wynkoop

Lot: 1226   Owner: Mrs. Thomas M. Fendall
               & Mrs. Anna A.R. Harkness   Purchased: 1948/06/02
Site 3   Thomas Miller Fendall   Age: 72 years
         Birth: 1875   Death: 1948/06/02   Burial: 1948/06/04
Site 4   Mrs. Lily Lawrence Rust Fendall   Age: 92 years
         Birth: 1880   Death: 1973/01/28   Burial: 1973/01/30
         Place: Leesburg, VA   On stone with Thomas Miller Fendall
Site 9   Rev. Norris William Harkness   Age: 83 years
         Birth: 1874/08/17   Death: 1958/01/01   Burial: 1958/01/03
         Place: Paeonian Springs, VA
Site 10 Anna Aylell Rust Harkness   On stone with Norris William Harkness
         Birth: 1877/02/04   Death: 1954/02/02
Site 11 Evelyn Harkness Corbell   Place: Lexington SC   Age: 70 years
         Birth: 1913/12/28   Death: 1984/01/15   Burial: 1984/01/19

Lot: 1227 E   Owner: Stanley Reed   Purchased: 1954/06/23
Site 7   Charles Frank Reed   Place: Leesburg, VA   Age: 76 years
         Birth: 1882   Death: 1959/10/26   Burial: 1959/10/28
Site 7   Mrs. Edna Mae Reed   Age: 80 years
         Birth: 1884   Death: 1964/12/01   Burial: 1964/12/03
         Place: Leesburg, VA   On stone with Charles Frank Reed
Site 8   Gordon Edward Warner Place: Leesburg, VA   Age: 73 years
         Birth: 1897   Death: 1970/10/07   Burial: 1970/10/10
Site 9   Mrs. Geneva H. Reed   Place: Leesburg, VA   Age: 54 years
         Birth: 1916/10/26   Death: 1971/03/18   Burial: 1971/03/26

Lot: 1227 W Owner: Lawrence Muse   Purchased: 1954/06/23
Site 1   George H. Morrison   Place: Leesburg, VA
         Birth: 1965/06/28   Death: 1995/03/09   Burial: 1995/03/13

Site 1 Gentry Lawrence Muse   Age: 69 years
       Birth: 1889   Death: 1958/12/09   Burial: 1958/12/11
       Cause: Heart   Place: L.C.H. Leesburg, VA
Site 2 Ruby M. Muse   Place: Leesburg, VA Age: 83 years
       Birth: 1897   Death: 1981/02/13   Burial: 1981/02/16
Site 3 J. Lawrence Muse   Age: 64 years
       Birth: 1918   Death: 1983/06/14   Burial: 1983/06/17
       Cause: Heart   Place: Leesburg, VA

Lot: 1228 E   Owner: J. Lincoln & Massie M. Chapin   1953/10/19
Site 7 John Lincoln Chapin   Place: DE   Age: 84 years
       Birth: 1888/12/20   Death: 1973/06/22   Burial: 1973/06/25
Site 8 Massie O. Moore Chapin   Age: 92 years
       Birth: 1893/01/18   Death: 1984/07/04   Burial: 1984/07/07
       Place: Haverford, DE   TS: Wife of John Lincoln Chapin
Site 9 Laura B. Nichols Moore   Age: 84 years
       Birth: 1868/05/24   Death: 1953/08/01   Burial: 1953/10/19
       TS: Wife of Arthur L. Moore   Disinterment

Lot: 1229   Owner: Clarence R. & Tillie A. Ahalt   1955/04/18
Site 2 Alice Ahalt Hays   Place: Arlington, VA Age: 47 years
       Birth: 1917/08/18   Death: 1965/02/14   Burial: 1965/02/17
Site 3 Clarence Randolph Ahalt Place: Leesburg, VA Age: 74 years
       Birth: 1888/05/28   Death: 1962/10/14   Burial: 1962/10/17
Site 5 Tillie Alice Ahalt   Age: 89 years
       Birth: 1889/09/09   Death: 1979/01/21   Burial: 1979/01/24
       Place: Leesburg, VA   On stone with Clarence Randolph Ahalt
Site 8 Thomas Spencer Hays   Place: Atlanta, GA   Age: 30 years
       Birth: 1943/10/07   Death: 1973/12/30   Burial: 1974/01/03

Lot: 1230 E   Owner: Hettie B. Cook   Purchased: 1955/02/24
Site 7 Thomas Franklin Bryant Place: Farmville, VA Age: 79 years
       Birth: 1876   Death: 1955/06/26   Burial: 1955/06/26
Site 8 Cora McCann Bryant   Age: 85 years
       Birth: 1876   Death: 1961/12/02   Burial: 1961/12/04
       Place: Fairfax, VA   On stone with Thomas Franklin Bryant
Site 12 Patricia Ellen Duke   Age: 4 hours
                              Death: 1956/04/11   Burial: 1956/04/12
       Place: Arlington Hosp., Arlington, VA   BP: Child of John M. Duke

Lot: 1230 W Owner: W. Boyd Bryant   Purchased: 1955/06/29
Site 1 Rev. William Boyd Bryant   Age: 74 years
       Birth: 1905   Death: 1979/11/19   Burial: 1979/11/23
       Place: Bedford, VA
Site 2 Mary Craun Bryant   On stone with Rev. William Boyd Bryant
       Birth: 1906   Death: 1979
Site 3 Ralph Leon Bryant   Place: Kansas City, MO Age: 47 years
       Birth: 1938   Death: 1985/06/03   Burial: 1985/06/07
       On stone with Rev. William Boyd and Mary Craun Bryant

Site 4 Walter Hugh Bryant   Place: Fairfax, VA   Age: 60 years
        Birth: 1908/02/28   Death: 1967/03/09   Burial: 1967/03/13

Lot: 1231 E Owner: Herbert Edwards   **Purchased: 1955/06/16**
Site 7 Herbert Tunis Edwards Jr.   Age: 15 years
        Birth: 1940/02/05   Death: 1955/06/15   Burial: 1955/06/15
        Place: Waterford, VA   TS: Sonny
Site 8 Herbert Tunis Edwards Place: Leesburg, VA   Age: 71 years
        Birth: 1915/08/26   Death: 1987/03/26   Burial: 1987/03/30

Lot: 1231 W Owner: Ernest M. Edwards, Sr.   **1955/07/27**
Site 1 Ernest M. Edwards Jr. Place: Charlottesville, VA   Age: 44 years
        No stone   Death: 1971/12/12   Burial: 1971/12/15
Site 2 Sarah Edwards   No stone   Age: 33 years
        Place: Leesburg, VA   Death: 1966/10/11   Burial: 1966/10/13
Site 3 Ernest Mosby Edwards Sr.   Age: 67 years
        Birth: 1888/02/19   Death: 1955/09/20   Burial: 1955/09/20
        Place: Leesburg, VA
Site 4 Sara E. Edwards   Age: 84 years
        Birth: 1887/09/12   Death: 1972/06/24

Lot: 1232 E Owner: Miscellaneous
Site 7 Joseph I. Grehan   Place: Fairfax, VA
        Birth: 1919/07/29   Death: 1995/10/24   Burial: 1995/10/27
Site 8 Margaret W. Grehan
        Birth: 1918/01/21   Death: 1993/08/06   Burial: 1993/08/09
        Place: Leesburg, VA   On stone with Joseph I. Grehan
Site 10 Hazel L. Davis   Place: Leesburg, VA   No stone
        Birth: 1917/01/12   Death: 1995/07/29   Burial: 1995/07/31
Site 11 Earl A. Raymond   Place: Hamilton, VA   Age: 63 years
        Birth: 1921/04/12   Death: 1984/11/29   Burial: 1984/12/03

Lot: 1232 W Owner: Emory Wilson Solomon   **1955/12/29**
Site 5 Stephen Lester Solomon TS: Son of E. Mason & Nancy L. Solomon
        Birth: 1963/10/14   Death: 1963/10/14   Burial: 1963/10/16
        Cause: Stillborn   Place: Leesburg, VA
Site 6 Linda Marie Solomon   Place: Ashburn, VA   Age: 13 days
        Birth: 1955/12/16   Death: 1955/12/29
        TS: Daughter of E. Mason & Nancy L. Solomon

Lot: 1233   Owner: Richard L. Carter & Mary V. Carter
                                               Purchased: 1955/06/06
Site 2 Paul Haynes Carter   Place: Leesburg, VA   Age: 93 years
        Birth: 1880/02/28   Death: 1973/10/26   Burial: 1973/10/29
Site 3 Mary Lucretia Drake Carter   Age: 69 years
        Birth: 1886/05/09   Death: 1955/09/26   Burial: 1955/09/26
        Place: Leesburg, VA
Site 5 James Bedford Blitch   Place: Fairfax, VA   Age: 58 years
        Birth: 1909/10/24   Death: 1966/04/23   Burial: 1966/04/25

Site 7 Richard Leigh Carter   Age: 58 years
       Birth: 1914/07/15   Death: 1972/08/23
Site 8 Janet Miller Carter
       Birth: 1916/10/28   Death: 1993/09/03   Burial: 1993/09/06
       Place: Richmond, VA   On stone with Richard Leigh Carter

Lot: 1234 E   Owner: Raymond W. Hollidge   Purchased: 1955/08/29
Site 7 Irving Weed Hollidge   Age: 69 years
        Birth: 1886/05/01   Death: 1955/08/28   Burial: 1955/08/29
Site 8 Raymond W. Hollidge   Place: Charlottsville, VA   Age: 75 years
        Birth: 1891/01/26   Death: 1966/10/27   Burial: 1966/11/01
Site 9 Lucy B. Hollidge   No dates on stone   Age: 86 years
                                 Death: 1972/06/11
Site 11 Charles W. Sydnor   Place: Leesburg, VA   Age: 62 years
        Birth: 1903/04/06   Death: 1965/11/13   Burial: 1965/11/16
Site 12 Velma W. Sydnor   Place: Leesburg, VA   Age: 69 years
        Birth: 1907/02/22   TSDeath: 1974/03/09

Lot: 1234 W   Owner: Henry & Nevelle Rinker   1954/01/27
Site 5 Henry E. Rinker   Place: Leesburg, VA   Age: 37 years
        Birth: 1938/10/02   Death: 1976/01/09   Burial: 1976/01/11
Site 6 Betty Rose Rinker   Age: 2 years
        Birth: 1951/08/26   Death: 1954/01/25   Burial: 1954/01/27
        Cause: Lead Intoxication   Place: Washington, DC

Lot: 1235   Owner: Miscellaneous
Site 1 Amos H. Barnhouse   Place: Leesburg, VA   Age: 73 years
        Birth: 1916/05/17   Death: 1990/02/18   Burial: 1990/02/21
Site 3 Lester C. Newton   Place: Leesburg, VA   Age: 72 years
        Birth: 1906   Death: 1978/08/02   Burial: 1978/08/05
Site 4 Bessie L. Newton   Age: 83 years
        Birth: 1907   Death: 1990/10/04   Burial: 1990/10/08
        Place: Winchester, VA   On stone with Lester C. Newton
Site 5 George I. Newton   Place: Leesburg, VA   Age: 66 years
        Birth: 1903/11/29   Death: 1970/03/06   Burial: 1970/03/09
Site 6 Nora V. Newton   Age: 81 years
        Birth: 1907/09/16   Death: 1989/03/18   Burial: 1989/03/22
        Place: Winchester, VA   On stone with George I. Newton

Lot: 1236   Owner: Miscellaneous
Site 4 Frances Fuller Sprague   Age: 65 years
        Birth: 1909   Death: 1973/12/19   Burial: 1977/05/07
        Removed from Danville, VA.   TS: of Pittsylvania Co.

Lot: 1237   Owner: Miscellaneous
Site 9 Charles Wesley Best   Place: Leesburg, VA   Age: 60 years
        Birth: 1929/01/03   Death: 1989/05/19   Burial: 1989/05/24

Lot: 1238   Owner: Miscellaneous
Site 7   Ronald M. Christopherson   Age: 41 years
         Birth: 1937/12/16   Death: 1978/08/12   Burial: 1978/08/17
         Place: Kansas, MO   TS: US Army Korea
Site 10 Carl Lee Dickens   Age: 37 years
         Birth: 1952   Death: 1990/03/20   Burial: 1990/03/23
         Place: Nassau Bay, TX   TS: Son
Site 10 Edgar G. Dickens   Place: Washington, DC   TS: US Army WWII
         Birth: 1920/02/14   Death: 1994/07/01   Burial: 1994/07/04
Site 11 Lynn W. Byrd   Place: Washington, DC   Age: 70 years
         Birth: 1909/07/13   Death: 1980/05/20   Burial: 1980/05/23

Lot: 1239   Owner: C.T. & Katherine O. Tavenner   1950/02/13
Site 1   Cloyd T. Tavenner   Place: Leesburg, VA   Age: 75 years
         Birth: 1887/03/09   Death: 1962/06/23   Burial: 1962/06/26
Site 2   Kathryn Orrison Tavenner   Age: 71 years
         Birth: 1890/02/22   Death: 1961/11/25   Burial: 1961/11/29
         Place: Leesburg, VA
Site 3   June T. Potterfield   Place: Leesburg, VA   Age: 69 years
         Birth: 1920/06/01   Death: 1988/03/03   Burial: 1988/03/07
Site 4   Robert Lee Potterfield Jr.   Age: 61 years
         Birth: 1918/04/09   Death: 1979/12/09   Burial: 1979/12/12
         Place: Leesburg, VA   TS: TEC4 US Army WWII
Site 9   Mrs. Patricia Tavenner Gillespie   Age: 30 years
         Birth: 1942/06/29   Death: 1973/04/15   Burial: 1973/04/19
                                   Place: Falls Church, VA

Lot: 1240   Owner: Roy M. & C.U. Flippo   Purchased: 1951/06/29
Site 1   Edgar Lee Upton   Age: 80 years
         Birth: 1871   Death: 1951/06/29   Burial: 1951/07/01
Site 2   Minnie B. Upton   Removal   On stone with Edgar Lee Upton
         Birth: 1877   Death: 1948   Burial: 1951/07/24
Site 3   Roy Monroe Flippo   Place: Leesburg, VA   Age: 66 years
         Birth: 1894   Death: 1960/11/29   Burial: 1960/12/01
Site 4   Charlsie W. Flippo   Place: Leesburg, VA   No stone
         Birth: 1903/08/12   Death: 1995/11/20   Burial: 1995/11/24
Site 6   Baby Wall   Death: 1958/09/22   Burial: 1958/09/23
         Cause: Stillborn   Place: L.C.H. Leesburg, VA
         TS: Infant daughter of James & Ellen Wall

Lot: 1241   Owner: C. Maloy & Ruth L. Fishback   1958/10/21
Site 1   Charles Maloy Fishback   Place: Leesburg, VA   Age: 59 years
         Birth: 1910/01/06   Death: 1969/04/22   Burial: 1969/04/24
Site 2   Ruth Tavenner Fishback   Place: Leesburg, VA   Age: 78 years
         Birth: 1912/02/05   Death: 1990/12/08   Burial: 1990/12/11

Lot: 1242   Owner: Frances Titus McCann   1957/10/16
Site 3   James Morgan McCann   Age: 48 years
         Birth: 1909/09/13   Death: 1957/10/15

Site 12 William Frank Thyson Place: Leesburg, VA Age: 39 years
Birth: 1944/08/07 Death: 1984/04/22 Burial: 1984/04/24

Lot: 1243 Owner: Miscellaneous
Site 3 Harry Umbaugh Place: Hamilton, VA Age: 82 years
Birth: 1881/02/06 Death: 1963/07/09 Burial: 1963/07/13

Lot: 1244 E Owner: Miscellaneous
Site 11 Milton C. Reed Place: Berkley Springs, WV Age: 77 years
Birth: 1911 Death: 1988/10/09 Burial: 1988/10/12
Site 12 Bertha B. Reed Place: Berkley Springs, WV Age: 70 years
Birth: 1913 Death: 1984/01/03 Burial: 1984/01/06

Lot: 1244 W Owner: Joseph H. Willingham Purchased: 1959/07/23
Site 1 Roy Nathan Willingham Place: Fairfax, VA Age: 68 years
Birth: 1917 Death: 1986/01/09 Burial: 1986/01/13
Site 3 Joseph Herbert Willingham Age: 74 years
Birth: 1889 Death: 1963/11/07 Burial: 1963/11/09
Place: Fairfax, VA
Site 4 Alice Virginia Willingham Age: 81 years
Birth: 1892 Death: 1973/04/06 Burial: 1973/04/09
Place: Fairfax, VA

Lot: 1245 E Owner: J. Fred & Richard Howser Purchased:
Site 10 James Frederick Howser Place: Leesburg, VA Age: 86 years
Birth: 1884/09/01 Death: 1971/05/09 Burial: 1971/05/12
Site 11 Maude May Howser Age: 60 years
Birth: 1898/01/22 Death: 1958/10/15 Burial: 1958/10/18
Place: L.C.H. Leesburg, VA On stone with James Fred Howser

Lot: 1245 W Owner: Kemper C. Rust Purchased: 1958/08/18
Site 5 Irene Hardy Rust Age: 65 years
Birth: 1892/12/09 Death: 1958/08/16 Burial: 1958/08/19
Place: Doubs, MD On stone with Kemper Clay Rust
Site 5 Kemper Clay Rust Place: Frederick, MD Age: 88 years
Birth: 1894/08/09 Death: 1982/10/11 Burial: 1982/10/14

Lot: 1246 Owner: Mrs. Lela T. McKimmey 1956/03/26
Site 1 Charles B. McKimmey Place: Leesburg, VA Age: 62 years
Birth: 1919/08/15 Death: 1982/01/09 Burial: 1982/01/12
Site 4 Birtrand Willard McKimmey Age: 66 years
Birth: 1889/09/03 Death: 1956/03/24 Burial: 1956/03/25
Place: Leesburg, VA
Site 4 Francie M. Wenner Place: Leesburg, VA Age: 67 years
Birth: 1912/11/10 Death: 1980/08/02 Burial: 1980/08/05
Site 6 Lela T. McKimmey Place: Leesburg, VA Age: 70 years
Birth: 1889/06/04 Death: 1960/01/22 Burial: 1960/01/25

Lot: 1247 E   Owner: Flossie McKimmey Herndon   1958/07/28
Site 7 Havard Burton Herndon   Age: 56 years
        Birth: 1902   Death: 1958/07/27   Burial: 1958/07/29
        Cause: Suicide   Place: Waterford, VA

Lot: 1247 W Owner: Mrs. Charles W. Hamilton   1956/06/02
Site 1 Charles W. Hamilton   Place: Ashburn, VA   Age: 52 years
        Birth: 1904   Death: 1956/05/31   Burial: 1956/06/02
Site 2 Lillian M. Hamilton   Place: Leesburg, VA   Age: 69 years
        Birth: 1906   Death: 1976/09/07   Burial: 1976/09/10
Site 3 Ronald Steven McGowen
        Birth: 1959/09/24   Death: 1992/01/24   Burial: 1992/01/28
        Place: Leesburg, VA   TS: Son, Brother, Friend

Lot: 1248   Owner: Miscellaneous
Site 3 Robert Edward Swank   Place: Manassas, VA   Age: 57 years
        Birth: 1924/02/29   Death: 1981/04/21   Burial: 1981/04/24

Lot: 1249   Owner: Miscellaneous
Site 3 Robert Kilgour Lanham   Age: 60 years
        Birth: 1922/02/07   Death: 1982/10/21   Burial: 1982/10/24
        Place: Leesburg, VA   TS: US Army WWII

Lot: 1250   Owner: Miscellaneous
Site 1 William E. Donohoe   Place: Leesburg, VA   Age: 70 years
        Birth: 1891   Death: 1961/12/12   Burial: 1961/12/14
Site 2 Carrie C. Donohoe   Age: 79 years
        Birth: 1890   Death: 1969/11/08   Burial: 1969/11/11
        Place: Leesburg, VA   On stone with William E. Donohoe
Site 6 Edna Conrad Donohoe   Place: Leesburg, VA
        Birth: 1915/09/11   Death: 1995/06/19   Burial: 1995/06/23
Site 11 Barbara Jane Sergison Richards
        Birth: 1914/04/09   Death: 1993/02/21   Burial: 1993/02/27
        Place: MD   TS: Surrey, England
Site 12 Arget (Dick) Richards   Place: MD   TS: Scottish Border
        Birth: 1913/04/09   Death: 1992/12/29   Burial: 1993/01/02

Lot: 1251   Owner: Miscellaneous
Site 2 Carroll E. Russell   Place: Woodbridge, VA   Age: 70 years
        Birth: 1916/06/18   Death: 1986/12/31   Burial: 1987/01/03
Site 4 David B. Kehr   Place: Ashburn, VA   Age: 47 years
        Birth: 1938   Death: 1986/06/29   Burial: 1986/07/02
        TS: Married Barbara N. Kehr February 14, 1959
Site 6 Clifton E. Lemarr Sr.   Place: Leesburg, VA   Age: 50 years
        Birth: 1933/10/12   Death: 1984/03/16   Burial: 1984/03/19
Site 7 John R. Potter   Place: Leesburg, VA   Age: 46 years
        Birth: 1943/05/08   Death: 1989/05/27   Burial: 1989/05/31
Site 10 Pauline W. Jones   Place: Leesburg, VA   Age: 62 years
        Birth: 1924/09/02   Death: 1987/03/17   Burial: 1987/03/20

Lot: 1252 Owner: Miscellanous
Site 2 Elsa Tomat Braidotti Place: Leesburg, VA Age: 77 years
Birth: 1914/01/21 Death: 1991/06/07 Burial: 1991/06/10

Lot: 1253 Owner: Miscellaneous
Site 3 Arnold E. Craighead Sr. Place: Leesburg, VA Age: 70 years
Birth: 1916/09/03 Death: 1987/04/10 Burial: 1987/04/13
TS: Married Syble F. Craighead September 4, 1937

Lot: 1254 E Owner: Miscellaneous
Site 7 James S. Ketchum Place: Silver Spring, MD Age: 55 years
Birth: 1923/12/12 Death: 1979/07/11 Burial: 1979/07/14
Site 9 John Preston Stocks Age: 55 years
Birth: 1923/10/13 Death: 1979/07/20 Burial: 1979/07/23
Place: Glen Ridge, NJ TS: PFC US Army WWII
Site 10 Richard Junior Stocks Age: 53 years
Birth: 1926/11/03 Death: 1980/06/30 Burial: 1980/07/02
Place: Leesburg, VA TS: TEC4 US Army WWII
Site 11 Edwin Arthur Boland III Place: Leesburg, VA Age: 20 years
Birth: 1959/06/07 Death: 1979/08/28 Burial: 1979/09/01

Lot: 1254 W Owner: Pauline C. Wippel Purchased: 1979/05/26
Site 1 Linus W. Wippel Age: 67 years
Birth: 1911/08/28 Death: 1979/05/20
Site 2 Pauline Lee Wippel Place: CA On stone with Linus W. Wippel
Birth: 1913/03/23 Death: 1991/02/03 Burial: 1991/02/09
Site 6 Elsie C. Witt Place: Ft. Lauderdale, FL Age: 97 years
Birth: 1889 Death: 1987/01/10 Burial: 1987/01/13

Lot: 1255 E Owner: Mrs. Homer H. Slaughter Purchased:
Site 7 Homer H. Slaughter Age: 68 years
Birth: 1885 Death: 1953/12/21 Burial: 1953/12/24
Cause: Pul. Infarct. Place: Washington, DC
TS: Colonel US Army USMA 1908
Site 8 Isma E. Slaughter Age: 88 years
Birth: 1889 Death: 1977/02/18 Burial: 1977/02/21
Place: Frederick, MD On stone with Homer H. Slaughter

Lot: 1255 W Owner: Newell H. Wright
**   & Susan Eidson Wright Purchased: 1955/12/21**
Site 1 John West Eidson Place: Leesburg, VA Age: 79 years
Birth: 1877/02/26 Death: 1956/04/08 Burial: 1956/04/09
Site 2 Mrs. Lillie Bell Eidson Age: 79 years
Birth: 1876/03/18 Death: 1955/12/20 Burial: 1955/12/21
Place: Leesburg, VA On stone with James W. Eidson
Site 3 Susan Etta Wright Place: York, PA
Birth: 1907/02/08 Death: 1992/01/13 Burial: 1992/01/18
Site 5 Mary Eidson Reynolds Age: 39 years
Birth: 1940 Death: 1980/08/01 Burial: 1980/08/06
Cause: Auto Accident Place: Arlington, VA

Lot: 1256E   Owner: Thomas M.
& Kathleen E. Courtney   Purchased: 1951/04/24
Site 9   Thomas Moore Courtney   Age: 79 years
         Birth: 1882/06/14   Death: 1962/04/07   Burial: 1962/04/09
         Place: L.C.H. Leesburg, VA
Site 9   Kathleen Everest Courtney   Age: 86 years
         Birth: 1884/05/19   Death: 1971/02/13   Burial: 1971/02/16
         Place: Leesburg, VA
Site 11 William Dunlap Courtney   Age: 72 years
         Birth: 1846/08/07   Death: 1919/07/15   Burial: 1953/10/16
         Cause: Apoplexy   Place: Canton, OH   Disinterment
Site 12 Sarah Jones Courtney Place: Purcellville, VA   Age: 98 years
         Birth: 1854/03/02   Death: 1953/01/04   Burial: 1953/01/07

Lot: 1257   Owner: Miscellaneous
Site 5   Collis Grant Polen   Age: 87 years
         Birth: 1891/06/10   Death: 1978/08/03   Burial: 1978/08/05
         Place: Leesburg, VA   TS: Cook US Army WWI
Site 6   Mrs. Sarah E. Polen   Age: 73 years
         Birth: 1891/08/10   Death: 1964/12/07   Burial: 1964/12/10
         Place: Hillsboro, VA   On stone with Collis Grant Polen
Site 11 Edward P. Polen   Place: Leesburg, VA   Age: 60 years
         Birth: 1925/09/23   Death: 1985/12/21   Burial: 1985/12/24
Site 12 Mrs. Mary Frances Polen   Cause: Cancer   Age: 47 years
         Birth: 1926/05/19   Death: 1972/11/20   Burial: 1972/11/22
         Place: Leesburg, VA   On stone with Edward P. Polen

Lot: 1258   Owner: Miscellaneous
Site 1   Winfred W. Fishback Place: Martinsburg, WV   Age: 73 years
         Birth: 1916   Death: 1989/10/21   Burial: 1989/10/24
Site 2   Virginia C. Fishback   Age: 60 years
         Birth: 1919   Death: 1979/05/10
         On stone with Winfred W. Fishback
Site 7   Lula Casilear Fetzer Place: Leesburg, VA   Age: 69 years
         Birth: 1909/08/17   Death: 1979/02/05   Burial: 1979/02/08

Lot: 1259   Owner: Miscellaneous
Site 1   Lilly Mae Jackson   Place: Winchester, VA   Age: 97 years
         Birth: 1881/02/16   Death: 1978/08/01   Burial: 1978/08/04
Site 9   Benjamin F. (Bennie) Jackson   Age: 71 years
         Birth: 1915/07/17   Death: 1986/11/12   Burial: 1986/11/14
         Place: Leesburg, VA

Lot: 1260   Owner: Miscellaneous
Site 1   John C. Hope   Age: 20 years
         Birth: 1941/01/06   Death: 1961/10/23   Burial: 1961/10/26
         Cause: Cancer   Place: Frederick, MD
Site 4   Lillie Virginia Hope Place: Knoxville, MD   TS: Mother
         Birth: 1918/04/16   Death: 1995/03/28   Burial: 1995/03/30

Lot: 1261   Owner: Miscellaneous
Site 4   Ethel Ryan Hope   Place: Waterford, VA   Age: 79 years
         Birth: 1906/11/16   Death: 1985/12/18   Burial: 1985/12/21

Lot: 1262   Owner: Miscellaneous
Site 1   Forrest G. Moler   Place: Frederick, MD   Age: 61 years
         Birth: 1899   Death: 1960/07/19   Burial: 1960/07/21
Site 9   Ernest H. Thompson   Place: Annandale, VA   Age: 79 years
         Birth: 1907/11/20   Death: 1987/02/07   Burial: 1987/02/10

Lot: 1263   Owner: Miscellaneous
Site 4   Samuel Powell Jones   Age: 57 years
         Birth: 1923/05/02   Death: 1980/10/01   Burial: 1980/10/04
         Cause: Heart   Place: Leesburg, VA
Site 5   Mrs. Madelaine Morgan Jenkins   Age: 46 years
         Birth: 1921/10/15   Death: 1969/11/11   Burial: 1969/11/13
         Cause: Cancer   Place: Bethesda, MD
Site 6   Jay Stewart Jones   Cause: Auto Accident   Age: 13 years
         Birth: 1949/12/05   Death: 1963/01/25   Burial: 1963/01/28
Site 9   William J. George   Place: Leesburg, VA
         Birth: 1915/03/07   Death: 1994/04/19   Burial: 1994/04/22
Site 10 Louise R. George   Age: 69 years
         Birth: 1918/10/07   Death: 1988/04/05   Burial: 1988/04/08
         Place: Leesburg, VA   On stone with William J. George
Site 11 Robert N. Ramsey Jr.   Place: Charlottesville, VA   Age: 61 years
         Birth: 1914   Death: 1975/01/05   Burial: 1975/01/09
Site 12 Mrs. Evie K. Ramsey   Age: 74 years
         Birth: 1888/11/01   Death: 1963/03/13   Burial: 1963/03/37
         Place: Leesburg, VA   TS: Mother

Lot: 1264   Owner: Miscellaneous
Site 1   Harry Wise Cunningham   Age: 50 years
         Birth: 1914/06/18   Death: 1964/10/24   Burial: 1964/10/27
Site 2   Elinor M. Cunningham
         Birth: 1923/08/26   Death: 1994/05/12   Burial: 1994/05/16
         Place: Sterling, VA   On stone with Harry Wise Cunningham
Site 5   Elijah F. Myers   Place: Leesburg, VA   Age: 73 years
         Birth: 1892/03/11   Death: 1965/09/05   Burial: 1965/09/07
Site 6   Pearl M. Myers   Place: Washington, DC   Age: 59 years
         Birth: 1905/12/30   Death: 1964/11/19   Burial: 1964/11/22
Site 8   G. Shirley Myers   Place: Leesburg, VA   Age: 67 years
         Birth: 1894/07/08   Death: 1963/04/29   Burial: 1963/05/01

Lot: 1265   Owner: Miscellaneous
Site 5   Joseph B. Ballo   Place: Leesburg, VA   Age: 64 years
         Birth: 1915/07/24   Death: 1980/05/27   Burial: 1980/05/30
Site 6   Gertrude C. Ballo
         Birth: 1916/09/05   Death: 1995/04/05   Burial: 1995/04/10
         Place: Leesburg, VA   On stone with Joseph B. Ballo

Site 7 Penny Jean Phillips   Age: 7 years
        Birth: 1964/06/25   Death: 1972/03/11   Burial: 1972/03/13
        Cause: Bone Cancer   Place: Bethesda, MD

Lot: 1266   Owner: Miscellaneous
Site 1 William L. Rollins   Place: Alexandria, VA   Age: 75 years
        Birth: 1911/11/25   Death: 1987/01/01   Burial: 1987/01/05
Site 7 Lola B. Crampton   Age: 71 years
        Birth: 1915   Death: 1987/02/17   Burial: 1987/02/19
        Place: Arlington, VA   On stone with John W. Crampton
Site 8 John W. Crampton   Birth: 1911/01/29   Death: 1992/09/28
Site 9 Elizabeth L. Ambry   Place: Leesburg, VA   Age: 100 years
        Birth: 1887   Death: 1987/04/14   Burial: 1987/04/15
Site 9 Vincent R. Ambrey   Place: Leesburg, VA   Age: 75 years
        Birth: 1911   Death: 1987/06/18   Burial: 1987/06/20
Site 11 Genevieve Ann Hutton   Age: 76 years
        Birth: 1910   Death: 1987/02/24   Burial: 1987/02/26
        Place: Leesburg, VA   TS: US Navy

Lot: 1271 E Owner: C.H. Arnold & Robert L. Arnold   1963/01/25
Site 7 Cleveland H. Arnold   Place: Leesburg, VA   Age: 82 years
        Birth: 1884/01/07   Death: 1966/08/13   Burial: 1966/08/16
Site 8 Mamie C. Arnold   Age: 78 years
        Birth: 1884/04/12   Death: 1963/01/01   Burial: 1963/01/04
        Place: Baltimore, MD   On stone with Cleveland H. Arnold

Lot: 1271 W Owner: Mr. & Mrs. Walter E. Grant   1954/07/30
Site 1 Walter Enders Grant   Place: Hamilton, VA   Age: 73 years
        Birth: 1881/04/17   Death: 1955/01/06   Burial: 1955/01/08
Site 2 Mrs. Sarah W. Grant
        Birth: 1884/03/20   Death: 1971/04/12   Burial: 1971/04/14
        Place: Leesburg, VA   On stone with Walter E. Grant
Site 3 Mary Jane Grant Brownrigg   Age: 65 years
        Birth: 1914/01/06   Death: 1979/07/17   Burial: 1979/07/20
        Place: Leesburg, VA   On stone with Philip Parker Brownrigg
Site 4 Philip Parker Brownrigg Place: Leesburg, VA   Age: 79 years
        Birth: 1908/10/10   Death: 1987/12/29   Burial: 1988/01/02

Lot: 1272   Owner: Miscellaneous
Site 1 Owen Lewis McNey   Place: Bethesda, MD   Age: 70 years
        Birth: 1896/06/06   Death: 1967/05/25   Burial: 1967/05/29
Site 9 William Joseph McDonald   Place: Leesburg, VA
        Birth: 1921/09/19   Death: 1991/08/02   Burial: 1991/08/05
Site 9 William Joseph McDonald Jr.   Age: 1day
        Birth: 1950/03/16   Death: 1950/03/17   Burial: 1991/10/15
        Place: Baltimore, MD

Lot: 1273   Owner: Miscellaneous
Site 1 Elijah B. White   Place: Leesburg, VA   Age: 81 years
        Birth: 1910/09/10   Death: 1991/09/09   Burial: 1991/09/13

Lot: 1274   Owner: Miscellaneous
Site 1   Rev. Charles W. Caulkins   Age: 80 years
         Birth: 1899/01/12   Death: 1979/03/12   TS: Capt. US Army WWI
Site 2   Eunice A. Caulkins   Age: 82 years
         Birth: 1899   Death: 1982/01/02   Burial: 1982/01/05
         Place: Leesburg, VA   On stone with Rev. Charles W. Caulkins
Site 6   M. Hawthorne Granger III, MD   Age: 44 years
         Birth: 1946/08/01   Death: 1990/08/29   Burial: 1990/08/31
         Place: Leesburg, VA
Site 7   Judge Franklin Shry   Place: Lucketts, VA   Age: 86 years
         Birth: 1890/01/03   Death: 1976/08/06   Burial: 1976/08/09
Site 8   Mrs. Anna Arlene Shry   Age: 73 years
         Birth: 1892/12/26   Death: 1965/12/06   Burial: 1965/12/09
         Place: Lucketts, VA   On stone with Judge Franklin Shry
Site 9   Marshall Franklin Shry   Place: Leesburg, VA   Age: 58 years
         Birth: 1929/05/22   Death: 1988/03/30   Burial: 1988/04/02

Lot: 1275   Owner: Miscellaneous
Site 6   Thomas J. Graves   Place: Winchester, VA   Age: 80 years
         Birth: 1902/03/11   Death: 1982/06/12   Burial: 1982/06/14
         TS: Married Wanda L. Graves February 19, 1927
Site 7   Sharon Arleen Sutler   Age: 20 years
         Birth: 1962/12/15   Death: 1983/05/31   Burial: 1983/06/03
         Cause: Auto Accident   Place: Washington, DC
Site 9   Charles Emil Felix   Place: Leesburg, VA   Age: 84 years
         Birth: 1900/03/25   Death: 1984/06/13   Burial: 1984/06/16
Site 10 Anne Walsh Felix   Place: Fairfax, VA   Age: 76 years
         Birth: 1906/09/08   Death: 1983/06/24   Burial: 1983/06/27

Lot: 1276   Owner: Miscellaneous
Site 8   Mary Irene Fletcher   Place: Leesburg, VA
         Birth: 1911/04/08   Death: 1991/04/23   Burial: 1991/04/27
Site 9   Mary Lane Isaacs   Place: Leesburg, VA   Age: 69 years
         Birth: 1912/04/19   Death: 1981/06/15   Burial: 1981/06/17
Site 9   Col. George E. Isaacs   Place: FL   TS: Col. US Army WWII
         Birth: 1902/07/29   Death: 1991/09/21   Burial: 1991/09
Site 10 Elmer Clifton Johnson   Place: Leesburg, VA   Age: 74 years
         Birth: 1906/10/02   Death: 1981/07/16   Burial: 1981/07/18
Site 11 Mary Mills Johnson   Place: Leesburg, VA
         Birth: 1917/02/06   Death: 1994/03/11   Burial: 1994/03/14
         Married Elmer Clifton Johnson August 17, 1938
Site 12 Segundo Luis Adolfo Ayala   Age: 71 years
         Birth: 1910/02/18   Death: 1981/10/02   Burial: 1981/10/04
         Place: Leesburg, VA

Lot: 1277   Owner: Miscellaneous
Site 1   Sterling Jennings   Place: Leesburg, VA
         Birth: 1911/02/26   Death: 1994/04/08   Burial: 1994/04/11

Site 2   Helen C. Jennings   Place: Leesburg, VA   Age: 78 years
         Birth: 1910/10/22   Death: 1989/08/05   Burial: 1989/08/08
         Cause: Cancer   On stone with Sterling Jennings
Site 3   Eda Mae Jennings Wine   Place: Washington, DC   Age: 36 years
         Birth: 1932/08/01   Death: 1968/11/21   Burial: 1968/11/23
Site 7   Clark E. Stream   Place: Leesburg, VA
         Birth: 1910/05/15   Death: 1993/10/14   Burial: 1993/10/16
Site 8   Annie R. Stream
         Birth: 1912/07/18   Death: 1992/07/29   Burial: 1992/08/01
         Place: Leesburg, VA   On stone with Clark E. Stream
Site 11 Robert P. Burkart   Age: 29 years
         Birth: 1952/08/29   Death: 1981/08/30   Burial: 1981/09/02
         Place: Ashburn, VA   TS: Born WI
Site 12 Baby Burkart   No stone   Age: 6weeks
         Place: Fairfax, VA   Death: 1984/03/28   Burial: 1984/03/31

Lot: 1278   Owner: Miscellaneous
Site 3   Raymond Barron   Age: 61 years
         Birth: 1902   Death: 1964/04/26   Burial: 1964/04/29
         Cause: Heart Attack   Place: Leesburg, VA
Site 4   Louise H. Legard   Place: Herndon, VA   No stone
         Birth: 1912/08/10   Death: 1994/06/06   Burial: 1994/06/08
Site 5   Mary Esther W. Hinton   Place: Gadsden, AL   Age: 81 years
         Birth: 1890   Death: 1971/09/26   Burial: 1971/09/29
Site 7   Maurice R. Wine   Place: Front Royal, VA   Age: 67 years
         Birth: 1898/12/25   Death: 1966/04/15   Burial: 1966/04/18
Site 8   Ruth M. Wine   Place: Alexandria, VA   Age: 77 years
         Birth: 1902/09/27   Death: 1980/02/21   Burial: 1980/02/24

Lot: 1279   Owner: Mrs. Helen A. Herndon   1966/06/19
Site 2   Calvin Herndon   Place: Charlottesville, VA Age: 35 years
         Birth: 1942/08/13   Death: 1977/11/16   Burial: 1977/11/19
Site 3   William A. Herndon   Place: Washington, DC   Age: 58 years
         Birth: 1907/10/21   Death: 1966/06/02   Burial: 1966/06/05
Site 3   Helen A. Herndon   Place: Leesburg, VA   Age: 75 years
         Birth: 1912/07/09   Death: 1987/10/09   Burial: 1987/10/11
Site 5   George Jack Montgomery   Age: 28 years
         Birth: 1943/06/01   Death: 1972/04/13   Burial: 1972/04/17
         Cause: Plane crash   Place: CT

Lot: 1280   Owner: Miscellaneous
Site 3   Clayton O. Church   Place: Fairfax, VA   Age: 59 years
         Birth: 1923/05/21   Death: 1982/07/21   Burial: 1982/07/24
Site 11 William Burton Miller   Place: Frederick, MD   Age: 76 years
         Birth: 1914/02/16   Death: 1990/11/17   Burial: 1990/11/20
Site 12 Elizabeth K. Miller   Age: 62 years
         Birth: 1916/06/28   Death: 1979/06/07
         On stone with William Burton Miller

Lot: 1281   Owner: Miscellaneous
Site 1 Douglas H. Cline   Place: Fredericksburg, VA   Age: 20 years
        Birth: 1958/12/23   Death: 1979/07/15   Burial: 1979/07/18
Site 2 Stanley W. Pangle Sr.   TS: PFC US Army WWII.   Age: 63 years
        Birth: 1926/10/14   Death: 1989/11/01   Burial: 1989/11/04
        Married Evelyn B. Pangle February 22, 1945
Site 4 Roland O. Keyes   Age: 70 years
                                  Death: 1979/08/23   Burial: 1979/08/27
        Cause: Heart   Place: Leesburg, VA   No stone

Lot: 1282 E   Owner: Miscellaneous
Site 8   Rose M. Foth   Place: Leesburg, VA   Age: 63 years
         Birth: 1915   Death: 1979/06/29   Burial: 1979/07/02
         TS: Married Erich A.W. Foth 1937 N.Y.C. Born PA
Site 9   William Proctor   Place: Stevenson, VA   Age: 78 years
         Birth: 1913   Death: 1991/05/23   Burial: 1991/05/27
Site 10 Cathrine F. Proctor   Age: 60 years
         Birth: 1918   Death: 1979/09/15   Burial: 1979/09/18
         Place: Leesburg, VA   On stone with William Proctor

Lot: 1282 W Owner: Lewis E. Flynn   Purchased:
Site 1 Lewis E. Flynn   Place: Leesburg, VA   Age: 77 years
        Birth: 1904   Death: 1981/07/22   Burial: 1981/07/24
Site 2 Bessie Elizabeth Flynn   Age: 74yers
        Birth: 1912   Death: 1986/08/17   Burial: 1986/08/20
        Place: Leesburg, VA   On stone with Lewis E. Flynn
Site 3 Lewis A. Flynn   Place: Leesburg, VA   No stone
        Birth: 1928/01/28   Death: 1992/11/19   Burial: 1992/11/21
Site 4 James Milton Flynn   No stone   Age: 61 years
        Place: Winchester, VA   Death: 1969/02/02   Burial: 1969/02/05

Lot: 1287   Owner: Miscellaneous
Site 0   Inez Hope Greene   Death: 1921/04/02
Site 1   Stanley T. Greene   Place: Leesburg, VA   Age: 80 years
         Birth: 1887/10/18   Death: 1968/07/17   Burial: 1968/07/19
Site 2   Mrs. Inez E. Greene   Place: Fairfax, VA   Age: 76 years
         Birth: 1898   Death: 1974/12/19   Burial: 1974/12/31
Site 7   Frances M. Durfey   Place: Leesburg, VA   Age: 88 years
         Birth: 1900/09/17   Death: 1989/07/02   Burial: 1989/07/06
Site 11 George J. Durfy   Age: 85 years
         Birth: 1890/01/23   Death: 1975/10/22   Burial: 1975/10/25
         Place: Leesburg, VA   TS: 1st Lt. US Army WWI

Lot: 1288   Owner: Miscellaneous
Site 1 C. Frank Atwell   Place: Ryan, VA   Age: 86 years
        Birth: 1883   Death: 1969/12/08   Burial: 1969/12/10
Site 2 Eunice H. Atwell   Age: 82 years
        Birth: 1891   Death: 1973/10/24   Burial: 1973/10/26
        Place: Leesburg, VA   On stone with C. Frank Atwell

Lot: 1289   Owner: Miscellaneous
Site 1   James Edward Wilson Sr.   Age: 80 years
         Birth: 1897/11/14   Death: 1978/10/07   Burial: 1978/10/10
         Place: Bethesda, MD   TS: "PAW"
Site 2   Ethel E. Wilson   Place: Gaithersburg, MD   Age: 72 years
         Birth: 1907/08/14   Death: 1980/03/15   Burial: 1980/03/19
         TS: "MAW"   On stone with James Edward Wilson Sr.
Site 8   Jo Ann W. Thomson   Place: MD   Age: 59 years
         Birth: 1931/06/30   Death: 1990/11/08   Burial: 1990/11/12

Lot: 1290   Owner: Miscellaneous
Site 1   Clarence Jennings Fry   Place: Lucketts, VA   Age: 75 years
         Birth: 1897/07/31   Death: 1971/08/01   Burial: 1971/08/04
Site 2   Bessie Grafton Fry   Age: 86 years
         Birth: 1889/07/19   Death: 1975/08/13   Burial: 1975/08/16
         Place: Leesburg, VA   On stone with Clarence Jennings Fry

Lot: 1291   Owner: Miscellaneous
Site 1   Chet B. Hucks   Place: Belmont, NC   Age: 3 years
         Birth: 1965   Death: 1968/07/30   Burial: 1968/08/01
Site 10 Charlie M. Kestner   Place: Fairfax, VA   Age: 72 years
         Birth: 1912/02/18   Death: 1984/11/07   Burial: 1984/11/10
         TS: Married Mary J. Kestner November 2, 1960

Lot: 1292   Owner: Miscellaneous
Site 1   Bruce Ryan Coughlin   Age: 64 years
         Birth: 1907/12/22   Death: 1972/06/25   Burial: 1972/06/28
Site 2   Alice Wilt Coughlin   Place: Leesburg, VA
         Birth: 1909/10/24   Death: 1992/10/13   Burial: 1992/10/16
Site 8   Janet J. Keene   Place: Berryville, VA
         Birth: 1929/12/10   Death: 1992/04/30   Burial: 1992/05/04

Lot: 1293   Owner: Miscellaneous
Site 1   Francis J. Reed   Place: FL
         Birth: 1915/08/31   Death: 1993/01/01   Burial: 1993/01/07
Site 4   Golena M. Simpson   Place: Fairfax, VA   Age: 68 years
         Birth: 1925/03/04   Death: 1987/05/30   Burial: 1987/06/01
Site 6   Marianne S. Greenfield Place: Leesburg, VA   Age: 59 years
         Birth: 1929/04/29   Death: 1989/02/20   Burial: 1989/02/23
Site 7   William Claiborne Hayes Place: Leesburg, VA   Age: 63 years
         Birth: 1924/10/06   Death: 1988/02/20   Burial: 1988/02/22
Site 9   Rita Diamante Bohumil   Place: Fairfax, VA   Age: 63 years
         Birth: 1926   Death: 1989/05/19   Burial: 1989/05/23
Site 10 Ronald J. Rogers   Place: Chester, MD   Age: 55 years
         Birth: 1934   Death: 1989/09/30   Burial: 1989/10/03
Site 12 Gloria A. Schriver   Place: Leesburg, VA   Age: 58 years
         Birth: 1929/11/30   Death: 1988/02/27   Burial: 1988/03/02

Lot: 1294 Owner: Miscellaneous

Site 1 Walter D. Craighead Place: Cherry Hill, NJ Age: 66 years
Birth: 1919 Death: 1985/11/28 Burial: 1985/12/02

Site 2 Alma N. Craighead
Birth: 1913/11/15 Death: 1993/06/15 Burial: 1993/06/18
Place: Marlton, NJ On stone with Walter D. Craighead

Site 3 Robert O. Comstock Place: Leesburg, VA Age: 65 years
Birth: 1921/02/18 Death: 1986/06/27 Burial: 1986/06/30

Site 4 Flavilla I. Fox Age: 88 years
Birth: 1902/10/18 Death: 1991/08/22 Burial: 1991/08/26
Place: Leesburg, VA On stone with Robert O. Comstock

Site 5 William R. Roderick Place: Leesburg, VA Age: 82 years
Birth: 1903 Death: 1985/11/27 Burial: 1985/11/30

Site 6 Amy C. Roderick Age: 88 years
Birth: 1904 Death: 1992/09/20 Burial: 1992/09/23
Place: Leesburg, VA On stone with William R. Roderick

Site 10 Kathleen G. Sutphin Place: Leesburg, VA
Birth: 1911/04/25 Death: 1992/03/17 Burial: 1992/03/20

Lot: 1295 Owner: Miscellaneous

Site 1 Harry C. Amos Jr. Age: 29 years
Birth: 1939 Death: 1969/01/23 Burial: 1969/01/25
Cause: Suicide Place: Leesburg, VA

Site 4 Harry C. Amos Sr. Place: Leesburg, VA Age: 78 years
Birth: 1896 Death: 1974/10/28 Burial: 1974/11/03

Site 5 Ethel Mae A. Amos Place: MD
Birth: 1906/08/04 Death: 1991/02/11 Burial: 1991/02/14

Site 7 Alfred M. Furr Age: 59 years
Birth: 1910 Death: 1970/04/15 Burial: 1970/04/18
Place: Leesburg, VA TS: Daddy Allie

Site 12 Mrs. Lucy B. Furr Place: Leesburg, VA Age: 73 years
Birth: 1898/05/12 Death: 1972/01/05 Burial: 1972/01/08

Lot: 1296 Owner: Miscellaneous

Site 1 Leonard James Wright Place: Leesburg, VA Age: 51 years
Birth: 1926/10/26 Death: 1978/01/06 Burial: 1978/01/09

Site 5 Robert E. Baker Place: Leesburg, VA Age: 60 years
Birth: 1917 Death: 1978/05/11 Burial: 1978/05/14

Site 6 Ada Mae Baker
Birth: 1920/04/09 Death: 1995/09/05 Burial: 1995/09/07
Place: Leesburg, VA On stone with Robert E. Baker

Site 7 Hubert F. McWilliams Place: Leesburg, VA Age: 77 years
Birth: 1900 Death: 1978/01/28 Burial: 1978/01/31

Site 8 Mary E. McWilliams Age: 80 years
Birth: 1900 Death: 1981/10/30 Burial: 1981/11/02
Place: Leesburg, VA On stone with Hubert F. McWilliams

Site 9 James H. Caddell Sr. Place: Leesburg, VA Age: 67 years
Birth: 1911 Death: 1978/02/03 Burial: 1978/02/06

Site 11 Wilma Dianne Gowans   Age: 31 years
         Birth: 1946/06/12   Death: 1978/03/20   Burial: 1978/03/24
         Cause: Cancer   Place: Arlington, VA

Lot: 1296 1/2 Owner: Miscellaneous
Site 1 Louis Roula Furr   Age: 72 years
        Birth: 1906   Death: 1978/10/28   Burial: 1978/10/31
        Place: Leesburg, VA   TS: TEC4 US Army WWII
Site 1 Hortence Lloyd Furr
        Birth: 1903/03/27   Death: 1994/07/25   Burial: 1994/07/28
        Place: Winchester, VA   TS: Wife of Louis Roula Furr

Lot: 1297 Owner: Miscellaneous
Site 1 John W. Cooper   Place: Leesburg, VA   Age: 73 years
        Birth: 1914   Death: 1988/02/20   Burial: 1988/02/23
Site 3 Lester A. Jenkins   Place: Eustis, FL   Age: 91 years
        Birth: 1899   Death: 1991/08/21   Burial: 1991/08/26
Site 7 Joseph C. Dickinson   Place: Leesburg, VA   Age: 66 years
        Birth: 1915   Death: 1981/06/03   Burial: 1981/06/05
Site 8 Virginia Bentley Mays   Place: Leesburg, VA
        Birth: 1933/04/19   Death: 1991/01/17   Burial: 1991/01/20

Lot: 1298 Owner: Miscellaneous
Site 3 C. Russell Tillett   Age: 77 years
        Birth: 1901/12/28   Death: 1979/03/11
Site 4 Tessie Penn Tillett
        Birth: 1904/04/03   Death: 1995/01/21   Burial: 1995/01/25
        Place: Leesburg, VA   On stone with C. Russell Tillett

Lot: 1299 Owner: B.H. Bratney   Purchased: 1949/01/10
Site 1 Mrs. Elizabeth Bratney Holcombe   Age: 86 years
        Birth: 1884/08/13   Death: 1970/12/03   Burial: 1970/12/05
                                Place: Charleston, SC
Site 2 Grace Bardetta Bratney Place: Leesburg, VA   Age: 78 years
        Birth: 1882/09/24   Death: 1961/06/26   Burial: 1961/06/28
Site 3 Mrs. Sara Mitchell Bratney   Age: 89 years
        Birth: 1860/09/22   Death: 1949/12/06   Burial: 1949/12/08
Site 4 John Frederick Bratney   Age: 68 years
        Birth: 1880/10/08   Death: 1949/01/15   Burial: 1949/01/17
Site 6 Bertrand H. Bratney   Place: Charleston, SC   Age: 79 years
        Birth: 1894/05/03   Death: 1974/02/09   Burial: 1974/02/12

Lot: 1300 Owner: Miscellaneous
Site 2 Horace Manson Hallett
        Birth: 1914/07/04   Death: 1988/10/21   Burial: 1989/02/27
        Place: FL   TS: Husband of Helen Drinkwater Hallett
Site 3 Nanci Hallett Wastie   Cause: Cancer   Age: 30 years
        Birth: 1944/02/29   Death: 1974/04/24   Burial: 1974/04/27
        Place: Columbia, MD   TS: Wife of Peter A. Wastie

Site 4　Helen Drinkwater Hallett
　　　　Birth: 1908/09/11　　Death: 1988/11/24　　Burial: 1989/02/27
　　　　Place: FL　　　　　　TS: Wife of Horace Manson Hallett
Site 5　Frank Earl Mason　　Place: Leesburg, VA　　Age: 86 years
　　　　Birth: 1893　　　　　Death: 1979/06/16　　Burial: 1979/09/04
Site 6　Ellen Thomsen Mason　　　　　　　　　　　Age: 80 years
　　　　Birth: 1896　　　　　Death: 1976/05/10　　Burial: 1979/09/04
　　　　Place: Leesburg, VA　　　　On stone with Frank Earl Mason
Site 8　Adele Monges Davison　Place: Leesburg, VA　Age: 64 years
　　　　Birth: 1909　　　　　Death: 1973/08/03　　Burial: 1973/08/06

Lot: 1301　Owner: Miscellaneous
Site 3　Marvin H. Everhart Sr.　Place: Leesburg, VA　Age: 83 years
　　　　Birth: 1904/07/16　　Death: 1988/04/17　　Burial: 1988/04/21
Site 4　Lelia E. Everhart　　Place: Charles Town, WV　Age: 66 years
　　　　Birth: 1909/10/11　　Death: 1976/07/04　　Burial: 1976/07/07
Site 5　Marvin H. Everhart Jr.　　　　　　　　　　　Age: 45 years
　　　　Birth: 1940/07/23　　Death: 1985/12/10　　Burial: 1985/12/14
　　　　Place: Washington, DC　　　　　　　　　　　TS: Captain
Site 7　John Wayne McDonald　　　　　　　　　　　Age: 23 years
　　　　Birth: 1950/08/26　　Death: 1973/10/26　　Burial: 1973/10/29
　　　　Cause: Killed by truck　Place: NY

Lot: 1302　Owner: Miscellaneous
Site 7　John Ira Burton　　　　　　　　　　　　　Age: 88 years
　　　　Birth: 1889/03/06　　Death: 1978/02/25　　Burial: 1978/03/18
Site 8　Grace Woodson Burton　Place: Leesburg, VA　Age: 100 years
　　　　Birth: 1888/09/20　　Death: 1988/12/16　　Burial: 1988/12/18
Site 9　Anne Burton Dudley　Place: Reston, VA　　Age: 58 years
　　　　Birth: 1922/06/17　　Death: 1980/12/23　　Burial: 1980/12/29

Lot: 1303　Owner: Miscellaneous
Site 1　Edwin C. Myers　　　Place: Alexandria, VA　Age: 73 years
　　　　Birth: 1900/12/18　　Death: 1974/09/01　　Burial: 1974/09/04

Lot: 1304　Owner: Miscellaneous
Site 5　Maureen Crooks Wortman　　　　　　　　　Age: 22 years
　　　　Birth: 1954　　　　　Death: 1977/10/06　　Burial: 1977/10/08
　　　　Cause: Cancer　　　　Place: Leesburg, VA
Site 7　Andrew Michael Taylor　TS: "Andy"　　　　Age: 13 months
　　　　Birth: 1980/08/28　　Death: 1981/10/09　　Burial: 1981/10/10
　　　　Cause: Head. w.　　　Place: Baltimore, MD

Lot: 1305　Owner: Miscellaneous
Site 1　Ishmael Osborne Myers　Place: Leesburg, VA　Age: 73 years
　　　　Birth: 1914/10/17　　Death: 1987/12/12　　Burial: 1987/12/15
Site 2　Helen Hess Myers　　　　　　　　　　　　　Age: Infant
　　　　Birth: 1921/06/15　　Death: 1992/06/13　　Burial: 1992/06/16
　　　　Place: NC　　　　　　On stone with Ishmael Osborne Myers

Site 6   Barbar M. Palcic   Place: Hamilton, VA   Age: 68 years
         Birth: 1918/11/08   Death: 1987/08/09   Burial: 1987/08/11
Site 12 Sue Ella James   Age: 72 years
         Birth: 1914   Death: 1987/07/22   Burial: 1987/07/24
         Place: Leesburg, VA   Moved from Lot 777, site 12 1987/09/22

Lot: 1307   Owner: Thelma Holcomb & Bess Rutherford
                                                              1956/03/03
Site 1   Walter H. Chambers   Age: 65 years
         Birth: 1896   Death: 1961/03/20   Burial: 1961/03/22
         Place: Bristol, VA   TS: Son
Site 2   Bess C. Rutherford   Place: Hampton, VA   Age: 79 years
         Birth: 1899   Death: 1978/10/13   Burial: 1978/10/16
Site 3   Mary Ann Chambers   Place: Leesburg, VA   Age: 75 years
         Birth: 1877/01/23   Death: 1956/03/03   Burial: 1956/03/03
Site 10 Victoria Jo Boston   Place: NC   Age: 9 years
         Birth: 1978/10/27   Death: 1988/05/01   Burial: 1988/05/05
         TS: Daughter of Vickie Jo Holcombe Boston. "Tori Jo"

Lot: 1308   Owner: Miscellaneous
Site 8   Louise Morne Flynn   Place: Leesburg, VA
         Birth: 1912/05/20   Death: 1990/12/09   Burial: 1990/12/12

Lot: 1309   Owner: Miscellaneous
Site 7   Samuel C. Adrain   Place: Berryville, VA   Age: 78 years
         Birth: 1906   Death: 1984/11/09   Burial: 1984/11/12
Site 8   Virginia E. Adrain   Age: 66 years
         Birth: 1917   Death: 1984/04/11   Burial: 1984/04/13
         Place: Leesburg, VA   On stone with Samuel C. Adrain
Site 11 John Patrick Fennelly   Place: Arlington, VA   Age: 68 years
                                  Death: 1968/02/20   Burial: 1968/02/22
Site 12 Esther Adrain Fennelly   Age: 67 years
                                  Death: 1967/06/03   Burial: 1967/06/06
         Place: Arlington, VA   On stone with John Patrick Fennelly

Lot: 1310   Owner: Miscellaneous
Site 1   William Frear   Place: Leesburg, VA
         Birth: 1909/03/02   Death: 1993/05/24   Burial: 1993/05/27
Site 3   Frederick N. Phillips   Place: Martinsburg, WV   Age: 50 years
         Birth: 1919/05/28   Death: 1969/11/30   Burial: 1969/12/04
Site 4   Lucy B. Gibson Phillips Place: Round Hill, VA   Age: 47 years
         Birth: 1923/02/15   Death: 1970/04/10   Burial: 1970/04/13
Site 11 Percy C. Crabill   Birth: 1902/05/26   Death: 1992/01/02
Site 12 Helen L. Crabill
         Birth: 1911/02/07   Death: 1992/11/22   Burial: 1992/11/24
         Place: Richmond, VA   TS: Wife of Percy C. Crabill

Lot: 1311   Owner: Miscellaneous
Site 1   Henry Halsted Harvey   Place: Winchester, VA   Age: 84 years
         Birth: 1891/07/30   Death: 1976/01/16   Burial: 1976/01/20

Site 2 Edith Denham Harvey Age: 81 years
Birth: 1900/08/31 Death: 1981/10/08 Burial: 1981/10/12
Place: Rockville, MD On stone with Henry Halsted Harvey
Site 3 Esther Denham Schwertner Age: 76 years
Birth: 1900/08/31 Death: 1976/10/25 Burial: 1976/10/26
Place: Montgomery, MD
Site 4 Herman Schwertner Place: Rockville, MD Age: 82 years
Birth: 1898/12/28 Death: 1981/08/05 Burial: 1981/08/10

Lot: 1312   Owner: Miscellaneous
Site 1 Gerald F. Kline Jr. Place: Fairfax, VA
Birth: 1941/06/25 Death: 1992/01/11 Burial: 1992/01/15
Site 7 Alfred D. Leone Place: Sterling, VA
Birth: 1918/03/27 Death: 1992/07/09 Burial: 1992/07/13
Site 8 Evelyn Leone Age: 72 years
Birth: 1917/10/26 Death: 1990/03/11 Burial: 1990/03/15
Place: Winchester, VA On stone with Alfred D. Leone

Lot: 1313   Owner: Miscellaneous
Site 1 Virginia Wilkerson Mechling Age: 66 years
Birth: 1923 Death: 1990/09/20 Burial: 1990/09/22
Place: Winchester, VA
Site 1 Mrs. Creola Daniel Wilson Age: 89 years
Birth: 1901/12/17 Death: 1991/03/13 Burial: 1991/03/18
Place: Heritage Hall, Leesburg, VA
Site 1 Samuel Robert Niccolls Place: Leesburg, VA Age: 20 years
Birth: 1971/03/04 Death: 1991/12/23 Burial: 1991/12/25
Site 1 Esmeralda G. Niedercorn Place: Santa Monica, CA
Birth: 1901/05/27 Death: 1992/07/26 Burial: 1993/03/29
Site 2 Arthr Michael Shorey Age: 83 years
Birth: 1908/10/29 Death: 1992/05/05 Burial: 1992/08/14
Place: Leesburg, VA TS: CPL US Army Air Corps WWII
Site 2 Virginia R. Kennedy Place: Fairfax, VA
Birth: 1907/09/16 Death: 1995/08/14 Burial: 1995/09/27
Site 7 Harry Alan Scarr Place: Leesburg, VA
Birth: 1934/05/04 Death: 1995/11/12 Burial: 1995/12/16

Lot: 1314   Owner: Miscellaneous
Site 1 Frances G. Heflin Place: Leesburg, VA Age: 61 years
Birth: 1918/07/28 Death: 1980/05/08 Burial: 1980/05/12

Lot: 1315   Owner: Miscellaneous
Site 7 Matthew L. Kohlhoss Sr. Place: Leesburg, VA Age: 78 years
Birth: 1903/09/17 Death: 1982/05/19 Burial: 1982/05/23

Lot: 1316   Owner: Miscellaneous
Site 2 Dorothy M. Wright Place: Berryville, VA
Birth: 1913/01/12 Death: 1992/12/05 Burial: 1992/12/08
Site 3 Ella Royston Udall Place: McLean, VA Age: 59 years
Birth: 1929/02/09 Death: 1988/08/13 Burial: 1988/08/16

Site 7   William Alger Heflin   Place: Montgomery, MD   Age: 56 years
         Birth: 1910   Death: 1967/01/16   Burial: 1967/01/18

Lot: 1317 E   Owner: Miscellaneous
Site 8   Allen K. Shreve Sr.   Place: Leesburg, VA
         Birth: 1919/06/21   Death: 1992/04/22   Burial: 1992/04/25
Site 11 Gertrude M. Christensen   Place: Leesburg, VA
         Birth: 1910/09/28   Death: 1995/06/11   Burial: 1995/06/14

Lot: 1317 W Owner: Frank & Edith Elliott
            & Ethel & William O'Brien   Purchased: 1960/08/01
Site 1   Frank S. Elliott   Place: Leesburg, VA   Age: 78 years
         Birth: 1892   Death: 1970/01/14   Burial: 1970/01/16
Site 2   Edith Adrain Elliott   Age: 67 years
         Birth: 1892   Death: 1960/08/04   Burial: 1960/08/07
         Place: Leesburg, VA   On stone with Frank S. Elliott
Site 3   Kathleen R. (Howe) Corl Place: Yarmouth, ME   Age: 86 years
         Birth: 1904   Death: 1990/10/20   Burial: 1990/10/25
Site 4   William W. O'Brien   Age: 46 years
         Birth: 1914/04/09   Death: 1961/02/20   Burial: 1961/02/23
         Place: MD   TS: "Pat" Maryland SP11 US Navy WWII
Site 5   Ethel Adrain O'Brien
         Birth: 1903/04/19   Death: 1995/09/11   Burial: 1995/09/14
         Place: Sandy Spring, MD   On stone with William W. O'Brien

Lot: 1318   Owner: Matthew L. & Cora H. Kohlhoss   1951/04/07
Site 1   Charles Marshall Heflin Sr.   Age: 75 years
         Birth: 1888/01/30   Death: 1963/08/14   Burial: 1963/08/18
         Place: Lucketts, VA   TS: Father
Site 2   Nellie Atwell Heflin   Place: Lucketts, VA
         Birth: 1895/12/30   Death: 1960/04/28   Burial: 1960/05/01
         On stone with Charles Marshall Heflin   TS: Mother
Site 7   William Carter Heflin   Place: Leesburg, VA
         Birth: 1927/07/31   Death: 1993/11/27   Burial: 1993/12/01

Lot: 1362   Owner: Miscellaneous
Site 5   Thomas A. Daniel Jr.   Place: Winchester, VA   Age: 67 years
         Birth: 1922/10/28   Death: 1990/06/01   Burial: 1990/06/04
         TS: US Navy WWII 1942-1945   Served aboard US Jacob Jones.
         VA State Game Warden 1949-1987 Loudoun Co.
Site 7   Walter Justus Ware   Place: Leesburg, VA   Age: 67 years
         Birth: 1905   Death: 1973/07/09   Burial: 1973/07/11
Site 8   Orma Anna Ware   Age: 75 years
         Birth: 1909   Death: 1984/12/09   Burial: 1984/12/12
         Place: Fairfax, VA   On stone with Walter Justus Ware
Site 10 George Wilbur Trittipoe   Place: Leesburg, VA   Age: 69 years
         Birth: 1904   Death: 1973/11/08   Burial: 1973/11/10
Site 12 Frank C. Valdetara   Age: 28 years
         Birth: 1946/10/05   Death: 1974/11/02   Burial: 1974/11/05
         Place: Fairfax, VA   TS: EM2 US Navy

Lot: 1363   Owner: Miscellaneous
Site 1   Charles H. Rutherford   Place: Leesburg, VA   Age: 63 years
          Birth: 1911   Death: 1974/03/30   Burial: 1974/04/03
Site 2   Lillie V. Rutherford   Age: 79 years
          Birth: 1911/05/14   Death: 1991/04/27   Burial: 1991/05/01
          Place: Loudoun Co., VA   On marker with Charles H. Rutherford
Site 3   Perry A. Burgess   Place: Bethesda, MD   Age: 77 years
          Birth: 1896/01/03   Death: 1973/09/26   Burial: 1973/09/28
Site 7   Thomas Burke Howard   Place: Fairfax, VA   Age: 77 years
          Birth: 1898/03/30   Death: 1985/06/25   Burial: 1985/06/28
Site 8   Dorothy Breeding Howard   Age: 83 years
          Birth: 1900/07/25   Death: 1983/09/07   Burial: 1983/09/10
          Place: Fairfax, VA   On marker with Thomas Burke Howard
Site 9   Ralph William Ball   Place: Arlington, VA
          Birth: 1919/05/14   Death: 1995/05/02   Burial: 1995/05/05
Site 11 James F. Cooper   Place: Leesburg, VA   Age: 46 years
          Birth: 1927   Death: 1974/06/05   Burial: 1974/06/07

Lot: 1366   Owner: Miscellaneous
Site 1   Jessie C. Harrison   No stone   Age: 70 years
          Place: Rockville, MD   Death: 1973/01/06   Burial: 1973/01/10
Site 2   Ollie E. Harrison   No stone   Age: 44 years
          Place: Rockville, MD   Death: 1976/06/21   Burial: 1976/06/24
Site 3   Robert H. Benton   Place: Olney, MD   Age: 35 years
          Birth: 1937   Death: 1973/02/23   Burial: 1973/02/27
Site 5   Pearly L. Bumgardner
          Birth: 1901/12/26   Death: 1994/09/27   Burial: 1994/09/30
          Place: Waterford, VA   TS: Capt. US Army WWII
Site 6   Dorothy S. Baumgardner Place: Leesburg, VA
          Birth: 1904/05/24   Death: 1991/07/14   Burial: 1991/07/17
Site 7   Bessie Wilder Spurlock   Age: 77 years
          Birth: 1895/07/03   Death: 1973/04/23   Burial: 1973/04/25
          Place: Leesburg, VA   TS: Mother
Site 8   Elmo Spurlock   Age: 49 years
          Birth: 1926/12/26   Death: 1976/03/24   Burial: 1976/03/27
          Place: Leesburg, VA   TS: PFC US Army WWII
Site 10 Carroll D. Legge   Age: 62 years
          Birth: 1910/09/27   Death: 1973/05/14   Burial: 1973/05/20
          Place: Alexandria, VA   TS: Virginia TEC4 US Army WWII
Site 11 James V. Apperson   Place: Leesburg, VA   Age: 67 years
          Birth: 1905   Death: 1973/06/04   Burial: 1973/06/06
Site 12 Cleo Boone Apperson   Age: 72 years
          Birth: 1905   Death: 1978/08/08   Burial: 1978/08/11
          Place: Charles Town, WV   On marker with James V. Apperson

Lot: 1367   Owner: Miscellaneous
Site 1   Stanley J. Spurloch   Place: Leesburg, VA
          Birth: 1942/08/17   Death: 1995/11/14   Burial: 1995/11/17

Site 3　Gertrude Wetzel　　　Place: Silver Spring, MD　　Age: 48 years
　　　　No stone　　　　　　Death: 1988/08/01　　　　　Burial: 1988/08/04
Site 5　Evenly O. Ritnour　　　No stone　　　　　　　　Age: 77 years
　　　　Place: Frederick, MD　Death: 1990/06/02　　　　Burial: 1990/06/05
Site 8　Frederick W. Rollins　Place: Leesburg, VA　　　Age: 91 years
　　　　Birth: 1895　　　　　Death: 1986/02/16　　　　Burial: 1986/02/19
Site 9　Nellie V. Rollins　　　　　　　　　　　　　　　Age: 77 years
　　　　Birth: 1901　　　　　Death: 1979/06/26
　　　　On stone with Frederick W. Rollins
Site 12　James M. Horsman　　Place: Ashburn, VA　　　Age: 16 years
　　　　Birth: 1957　　　　　Death: 1974/06/07　　　　Burial: 1974/06/10

Lot: 1370　Owner: Miscellaneous
Site 1　William D. Cissell　　Place: Leesburg, VA
　　　　Birth: 1929/03/17　　Death: 1994/08/02　　　　Burial: 1994/08/05
Site 2　Jean Lynn Cissel　　　Place: Washington, DC　　Age: 18 years
　　　　Birth: 1962/11/25　　Death: 1981/01/27　　　　Burial: 1981/01/30
Site 3　Laura Lee Cissel　　　Place: York, PA　　　　　Age: 18 years
　　　　Birth: 1960/06/07　　Death: 1978/12/20　　　　Burial: 1978/12/23
Site 4　Joylyn Fountain　　　Place: Leesburg, VA　　　Age: 41 years
　　　　Birth: 1937/10/03　　Death: 1979/02/04　　　　Burial: 1979/02/08
Site 10　Rhoda Loutta Parsell　Place: Leesburg, VA　　　Age: 69 years
　　　　Birth: 1918/12/06　　Death: 1989/01/31　　　　Burial: 1989/02/03
　　　　Cause: Auto Accident　TS: Married William Dailey Parsell
　　　　June 1, 1934. Sons: Paul 1938, Cassell 1942, Alphonso 1947, Monty
　　　　1952, Wally 1959. Daughters Josephine 1936, Trula 1943, Henrietta
　　　　1948, Cathy 1968.

Lot: 1371　Owner: Miscellaneous
Site 8　Maude Elizabeth B. Kirkpatrick　　　　　　　　Place: Winchester, VA
　　　　Birth: 1915/03/10　　Death: 1992/10/10　　　　Burial: 1992/10/13
Site 9　Vincent Lyle Deimler Jr.　　　　　　　　　　　Age: 31 years
　　　　Birth: 1957/05/28　　Death: 1988/10/16　　　　Burial: 1988/10/20
　　　　Cause: Suicide　　　Place: Leesburg, VA

Lot 1372 or 1373 Miscellaneous
Site 0　Peggy A. Lee　　　　Birth: 1937/10/13　　　　Death: 1988/02/08
Site 0　Ronnie Allen Lee　　Birth: 1959/07/09　　　　Death: 1985/09/27

Lot: 1374　Owner: Miscellaneous
Site 1　Charles Russell Taylor　Place: Winchester, VA　Age: 63 years
　　　　Birth: 1915　　　　　Death: 1978/05/02　　　　Burial: 1978/05/05
Site 3　Charles W. Foglesong　　　　　　　　　　　　　Age: 40 years
　　　　Birth: 1938　　　　　Death: 1978/05/04　　　　Burial: 1978/05/06
　　　　Place: Winchester, VA　　　　　　　　　　　　　TS: "Bill"
Site 7　Mrs. Rose Anna Wilson　Place: Alexandria, VA
　　　　Birth: 1906/09/29　　Death: 1978/05/27　　　　Burial: 1978/05/30

Lot: 1375 Owner: Miscellaneous

Site 1 Paul Douglas Costello   Cause: Auto Accident   Age: 16 years
        Birth: 1962/08/21   Death: 1979/01/28   Burial: 1979/01/31
Site 5 Virginia E. Douglas
        Birth: 1902/08/26   Death: 1993/06/30   Burial: 1993/07/03
        Place: Waterford, VA   On marker with E. Lee Douglas
Site 6 E. Lee Douglas   Place: Leesburg, VA   Age: 83 years
        Birth: 1903/03/22   Death: 1986/10/15   Burial: 1986/10/17
Site 10 Mrs. Karen Byer Costello Place: Sterling, VA   Age: 24 years
        Birth: 1965/08/09   Death: 1989/12/17   Burial: 1989/12/21
        TS: Married John Albert Costello Jr. June 17, 1989

Lot: 1378 Owner: Miscellaneous

Site 1 James W. Cox   Age: 50 years
        Birth: 1925   Death: 1975/12/29   Burial: 1975/12/31
        Place: Leesburg, VA   TS: FLT 0 Army Air Forces WWII
Site 5 Albert A. Novatney   Place: Martinsburg, WV   Age: 74 years
        Birth: 1904   Death: 1979/10/23   Burial: 1979/10/25
Site 6 Bertie T. Novatney   Age: 71 years
        Birth: 1905   Death: 1977/09/15   Burial: 1977/09/18
        Place: Clarke Co.   On stone with Albert A. Novatney
Site 8 Gladys Mildred Michell Place: Leesburg, VA
                                Death: 1977/10/28   Burial: 1977/10/31
Site 9 Theron E. (Ted) Lowe   Age: 66 years
        Birth: 1911   Death: 1978/03/24   Burial: 1978/03/27
        Cause: Cancer   Place: Leesburg, VA
Site 11 Virginia Gladys Curry   Place: Leesburg, VA   Age: 64 years
        Birth: 1914   Death: 1978/12/22   Burial: 1978/12/26
Site 12 Mrs. Susan L. Helmke Gilliland   Age: 28 years
        Birth: 1949/10/08   Death: 1977/10/28   Burial: 1977/11/01
        Cause: Cancer   Place: Bethesda, MD

Lot: 1379 Owner: Miscellaneous

Site 6 Michael Robey Simpson   Age: 37 years
        Birth: 1947/11/17   Death: 1985/06/14   Burial: 1985/06/17
        Cause: Cancer   Place: Leesburg, VA TS: US Army Vietnam
Site 7 Michael Allen Sisk   Age: 31 years
        Birth: 1950/03/14   TSDeath: 1981/08/17   Burial: 1981/08/21
        Cause: Auto Accident   Place: Leesburg, VA
Site 10 Calvin C. Sisk   Place: Leesburg, VA
        Birth: 1927/06/02   Death: 1993/04/25   Burial: 1993/04/28

Lot: 1382 Owner: Miscellaneous

Site 1 Hubert L. Lemarr   Place: Leesburg, VA   Age: 78 years
        Birth: 1911/04/27   Death: 1990/01/04   Burial: 1990/01/07
Site 6 Lowell L. Maguire   Age: 36 years
        Birth: 1938/08/28   Death: 1975/05/23   Burial: 1975/05/28
        Cause: Auto Accident   Place: The Plains, VA

Lot: 1383   Owner: Miscellaneous
Site 5   Simon J. Kraebel   Place: Leesburg, VA   Age: 78 years
         Birth: 1902   Death: 1981/02/23   Burial: 1981/02/26
Site 10 Kimberly Beth Hannahs   Place: Harrisonburg, VA   Age: 21 years
         Birth: 1968/01/14   Death: 1989/09/14   Burial: 1989/09/18
Site 11 Vince Lyle Deimler Sr.   Place: Charlestown, WV   TS: US Air Force
         Birth: 1933/05/03   Death: 1993/01/13   Burial: 1993/01/16

Lot: 1386   Owner: Miscellaneous
Site 1   Frank Fleming   Age: 50 years
         Birth: 1929/01/17   Death: 1979/05/13
Site 2   Forida Khan   Age: 54 years
         Birth: 1928   Death: 1979/01/02   TS: Karbala-Iraq
Site 6   Carol Herndon Leef Rider   Age: 52 years
         Birth: 1930/07/17   Death: 1983/06/24   Burial: 1983/06/27
         Place: Fairfax, VA
Site 7   Herbert D. Schuller   Place: Winchester, VA   Age: 66 years
         Birth: 1922/05/15   Death: 1988/05/27   Burial: 1988/05/29
Site 11 William H. Leef   Place: Leesburg, VA   Age: 80 years
         Birth: 1899/07/24   Death: 1979/12/22   Burial: 1979/12/24
Site 12 Alice H. Leef   Age: 73 years
         Birth: 1904/09/23   Death: 1978/06/27   Burial: 1978/06/29
         Place: Leesburg, VA   On stone with William H. Leef

Lot: 1387   Owner: Miscellaneous
Site 3   Michel David Thomas   Age: 16 years
         Birth: 1973/02/10   Death: 1989/08/30   Burial: 1989/09/03
         Cause: Auto Accident   Place: Leesburg, VA
Site 7   Kenneth E. Suits   Age: 52 years
         Birth: 1930   Death: 1982/08/06   Burial: 1982/08/09
         Cause: Suicide   Place: Fairfax, VA

Lot: 1390   Owner: Miscellaneous
Site 1   Harry B. Saunders   Place: Leesburg, VA
         Birth: 1917/07/13   Death: 1993/05/14   Burial: 1993/05/17
         TS: Married Mildred V. Saunders May 20, 1946.   T SGT US Army
Site 9   Roger T. Jenkins   Place: Leesburg, VA
         Birth: 1914/07/24   Death: 1993/04/26   Burial: 1993/04/28
Site 10 Nellie L. Jenkins
         Birth: 1916/10/12   Death: 1991/08/13   Burial: 1991/08/17
         Place: Leesburg, VA   On stone with Harry B. Jenkins
Site 12 Sally D. Jenkins   Place: Washington, DC
         Birth: 1954/04/13   Death: 1995/02/21   Burial: 1995/02/24

Lot: 1391   Owner: Miscellaneous
Site 2   Lois Annette Kimball   Place: Leesburg, VA
         Birth: 1966/01/21   Death: 1994/05/31   Burial: 1994/06/04
Site 5   Paulette Marie Howell   Place: Leesburg, VA   Age: 38 years
         Birth: 1952/11/15   Death: 1990/12/22   Burial: 1990/12/27

Site 6 Kenneth J. Howell   Place: Leesburg, VA
        Birth: 1951/11/22   Death: 1995/04/01   Burial: 1995/04/04
Site 7 Benjamin P. McDonald   Age: 62 years
        Birth: 1928/06/27   Death: 1991/02/23   Burial: 1991/02/25
        Place: Leesburg, VA   TS: TSGT US Air Force Korea Vietnam
Site 10 Randell W. Cooper   Place: WV   Age: 29 years
        Birth: 1962/12/29   Death: 1990/12/10   Burial: 1990/12/15

Lot: 1394   Owner: Harvey M. Ball   Purchased:
Site 1 Ida May Ball
        Birth: 1889/04/28   Death: 1924/05/10   Burial: 1950/08/10
        Removal from Hamilton, VA   TS: Wife of H.M. Ball
Site 2 Harvey MacDaniel Ball Place: Purcellville, VA Age: 81 years
        Birth: 1887/10/13   Death: 1969/07/12   Burial: 1969/07/15
Site 2 Anna B. Carter   No stone   Age: 64 years
        Place: FL   Death: 1989/01/02   Burial: 1989/01/07
Site 3 May Lodge Ball   Place: Berryville, VA Age: 94 years
        Birth: 1892/08/19   Death: 1987/01/10   Burial: 1987/01/13
Site 4 Gertrude Ball Pardew   Age: 56 years
        Birth: 1921/04/03   Death: 1978/03/30   Burial: 1978/04/03
        Place: Fort Lauderdale, FL   TS: Wife of Paul McLaren Pardew
Site 7 James Richard Adams   Age: 62 years
        Birth: 1910/01/31   Death: 1972/12/09   Burial: 1972/12/13
        Place: Middletown, VA TS: Husband of Ida Ball Adams

Lot: 1395   Owner: Miscellaneous
Site 2 Helen Ludell Buttery   Place: Leesburg, VA   Age: 57 years
        Birth: 1928/05/26   Death: 1985/06/12   Burial: 1985/06/16
Site 8 Janet Sue Evans   Place: Fairfax, VA
        Birth: 1935/08/30   Death: 1993/02/28   Burial: 1993/03/03
Site 9 Douglas W. Smith   Place: Waterford, VA
        Birth: 1907/01/12   Death: 1992/02/26   Burial: 1992/02/28

Lot: 1399   Owner: Miscellaneous
Site 3 Cheryl L. Meyer Arnett Place: DE
        Birth: 1968/02/23   Death: 1995/01/21   Burial: 1995/01/25
Site 7 Lloyd Goode Johnson
        Birth: 1917/10/14   Death: 1995/02/10   Burial: 1995/02/14
        Place: Leesburg, VA   TS: PVT US Army WWII

Lot: 1402   Owner: Miscellaneous
Site 3 Harry W. Merchant   Place: Arlington, VA
        Birth: 1911/03/29   Death: 1995/11/11   Burial: 1995/11/14
Site 5 Harry William Merchant   Age: 57 years
        Birth: 1934/11/26   Death: 1992/04/17   Burial: 1992/04/21
        Place: Leesburg, VA   TS: US Navy. "Bill"
Site 7 Walter C. Pine   Place: Annandale, VA   Age: 83 years
        Birth: 1904/01/29   Death: 1987/06/19   Burial: 1987/06/24

Lot: 1403   Owner: Miscellaneous
Site 9   Stanley Paul Jewell
    Birth: 1919/01/11   Death: 1992/05/22   Burial: 1992/05/25
    Place: Bluemont, VA   TS: TEC 5 US Army WWII

Lot: 1406   Owner: Clara J. & Richard L. James   1957/12/10
Site 1   Richard L. James   Place: Leesburg, VA
    Birth: 1920/05/26   Death: 1993/05/15   Burial: 1993/05/18
Site 4   Minor Linwood James   Age: 64 years
    Birth: 1893/05/17   Death: 1957/12/09   Burial: 1957/12/11
    Cause: Heart Failure   Place: Leesburg, VA
Site 6   Clara Jane James   Age: 65 years
    Birth: 1892/10/01   Death: 1958/05/25   Burial: 1058/05/27
    Cause: Heart   Place: Purcellville, VA
Site 9   Michael Arl Curry   Age: 36 years
    Birth: 1948/04/09   Death: 1984/11/06   Burial: 1984/11/09
    Cause: Plane crash   Place: near Waterford, VA

Lot: 1407   Owner: Miscellaneous
Site 7   Mark S. Peer   Age: 23 years
    Birth: 1961/10/03   Death: 1984/11/17   Burial: 1984/11/20
    Cause: Auto Accident   Place: near Arcola, VA
Site 8   Robert B. Hissam   Place: Fairfax, VA   Age: 58 years
    Birth: 1928   Death: 1985/01/12   Burial: 1985/01/16
Site 11 Richard Lee Clem   Place: Leesburg, VA   Age: 38 years
    Birth: 1946/09/16   Death: 1985/01/06   Burial: 1985/01/09

Lot: 1410   Owner: Miscellaneous
Site 1   Karl Kadic   Place: Bethesda, MD   Age: 86 years
    Birth: 1901/09/24   Death: 1988/07/18   Burial: 1988/07/21
Site 2   Fanny Laycock Kadic   Age: 76 years
    Birth: 1900/04/17   Death: 1976/05/14   Burial: 1976/05/17
    Place: Bethesda, MD   On stone with Karl Kadic
Site 6   Clayton Benjamin Sherwood   Age: 58 years
    Birth: 1902   Death: 1963/05/22   Burial: 1963/05/23
    Place: Miami, FL
Site 6   Nannie Laycock Sherwood   Age: 62 years
    Birth: 1906   Death: 1968/05/19   Burial: 1968/05/23
    Place: Leesburg, VA   On stone with Clayton Benjamin Sherwood

Lot: 1411   Owner: Miscellaneous
Site 1   Clem D. Robey   Place: Berryville, VA   Age: 71 years
    Birth: 1913/04/30   Death: 1984/09/19   Burial: 1984/09/21
Site 2   Nellie V. Robey
    Birth: 1912/09/17   Death: 1991/04/20   Burial: 1991/04/22
    Place: Winchester, VA   On stone with Clem D. Robey
Site 3   Elsie L. Healey   Place: Winchester, VA   Age: 74 years
    Birth: 1908   Death: 1982/10/21   Burial: 1982/10/23
Site 6   Beverly J. Fromm   Place: Waterford, VA   Age: 52 years
    Birth: 1937/04/13   Death: 1989/04/14   Burial: 1989/04/18

Site 10 Jeffrey Alan Jones   Place: Leesburg, VA   Age: 19 years
         Birth: 1961/06/15   Death: 1980/09/19   Burial: 1980/09/23
Site 11 Roland H. Robey   Cause: Killed by bull   Place: Berryville, VA
         Birth: 1935/10/13   Death: 1994/08/28   Burial: 1994/09/01

Lot: 1414   Owner: Miscellaneous
Site 1 West Mansfield Maddox   Age: 73 years
         Birth: 1911   Death: 1984/09/09   Burial: 1984/09/11
         Place: Leesburg, VA   TS: PFC US Army WWII
Site 4 Willie Clay Denny   Place: Richmond, VA   Age: 68 years
         Birth: 1906/01/24   Death: 1974/12/28   Burial: 1974/12/31
Site 5 Gibson F. Rinker   Place: Ransom, WV
         Birth: 1919/03/15   Death: 1994/01/05   Burial: 1994/01/07
Site 7 Arnold G. Phillips Jr. Place: Bethesda, MD   Age: 55 years
         Birth: 1923   Death: 1978/06/24   Burial: 1978/06/27
Site 8 Gary Wayne Phillips   Place: Bethesda, MD   Age: 21 years
         Birth: 1960/02/26   Death: 1981/09/24   Burial: 1981/09/28
Site 9 Charles Ricketts   Place: Martinsburg, WV   No stone
         Birth: 1928/03/25   Death: 1993/06/18   Burial: 1993/06/22

Lot: 1414 1/2   Owner: Miscellaneous
Site 6 Sofia M. Bialasik   Place: Elizabeth, NJ   Age: 69 years
         Birth: 1911/05/21   Death: 1980/08/13   Burial: 1980/08/15
Site 11 Konstantin Bialasik   Place: Reston, VA
         Birth: 1912/03/10   Death: 1992/01/23   Burial: 1992/01/25

Lot: 1415   Owner: Miscellaneous
Site 1 Marsha Ann Bliss   Place: Leesburg, VA   Age: 35 years
                                Death: 1980/03/08   Burial: 1980/03/11
         Disinterred 10/25/88-Catholic Cemetery   No stone
Site 5 Jeanne Mary Branan   Place: Winchester, VA   Age: 36 years
         Birth: 1943/12/26   Death: 1980/06/12   Burial: 1980/06/15
Site 6 Stephen Michael Gooding Johnston   Age: 23 years
         Birth: 1957/11/27   Death: 1981/05/11   Burial: 1981/05/15
         Cause: Auto Accident Place: Leesburg, VA
Site 8 Monica Elizabeth Barney Place: Leesburg, VA   Age: 75 years
         Birth: 1909/05/06   Death: 1984/10/14   Burial: 1984/10/22
Site 8 Esther Barney Prather Place: Leesburg, VA
         Birth: 1907/01/25   Death: 1992/10/25   Burial: 1992/10/28
Site 9 Pat C. Patty   Age: 55 years
         Birth: 1925   Death: 1981/01/08   Burial: 1981/01/11
         Place: Leesburg, VA   TS: US Army
Site 11 Teresa E. Garrison   Place: Leesburg, VA   Age: 27 years
         Birth: 1953/08/15   Death: 1981/01/05   Burial: 1981/01/07
Site 12 William H. Fling   Age: 62 years
         Birth: 1918   Death: 1980/09/14   Burial: 1980/09/16
         `Place: Annandale, VA   TS: US Army

UNION CEMETERY
LEESBURG, LOUDOUN CO., VA

PLAT NEW

Lot: 1 Owner: Miscellaneous
Site 1 James R. Cooper   Age: 39 years
        Birth: 1936   Death: 1975/04/11   Burial: 1975/04/15
        Cause: Cancer   Place: Woodbridge, VA
Site 2 Geraldine A. Cooper   Place: Fairfax, VA
        Birth: 1939/05/16   Death: 1994/07/30   Burial: 1994/08/02
Site 3 Richard Wayne Tavenner Place: Lincoln, VA   Age: 19 years
        Birth: 1956/01/31   Death: 1975/08/04   Burial: 1975/08/07
        Cause: Lightning   TS: SR US Army Vietnam
Site 4 William Carskaden   Place: Leesburg, VA   Age: 77 years
        Birth: 1897/01/13   Death: 1975/06/02   Burial: 1975/06/05
Site 5 Corrine Carskaden   Place: Leesburg, VA   Age: 74 years
        Birth: 1900/07/18   Death: 1975/02/15   Burial: 1975/02/17
Site 6 Alva S. Wright   Age: 58 years
        Birth: 1922   Death: 1980/12/13   Burial: 1980/12/16
        Place: Leesburg, VA   TS: Mother
Site 8 Rebecca P. Quirk   Place: Washington, DC   Age: 69 years
        Birth: 1907   Death: 1976/08/19   Burial: 1976/08/21

Lot: 2 Owner: Miscellaneous
Site 1 Ottie L. Bentley   Age: 68 years
        Birth: 1919   Death: 1988/06/05   Burial: 1988/06/07
        Cause: Cancer   Place: Ashburn, VA
Site 3 Katherine R. Rutherford Place: Leesburg, VA   Age: 62 years
        Birth: 1915   Death: 1977/11/07   Burial: 1977/11/10
Site 4 Ralph T. Spring   Place: Lucketts, VA   Age: 59 years
        Birth: 1917   Death: 1976/10/07   Burial: 1976/10/10
Site 6 William Arthur Ware   Age: 36 years
        Birth: 1941   Death: 1977/11/21   Burial: 1977/11/25
        Place: Sterling, VA   TS: US Army
Site 9 Lawrence E. Turner   Age: 56 years
        Birth: 1920/10/22   Death: 1977/02/20   Burial: 1977/02/23
        Place: Leesburg, VA   TS: SGT US Army WWII
Site 10 Walter Dyson Sr.   Place: Staunton, VA   Age: 74 years
        Birth: 1905   Death: 1980/04/14   Burial: 1980/04/19

Lot: 3 Owner: Miscellaneous
Site 1 Teddy Lee Long   Age: 24 years
        Birth: 1965/03/09   Death: 1989/08/02   Burial: 1989/08/05
        Cause: Killed by truck   Place: Leesburg, VA
Site 2 Ruby Maddox Clyburn   Place: Manassas, VA   Age: 91 years
        Birth: 1898   Death: 1990/06/14   Burial: 1990/06/16

Site 5	James Benton Pelasara		Age: 20 years
	Birth: 1959	Death: 1979/10/03	Burial: 1979/10/05
	Cause: Auto Accident	Place: Fairfax, VA	
Site 8	Doris C. Dockery	Place: Warrenton, VA	
	Birth: 1936/01/01	Death: 1991/07/16	Burial: 1991/07/19
Site 9	John A. Cooper	Place: Leesburg, VA	
	Birth: 1912/08/14	Death: 1993/08/21	Burial: 1993/08/23

Lot: 4   Owner: Miscellaneous

Site 1	William H. Powell Jr.	Place: Leesburg, VA	
	Birth: 1949/07/29	Death: 1993/09/18	Burial: 1993/09/21
Site 2	Audrey Kasza	Place: Leesburg, VA	
	Birth: 1926/05/23	Death: 1993/04/02	Burial: 1993/04/05
Site 5	Norma Jean Ware Trittipoe		Age: 46 years
	Birth: 1938	Death: 1985/06/28	Burial: 1985/07/02
	Place: Leesburg, VA		
Site 6	Lisa M. Holden		Age: 17 years
		Death: 1985/06/03	Burial: 1985/06/06
	Cause: Auto Accident	Place: Frederick Co., MD	No stone
Site 9	Robert S. Jarmens		Age: 65 years
	Birth: 1920/05/27	Death: 1986/03/03	Burial: 1986/03/06
	Place: Manassas, VA		TS: PFC US Army WWII

Lot: 5   Owner: Miscellaneous

Site 1	Ray Spurloch	Place: Martinsburg, WV	
	Birth: 1920/04/23	Death: 1995/06/24	Burial: 1995/06/28
Site 5	Leroy E. Cooper		Age: 34 years
	Birth: 1951	Death: 1986/05/10	Burial: 1986/05/14
	Cause: Changing tire on truck		Place: Lucketts, VA

Lot: 18   Owner: Miscellaneous

Site 1	Floyd L. Johnson	Place: Paeonian Springs, VA	Age: 85 years
	Birth: 1903/10/08	Death: 1988/10/13	Burial: 1988/10/15
Site 2	Louise R. Johnson	Place: Paeonian Springs, VA	
	Birth: 1906/08/20	Death: 1994/06/10	Burial: 1994/06/13
Site 3	Frank G. Caslar	Place: Leesburg, VA	Age: 66 years
	Birth: 1909/11/03	Death: 1974/11/05	Burial: 1974/11/09
Site 5	Billy Martin Jr.		Age: 20 years
	Birth: 1958/10/30	Death: 1979/03/30	
Site 6	Raymond Gillum		Age: 46 years
	Birth: 1928/08/29	Death: 1975/04/16	Burial: 1975/04/19
	Place: Martinsburg, WV		TS: CPL US Army Korea
Site 8	Elbert Eugene Hough	Place: Charlottesville, VA	Age: 45 years
	Birth: 1929	Death: 1975/06/28	Burial: 1975/07/01
Site 10	Dennis L. Wright	Place: Fairfax, VA	Age: 19 years
	Birth: 1956	Death: 1975/07/17	Burial: 195/07/19

Lot: 19   Owner: Miscellaneous

Site 4	Ralph Edward Bradley	Place: Leesburg, VA	Age: 49 years
	Birth: 1928/03/03	Death: 1977/09/04	Burial: 1977/09/07

Site 6   Santiago E. Millian   Place: Alexandria, VA   Age: 81 years
         Birth: 1898   Death: 1979/09/20   Burial: 1979/09/22
Site 10 Susan Rebecca Payne   Place: Leesburg, VA   TS: "Susi"
         Birth: 1961/05/29   Death: 1993/01/23   Burial: 1993/01/25

Lot: 20   Owner: Miscellaneous
Site 1   Mervin A. Marshall   Place: Purcellville, VA   Age: 29 years
         Birth: 1950   Death: 1980/05/04   Burial: 1980/05/08
Site 2   Alva R. Marshall   Place: Leesburg, VA   Age: 89 years
         Birth: 1902   Death: 1992/03/07   Burial: 1992/03/10
Site 5   Linda E.M. Peacoe   Age: 39 years
         Birth: 1946   Death: 1985/07/11   Burial: 1985/07/15
         Cause: Killed by husband   Place: Fairfax, VA
Site 6   Joseph Edward Rutherford   Age: 3 years
         Birth: 1979   Death: 1982/03/31   Burial: 1982/04/03
         Place: Washington, DC   TS: "Joey"
Site 7   Carol Sue Martin   Place: Front Royal, VA   Age: 38 years
         Birth: 1945/08/30   Death: 1983/01/01   Burial: 1983/01/04
Site 8   Nina Alice Cook   Place: Leesburg, VA   Age: 73 years
         Birth: 1909/11/15   Death: 1983/04/15   Burial: 1983/04/18
Site 10 Raymond Spurlock   No stone   Age: 49 years
         Place: Reston, VA   Death: 1987/10/03   Burial: 1987/10/06

Lot: 21   Owner: Miscellaneous
Site 1   Alyssa Erin Blaylock   Place: Fairfax, VA
         Birth: 1991/02/05   Death: 1993/03/28   Burial: 1993/03/03

Lot: 34   Owner: Miscellaneous
Site 5   Brett Everett Entsminger   Age: 19 years
         Birth: 1971/09/27   Death: 1991/11/07   Burial: 1991/11/18
         Cause: Murdered   Place: Washington, DC   No stone

Lot: 35   Owner: Miscellaneous
Site 1   Peggy Ann Leith Lee   Place: Leesburg, VA   Age: 50 years
         Birth: 1937/10/13   Death: 1988/02/08   Burial: 1988/02/11
Site 2   Ronnie Allen Lee   Age: 26 years
         Birth: 1959/07/09   Death: 1985/09/27   Burial: 1985/10/01
         Cause: Suicide   Place: Harpers Ferry, WV
Site 8   Debra Ann Reynolds   Age: 23 years
         Birth: 1956   Death: 1979/06/28

Lot: 52   Owner: Miscellaneous
Site 1   Alan Lee Rollins   Place: Arlington, VA   Age: 37 years
         Birth: 1951/01/05   Death: 1987/06/14   Burial: 1987/06/17

Lot: 53   Owner: Miscellaneous
Site 1   Jad Jaghab   Place: Leesburg, VA   No stone
         Birth: 1950/06/11   Death: 1994/10/04   Burial: 1994/10/08

Lot: 69   Owner: Miscellaneous
Site 1   William E.(Bill) Wright   Place: Leesburg, VA   Age: 54 years
         Birth: 1935/12/08   Death: 1990/01/03   Burial: 1990/01/06
Site 4   David B. VanHooser   Place: Arlington, VA
         Birth: 1943/05/04   Death: 1993/01/20   Burial: 1993/01/23

Lot: 70   Owner: Miscellaneous
Site 6   William Joseph Stokes   Place: Leesburg, VA
         Birth: 1925/05/31   Death: 1994/07/31   Burial: 1994/08/04

Lot: 86   Owner: Miscellaneous
Site 1   William L. Callaghan   Place: FL   Age: 64 years
         Birth: 1926/04/14   Death: 1990/12/25   Burial: 1990/12/28
Site 4   Dean S. Smith Sr.   Place: Leesburg, VA
         Birth: 1925/10/20   Death: 1994/08/15   Burial: 1994/08/18
Site 4   Margaret H. Smith   Place: Leesburg, VA   TS: "Faye"
         Birth: 1939/06/30   Death: 1993/03/25   Burial: 1993/03/28

Lot: 87   Owner: Miscellaneous
Site 4   Ryan Michael Shawen   Age: Infant
         Birth: 1995/02/11   Death: 1995/03/13   Burial: 1995/03/16
         Place: Washington, DC   No stone
Site 5   Evelyn May Boyd   Place: Leesburg, VA
         Birth: 1907/03/14   Death: 1994/10/31   Burial: 1994/11/03

Lot: 120   Owner: Miscellaneous
Site 2   Gwendolyn E. Smith   Place: Leesburg, VA
         Birth: 1919/09/25   Death: 1995/07/11   Burial: 1995/07/14
Site 4   William Gordon Huffman   Place: Leesburg, VA   Age: 64 years
         Birth: 1929/08/08   Death: 1994/03/08   Burial: 1994/03/11

Lot: 121   Owner: Miscellaneous
Site 1   William (Bill) Earl Doggett
         Birth: 1928/01/02   Death: 1994/04/15   Burial: 1994/04/18
         Place: Leesburg, VA   TS: US Marine Corp

Lot: 139   Owner: Miscellaneous
Site 1   Angus Stewart Whitehurst Treviranus
         Birth: 1966   Death: 1983
Site 2   Thomas Bedford Grey
         Birth: 1917/10/15   Death: 1995/06/16   Burial: 1995/06/20
         Place: Leesburg, VA   TS: PFC US Army WWII

Lot: 192   Owner: Miscellaneous
Site 1   Cary A. Perdue   Place: Sterling, VA
         Birth: 1904/10/06   Death: 1988/09/01   Burial: 1988/09/03
Site 2   Kate L. Perdue   Place: NC
         Birth: 1909/08/14   Death: 1993/06/11   Burial: 1993/06/14

Lot: 217 Owner: Miscellaneous
Site 1　Harry H. Hanson　　　Place: Lucketts, VA　　　Age: 71 years
　　　　Birth: 1912　　　　　　Death: 1983/12/19　　　Burial: 1983/12/21

Lot: 230 Owner: Miscellaneous
Site 1　Leah Faith Smith　　　Place: Winchester, VA　　Age: 5 months
　　　　Birth: 1990/Apr.　　　　Death: 1990/07/26　　　Burial: 1990/07/28
Site 1　Samantha Jo McKinnon　Place: Lovettsville, VA　Age: 3 months
　　　　Birth: 1990/05/29　　　Death: 1990/09/15　　　Burial: 1990/09/19
Site 1　Victor Lawrence Ament II　　　　　　　　　　　Age: Infant
　　　　Birth: 1992/03/30　　　Death: 1992/03/30　　　Burial: 1992/03/30
　　　　Cause: Stillborn　　　　Place: Fairfax, VA
Site 1　Zachary Scott Fritts　　Place: Washington, DC
　　　　Birth: 1993/06/25　　　Death: 1993/07/26　　　Burial: 1993/07/29
Site 2　B.C. Comber　　　　　Cause: Stillborn　　　　Place: Leesburg, VA
　　　　　　　　　　　　　　　Death: 1992/08/16　　　Burial: 1992/08/20
Site 2　Glenn L. Baker　　　　Place: Sterling, VA
　　　　Birth: 1905/05/03　　　Death: 1993/05/24　　　Burial: 1993/05/28
Site 2　Carolyn Ann George　　Death: 1995/01/19　　　Burial: 1995/01/24
　　　　Cause: Stillborn　　　　Place: Leesburg, VA　　　No stone
Site 3　Triplets of Hogan　　　Death: 1995/02/16　　　Burial: 1995/03/11
　　　　Cause: Premature Birth　Place: GA　　　　　　　No stone

Lot: 248 Owner: Miscellaneous
Site 1　Alphonse Billand　　　Place: MI　　　　　　　Age: 86 years
　　　　Birth: 1903/07/16　　　Death: 1990/05/13　　　Burial: 1990/05/19
Site 2　Eleanor N. Billand　　　　　　　　　　　　　Age: 77 years
　　　　Birth: 1909/10/21　　　Death: 1986/12/28　　　Burial: 1986/12/30
　　　　Place: Leesburg, VA　　On stone with Alphonse C. Billand
Site 3　Thomas Eugene Hart　Place: Leesburg, VA　　　Age: 32 years
　　　　Birth: 1954/08/16　　　Death: 1987/01/17　　　Burial: 1987/01/20

Lot: 249 Owner: Miscellaneous
Site 1　William R. Dayen　　　Place: Reading, PA　　　Age: 67 years
　　　　Birth: 1920　　　　　　Death: 1988/02/13　　　Burial: 1988/02/17

Lot: 266 Owner: Miscellaneous
Site 2　Rosemary C. Murawski　Place: Fairfax, VA　　　Age: 48 years
　　　　Birth: 1937　　　　　　Death: 1986/08/22　　　Burial: 1986/08/25
Site 5　Floyd C. Peer　　　　　　　　　　　　　　　　Age: 86 years
　　　　Birth: 1918/04/22　　　Death: 1987/03/22　　　Burial: 1987/03/26
　　　　Place: Leesburg, VA　　　　　　　　　　　　　TS: US Navy WWII

Lot: 267 Owner: Miscellaneous
Site 4　Mrs. Mary G. Harris　　Place: Leesburg, VA　　Age: 78 years
　　　　Birth: 1911/10/23　　　Death: 1990/05/29　　　Burial: 1990/06/01

Lot: 270 Owner: Miscellaneous
Site 1　Janet Harrison Harrison　Place: Leesburg, VA　Age: 74 years
　　　　Birth: 1915/09/22　　　Death: 1990/03/11　　　Burial: 1990/03/14

Lot: 271 Owner: Miscellaneous
Site 1 Deborah Ashley Simpson   Age: 18 years
        Birth: 1968/04/01   Death: 1986/07/25   Burial: 1986/07/28
        Cause: Auto Accident   Place: Waterford, VA
Site 5 Elise R. Blair   Place: Takoma Park, MD Age: 83 years
        Birth: 1902/09/29   Death: 1986/07/06   Burial: 1986/07/09

Lot: 272 Owner: Miscellaneous
Site 5 Kelly F. Baynard   Age: 78 years
        Birth: 1909/02/15   Death: 1987/08/02   Burial: 1987/08/06
        Cause: Auto Accident   Place: Reston, VA
Site 6 Martha Linda Baynard   Age: 55 years
        Birth: 1930/10/07   Death: 1986/02/13   Burial: 1986/02/17
        Place: Arlington, VA   Married Kelly F. Baynard June 28, 1952
Site 7 Ferrell T. Williams   Place: Leesburg, VA   Age: 69 years
        Birth: 1916/10/02   Death: 1986/02/18   Burial: 1986/02/22
Site 8 Cecilia Williams   Age: 74 years
        Birth: 1913/09/12   Death: 1988/01/17   Burial: 1988/01/20
        Place: Clark County   On stone with Ferrell T. Williams

Lot: 291 Owner: Miscellaneous
Site 4 Malachi G. Spence   Place: Leesburg, VA   Age: 83 years
        Birth: 1902/02/15   Death: 1985/04/23   Burial: 1985/04/25
Site 6 Nellie B. Jackson   Age: 63 years
        Birth: 1918/11/22   Death: 1982/09/24
Site 7 Herbert Socks   Place: Leesburg, VA   Age: 75 years
        Birth: 1911/02/16   Death: 1986/06/16   Burial: 1986/06/18
Site 8 George R. Mackinnon   Place: Reston, VA   No stone
        Birth: 1912/05/22   Death: 1995/12/06   Burial: 1995/12/09

Lot: 292 Owner: Miscellaneous
Site 5 Helen Eloise Roland   Place: Ashburn, VA   Age: 74 years
        Birth: 1912   Death: 1985/07/16   Burial: 1985/07/18
Site 6 George F. Casey   Place: Washington, DC   Age: 69 years
        Birth: 1916   Death: 1985/12/08   Burial: 1985/12/10

Lot: 311 Owner: Miscellaneous
Site 1 William Bishop   No stone   Age: 75 years
        Place: Leesburg, VA   Death: 1987/03/10   Burial: 1987/03/13
Site 5 William R. Hayes   Age: 93 years
        Birth: 1917/04/24   Death: 1982/09/10   Burial: 1982/09/13
        Place: Leesburg, VA   TS: Married Pauline D. Hayes June 15, 1946
Site 7 Charles E. Doyle   Age: 64 years
        Birth: 1917/08/09   Death: 1982/05/29   Burial: 1982/06/01
        Place: Sterling, VA   TS: US Army WWII

Lot: 312 Owner: Miscellaneous
Site 1 Raymond W. Markham   Place: Leesburg, VA   Age: 56 years
        Birth: 1927/10/21   Death: 1984/03/02   Burial: 1984/03/06

Site 7 Howard C. Philyaw Age: 47 years
Birth: 1930/09/26 Death: 1978/08/11 Burial: 1985/08/22
Removed from National Memorial Park, Falls Church, VA

Lot: 330 Owner: Miscellaneous
Site 7 Joseph F. Mallon No stone Age: 83 years
Place: Leesburg, VA Death: 1983/11/19 Burial: 1983/11/22
Site 8 Genevieve C. Mallon Place: Middletown, PA No stone
Birth: 1902/01/01 Death: 1995/04/15 Burial: 1995/04/19
Site 8 Joseph F. Mallon III Age: 64 years
Birth: 1929/07/26 Death: 1993/12/15 Burial: 1993/12/18
Place: Leesburg, VA TS: US Army Korea

Lot: 332 Owner: Miscellaneous
Site 1 John Collins James Place: Tahuya, WA
Birth: 1915/11/02 Death: 1995/05/02 Burial: 1995/06/14
Site 2 Margaret Ann Moffett James Age: 59 years
Birth: 1976/10/07 Death: 1985/11/06 Burial: 1985/11/09
Place: Bethesda Naval Hosp., MD

UNION CEMETERY
LEESBURG, LOUDOUN CO., VA

APPENDIX A
Corrections to PLATS A & B

Lot: 85   Site 12   Della J. Mercer   Place: GA
          Birth: 1918/01/14   Death: 1995/12/29   Burial: 1996/01/02
Lot: 94   Site 1   Gertrude E. Johnson   Place: Silver Spring, MD
          Birth: 1907/05/24   Death: 1995/05/22   Burial: 1995/05/26
Lot: 166 Site 1   Edgar L. Carter   Place: Leesburg, VA
          Birth: 1910/08/14   Death: 1995/07/14   Burial: 1995/07/17
Lot: 180 Site 11   Jeremy Joseph Reeder   Place: Fairfax, VA
          Birth: 1992/12/05   Death: 1993/08/12   Burial: 1993/08/17
Lot: 220 Site 9   Leona M. Stevens   Place: Fairfax, VA
          Birth: 1910/07/06   Death: 1993/10/10   Burial: 1993/10/13
          Site 12   Patricia Petrykanyn   Place: Reston, VA
          Birth: 1939/08/07   Death: 1994/05/13   Burial: 1994/05/16
Lot: 274 Site 2   Helen G. Passapae   Place: NC
          Birth: 1913/07/15   Death: 1995/09/21   Burial: 1995/09/26
Lot: 286 Site 11   Charles Albert English Cole   Place: Leesburg, VA
          Birth: 1913/09/03   Death: 1993/07/25   Burial: 1993/07/28
Lot: 292W Site 5   Elizabeth Gormley Ford   Place: Rockville, MD
          Birth: 1904/09/18   Death: 1995/02/17   Burial: 1995/02/24
Lot: 297 Site 6   Clayton O. Kephart   Place: Leesburg, VA
          Birth: 1902/01/25   Death: 1993/02/28   Burial: 1993/03/03
Lot: 310 Site 5   Alfred Burdon Seccombe
          Birth: 1912/09/15   Death: 1993/05/03   Burial: 1993/05/06
          Place: Leesburg, VA   TS: Born Beverly, MA. Died Leesburg, VA
Lot: 315 Site 11   William Hall Harris III
          Birth: 1907/01/11   Death: 1994/01/30   Burial: 1994/02/03
          Place: Baltimore City, MD   TS: Husband of Sarah Louise Fairfax
Lot: 321 Site 12   Jane Herndon   Place: Leesburg, VA
          Birth: 1893/09/01   Death: 1995/12/12   Burial: 1995/12/15
Lot: 340 E Site 7   Clarence E. Alexander   Place: Arlington, VA
          Birth: 1902/12/23   Death: 1995/04/28   Burial: 1995/05/02
Lot: 345 Site 5   Douglas Davis Fairfax
          Birth: 1913/05/17   Death: 1994/01/21   Burial: 1994/01/26
Lot: 365 Site 6   Dorothy M. Beatty   Place: Burke, VA
          Birth: 1911/02/20   Death: 1994/08/30   Burial: 1994/09/02
Lot: 430 1/2 Site 2 Alice R. Loudermilk   Place: Fairfax, VA
          Birth: 1913/01/10   Death: 1993/12/19   Burial: 1993/12/22
Lot: 447 Site 2   Mary E. Kirkpatrick   Place: Leesburg, VA
          Birth: 1904/12/08   Death: 1993/04/30   Burial: 1993/05/05
          TS: On stone with J. Emory Kirkpatrick
Lot: 459 Site 5   James Stanley Cox   Died: ME
          Birth: 1909/11/27   Death: 1994/12/17   Burial: 1994/12/22

Lot: 461W Site 4	Mable Kane	Died: Leesburg, VA
	Death: 1993/09/11	Burial: 1993/09/15
Lot: 469W Site 2	Mary E. Hall Lowe	Died: Leesburg, VA
Birth: 1897/03/29	Death: 1995/05/17	Burial: 1995/05/22
Lot: 476 Site 9	Martha Gray Herndon	Died: Martinsburg, WV
Birth: 1923/09/01	Death: 1995/12/02	Burial: 1995/12/05
Lot: 480 Site 11	Doris B. White	Died: CT
Birth: 1903/05/04	Death: 1995/10/11	Burial: 1995/10/21
Lot: 482 1/2 Site 12	Laurie L. Ward	Died: AZ
Birth: 1902/05/03	Death: 1995/08/28	Burial: 1995/09/02
Lot: 518 Site 7	Robert C. Myers	Died: Berryville, VA
Birth: 1907/02/08	Death: 1995/07/07	Burial: 1995/07/11
Lot: 527 Site 2	Grace Lucille Ryan	Died: Leesburg, VA
Birth: 1905/04/12	Death: 1993/09/29	Burial: 1993/10/02
Site 8	Helen R. Ryan	Died: Ashland, VA
Birth: 1916/09/09	Death: 1993/10/30	Burial: 1993/11/02
Lot: 528 Site 3	Isaac Adelbert Long	
Birth: 1899/08/08	Death: 1993/11/15	Burial: 1994/01/15
Died: Richmond Heights, MO		
Lot: 529 Site 6	Constance E. Beach	Died: Alexandria, VA
Birth: 1906/12/17	Death: 1993/02/28	Burial: 1993/03/05
Lot: 536 Site 11	Evelyn L. Ford	Died: Annandale, VA
Birth: 1915/10/18	Death: 1993/10/13	Burial: 1993/10/16
Lot: 540E Site 9	Ruth W. Spitler	Died: Winchester, VA
Birth: 1912/02/05	Death: 1993/11/10	Burial: 1993/11/13
On stone with J. Quinter Spitler		
Lot: 553 W Site 6	Emily Lewis Wieland	
Birth: 1916/05/31	Death: 1993/04/10	Burial: 1993/04/17
Died: Charlottesville, VA		
Lot: 556W Site 6	Nellie C. Powell	Died: Warrenton, VA
Birth: 1904/09/03	Death: 1993/12/22	Burial: 1993/12/24
On stone with Herbert M. Powell		
Lot: 563 Site 6	Jane Wire Rhodes	Died: Arlington, VA
Birth: 1920/05/16	Death: 1993/06/11	Burial: 1993/06/14
Site 10	Anna H. Conard	Died: Washington, DC
Birth: 1905/02/01	Death: 1995/11/08	Burial: 1995/11/15
Lot: 564 Site 6	Jessie D. Quinn	Age: 104 years
Birth: 1890/07/28	Death: 1994/09/05	Burial: 1994/09/08
Died: Lake Ridge, VA		
Lot: 567 Site 9	Carrie Lee Herndon	Died: Leesburg, VA
Birth: 1903/05/11	Death: 1994/06/17	Burial: 1994/06/20
Lot: 569W Site 4	Edna G. Carlisle	Died: Woodstock, VA
Birth: 1899/07/30	Death: 1993/11/17	Burial: 1996/11/19
On stone with Jess Carlisle		
Lot: 571 Site 9	Grace Morris	Died: Colonial Hts., VA
Birth: 1892/11/12	Death: 1995/09/04	Burial: 1995/09/08
Lot: 578 Site 1	Roger B. Trussell	Died: FL
Birth: 1905/06/01	Death: 1995/02/18	Burial: 1995/02/22

Lot: 579 Site 11   Earl E. McNealea   Died: Alexandria, VA
   Birth: 1925/01/01   Death: 1994/01/25   Burial: 1994/01/28
Lot: 591 Site 1   Frank E. Winingder   Died: Reston, VA
   Birth: 1917/10/03   Death: 1995/09/02   Burial: 1995/09/05
Lot: 600 Site 5   Alma Jenkins   Died: Leesburg, VA
   Birth: 1899/06/21   Death: 1994/11/01   Burial: 1994/11/04
Lot: 613 Site 12   William Hunter Moore Jr.   Died: DE
   Birth: 1916/10/29   Death: 1993/12/10   Burial: 1993/12/16
Lot: 614 Site 7   George Taylor Gibson   Died: Richmond, VA
   Birth: 1920/08/03   Death: 1994/01/11   Burial: 1994/01/15
          Site 12   Lillian Brock   Died: Leesburg, VA
   Birth: 1904/05/31   Death: 1993/03/16   Burial: 1993/03/19
          Site 12   Fred A. Brock   Age: 95 years
   Birth: 1898/09/21   Death: 1994/02/10   Burial: 1994/02/19
   Died: Leesburg, VA   TS: US Army WWI
Lot: 628W Site 1   George Wendell Robinson Jr.
   Birth: 1916/06/10   Death: 1993/03/06   Burial: 1993/03/09
   Died: Manassas, VA
Lot: 641 Site 10   Virginia McCabe Hawkins
                           Death: 1995/01/03   Burial: 1995/01/11
   Died: Washington, DC
Lot: 648 Site 9   Anne Rea Shiring   Died: MD
   Birth: 1911/08/17   Death: 1993/03/22   Burial: 1993/03/26

INDEX

—A—

Abell	
Arthur J., Sr.	142
Dixie M.	142
Holly Sue	142
William Dennis	142
Ackad	
Kalil D.	137
Rose G.	137
Adams	18
Harry C.	88
James Richard	217
James Sterling	151
Mae Trittipoe, Mrs.	151
Mary C.	88
Steven William, Jr.	102
Addison	
Nellie Johnson	99
Robert Lawrence	99
Adrain	
Lucy Edna	89
Samuel C.	210
Virginia	101
Virginia E.	210
Adrian	
Allen Mercer	171
Eugene Howard	172
Eugene S.	171
James Emanuel	183
Lillian H., Mrs.	172
Ahalt	
Clarence Randolph	193
Tillie Alice	193
William H., Sr.	45
Ainsworth	
Humphrey L.	124
Airlines Corp. Penn	19
Akers	
Eliza Agnes	59
Elizabeth Florence	59
Fannie Louise	59
Ida Hedge	125
James Monroe	59
John Brown	59
Wilbert Ezra	125
Alderman	
John D.	118
Alexander	
Carrie	77
Clarence E.	227
Edward	77
Thomas	77
Allen	
Ann Hubbard	119
G. Dudley	132
Gladys A.	132
Robert H.	119
Allensworth	
Nellie Bell	81
Walter Scott	81
Allison	
Arthur W.	133
Barbara A.	175
Charles Lochte	159
George W., Jr.	175
Georgia Belle, Mrs.	36
Judy Ann	36
Olive M.	133
Thomas Ryan	175
William Calvin	36
Ambrey	
Vincent R.	202
Ambry	
Elizabeth L.	202
Ament	
Victor Lawrence, II	224
Amos	
Ethel Mae A.	207
Harry C., Jr.	207
Harry C., Sr.	207
Anderson	
Child of Webb	79
Edythe E.	144
Harry Gilmore	171
James B.	143, 144
Margaret L.	79
Mary Louise	171
Apperson	
Cleo Boone	213
James V.	213

Applegate
   Katie Lynn   92
Armack
   Jane Hammerly   45
Armour
   Merrill   3
Arnett
   Cheryl L. Meyer   217
   Frances G.   110
   Mary L.   110
Arnold
   Cleveland H.   202
   Ella M.   166
   Etta Leola   162
   Forest Anne   166
   Forest Inez   166
   James E., Sr.   166
   James Edwin, Jr.   117
   Jason   166
   John William   166
   Katherine Bondeena   166
   Mahlon David   162
   Mamie C.   202
   Patricia Ann   166
   Richard Wayne   166
   Richard Yakey   166
Ashby
   Warren D.   168
Ashton
   Baby Girl   36
   William U.   128
Atchley
   Marie S.   170
Athey
   Alta Leona   40
   Andrew Fillmore   176
   Charles F.   176
   Ervin Preston   40
   Frances Leona   40
   Harry Thomas   40
   J.W. & N.M.   40
   James Aubrey   180
   John Donald   78
   Kathleen R., Mrs.   170
   Mary Estell, Mrs.   176
   Maude L.   40
   Mildred F.   177
   Myrtle Myers   78
   Norman Andrew   176

Atwell
   Arthur B.   93
   C. Frank   205
   Charles Roland   135
   Cora   93
   Edward Hugh   29
   Eunice H.   205
   Hugh E.   10
   John G., Sr.   123
   Kathleen P.   123
   Louis F.   145
   Mary Waters   145
   Maurice D.   166
   Sara Arnold   166
   Virginia Wilson   135
Austin
   Tex Hunter   91
Ayala
   Segundo Luis Adolfo   203

—B—

Babson
   Keith   59
Bailey
   Elizabeth M., Miss   75
   George T.   75
   John T.   75
   Lula Temple   75
   Mary Elizabeth   75
   Thomas   75
   William M.   75
Baker
   Ada Mae   207
   Adolphus Bartlett   66
   Baby   99
   Christopher Brandenburg   185
   D.B.   66
   Ernesy L.   31
   Frances M.   66
   Glenn L.   224
   Harry F.   122
   Harvey Rollins   66
   Mark Peter   185
   Mary Loy   31
   Mattie May   122
   Minnie E.   90
   Nellie Hellen   125
   Otho D.   90

Paul Bliss	125
Pearl E.	88
Robert E.	207
Roger, Dr.	185
Ball	
Bessie W.	104
Dolly McPherson, Mrs.	71
Edna Irene	164
Fred L., Jr.	164
George H.	71
Grace G., Mrs.	108
Harry G.	71
Harvey Hamilton	108
Harvey MacDaniel	217
Ida May	217
Mary D.	71
May Lodge	217
Ralph William	213
William E.	71
William Joseph	104
Ballenger	
Clifton	9
Clinton	141
Daisy C. Wallace	9
H.W., Mrs.	9
Henry W.	9
India G.	141
Lawrence D.	10
Mary V.	10
Mildred Elona	9
Paul P.	9, 10
William G.	130
Ballo	
Gertrude C.	201
Joseph B.	201
Barclay	
Madge Venable	122
Bark	
Edw. & Eliz.	103
Vicki Angela	103
Barker	
Robert Lee	117
Barnes	
Gene Wayne	114
Harry Garth	125
Barnette	
Baby Boy	101
Barney	
Monica Elizabeth	219
Barnhouse	
Amos H.	195
Edgar	94
Harry Edgar	83
Irving F.	83
Lovetta C.	94
Mary Agnes S.	94
Raymond B.	94
Barron	
Raymond	204
Bartee	
Pattie Downs	103
Bartel	
Hannah E.	130
Louis	130
Bassell	
John Young	143
Rebecca Gray Benedict	143
Baumgardner	
Dorothy S.	213
Baynard	
Kelly F.	225
Martha Linda	225
Beach	
Bertha W., Mrs.	104
Constance E.	228
Louis E.	127
Samuel Messina	128
Shirley Randolph	104
Steave S.	36
Beales	
Catherine K.	15
Dale	129
Henry	186
Richard Henry (Dick)	129
Beall	
Charles Richard	24
Ernest Ellsworth	189
Ernest M.	188
Lela Grace	189
Orra L.	25
Beals	
Mabel Carlisle Pierce	186
Beasley	
Louise Scales	60
Lucius Scales	60
Oscar Hill, Sr.	60
Patricia Wall	60
Beatty	

Audrey	146	Ann Breed	85
Dorothy M.	227	Ann Catherine Drake	85
Beauchamp		Anne Leiper Martin Breed	85
Baby Boy	20	Marie Constance, Mrs.	85
Dorthy Isable Scott	20	Ottie L.	220
Beaver		Richard Mongomery	85
Anna G.	147	Robert Henry	114
Edwin E.	147	Robert L.	85
John Andrew	83	Robert L., Jr	85
Louise Huger	83	Robert Longden	85
Beavers		Robert Longden, III	85
Enos	77	Robert Longden, Jr.	85
Beckner		Benton	
Ella V.	15	Robert H.	213
Marcus L., Jr.	15	Berger	
Marcus L., Sr.	15	Clift P., Dr.	155
Beggs		Dorothy R.	155
Bessie Mae D.	128	Berry	
Vernon L.	128	Lucille A.	13
Bell		Best	
Annie I.	117	Alice Skenker	20
Arch Samuel	177	Charles Wesley	195
Catherine Jane, Mrs.	105	Elton McCoy	83
Clarence D., Jr.	17	John Spencer, Sr.	35
Clarence Duke	119	Phoebe Ann Thompson	18
Eleanor S.	91	William V.	18
Mary Alice M.	177	Betterly	
Monnie P.	177	Infant Boy	103
Oliver S.	91	Bettis	
Robert B.	105	Child	65
Rufus R.	177	Jennie Virginia	65
Samuel C.	177	William Irving	65
Susie L. Kitts	119	Beverly	
Tyler Eugene	119	James B.	vi
William T.	137	Bialasik	
William Thomas, II	137	Konstantin	219
Belt		Sofia M.	219
Annie Thrift	43	Biggs	
Benjamin T.	43	Cora L.	54
Nellie Carr	43	Elmer B.	53
Paul	43	Margaret	53
Samuel Phillips	43	Robert H.	53
Townsend N.	43	Billand	
Townsend W., Jr.	43	Alphonse	224
Benford		Eleanor N.	224
Betty H.	132	Billy	
Benjamin		Heidi Theresa	131
Ray	178	Joel John	131
Bentley		Bilson	

Albert Clogan	123
Bishel	
Dale Lee	118
Bishop	
Ethel L.	169
Francis	169
Francis E.	169
Genevieve K.	144
Henry R., Sr.	144
William	225
William Edward	154
Bitzer	
John W.	7
Leah, Mrs.	7
Leonora Goodhart, Mrs.	7
Bjornson	
Ben	2
Infant Daughter	2
Louise E.	2
Blackwell	
Rosalie Steadman	156
Blair	
Edward M.	90
Elise R.	225
May Powell	186
Nancy S.	63
Smith	186
Blankenship	
Bacil F.	122
Edward H.	122
Blantz	
Child	17
Blaylock	
Alyssa Erin	222
Baby	92
Blincoe	
John H.	189
Bliss	
Marsha Ann	219
Blitch	
James Bedford	194
Blue	
Charles W., Capt.	173
Bly	
Chloe Cluxton, Mrs.	27
Coral Erickson	26
Merwyn Cluxton	26
Robert Tuthill	27
Vincent Tuthill	27

Bobbitt	
Anna Peters	139
Harold	139
Bodine	
Grace May	101
Henry C.	81
John F.	101
Bodmer	
Elmer Augustus	97
Henrietta	38
Louis A.	94
Louise Orr	64
Ruby C.	94
Susie Virginia	111
Thomas E.	111
Thomas Edward	38
William Page, Dr.	64
Bohumil	
Rita Diamante	206
Boland	
Edwin Arthur, III	199
Bond	
Alice J.	83
Paul S.	83
Boone	
John Oscar	127
Boston	
Vickie Jo Holcombe	210
Victoria Jo	210
Bourke	
Anne Rosaleen	140
Josephine Ott	140
Bowers	
Harry Samuel	22
Izetta Gardner	22
Bowman	
Ora Lee Marion	53
Boyd	
Evelyn May	223
John Michael	180
Bozel	
George B.	190
Brackett	
William	124
Braden	
Carrie E., Mrs.	62
Gabriel V.	62
Gladys Smoot	62
Robert Furr	62

Sallie F., Mrs.	62
Bradfield	
Edward Neville	152
Ruth Crim	152
Bradley	
Ralph Edward	221
Woodrow	68
Bradshaw	
Helen Margaret, Infant	134
Hugh M.	134
Lydia J., Mrs.	134
Brady	
Amos H.	131
Charles H.	149
Charles Henry	130
Helen J.	50
James Robert	50
Lovie Newton	149
Norris W.	131
Braidotti	
Elsa Tomat	199
Branan	
Jeanne Mary	219
Bratney	
Bertrand H.	208
Grace Bardetta	208
Hester Ann LeFevre Harrison	191
John Frederick	208
Sara Mitchell, Mrs.	208
Breckenridge	
Frances A.	2
Harriett R.	2
Nelson W.	2
Breed	
Charles Henry, Dr.	85
Frances deForest Martin.	85
Brewster	
Jeremie Lynwood	91
Jerry, Jr.	92
Briggs	
Thomas W.	125
Bristow	
Joseph Quayle	138
Rosamond Ingalls	138
Brock	
Fred A.	229
Lillian	229
Broderick	
George L.	17
Brooks	
Milton Hope, Jr.	76
Olive	133
Brown	
Addison	160
Della A.	126
Elizabeth Fitzhugh Rust	160
Emma Eugene Herndon, Mrs.	48
Esther M.	13
George Thomas	126
Helen Carpenter Gaskin	160
Margory	154
Stanley Noel	160
Brownrigg	
Mary Jane Grant	202
Philip Parker	202
Bruck	
Bessie, Mrs.	29
Brundage	
Robert Vernier	160
Brunner	
Jane Eppes	179
Bryan	
John Lewis	48
Rolande (Tinia) Hancock	48
Bryant	
Cora McCann	193
Mary Craun	193
Ralph Leon	193
Thomas Franklin	193
Walter Hugh	194
William Boyd, Rev.	193
Buchanan	
James Robert	94
Bugher	
Frederick McLean	143
Henrietta Benedict Bassell	143
Bullard	
Edith M. Jones	77
Bullock	
Alfred	69
Bumgardner	
Pearly L.	213
Burbank	
Richard Willoughby, Sr.	136
Burch	
Edgar Francis	140
Olga Crandall	140
William Thompson, Dr.	140

Burdick			Callaghan	
Anna Lazenby	110		William L.	223
Burger			Campbell	
Bessie Louise Costello	35		Aletha Whetsell	102
Burgess			Ellen C.	107
Perry A.	213		John M., Jr.	170
William E.	111		John N.	169
Burkart			Lee	155
Baby	204		Lillie Rufus, Mrs.	99
Robert P.	204		Ray N.	107
Burke			Ruth Lee	155
Mary J.	56		Stephenson C.	99
Burton			Capital Airlines Inc.	109
Grace Woodson	209		Carlisle	
Hampton E., Jr.	148		Albert N.	97
John Ira	209		Anna Lee	97
Norman Lee	124		Edna G.	228
Ruth Van Waters	124		Myrtle R.	97
William R.	148		Carlson	
Bushong			Agnes H.	146
Charles Edward	76		Carnes	
Elizabeth W.	77		George L.	101
John Albert	76		Henry Lee	177
Minnie B.	77		Kenneth Wayne	187
Pearl Rake	76		Maurice L.	180
Virgil S.	77		Ruby V.	180
Bussinger			Carpenter	
Clarence Michael	120		Christopher S.	92
Buttery			Carper	
Child	53		Florence Carlson	132
Helen Ludell	217		Carr	
Buttlery			Edward R.	158
Annie F. Enery	19		Elizabeth Hume	172
Byrd			Emma B.	159
Lynn W.	196		Evelyn Loveless	157
			James W.	66
			Josephine VanD.	66
—C—			William B., Dr.	158
			Carroll	
Caddell			William J.	95, 98
James H., Sr.	207		Carskaden	
Calef			Corrine	220
Patricia Martzell	90		William	220
Calhoun			Carson	
Carl S.	70		Ann Orrison	30
Hencil M.	133		Florence Lillian, Mrs.	88
Mervin Francis	133		George B.	87
Calkins			Carter	
Infant of A.	11		Anna B.	217
Lillie Bell	11			

Baby Girl	35	Mary Ellen	184
Donna Louise	81	Chapin	
Edgar L.	227	John Lincoln	193
Fred, Mr. & Mrs.	102	Massie O. Moore	193
George C.	24	Chastain	
Janet Miller	195	Baby	103
Mary E., Mrs.	5	Chatard	
Mary Eyre	24	Alice Whelan	85
Mary Lucretia Drake	194	Ferdinand E & Constance	85
Paul A.	180	Ferdinand Edme	85
Paul Haynes	194	Mary	85
Richard Leigh	195	Chatel	
Ronald Keith	102	Jean Charles	130
Cary		Chatfield	
Hugh William	15	Edna Saunders	47
Lillian H.	15	Frederick R., Jr.	47
Casey		Frederick Rupert	47
George F.	225	Shirley Oswalt	47
Casilear		Cheney	
Martha E.	30	Mary Lucille	131
Raph A.	30	Chittenden	
William B.	30	Henry Treat	143
Caslar		Christensen	
Frank G.	221	Gertrude M.	212
Castle		Christian	
Rose Frances, Mrs.	105	Orville S.	185
Walter Elias	105	Christopherson	
Caulkins		Ronald M.	196
Charles W., Rev.	203	Church	
Eunice A.	203	Belva B.	6
Caylor		Clayton O.	204
Charlcie B.	90	James M.	6
Eugene G.	97	Chwalowski	
Evelyn B. (Puddin)	110	Zofia	30
Lawrence E.	83	Cissel	
Mary	83	Jean Lynn	214
Milton E.	82	Laura Lee	214
Ralph H. (Tommy)	110	Cissell	
Warren Granville	67	William D.	214
Chambers		Clagett	
Mary Ann	210	Sarah Ellen	184
Walter H.	210	Vernon Lee	184
Chamblin		Clapp	
Daniel S. & Ernestine F.	186	Stephen	122
Ernestine Fox	136	Clark	
Helen Elizabeth Phillips, Mrs.	157	Anna T.	168
Kathryn H.	186	Ralph A.	168
Mildred Lee	186	Richard T.	168
Champion		Clarke	

Addison H.		vi	Colbert	
Claypool			Ellen	191
Katrina E.		91	John E.	191
Cleaver			Cole	
Charles & Diana		8	Charles Albert English	227
Clem			Glen Perry, Jr.	51
Richard Lee		218	Howard Eeton	161
Clemens			Sarah E.	161
C.H. & Leona S.		61	Coleman	
Christian H.		63	Henry Paris	56
Emma S.		61	Myrtle E., Mrs.	57
Hattie Cambell		97	William P.	57
Hattie Jenkins		61	Collins	
Infant daughter		61	Douglas Ray	152
John R.		63	May Virginia	107
John Robert		60	Stacy R., Sr.	154
John William		63	Comber	
Leona Shroy		63	B.C.	224
Lorenzo D., Jr.		125	Comer	
Lorenzo Daw, Sr.		97	James R. L.	107
Mary E., Mrs.		61	Ralph & Hazel	107
William Hendrie		61	Compher	
Cline			Doris H.	70
Douglas H.		205	Comstock	
Cloud			Robert O.	207
Irva Sutton, Mrs.		73	Conard	
James Walter		73	Anna H.	228
Clyburn			Connelly	
Ruby Maddox		220	Marie Louise	140
Coates			Connor	
Calvin D.		36	Anna S.	63
Coburn			C. Fenton	169
Alice Hilton		160	Cecil	169
Harry W.		160	Edna Fadeley	169
Cochran			Hattie E.	23
Ethel E.		45	James Arthur	63
Roland C.		45	John William	23
Cockerell			Margaret Helen	23
Nannie Florence Newlon		176	William Jerome	23
Cockerille			Conrad	
Grace Hough		68	Benj. F. & Elizabeth Stuart	76
Kermit E.		68	George W.	101
Cockrell			James E.	98
Harvey M.		51	Mabel C.	101
Shirley Ann		119	Cook	
Cocroft			Gloria J.	82
Reginald Bifield, Jr.		111	Hettie B.	193
Coffey			Nina Alice	222
Dillard E., Jr.		81	Peggy Ray	112

Cooke		Robert H.	185
John W. & Betty L.	188	Costello	
John W., III	188	Charles Oscar	34
Cooksey		Ello, Miss	5
Eva H.	38	Elsie	17
J. Robert	38	George Robert	74
Lawrence Hickam	38	John Albert	215
Lawrence Thomas	38	Karen Byer, Mrs.	215
Cooper		Katherine N.	134
Adley C.	24	Louisa F., Mrs.	36
Albert C.	131	Marjorie	5
Clarence Leroy	69	Marshall E.	36
David W.	54	Mary Ellen	60
Dorcas Ann, Mrs.	54	Oliver T.	58
Dorothy A. (Dolly)	54	Oscar A.	35
Eva C.	69	Paul Douglas	215
Evelyn M.	131	Rebecca D. Symons	58
Flossie	188	Rosalie M.	74
Geraldine A.	220	William T.	60
Helen N.	108	Coster	
Irving Thomas	188	Florence Anne Smoot	165
James A.	220	Cotton	
James F.	213	George Bruce	117
John A.	221	Robert Bruce	117
John W.	208	Coughlin	
John Wesley	54	Alice Wilt	206
John William	70	Bessie Virginia	31
Joseph Henry	33	Bruce Ryan	206
Kenneth Lee	92	William M.	31
Leroy E.	221	Courtney	
Letitia M., Mrs.	33	Kathleen Everest	200
Lillie Mae Hough	2	Sarah Jones	200
Lula May F.	69	Thomas Moore	200
Mary Perry	24	Undred T.	95
Maurice A.	176	William Dunlap	200
Michael A.	146	Cowart	
Ollie L. Atwell	99	William Lawson	136
Randell W.	217	Cowne	
Raymond A.	107	Dorothy K.	108
Robert G.	99	Leroy J.	108
Corbell		Cox	
Edna Wright	170	James Stanley	227
Evelyn Harkness	192	James W.	215
Robert Thruston	170	Jane Rust	160
Corl		William Junkin	160
Kathleen R. (Howe)	212	Crabill	
Corley		Helen L.	210
Helen Lee	21	Percy C.	210
James R. & Carrie	21	Crabites	

Frederica diZerega	62		James Volney	2
Henry Berlin	62		M. Elizabeth	2
Craighead			Maude Helen	2
Alma N.	207		Cunningham	
Arnold E., Sr.	199		Alfred Lee	3
Syble F.	199		Dolph N.	65
Walter D.	207		Elinor M.	201
Craighill			Harold W.	70
Anne Macdonald	171		Harry Wise	201
Children of Payton & Anne	171		Infant	65
George Peyton	171		Marjorie	65
Robert Macdonald	171		Mary M.	70
Crampton			Millard	65
Lola B.	202		Curry	
Craun			Michael Arl	218
Stella Q.	177		Virginia Gladys	215
William W.	177		Curtin	
Creamer			Mary Virginia	31
Mary Ruth Scott	20			

—D—

Crighton			Dailey	
Elizabeth, Mrs.	78		Elizabeth M. Love	11
Lily B., Miss	78		Frank T.	11
William	78		Daniel	
Crogham			Anita Frasier	134
Harry C.	109		Clellie C.	137
Crooker			Elizabeth, Mrs.	84
Arleigh T.	127		Harry C.	137
Sylvan J.	127		Harry Camel	137
Crosen			John Orr	134
Andrew Noland	89		John William	134
Croson			Mary A.	134
Minnie M.	89		Orville	84
Cross			Thomas A., Jr.	212
Martin	115		Danner	
Sylvester Glenn	115		George F.	110
Crouch			Teresa Lynn	92
Clarence Copeland	65		Darby	
Emory C.	90		Glen Alan	15
Eva Jeanette, Mrs.	65		Darne	
Henry Pendleton	65		Floyd Foster	16
Raymond L.	31		Lillie P.	16
Cullen			Darnes	
George Franklin	167		Horace E.	177
Mary Gertrude	167		Joseph A.	176
Ruth Howser	167		Rensler E.	176
Walter Franklin	167		Rosa Lucille U.	177
Cummings			Stilson Wendell	176
D.V.	2			
David V.	2			

Davetson
   Anders Hanan   98
Davidson
   Harry Th.   108
   Infant Son   107
   Peter Hilderbrand   108
Davis
   Elva M.   119
   Hazel L.   194
   Louisa   43
   Mary E.   144
   Myrtle Gulick, Mrs.   46
   Virgil C.   46
   William Dana   43
Davison
   Adele Monges   209
Dawson
   Annie E.   68
   Cora V.   18
   David   119
   Dorothy S.   100
   Edward S.   100
   James C.   68
   James L.   81
   Larry Allen   98
   Ray C.   54
   Robert Amos   122
   William T.   18
Day
   Frederick F.   154
   Harold L.   97
   Jewell Jane   154
   Julia D.   97
Dayen
   William R.   224
Daymude
   Athoel Edward   22
   Cecil G.   159
   Edward L.   22
   James J.   22
   James Lowe   22
   Luvenia Augusta, Mrs.   22
   Mary E.   22
   Nettie A.   22
   Willie J., Jr.   22
   Willie Jacob   22
de Balla
   Ann Katherine Drake Bentley 86
   Valentine, Dr.   86

Deans
   Baby Boy   105
Dearden
   Jennifer Dawn   103
DeCray
   Dorothea Peters   109
DeHart
   Claude Henry   21
   Claude William   119
   Gerald C.   119
   Infant   21
   L. G.   21
   Martha A.   21
   Paul G.   21
   Paul L.   21
   Robert   21
   Ruth E., Mrs.   21
Deibel
   Madelyn Sarah   80
Deimler
   Vince Lyle, Sr.   216
   Vincent Lyle, Jr.   214
DeJonghe
   Albert A.   107
Denny
   Willie Clay   219
DeSilva
   Eulogia L.   111
Detrick
   Ada V.   125
Dewar
   John H., Mrs.   109
di Zerega
   Agnes Green   189
   Augustus   189
   Elizabeth J.   189
   Emile A.   189
   John P. H.   189
   Louis Augustus   189
   Olivia Tyler   189
   William Luck   190
Dickens
   Carl Lee   196
   Edgar G.   196
Dickinson
   Joseph C.   208
Dickson
   Ruth Fowler Johnston   147
diZerega

Alfred L.B. & Alice A.	62	Downs		
Frederica, Mrs.	61	Grover H.		164
Gasquet	61	Inola		164
Martha Alice	62	James A.		78
William Irvine	62	John Noland		78
Dockery		Mary Darnes		78
Doris C.	221	Walter N.		86
Dodd		Doyle		
Ada Bridges	163	Charles E.		225
Charles Grey	163	Drake		
John G.	163	Elsie C.		47
Joseph Foster	163	Eugene H., Dr.		47
Laura V.	163	Eugene Harvey, Jr.		47
Mae W.	163	Joseph C.		47
Paul	163	Dripps		
Wesley F.	163	J. M.		17
Doggett		Drish		
William (Bill) Earl	223	Harriett		vi
Doman		William		vi
Richard A.	81	Dudley		
Donaldson		Aldrich, Sr.		43
Frederick Lee	111	Anne Burton		209
Donley		Louise Littig		43
Michael A.	87	Margaret Titus		149
Donohoe		Duff		
Carrie C.	198	James		7
Edna Conrad	198	Martha Boyd Tompkins, Mrs.		6
Hilda G.	159	Martha Elizabeth		7
John K., Jr.	59	Mary M.		7
Thomas	159	R.C.		6
William E.	198	Robert Cecil		6
Donovan		Robert Cecil, Jr.		7
Hilda R. Cunningham	70	Virginia Barbara		6
Douglas		Duke		
E. Lee	215	John M.		193
John Moore	181	Patricia Ellen		193
Virginia E.	215	Dulaney		
William B.	135	Polly Venable		122
Douglass		Robert L.		122
James Edwards	181	Dulin		
John M.	181	Alfred		184
Martha Strother	181	Mary Alice		184
Nellie V.	67	Duncan		
Dove		Edward Lee		114
Cleopatra	181	Grace M.		114
Dollie A., Mrs.	101	Timothy Allen		114
Frederick M.	181	Tony		114
John A.	181	Dunn		
Richard A.	101	Blanche C.		188

Carroll Edwin	188	Eidson	
John Daniel	176	John West	199
Julia L.	176	Lillie Bell, Mrs.	199
Martin G.	68	Elder	
William	188	Alice	81
Durfey		Elgin	
Frances M.	205	John H., I	76
Durfy		Norman B.	98
George J.	205	Elliott	
Duryea		Charles Edwin	71
Mary Scott	2	Edith Adrain	212
Dwyer		Emily Cox, Mrs.	71
Daisy M.	59	Frank S.	212
John G.	59	James William	98
John G., Jr.	59	Lewis H.	65
Maurice J.	59	Marie C.	98
Dyson		Sarah Elizabeth	65
Walter, Sr.	220	William H.	65
		Ellis	
—E—		Baby Girl	98
		Lincoln Paul, Dr.	128
Eamich		Mattie K.	129
Wanda R.	112	Ellmore	
Early		Amos	89
Lee Child of James	36	Bertha Aldridge	44
Ector		Charles A.	45
Carolyn E.	161	Charles Henry	44
Hannah A.	161	Emory Staley, Rev.	137
Robert Warren	161	John Franklin	89
Edelen		Lena	11
Naomi F. Bell	137	Mary Virginia	45
Edmondson		Murphy D., Rev.	11
Andrew Davis	162	Robert Franklin	45
Carrie Jane Preston	162	Sarah Cecelia	45
John B.	190	Susie T.	45
Marie T.	162	Virginia Grey	11
Mildred M.	191	Ely	
Robert William	162	Alexander M.	43
Edmonston		Elizabeth L. Richmond, Mrs.	43
Elizabeth J. Fry	60	John C.	44
Edwards		Manny Lee	43
Ernest M., Jr.	194	Melvinia Orlena Bales	44
Ernest Mosby, Sr.	194	Embrey	
Florence Alma Akers	59	Charlie R.	168
Herbert Tunis	194	English	
Herbert Tunis, Jr.	194	Horace L.	84
Sara E.	194	Lelia Steiner	85
Sarah	194	Ennis	
Zelda A.	92	Barbara	102

Entsminger	
Brett Everett	222
Eppes	
Charles Gibson	179
Frank Gibson	179
Sally Joe	179
Espey	
Annie E.	83
Evans	
Ann Sutherland	63
Janet Sue	217
Everhart	
Anne Morris	47
Frances E.	5
George N.	90
John Philip	47
Lelia E.	209
Lydia M.	5
Marvin H., Jr.	209
Marvin H., Sr.	209
Mildred Jane	90
Ewing	
Henry Charles T.	185
Lucy Litton	185

—F—

Fagan	
Josephine Raflo	121
Fairall	
George G.	147
Geraldine	147
Virginia	147
Fairfax	
Douglas Davis	227
Lula A. Filler, Mrs.	174
Sarah Louise	227
Fanning	
Nannie K.	69
Farmer	
Child	53
Donald Norman	70
Emmett O.	99
Emmitt	119
Herbert T.	101
Lucy V., Mrs.	99
Rosie F., Mrs.	101
Velma Patricia, Mrs.	124
Farnie	

Mabel T. Shryock	61
Farris	
Donald Lee	156
Matthew E., Sr.	156
Myrtle Elizabeth	156
Fath	
Edouard J.	145
Fauver	
Orbrey J.	92
Feagans	
Florida Fling, Mrs.	98
Feeney	
Marjorie A.	142
Feezle	
Jennifer	76
Felix	
Anne Walsh	203
Charles Emil	203
Fendall	
Lily Lawrence Rust, Mrs.	192
Thomas Miller	192
Fennelly	
Esther Adrain	210
John Patrick	210
Ferguson	
Bertha Jane	64
E. Hazel, Mrs.	64
Estelle L.	64
J.S. & N.G.	132
Lacey M.	64
Lulah Blanche	64
Paul W.	73
Stella Galleher	73
Fetzer	
Ernest Lee	92
Ivy M. Carlisle	105
Leslie G.	149
Louise R.	149
Lula Casilear	200
Mervin T. (Pete)	105
Robert T.	149
Robert Thrift, Jr.	104
Robert William	149
William W.	149
Filler	
Drucella H.	174
James Robert	174
Nina E.	174
William Michael	174

Finney	
William Roy	81
Firestone	
Shannon Dale Warf	119
Fishback	
Charles Maloy	196
Ruth Tavenner	196
Virginia C.	200
Winfred W.	200
Fisher	
Nellie May	119
Fiske	
Charles W.	136
Elizabeth May	136
John William	136
Fitzgerald	
Troy M.	154
Flagg	
Virginia Peyton	91
Flanagan	
Pearl Ellmore	45
Thomas James	44
Fleenor	
Eugene H.	120
Fleming	
Ashley Michelle	186
Charles Preston	101
Edith K.	159
Frank	216
Glennie M.	101
Grace Elizabeth	32
Grace Leslie	32
Jack W., Sr.	159
Jack West	159
James Clayton	161
Katherine	32
Margaret Craig	161
Robert Lee	32
Thomas P.	83
Fletcher	
Albertha D.	181
Baby	98
Benjamin James	25
Bertha F.	25
Carlie James	181
Charles F.	31
Charlotte Ellen Harding	31
Child	99
Christopher Eugene	118
Deborah Lee	181
Dorothy Russell	181
Edward C.	29
Elizabeth Mae	53
Frank Robert	122
Geneva M. (Eva)	181
George L.	74
Helena R.	74
James H.	25
James M.	181
Lester Ely	180
Lillian Rebecca	88
Loretta Ann	98
Mary Irene	203
Minnie Ellen	31
Minnie Myers, Mrs.	31
Robert Lee	181
Terry Lee	181
Vivian Ann	122
W. Luck	110
William Essie	180
Fling	
C.A.	17
Clarence Ashby	128
Clifford Ashby	128
Infant Ashby	17
William H.	219
Flint	
Margie D.	134
Roland B.	134
Flippo	
Charlsie W.	196
Christopher Burton	182
Frank B., Sr.	182
Martha C. (Mattie)	182
Monroe	182
Nina Elizabeth	182
Roy Monroe	196
William Clifton	182
Flynn	
Ada K.	76
Bessie Elizabeth	205
Betty Pauline, Miss	53
Clarence F.	128
Clinton William	76
Dorothy Louise	80
Edith M.	128
Elizabeth Anne, Mrs.	51
Hugh G.	68

James Milton	205		Thelma J.	106
Katherine Marie	37		Franklin	
Lewis A.	205		A. Fannie	3
Lewis E.	205		Barbara Burch	3
Louise Morne	210		Benjamin Willard	86
Robert Franklin	51		C. Lee	178
Shirley M.	80		Corbin H.	12
Focer			Corbin Hunter	178
Ethyl Valerie	133		Emma Shaffar	86
Foglesong			Frederick H.	12
Charles W.	214		Hattie Sowers	12
Follin			James M.	2
Albert Fox	169		John A.	23
Foote			John G.	20
Irvin V.D.	127		Lena D.	23
Michel	127		Mary Louise Hoskinson, Mrs.	23
Ford			Newton	3
Doolin Dewitt	105		Rebecca Fannie	20
Elizabeth Gormley	227		Thomas F.	20
Evelyn L.	228		Vernon G.	23
Winnie D.	105		Frasca	
Fornshill			Modestino J.	153
Betty Ann Rogers	40		Frear	
Kenneth B.	40		William	210
Kenneth D. B.	40		Fred	
Forry			Barbara S.	140
Nina Fletcher	25		Barbara Stewart	132
Foss			Hugh Wharton	139
Catharine Clemens	63		Rogers	139
Foster			Ruby W., Mrs.	139
James Carrington	140		Freehof	
Katherine E.	140		Elizabeth	91
Foth			Mortimer E.	91
Erich A.W.	205		Freilinger	
Rose M.	205		Corinne W.	75
Fouche			Matthew C., Dr.	75
Elva Lee	173		Matthew W.	75
George Emory	49		French	
Hubert Alvin	49		Alexander B.	190
John W.	173		Bruce A.	190
Fountain			Emma Jane	190
Joylyn	214		Fritts	
Fox			Zachary Scott	224
Flavilla I.	207		Frizzell	
Gustave Elizabeth Moran, Mrs.	72		John C.	126
Margaret Elizabeth	106		Fromm	
Robert & Katherine	150		Beverly J.	218
Roger Willis	106		Fry	
Ronald L.	150		Alma P. George	7

Anne May	14	Mary Naomi, Mrs.	71
Archie Linwood	158	Millard W.	58
Arthur S.	118	Norman C., Sr.	190
Bela McCann	72	Paul S.	118
Bertha Magaha, Mrs.	72	Robert W., Sr.	111
Bessie Grafton	206	Ruby M.	58
Charles William	84	Terry Lee	111
Clarence Jennings	206	Theresa F.	58
Clark L.	72	Viola Mary	116
Clifford N.	118	Wilbur R.	170
Cora Osborn	158	Funk	
Eileen, Mrs.	116	Norman W.	81
Elizabeth E.	59	Furr	
Ella B.	7	Alfred M.	207
Gracie M.	118	Carrie Lee	100
Hannah (Nannie) Ann	5	Dorothy Ellen Keyes, Mrs.	88
Herbert J.	7	Forest	88
Ida J.	60	Hortence Lloyd	208
J. Frank	5	John Henry	100
Kathy Loretta	116	Louis Roula	208
Kaye Irene	72	Lucy B., Mrs.	207
Leo	116	Milton H.	180
Maggie Roberta, Mrs.	84	Pauline V.	180
Marshall Herbert	7		
Mary Paver	116	—G—	
Melvin C.	84		
Nellie M.	7	Gaines	
Roger Clifton	72	Alice Newlon	176
Roy L.	190	Elenita Charlotte	118
Samuel W.	60	Eva W.	152
W.T.	13	Joseph Patrick	118
William N.	14	Nellie R.	32
William Thomas	14	Peggy Lou	33
Frye		Stanley Newlon	175
Blanche W.	153	Stanley Tyler	175
Clarence J.	116	Vivian A.	33
Columbus Berkley	36	William E.	32
Daisy S.	173	Galleher	
Delia Theresa	116	Agnes Barbara	73
Edward Penn	71	Edmund Randolph	149
Edward Pennrose	71	Elinor Hutchison	58
Elbert H.	170	George Raymond	147
Eugene D.	173	Leila Hickman	150
Grace C.	39	Martha Jordan, Mrs.	73
Jesse Woodrow	172	Robert Lee	136
Joseph M.	38	Thomas Raymond	58
Kathleen Athey	170	William R.	73
Lloyd E.	153	Gamble	
Lovie R.	170	William Henry, Jr.	122

Gandee	
Charles E., II	92
Gandolph	
Infant J. O.	35
Joseph O.	142
Gant	
Harm	54
Gardner	
Brian Keith	185
Walter G.	115
Garretson	
Robert K.	109
Garrett	
Agnes Dibrell	25
Catherine Cox	25
Edwin Enoch	25
Edwin Enoch, Jr.	25
Margaret F.	25
Mary E., Mrs.	60
Paul Willis	60
Rosa Virginia	25
William Francis	25
Garrison	
Elizabeth Mrs.	vi
James	vi
Teresa E.	219
Gates	
George W.	127
Kathryn D.	127
Gault	
Marjorie Craik	108
Perceval Stanway	108
Geiman	
Mazie Pearson	99
Wade B.	99
George	
Annie, Child of Wallace	25
Carolyn Ann	224
Charles G.	27
Edward Clayton	26
Flora Louisa, Mrs.	27
James E.	153
James W.	27
Louise R.	201
Mary E.	27
Norman	26
Sallie E.	26
Thelma T.	153
Wallace West, Sr.	26
Wallace, Sr.	26
William J.	201
Gerndt	
Julia Johnston	181
Gibbs	
Bessie V.	29
Henry H.	29
Gibson	
Bessie George	27
Edward C.	27
George Taylor	229
Harriet T. Hutchison	95
Infant of E.C. & B.C.	27
James Wallace, Dr.	62
Mary R.	168
Milton R.	168
Robert William	168
Taylor William, III	68
Gilbertz	
Lois Walker	190
Gill	
Charles Henry	51
Charles Lee	19
Charles W.	51
Cora B.	20
Emma F.	19
Essie May	19
George R., 3rd	19
George W.	19
George W., Jr.	20
Joseph W.	191
Luther W.	19
Margaret E.	191
Pearl Gertrude, Mrs.	51
Vava Reed	52
Violet	69
Gillespie	
Patricia Tavenner, Mrs.	196
Gilley	
Charles M.	53
Mamme R.	53
Gilliland	
Susan L. Helmke, Mrs.	215
Gillum	
Raymond	221
Ginn	
Joff C.	91
Joffrion M., Mrs.	91
Girard	

Justine	102	Pearl Kephart	101
Glasscock		Robert	141
Elizabeth	134	Robert Edward Lee, Jr.	141
Godbold		Robert H.	vi
Edwin Joslyn	21	Roy Preston	101
Mary D.	21	Sally Josephine	116
Mary H.	21	William H.	vi
Godfrey		William M.	116
Arthur M.	140	Green	
Arthur Morton	140	Child	105
Mary B.	140	Greene	
Goetz		Alice, Mrs.	29
Peter Y.	117	Frank I.	29
Goff		Inez E., Mrs.	205
Eugene Douglas	142	Inez Hope	205
Gooden		Mary Alice	29
Floyd L., III	129	Stanley T.	205
Goodhart		Greenfield	
Winfred Lee, Mrs.	23	Marianne S.	206
Gordon		Nancy K.	107
Child of Mr.	17	Norman D.	106
Gore		Greenwade	
Coleman C.	146	Charles E.	1
John Coleman	146	Victoria Belle	1
Lucy Jackson	146	Virginia Anna	1
Gowans		William T.	130
Wilma Dianne	208	Greenway	
Graham		Child	1
Charles M., Sr.	142	Gregg	
Kathleen A.	142	George	18
Two Baby Boys	170	Grehan	
Grammer		Joseph I.	194
Elizabeth	161	Margaret W.	194
Frederick Louis	161	Grey	
Harriet McK.	161	Francis	188
Granger		Martha L.	188
M. Hawthorne, III, MD	203	Mildred Lee	93
Grant		Shirley P., Sr.	188
Jack Ellis	143	Thomas Bedford	223
Sarah W., Mrs.	202	Welby	93
Walter Enders	202	Grimes	
Graves		Calvin C.	118
Thomas J.	203	John Robert	138
Gray		Lena L.	139
Anna Belle, Mrs.	46	Mary Ellen	131
Dexter C.	116	Nettie	78
Geo. T.	46	Percy R.	78
Marie R.	116	Raymond E.	74
Maude B.	63	Ruth S.	148

Samuel Houston, Jr.	148		Helen Drinkwater	209
Towney R., Sr.	131		Horace Manson	208
Grimsley			Hamilton	
Evelyn B. (Dorothy)	126		Charles W.	198
George H. (Tex)	126		David Wayne	177
George H., Jr.	126		Lillian M.	198
Groff			Louise A.	177
Reginald C.	120		William E.	177
Groot			William Hall	177
Gertrude W.	55		Hammat	
Grubbs			Edward	vi
Annie Carson	185		Hammer	
Betty J. (Bonnie)	117		Michael Lynn	75
Gualtieri			Hammerly	
Thomas, Dr.	112		Adelaide Jessie	45
Gulick			Charles Decatur	45
Flora Gertrude Saffer, Mrs.	46		Elizabeth W.	45
Gladys	46		Esther Rhodes	187
John Allen	46		George P., Jr.	187
John Frank	46		George Preston	187
Myrtle Thompson	46		Jesse M.	45
Gum			Margaret J.	45
Dyer	158		Mary Lewis Murray	45
Gertie E., Mrs.	158		Nellie Blanch	45
Isaac Dyer	158		Ruth	45
Leroy Dyer	158		Hammes	
Mary P.	10		George K.	126
Pinckney L.	10		James C.	126
Gunn			Hancock	
Pauline Willson	142		Robert Franklin	53
Gunnells			Hanes	
Judith Ann	52		John H.	100
Judith H.	52		Mary Georgia	100
			Hanger	
			Carrie E.	162
—H—			Carrie E. Lowenbach	162
			John T.	162
Hagenbuch			Hannahs	
Grace O.	93		Kimberly Beth	216
Roy Phinis	93		Hanson	
Hagins			Harry H.	224
Almeda Jane, Mrs.	44		Harding	
Daniel Floyd	44		Arthur C., Sr.	31
Hall			Charlotte Ellen	31
Ann T.	94		Donald O., Pvt.	55
Child	18		Dorothy Lee	80
Clarence William	115		Edna C.	55
Katryna Anne	91		Eleanora Gray	31
Wilbur C.	vi		Emma Lee	168
Hallett				

Ernest T.	178
Infant of Mr. William	55
Leslie	55
Paul Palmer	178
Pauline Ethel	178
Russell B.	80
Victor Buford	168
William	55
William Walter Kenneth	55
Hardy	
Adolphus L.	70
Alvarado	25
Beulah Belle, Mrs.	70
Clarence E.	130
Earl W.	40
Hattie Jane, Mrs.	25
Helen J.	80
Lena P., Mrs.	131
Leonard Gray	25
Lucenda May	40
Mildred May	70
Robert	1
Roy Wilson	80
William H.	40
Winfred C.	70
Harkleroad	
Peggy A.	80
Harkness	
Anna Aylell Rust	192
Norris William, Rev.	192
Harman	
Elizabeth S.	111
Harmon	
Roger William	111
Harper	
Janet Virginia	186
Leon C.	186
Mary Ellen	33
Mattie May	108
R.E.	21
Robert Edwin	33
Robert Lewis	179
Harr	
Shayne William K.	81
Harris	
Clinton H., Jr.	108
Clinton Henry, Sr.	108
Eliza V.	148
James F.	96
James S.	vi
Mary Elizabeth Ramsey	108
Mary G., Mrs.	224
Maude S., Mrs.	54
Milton A.	54
Milton E. Alonzo	54
Richard Lee	7
Robert M.	148
Sarah Margaret	7
William Hall, III	227
Harrison	
Alma L.	52
Baby	103
Charles F., Jr.	191
Charles Fauntleroy	191
Child	3
Edwin T., Jr.	189
Eugene	52
Frances Dora	189
Henry T.	vi
Herbert	3
Herbert Lester	3
Infant of Herbert	3
James E.	52
Janet F. Harrison	224
Jessie C.	213
Lelia W.	24
Lillie Lee	38
Mary Arthur Fendall	191
Mary B.	24
Mary E. Carter	3
Ollie E.	213
Sarah Powell	24
Shirley Arlene, Miss	52
Stirling Murray	191
Walter T.	38
William Burr, Maj.	24
Hart	
Anne Luckett Keys	80
Thomas Eugene	224
Harvey	
Edith Denham	211
Henry Halsted	210
John Lacey	147
Harvich	
Elizabeth A.	132
Hashemizadeh	
Rozit A.	114
Hass	

Delores C.	154	William C.	67
Loysciel V.	154	Hays	
Hatcher		Alice Ahalt	193
Naomi Pierce	113	Thomas Spencer	193
Thomas Joshua	113	Hazel	
Havener		Jean	29
John R.	137	Head	
Marion F.	137	George R.	vi
Hawes		Healey	
Bessie Lee	4	Elsie L.	218
Charles R.	4	Heckel	
Charles Ruebin	4	Helen	43
Ethel M.	66	Heffelfinger	
Harry O.	4	Melcinia Burbank	136
Irene Virginia	36	Heflin	
James Alexander	66	Charles Marshall, Sr.	212
James Elmer	4	Frances G.	211
Mary	4	Nellie Atwell	212
Mary E. Tavenner	69	William Alger	212
Mishia	4	William Carter	212
Pearl A.	4	Heline	
Hawkins		Masty L.	92
Arbie Harrison	105	Henderson	
Arville	111	Carroll E.	4
Emmett	105	Dorothy M.	4
Jesse Anthony (Tony)	120	Gladys Bell	81
Polly Belle	109	Mary Virginia	4
Virginia McCabe	229	Mrs. H. K.	4
Hawley		Henline	
Sean Patrick	123	Lorrie Ann	92
Hawthorn		Hensley	
Noah B.	86	Della M.	121
Hawthorne		Etta May	98
David E., Sr.	158	John W.	98
Dorothy I.	158	William O.	121
Hettie J. Grant, Mrs.	86	William O. (Billy)	121
James W.	86	Herczyk	
Katherine	148	Frank A., Jr.	122
Maria Parr	86	Herndon	
Mary Lucretia	86	Calvin	204
Hay		Carrie Lee	228
Henry Malcolm	86	Child	48
Hayes		Edgar J.	124
Daniel W.	92	Flossie McKimmey	198
William Claiborne	206	George W.	33
William R.	225	H.L. Payne, Mrs.	10
Haynes		Havard Burton	198
Aaron Michael	93	Helen A.	204
Bessie E.	67	**Jane**	227

Martha F.	33	Franklin Delano	59
Martha Gray	228	Martin Barbour, , Jr.	59
Mattie Perry, Mrs.	105	Martin Barbour, Dr.	59
Randolph	34	Mary Nelson Williams, Mrs.	59
Rebecca Sevilla	34	Higdon	
Richard T.	48	James L.	31
Robert Clay	92	Martha Alice	31
Robert Fred	107	Hilbert	
Shelby	34	Dorothy Rinda Coe	117
Vida L.	53	Philip Fox	117
William A.	204	Hill	
Herrell		Gene	151
Stanley D.	142	Theodore S.	151
Hershbach		Hillman	
Isabelle	35	Sidney Augustus	161
Hersperger		Hinckle	
Clare Louise	106	Franklin M.	127
Mary L.	106	Gloria Lee	127
Samuel Ahalt	106	Hindman	
Samuel Peerce	105	Raymond Olsen	182
Heskett		Raymond Olsen, Jr.	182
Carrie Lee	21	Rebecca Smale	182
George W.	66	Hinkle	
Grace M.	133	Dirk Handley	112
Pearl Moxley	69	Hinman	
Raymond C.	21	Annie V.	145
Roger Nathanial	66	Stanley	145
Sarah Catherine	66	Hinton	
Theodore R., Sr.	133	Mary Esther W.	204
William H.	69	Hipkins	
Hessick		Brian Allen	191
Annie C.	16	Hissam	
Edward W.	16	Robert B.	218
John E.	16	Hitt	
Hibbs		Aldridge Y.	123
Charles B.	151	Flossie L.	123
Charles H.	151	Hodson	
Elsie G.	151	Walter D.	109
Hickam		Hoffman	
Addie R.	41	John	vi
George F.	41	Hogan	
George Fred	41	Triplets of	224
Hickman		Holandsworth	
Donald L.	66	Philip James	34
Frances B.	70	Holcomb	
George William	66	Thelma	210
Lester A.	70	Holcombe	
Rachel B.	66	Elizabeth Bratney, Mrs.	208
Hiden		Holden	

Lisa M.	221
Ronald Glenn	65
Holland	
Baby Girl	103
Walter Scott	121
Hollandsworth	
Ceveria Ross	34
Daisy Gertrude	34
Kirby Winston	34
Holliday	
Arthur Henry	167
Baby Girl	2
Donald F.	133
Doris Lee	2
Edward M.	167
Mary S. Molly, Mrs.	167
Pearl E.	167
Hollidge	
Irving Weed	195
Lucy B.	195
Raymond W.	195
Holsinger	
Odessie M.	180
Holton	
Mary B.	43
Holtz	
John	174
Holtzclaw	
Arthur Lloyd	190
Austin M.	190
Carolyn Lee	190
Honicon	
Claude	133
Ethel G.	133
Hood	
Moselle R.	43
Hooper	
Thomas Hillman	147
Hooppaw	
Bessie	102
Cadle	102
Helene	102
Hope	
Alice Marjorie B.	178
Charles R., Sr.	173
Charles Randolph, Jr.	173
Cora May	5
Ethel Ryan	201
Forrest William (Billy)	5
John A.	5
John Alexander	5
John C.	200
Lillie Virginia	200
Margaret L.	5
Mary Pleasant	5
Miriam L. Lampe	173
Nora Howser	173
Paul H.	5
Ronald A.	178
Hopkins	
Claude H.	118
Elizabeth Hopper	164
Emma Skipwith	48
John	48
John C., III	46
John Guthrie	48
Marcus Clarence	51
Mary E. Howard	161
Mary Enos	48
Nancy Jane S.	118
Horn	
Rebecca Louise	83
Horsman	
James M.	214
Hoskinson	
Irwin G.	23
Hottel	
Rest Hipe	19
Hottle	
M. J., Mrs.	19
Hough	
Arthur Lee	96
Arthur S.	96
Bessie Pearl	96
Cora Virginia	96
Elbert	128
Elbert Eugene	221
Elizabeth C., Mrs.	128
George	8
George W.	5
J.F.	5
Joanna T.	5
Joe	5
John Wesley	96
Levin W.S.	vi
Louise	54
Louise V., Mrs.	106
Mary	5

Mary E.	5	Frank S.	131
Mary V. B.	96	Helen A.	188
Owen L.	120	Irene H.	14
Phoebe	8	James Frederick	197
Raymond L.	106	John S.	131
Sylvia C.	120	Lloyd M.	14
Houghton		Marshall C. Bush	14
Worthington Bowie	76	Maude May	197
Houpt		Prissilla G., Miss	14
George A.	8	R. Tweed	188
Henry J.	8	Richard	197
Sallie Ellen	8	William Henry	14
Sarah Louise	8	Hucks	
Susannah Wingert	8	Chet B.	206
Houston		Huffman	
Patricia	81	William Gordon	223
Howard		Huger	
Annie Hughart, Mrs.	28	Louise W.	83
Blaine L.	67	Hughes	
Carroll H.	159	George Robert	38
Child of J. F.	67	Hume	
Columbus Fletcher	67	Elsie Payne, Mrs.	172
Dorothy Breeding	213	Gray Walton	172
Ethel O., Mrs.	67	Gray Walton, III	172
Ethel V.	159	Gray Walton, Jr.	172
Herbert H., Sr., Dr.	161	Lillian Lawson	172
James A.	67	Hummer	
Josephine Page	28	Baby	102
Lillian M.	161	Humphreys	
M.W., Mrs.	27	George E.	183
Margaret Ellen	161	Huntley	
Oden Hughart	28	Harry H.	113
Ralph V.	67	Mabel F.	113
Sara Wharton	28	Hurst	
Sarah Page	28	Grace E.	14
Thomas Burke	213	Henry D.	14
William Alanson, Maj.	28	John Harry	14
William Spencer	27	Samuel Gibson	57
Howell		Tacie, Mrs.	57
Ethel	134	William (Bill) G.	14
Eugene D.	15	Hutchinson	
J. Howard	15	Elizabeth Howard	142
Kenneth J.	217	Lawrence S., Jr.	142
Paulette Marie	216	Hutchison	
Rosa Florence	15	Ada Leith	65
Howser		Alfred Owens	175
Cora Carena	14	Baby	142
Earl Vandon	52	Baby Girl	95
Ethel Virginia	131	Benjamin Barbour	48

Eligah C.	95
Elizabeth Howser	146
Eva Matthews, Mrs.	48
Frances Elizabeth	145
Gordon M.	48
Granville Randolph	146
Helen Megeath	174
James W.	163
James Walter	145
John S.	95
Lawrence S., Sr.	146
Leila Rankin	95
Lucile	65
Marion G.	64
Mary Ellen	145
Nell Cabell	146
Oscar C.	65
Thomas B.	174
William R.	95

Hutt
Marjorie Wood	90

Hutton
Genevieve Ann	202

Hyatt
David Wayne	159
Lori Jean	159

—I—

Ingalls
Rose Belknap	138

Irwin
Mary K.	102
Richard W., Jr.	101
Richard W., Sr.	101
Samuel	126

Isaacs
George E., Col.	203
Mary Lane	203

Isenberg
Helen Goldstrohm	151
Wilbur L., Sr.	151

Ish
Anna Goode	94
Samuel Thornton	94

—J—

Jackson
Albert G.	2
Asa	vi
Benjamin F. (Bennie)	200
Bernard W.	2
Bettie Ann	1
Daisy L.	65
Emma Jane Porter	2
Florence Keys	3
Harold Maurice, Dr.	41
Herbert	2
Herbert Griffith	2
Hildur E.	56
James	56
James H.	56
James Thomas, Dr.	112
Lauretta U.	56
Lilly Mae	200
Louise S., Mrs.	41
Mable J.	50
Maurice Stanley	41
Mrs. E.P.	2
Nellie B.	225
Patricia	114
Powell C.	56
Randolph M.	65
Robert Lee	2
Robert W.	120
Thomas Franklin	129
Victor Nelson	50
Wilber D.	77
William S.	92
William Stanley	41

Jacobs
Leonard W.	177
Lucy A.	18

Jaghab
Jad	222

Jamarik
Blair Dissette, Mrs.	80

James
Annie Elizabeth	51
Arthur A.	41
Arthur D.	50
Berkeley Lee	50
Child	2, 79
Clara Jane	218
Clarence B., Sr.	79
Cora Lee	50
Dora Bell Gray	46

Edna C.	41	Orra Lee	165
Elmer E., Sr.	79	Pearl Shreve	173
Emma Cecelia	42	Rebecca Lew	164
Helen L.	79	Roger T.	216
Herbert H.	50	Ruby A.	101
Herbert Harwood	50	Ruby T.	173
Jessie E. Jackson, Mrs.	79	Sally D.	216
John Collins	226	Scott B.	173
Lola Frances	2	William Herndon	165
Margaret Ann Moffett	226	William Smith	165
Minor Linwood	218	Jennings	
Nettie Mae	79	Allean Catherine	53
Nettie Rinker	79	Hattie E.	130
Oscar C.	79	Helen C.	204
Richard L.	218	James B.	130
Sue Ella	210	Sterling	203
William B.	50	Jerry	
William Carlyle	42	Cynthia	99
William V.	2	Jessee	
Jarmanes		Grover Roy	67
James William	52	Margurette Rebecca Flippo	182
Jarmans		Willie Vera, Mrs.	67
Annie Belle, Mrs.	36	Jewell	
Etta M.	53	Alfred H.	121
John Louis	53	Fannie, Mrs.	35
Jarmens		Genevieve	121
Infant of Robert	17	Gilbert Hunter	135
Robert S.	221	Henry C.	105
Jenkins		James Randolph	135
Alma	229	Janet Virginia	134
Arthur S.	173	Lila Virginia, Mrs.	105
Bessie Frances	97	Lina Lillian	135
Charles H.	147	Myron R.	134
Clinton Columbus	164	Raymond A.	130
Dorothy S.	104	Rosabell G.	135
Edith V.	147	Stanley Paul	218
Fannie Mae L.	173	Walter L.	35
Gene Montgomery	165	Jobe	
Harry C.	100	Anne E. McQuade	41
Harry M.	173	Johnson	
Hubert C.	103	Alexander R.	28
Inez Ashby Howser	164	Bedford Lee	175
Lester A.	208	Blanche	40
Lewis Edgar	164	Catherine L.	51
Madelaine Morgan, Mrs.	201	Deborah J.	175
Mary Anne	173	Dora K.	95
Michael Allen	148	Elmer Clifton	203
Michelle Lee	148	Ernest	16
Nellie L.	216	Esker Carl	175

Floyd L.	221	Hugh B.	38
Gertrude E.	227	Hugh Bell	38
Howard T.	95	James Edgar	79
James Chott	175	Jay Stewart	201
James Hubert	185	Jeffrey Alan	219
James M.	175	Kate, Mrs.	77
Jane Heath	185	M.L.	38
Jeannette Harding	185	Mary	102
John W.	175	Pauline W.	198
Julian Clark	107	Samuel Powell	201
Lena I.	28	Jordan	
Lloyd Goode	217	Bobby	126
Louise Mitchell	60	Harry, Sr.	37
Louise R.	221	Mary Elizabeth	37
Mac C.	51	Raymond M.	37
Mary Elizabeth	175	Thomas	37
Mary Mills	203	Jorman	
Mildred H.	189	John	17
Nicholas	189	Judd	
Reed	167	Ada M.	127
Richard Hubert	185	John R.	127
Robert E., Jr.	103		
Sonny Julian Clark	111	**—K—**	
Thomas Walter	68		
Vivian H.	107	Kadic	
Wanda	175	Fanny Laycock	218
William H.	40	Karl	218
William Henry, Jr.	40	Kane	
Wilton C.	95	Mable	228
Johnston		Kappa	
Alice Rebecca	30	Child	36
Beulah Neel	30	Kasza	
Bruce F.	145	Audrey	221
Infant of John A.	30	Kaufman	
Infant of John Allen & H.M.	30	Gilbert O. (Pete)	81
Infant of Samuel J. & B.N.	30	Kearns	
Madge W.	145	Betty Anne	17
Samuel J.	30	Keatts	
Stephen Michael Gooding	219	Dorothy	49
Stuart James	30	Durward S.	49
Jones		Keene	
Carroll T.	111	Janet J.	206
Cary C.	105	Kehr	
Della E.	111	Barbara N.	198
Dorothy H.	14	David B.	198
Elizabeth Frances, Mrs.	105	George B., Jr.	153
Emma Marie	38	Margaret L.	153
Frances Lee	38	Kelly	
Gary J.	81	Helen Veronica	129

William A., Jr.	129	Janet H., Mrs.	119
Kenman		Lee Thomas	143
Clifford L.	1	Lucille Lawson, Mrs.	93
Kennedy		Ludwell Alex.	3
Virginia R.	211	Randolph A., Sr.	119
Kent		Raymond	88
Nellie Alberta	124	Roland O.	205
Thomas Lewis	124	Rudolph F.	143
Kephart		Sarah E.	109
Clayton O.	227	Thomas L.	143
Elizabeth Ashley	81	Thomas Richard	109
John William	95	Viola May	88
Kern		Keys	
Child	17	Ella M. Finch	15
Mabel V.	17	Ray Osburne	35
Kerns		Khan	
Annabell	82	Forida	216
Betty	17	Kidwell	
Cecil J.	82	Baby Boy	187
Harry G.	81	Catherine Gill	187
James R., Jr.	82	James Israel	187
James Richard	82	Katie Ellen Arnette	187
John K.	20	Myrtle A.	182
John William	67	Paul Martin	187
Leona Mae	82	Kiley	
Lewis H., Jr.	55	Florence Elizabeth Marcus	112
Lillie Marshall	55	Killinger	
Robert J.	55	Virginia Charon	56
Sara Louise	67	Kimball	
Sarah I.	20	Lois Annette	216
Walter H.	55	Kimes	
William Henry	55	Carl Austin	12
Kerr		E. Harry	12
Floyd Nathaniel	64	Harry Egbert	12
Lillian Rhodes	64	Infant	12
Margaret Katharine	64	Lillie Jane, Mrs.	12
Kerwin		Olaf Douglas	12
Daniel F.	88	Ruth S.	12
Susan Bertha, Mrs.	88	Kincaid	
Kestner		Infant of J. F.	148
Charlie M.	206	John Franklin	148
Mary J.	206	John Franklin, Jr., MD	148
Ketchum		Nan Lin Anderson, Mrs.	148
James S.	199	King	
Keyes		Andrew	123
Ann U.	80	Wesley A.	123
Charlotte Ann	3	Kinser	
Elizabeth M. (Betty)	119	Lester Neal	99
James Howard	15	Ollie Goode	99

Kirby
   Anna May 44
   Clifton Register 144
   Fanny Lee Dyke 44
   Gettie S. 61
   Harrison Gibson 44
   Irene Myers 44
   Jennie Strother, Mrs. 44
   Luther D., Jr. 152
   Luther Delbert 44
   Paxton Marshall 44
   Woodrow Wilson 44
Kirk
   Linda 69
Kirkpatrick
   Annie E. 169
   Herbert N. 169
   Herbert Nelson, Jr. 169
   J. Emory 227
   James E. 54
   Mary E. 227
   Maude Elizabeth B. 214
Kitchen
   Rosa B., Mrs. 9
   Sarah Ellen 78
Kitts
   A. Eugene 97
   Andrew Clinton 96
   Carrie L. Moore 110
   Eva Bell, Mrs. 96
   George W. 35
   Ira Cecil 97
   John David 96
   Joseph I. 97
   Laura E. 109
   Lucy D. 97
   Walter Henry 109
   William T. 110
Kitzmiller
   Melanie Jean 176
Kline
   Albert M. 19
   Albert M., Jr. 19
   Gerald F., Jr. 211
   Gibson H. 19
   H. Wendell 63
   Lois Clemens 63
Klotz
   Robert G., Capt. 10

Klyn
   Dorothy Darroch 131
   Richard John 131
Knox
   Thomas P. vi
Kohlhoss
   Matthew L., Sr. 211
Kraebel
   Simon J. 216
Kyle
   Anna P. 55
   David Nathionale 55

—L—

Lacey
   Quintin H. 152
Lacy
   Harry 28
Lambert
   Emory B.W. 82
   Lourie F. 82
   William Perry 82
Lane
   Linda Kay 68
Langston
   Carl W. 92
Lanham
   Curtis 95
   Donald W. (Donnie) 89
   Irene, Mrs. 95
   Robert Kilgour 198
Larson
   Donald F. 135
Lasdins
   Martins 105
Laughlin
   Bessie Merritt, Mrs. 156
   John Page 156
Lawrence
   Mary Chase 117
Laws
   Clyde 92
Lawson
   Annie Ward, Mrs. 89
   Christopher Zane 88
   Clarence J. 89
   Elise Gray Hume 172
   Elizabeth Dora 189

Harry West (Buck)	89	Bessie Johnson	175
John William	89	Clifton E., Sr.	198
Jones Moore	172	Dorothy J.	175
Ora Belle	89	Gillis E.	175
Zane G.	88	Hubert L.	215
Lay		James	175
Irene Virginia (Moore)	143	Nancy Arlene J.	175
Lee		Lemert	
Bessie Keyes	15	Lee Roy	82
Julian R.	15	Lemmon	
Julian R., Mrs.	15	David	63
Kenneth I.	115	Mary M.	63
Larry Franklin	100	Leonard	
Pamela Sue	103	Montgomery G.	83
Peggy A.	214	Nina	83
Peggy Ann Leith	222	Leone	
Peggy D.	98	Alfred D.	211
Ronnie Allen	214, 222	Evelyn	211
Leef		LeRoy	
Alice H.	216	Mary M.	71
William H.	216	Leslie	
Leete		John Harrison (Harry)	86
Charles H.	112	Lewis	
Legard		Sarah Briggs	191
Louise H.	204	Light	
Legg		James B.	154
Dixie Bertha	180	Lightfoot	
Henry Murt	180	Bertha Helen Quilliam	84
John W.	106	Philip Howell, Sr.	84
Loretta V.	106	Lindquist	
Legge		Clarence A.R.	187
Carroll D.	213	James Peter	187
Lula Ellen	106	Zoe Roblin E., Mrs.	187
Spitler A.	180	Lintner	
LeGrys		Dorthy Maynard	37
Frederick G.	120	Frederick Wilhelm	38
Leighton		Henrietta Stanley	37
Heyl (Jack)	78	J. Harris S.	37
Leissering		Jules R., Jr.	38
Frederick Karl	3	Julius Ross	37
Leith		Mary Stonestreet, Mrs.	37
Benjamin F.	52	Newell Vanmeter	37
Child Clifton	35	Roy B.	37
Child of James	36	Littig	
Edward	35	James Gittings	43
James N., Jr.	99	Lula Ashby	43
John Dennis	35	Littleton	
Maude Mae A.	52	Frank Campbell	62
LeMarr		Frank Campbell, Jr.	62

Henrietta Olive Trowbridge	62
Trowbridge	62
Livesay	
Milam Earl	185
Lockwood	
Rick Owen	103
Lofgren	
Helen C.	30
Lomax	
Anthony John	126
Christine Ann	126
Sydney Evans	127
Long	
Bessie D.	32
Fred & Joyce	81
Henry Bowen	178
I.S.	14
Isaac Adelbert	228
John M., Mrs.	31
John W.	32
Morgan Marie	81
Robert Joseph	31
Ruby Kerwin	32
Ruth C.	178
Teddy Lee	220
Lorenz	
Annie Sutphin	116
Loucks	
Nelson A.	76
Ruth Saffer	76
Loudermilk	
Alice R.	227
Love	
Josephine M., Mrs.	11
Nora H.	11
S.H., Mrs.	11
Samuel Henry	11
Loveless	
George Ward	157
Irene	157
Lowe	
Jessica Corrine	146
Mary E. Hall	228
Preston Hamilton	146
Shirley L.	121
Theron E. (Ted)	215
William Henry	22
Lowenbach	
Kate Casilear, Mrs.	30
Lowry	
Beatrice M. Cortez, Mrs.	138
Harold L.	138
Loy	
Carl A.	31
Della T.	184
Edgar Calvin	184
Geneva L.	188
Leighton W.	50
Lester L.	188
Mary R., Mrs.	31
Mollie V.	50
Rosa S. Belle	50
William H.	50
Luckett	
Stephen Lee	80
Ludlow	
Chevalier H.	109
Luebben	
Gerold Edward	124
Ingeborg Wiener	124
Lueck	
Elizabeth Hawthorne	86
Lund	
Einor G.	3
Kathryn E.	3
Lunsford	
Lydia L. Winks	88
Maphis F.	88
Nelly Jane	88
Theodore Ashton	126
Lusby	
Charles I.	167
Goldie Catherine	167
Lynch	
Mary Clemens	61
Mary J.	61
Lynn	
Bessie F.	153
Charles W.	133
Margaret M.	133
Robert F.	132
Wade Hampton	153
Lyon	
Charles Edward	85
Fanny Moncure Nelson	85
James William	85
Jo Ann Vestal	85
M. Constance Bentley	85

Moncure Nelson	85	Mang	
Robert Bentley	85	H. Fredrick	10
		Hazel Grimes	10
—M—		Manning	
		Florence Graham	9
Mabe		Florence Louise, Mrs.	9
Audrey E.	90	J.T.	9
Henry P.D.	90	James Forrest	9
Macdonald		Mabel	9
Alastair S.	171	Marguerite	9
Augusta Lea, Mrs.	171	Robert D.	9
Robert	171	Marcum	
Mackinnon		Agnes	112
George R.	225	Annie Middleton	79
Maclaine		Arthur H.	79
Justin William	93	Charles R.	79
Maddox		Hessie	112
Dorthey Schulke	15	Ida Hawkins	79
James L.	15	John	112
Lemuel	1	Katherine	154
Mary B.	1	Robert E.	112
Mary Lena	1	Ronnie Lee	84
Nathaniel W.	104	Roy Fred	117
West Mansfield	219	Samuel L.	117
Madigan		Marion	
James B.	123	Charlie W.	53
John Andrew	123	Markham	
Maffett		Raymond W.	225
Bertie F.	3	Markland	
C.H.	3	Leonard Charles, Sr.	80
Charles Harry	3	Marks	
Henry	3	Barry A.	114
Marcellus L.	4	Marr	
Raymond C.	4	Francis (Frank)	123
Raymond Henry C.	4	Helen Cockrill	123
Sarah E.	4	Marriott	
Maguire		Alexander D.	137
Lowell L.	215	Lillian L.	137
Mahoney		Nannie Lavinia S.	29
Bernard J.	144	Marshall	
Eileen Hogan	144	Alva R.	222
Mallicoat		James Scott	118
Rollie Jay	63	James W., Dr.	10
Mallon		John Monroe	182
Genevieve C.	226	Katharine S., Mrs.	10
Joseph F.	226	Katharine Tennent	140
Joseph F., III	226	Mervin A.	222
Malloy		Rachel P.	10
Patricia Ann Tillett Warner	133	Reginald Ernest	23

Roland S.	140
Susannah R.	182
Martin	
Allie, Mrs.	104
Billy, Jr.	221
Carol Sue	222
Child	109
George M.	155
Kathleen Armentrout	108
L. Kinard	108
Marie V.	155
Norita S., Mrs.	155
William H., II	155
Wm. H.	155
Martindale	
Justin E.	171
Mason	
Ellen Thomsen	209
Frank Earl	209
Margaret B.	140
Ruth Virginia	149
Mathers	
Alfred F.	87
Sarah Belle	87
Mathews	
Arthur Wesley	104
Gracie Carmen, Mrs.	104
Marietta S.	111
Matthew	
Walton	154
Walton Janney	154
Warren Wentworth	154
Matthews	
C.B. & Rose S.	48
Cecile Hutchison	48
Charles Balthrop	48
Margaret Elgin	47
Mauran	
Antoine J.	55
Retta Douglas, Mrs.	55
Maxcy	
Charles J.	110
Coleman Aaron	110
May	
Philip Ashlin	117
Mayer	
Franklin A.	89
Lois Howard	99
William Francis	89

Mays	
Bena Virginia Poling	67
Imogene James	41
Julian Reid	41
Virginia Bentley	208
McCabe	
Cora Havener	9
Dorothy Hodson McCabe	9
Ethel Gray, Miss	9
J. Randolph	9
John R.	9
William H.	9
McCafferty	
Charles Haylett	109
McCann	
Frances Titus	196
James Morgan	196
John William	71
Mary Louise	71
McCarthy	
Bessie Roberta	143
Charles Raymond	144
Peggy	143
McCaughey	
William I.H.	190
McClellan	
Lester A.	128
McCool	
Kenneth D.	127
McCord	
Hilda O.	132
Lloyd	132
McCracken	
Anne Walker	114
James Terrence, Sr.	114
McDavid	
Elizabeth C.	67
McDonald	
Benjamin P.	217
John Wayne	209
William Joseph	202
William Joseph, Jr.	202
McDonough	
Clifton H.	183
Margaret T.	183
McFarland	
Ella Lee, Mrs.	167
Eppa Lee	167
Harry	104

McGaha		McWilliams	
Janie L.	94	Hazel Margaret	164
Stanley F.	94	Herbert James	100
McGavack		Hubert F.	207
A. Llewellyn	62	John Robert	164
Adeline Virginia, Mrs.	63	Mary E.	207
Andrew L.	62	Mechling	
McGhee		Virginia Wilkerson	211
Mary M.	103	Megeath	
McGowen		Alfred Leith	130
Ronald Steven	198	Mary Hardesty	130
McGrady		Melton	
Becky Ann	182	James Mason	152
McIlvain		Pearl Hughes, Mrs.	152
Flavia Baker	82	Mercer	
McIntosh		Della J.	227
Bruce	8	John D.	120
Infant son of James	8	John Nathaniel	120
Irene Bridges	8	Joseph E.	55
James Logan	8	Tabitha C.	91
James Logan, Jr.	8	Thomas E.	54
McKimmey		Merchant	
Birtrand Willard	197	Charles Edward	124
Charles B.	197	Harry W.	217
Lela T.	197	Harry William	217
Raymond F.	126	Mersinger	
McKinney		Marjorie M.	119
Raymond F.	126	Metzger	
McKinnon		Clare Briggs	191
Samantha Jo	224	Fanny Dawson	191
McLeod		Mary Tyson	191
Mary Ella	82	William (Billy)	191
McMorran		William Albert	191
Jennifer E.	112	William Baylor	191
McNealea		Michelet	
Earl E.	229	Karl Haus	145
McNealy		Michell	
Estella Geneva, Mrs.	104	Gladys Mildred	215
Howard H.	104	Middleton	
Maurice Bill	104	Baby Lester	98
McNey		Milbourne	
Owen Lewis	202	Baby	91
McPherson		Milburn	
Arthur H.	22	Milton B.	121
Earl Franklin	32	Miles	
Elmore Lee	22	Anna	151
Ida C.	22	Thomas D.	21
John W.	32	Miller	
Mary E.	32	Child	18

Dennis P.	154	Augustus Courtney, Jr.	153
Elizabeth K.	204	Ella J.	189
Franklin Perry	123	F.F.	189
Jean Coleman	56	Florence A.	3
Marian V.	168	George T.	153
William Burton	204	Harvey Hartgrove	189
Millian		Janie S. Tavenner	42
Santiago E.	222	Joseph E.	3
Mills		Joseph L.	3
Alice Tyler	129	Margaret C.	144
Margot H.	81	Margaret F.	189
Minard		Mary Lee	152
Russell L.	114	Mrs. Jos.	3
Miner		Mrs. Ruby G.	3
John W.	46	Roger I.	144
Minick		Roger P.	144
Alice R., Mrs.	127	William W.	42
John W.	127	Moland	
Minor		Charles Henry	73
Bernard	110	Edna E.	73
Bernard L.	73	Moler	
Infant of Jackson	46	Forrest G.	201
Jackson	46	Monaco	
John Brown	46	Joseph E., Sr.	122
Mary E., Mrs.	46	Montgomery	
Nellie W., Miss	46	George Jack	204
Rhua E., Mrs.	110	Mooney	
William T.	46	Eugenia F.	18
Miskell		Moore	
Lydia Maria	74	Anne J.	136
Mabel L.	74	Arthur L.	193
Winfield Scott	74	Baby	102
Mitchell		John W., Jr.	136
Annie M.	13	Laura B. Nichols	193
Eleanor R.	13	Lula F. Kitts	97
Harry	13	Scott, Mrs.	97
Henry	13	William Hunter	229
Llewellyn T.	13	Moran	
Rebecca J., Mrs.	60	Alice Bond Paxson	38
Moatz		Elbert M., Sr.	170
Wilma E.	132	Harmony Thomas	38
Mock		Herman F.	121
George William	18	James Sterling	170
Henry Russell	19	Joseph Richard	72
James H.	19	Lizzie E.	121
Lucy Lee Palmer	19	Nellie Bryant	170
Mary Elizabeth	19	Nora M.	72
Moffett		Sarah E.	72
Augustus Courtney	152	William Thomas	38

Morgan			Ruby M.	193
Child of James		109	Musgrave	
Moriarty			Bess D. Ridley	144
Thomas		127	George Harrison	144
Morris			Myer	
Catherine Elizabeth, Mrs.		47	Elizabeth Shreve	85
Ethel M.		47	Thomas Jacob	85
Grace		228	Myers	
John M.		46	Carrie L.	176
Mahlon		47	Charles Claude, Rev.	28
Margaret V.		53	Claggett O.	176
Rose Lee, Mrs.		46	Clara B.	162
Morrison			Daisey H.	28
George H.		192	Daisy M.	78
Moss			Daisy May	165
Frank Hazlett, Jr., Rev.		145	Douglas N., Mrs.	71
Moxley			Douglas Nelson	166
Bertha Newberry		82	Edward Bruce	165
Evelyn E.		48	Edward Bruce, Jr.	165
Margaret D.		49	Edwin C.	209
Mary Margaret		82	Elijah F.	201
Thomas Oden		49	Elmer C.	148
William T.		49	G. Shirley	201
Mullins			Georgia L.	168
Baby Girl		103	Grace Gum	162
Muncaster			Harry	78
John Edwin, Jr.		153	Helen Hess	209
Muncy			Ishmael Osborne	209
David Carton		125	James L.	68
Joann P.		125	Kate Lee	162
Maude Agnes		126	Leroy J.	162
Orville M.		126	Leslie Emerson	176
Munday			Mary Agnes Williams	28
Ernest L., Sr.		165	Nellie M.	176
Lula A., Mrs.		165	Pearl M.	201
Murawski			Robert C.	228
Rosemary C.		224	Ruby Lucille	69
Murphy			Victor Leon	167
James T.		61	Winifrede E.	166
Lester B.		61		
Mary Virginia		61	—N—	
Pamela Marie		121		
Patricia Ann Miller		121	Nalle	
Sarah Catherine, Mrs.		61	Bernard Franklin	181
Thaddeus H.		61	Leonora Preston	181
Muse			Neff	
Gentry Lawrence		193	Evelyn Frye	153
J. Lawrence		193	Neish	
Naomi M.		66	Devillo W.	152

Myrtle O.	152
Ness	
Percy John	109
Newcomb	
Charles S.	101
James W.	120
Vallie V.	101
Newlon	
Nannie Florence	176
W.R. & F.L.	176
Newman	
Mary Anne	130
Newton	
Archie R.	31
Bessie L.	195
Charles E., Jr.	136
Charles Edward	76
Charles M.	50
Clara Best, Mrs.	150
Della E.	30
Ethel B.	50
George I.	195
Harry Franklin	150
James Robert	150
Lester C.	195
Maggie B., Mrs.	76
Nora V.	195
Roy P.	76
Niccolls	
Samuel Robert	211
Nichols	
Baby	96
Dorothy Lillian, Mrs.	96
Edgar	1
Eugene E.	96
Hazel G.	96
James E., Sr.	96
Lillian May	96
Thurman H.	96
Thurman Henry, Jr.	96
Niedercorn	
Esmeralda G.	211
Nixon	
Lewis	156
Mary Doran	156
Naomi G.	73
Reginald Lee	73
Norfolk	
Bernard A.	116

Ira M.	116
Norman	
Anne R.	44
Lawrence L.	44
Mary Ely	44
Norris	
Beverly Marshall	140
Catherine Ann	171
Charles R.	39
Edward H. (Beans)	172
Edward Hammet	171
Elizabeth Newton	171
Ellen Gaines	172
Essie May Newton	171
Margaret E.	39
Mary F., Miss	171
Rata J.	39
Raymond Alan	140
William W.	39
Novatney	
Albert A.	215
Bertie T.	215
Noyes	
Catherine L.	138
Edmund, Maj.	138

—O—

O'Brien	
Ethel Adrain	212
William W.	212
O'Reilly	
Helen E.	97
Lorne	97
Ogburn	
Velvet C.	109
Oliver	
Frances E.	84
Joseph Nelson	84
William L.	84
Orr	
Mary Frances	140
Mary Page	64
Robert A., Dr.	140
William Clayton, Dr.	64
William Clayton, Jr.	64
Orrison	
Boxter Duncan	30
Cora Hazel	100

Edith Alma Tavenner	72	Nelson	95
Elmer Stanley	126	Passapae	
Frank Gordon, Sr.	125	Helen G.	227
Jeffrey Gordon	125	Patty	
Lynne Johnson	125	Pat C.	219
Robert Henry	72	Payette	
Robert Lee	109	Dorothy Crandall	136
T.L.	30	John Jay	136
Vernon L.	71	Richard C.	136
Virginia Rose	72	Robert C.	136
Ours		Payne	
Stephen Michael	180	Ewell J., Sr.	141
Overfelt		Forrest B., Sr.	58
Kristian Ann	92	Gibson S.	156
Owen		H. L., Mrs.	10
Garry Grant	129	Harry S.	153
William Garrett	129	Herman L.	10
Owens		Iva D., Mrs.	58
Clyde Delbert	61	Martha Ann	156
Thomas F.	90	Mary C.	153
		Mildred J., Mrs.	141
		Siddie Jane Kerrick	10
		Susan Rebecca	222

—P—

Painter		Peacock	
Azel A.	104	Arthur Raymond	41
Edna B.	31	Edgar	41
Maggie Myrtle	104	Lola M. Grubb	41
Robert S.	31	Mary Catherine	41
Palcic		Peacoe	
Barbar M.	210	Linda E.M.	222
Palmer		Pearce	
Elsie M.	21	Bertha	128
Harold E., Capt.	167	Claude	128
Louise L.	167	L.I.	168
Pangle		Pearson	
Stanley W., Sr.	205	Aubrey Linwood	169
Pardew		Carl L.	158
Gertrude Ball	217	Edith Royston (Minna)	169
Parker		Hattie L.	169
Leonard W.	118	John Carlton	16
Parsell		Joseph Samuel	169
Rhoda Loutta	214	Mary J.	158
William Dailey	214	Nannie B.	17
Parsons		Paul R.	169
Ella S. (Ethel Lula)	18	Peck	
James Z.	19	Elton L.	64
Partlow		Peebles	
Francis Elizabeth, Mrs.	95	James F., Sr.	153
Mary Ellen	83	Peer	

Floyd C.	224	Elizabeth Littlejohn	157	
Mark S.	218	Everett	167	
Pelasara		Frederick N.	210	
James Benton	221	Gary Wayne	219	
Peltonen		Geneva A.	141	
Robert Lee	122	John T.	155	
Pepin		Lonie John	132	
Joseph O.	143	Lucas Dallam	157	
Peppin		Lucy B. Gibson	210	
Child-Fred	105	Lucy Turman	167	
Perdue		Mary Sanderson, Mrs.	155	
Cary A.	223	Mazzie H.	34	
Kate L.	223	Nancy Musgrave	145	
Perfater		Penny Jean	202	
Rita Fox	100	Silas D.	141	
Perinis		Thomas Oxley	155	
Michael Phaethon	129	Philyaw		
Perry		Howard C.	226	
John William	24	Pierce		
Maud C.	24	James W.	186	
Peters		Joseph William	186	
Alma Estell	163	Raymond R.	186	
Cammie Louise	163	Pierpoint		
Carl Pack	139	Hugh Brown	184	
Charles W.	163	Piggott		
Jacob H.	87	Belle M.	48	
James Pack	139	Fenton L.	48	
James Walker, Sr.	163	John Burr, Dr.	48	
Lily Lorraine	40	Pine		
Mabel S.	40	Walter C.	217	
Sarah Alice	87	Pinner		
Petersen		Roy F.	116	
Imogene Colburn	118	Suzanner Rubel	116	
Joseph S., Jr.	118	Pirce		
Petrykanyn		Baby	102	
Patricia	227	Plaster		
Peyton		David Dixon	29	
Bartie C.	135	Helen Thompson	157	
Philips		James W.	29	
William Bryant, Jr.	34	Leiter Virginia	29	
Phillips		Marie F.	158	
Arnold	34	Sarah Marie	29	
Arnold G., Jr.	219	Tunis Henry	158	
Arnold I.	141	W. E.	28	
Avery James	34	William Emory	157	
Baby Boy	99	Polen		
Carrie Jane C.	155	Catherine	1	
Cecil Vernon	80	Collis Grant	200	
Child John M.	34	Edward P.	200	

George Robert	1		George Rutledge	95
Mary Frances, Mrs.	200		Leonora Johnston, Mrs.	181
Sarah E., Mrs.	200		Robert Lee	181
Poling			Proctor	
Laura Virginia	66		Cathrine F.	205
Virgil	66		Melissa	111
Poole			William	205
Carrie Bell	16		Promos	
James E.	16		Louis	118
Margaret Virginia	16		Provost	
Maurice	16		Elizabeth F.	115
Robert Burton	16		Pugh	
William Keith	16		Ann Hampton, Mrs.	84
Popkins			Marshall Braxton	83
Edwin W.	49		Pulliam	
George Washington, Rev.	49		Helen Jackson	56
Laura W. LeFever	49		Matthew	56
Ruth H.	49		Pumphrey	
Potter			Christopher Lawrence	184
John R.	198		Dorothy Barbara	184
Potterfield			James B.	103
June T.	196		John W., Sr.	183
Robert Lee, Jr.	196		Mary Herndon	184
Potters Field			Ruth Hannah	183
Remains	91			
Powell			—Q—	
Erma I.	11			
George Oden	11		Quackenbush	
Georgia Bell Allison (Nanny)	53		Donald	106
Grace Virginia (Peggy)	96		Leo	106
Herbert M.	228		Lucile H.	106
Marian T.	186		Quesenberry	
Maude M. Ellmore, Mrs.	11		Archie Lee	36
Nell M.	186		John H.	70
Nellie C.	228		John T.	134
Ruth Ellmore	11		Luvenia	70
Stanley H.	186		Mary Katherine	70
William	103		T.J.	70
William E., Sr.	53		William Scott	70
William H., Jr.	221		Quinn	
Powers			Jessie D.	228
Joseph A.	10		Quirk	
Lula Virginia	30		Rebecca P.	220
Vivienne Reinhart	10			
Prather			—R—	
Charles DeVault, Jr., Dr.	150			
Esther Barney	219		Racz	
Preston			Ernest David	94
Alice, Miss	95		Raflo	

Philip Brian	121
Rakes	
Cathrine M.	147
Edward S.	147
Ramsey	
Evie K., Mrs.	201
Robert N., Jr.	201
Raneri	
Carmelo	39
Sebastiana	39
Vincenzo	39
Rathrock	
William L.	19
Raush	
Emma, Mrs.	10
J.V.	8
Mary Emma H.	8
Rawlings	
Louise Perry	24
Raymond	
Earl A.	194
Reavis	
Steven Hampton	18
Redman	
Golden A.	20
Redmon	
George D.	51
Martha Ellen	51
Myrtle L.	51
Redmond	
Essie I. Slack	20
Reed	
Bertha B.	197
Charles Frank	192
Edna Mae, Mrs.	192
Francis J.	206
Geneva H., Mrs.	192
James Franklin	108
Milton C.	197
Stanley	192
Thomas Russell, Jr.	103
Reeder	
Jeremy Joseph	227
Rehker	
Ernest H.	1
Reisler	
Harold A.	92
Helen E.	92
Reno	
Donald Eugene, Sr.	178
Repass	
Gary Eugene	93
James B.	115
Joseph N.	93
Nannie R.	115
Raymond L.	17
Reynard	
Alma	1
Alma M.	90
Carl E.	1, 90
Carl, Jr.	1
Reynolds	
Debra Ann	222
Elizabeth T.	22
John H.	22
Mary Eidson	199
Rhea	
Frances Hooper Shelby	147
Rhodes	
Jane Wire	228
Richards	
Arget (Dick)	198
Barbara Jane Sergison	198
Ricketts	
Charles	219
Charles Alan	34
Riddle	
Catharine B.	112
Frances B., Mrs.	112
Morton, III	112
Rider	
Carol Herndon Leef	216
Ridgeway	
Dorothy E. Kearns Bullock	69
Robert N.	69
William B.	119
Willie Ann	120
Ridley	
Child of Robert B.	36
Rieley	
Ann Davies	129
Riley	
Elizabeth Brooks	133
John W.	106
Lowell Meeker, Col.	133
Mary E.	106
Rinker	
Betty Rose	195

Charles Theodore	114	Sally T.	138
Gibson F.	219	Samuel E.	74
Henry E.	195	Samuel E. & Elizabeth C.	74
Lawrence G.	35	Samuel H.	74
Lula Catherine P., Mrs.	84	Samuel Hamilton	75
Thomas S.	84	Willa Ashby	75
Ritenour		William Thomas Clagett	132
Harry Lucius	130	Roland	
Ritnour		Helen Eloise	225
Evenly O.	214	Rollins	
Robb		Alan Lee	222
Ambers	86	Clifford K.	72
Robert L. Bentley, Jr	85	Dorothy Steadman	4
Roberts		Esther Marshall	124
Grace Lee	32	Frederick W.	214
Larry W.	98	Ida Lucinda	7
Robertson		Kenneth Brady	149
Alice L.	12	Louis Charles	7
Carroll	12	Lucy, Mrs.	7
Eppa H.	12	Mary B.	149
Luther R.	12	Nellie V.	214
Margaret M., Mrs.	12	Vivian Ruth Smith, Mr.	124
Robey		William L.	202
Anna S., Mrs.	109	Rollison	
Clem D.	218	Clayton	13
Joseph Willard	108	Delbert	37
Nellie V.	218	Dinah Lee	37
Roland H.	219	Earl	88
Robinson		Edna L., Mrs.	99
Cathey Ellen	103	George C.	79
George Wendell, Jr.	229	George E.	174
Roderick		George W.	93
Amy C.	207	Jeannette Ann	37
William R.	207	Kenneth T.	174
Rodgers		Laurence Lee	13
Darrell E.	90	Lawrence E.	112
Rogers		Mattie B.	93
Anna Ferguson, Mrs.	132	Maude F.	13
Beulah Corbin	74	Maude K.	112
Child of	138	Mazie T.	174
Elizabeth Cochran	75	Nellie B.	37
Elizabeth Megeath, Miss	74	Neva M.	174
Howard Cochran	74	Rose Ella	88
Infant son	75	William H.	13
Jane Cochran	74	Rorrer	
Joseph Decatur, Dr.	74	Johnny C.	125
Lulu	74	Rose	
Richard A.	138	Annie Parsons	104
Ronald J.	206	John Franklin	104

Rosen		
C. Benton	4	
Ross		
John Anthony	179	
Marguerite Jenkins	179	
Rubel		
Gordon Richardson	117	
Marian Richardson	117	
Walter Louis	116	
Rush		
Berle Margaret	135	
Rusk		
Asa C., Jr.	69	
Edgar B.	155	
May Ernestine, Mrs.	155	
Roger Edgar	156	
Ruth Elizabeth, Mrs.	156	
Rusmiselle		
Lona Russell	155	
Russell		
Carroll E.	198	
Catherine Elizabeth, Mrs.	125	
Child	18	
Clifton Herbert	179	
Fannie M.	179	
Hilda Estella	52	
James Harrison	100	
James Michael	52	
Lester	52	
Linnie E.	100	
Mollie Compher	155	
Richard Lee, Sr.	125	
William Ellmore	180	
William O.	155	
Rust		
Armistead T.M.	159, 160, 161	
Elizabeth Watkins	160	
Ellsworth Marshall	161	
Eva Thompson	161	
Henry Bedinger	160	
Ida Lee	159, 160, 161	
Irene Hardy	197	
John C., Jr.	186	
Kemper Clay	197	
Margaret D.	160	
Mary E.L. Fleming	160	
Mary Hilton Coburn	160	
Myrtle Peacock	186	
S.M.	59	
Stirling Murray	159	
William Fitzhugh	160	
William Fitzhugh, Jr.	160	
Rutherford		
Bess C.	210	
Charles H.	213	
Child of William M.	79	
Joseph Edward	222	
Katherine R.	220	
Lawrence S.	115	
Lillie V.	213	
Rutter		
Mildred C.	98	
Sarah Elizabeth (Betty)	28	
William W., Sr.	98	
Ryan		
Grace Lucille	228	
Helen R.	228	
Henry Preston	149	
Millicent P.	149	
Odie Margaret	149	
Robert William	149	
Ryon		
Howard M., Sr.	57	
Lily Williams, Mrs.	110	

—S—

Saffer		
Caroline Porter, Mrs.	72	
Claude C.	72	
Claude Hunton	73	
Clinton Stuart	73	
Katherine (Katie) A. Jacobs	76	
Olive May Riticor	73	
Sadie A., Mrs.	163	
Walton Riticor	72	
William Clinton	162	
Sager		
Lawrence Kinsley	155	
Mary Phillips	155	
Sampsell		
C.T.	29	
Frank C.	29	
J. Nixon	29	
Maiza M., Mrs.	29	
Yulie M.	29	
Sampselle		
Frances R.	29	

Mary B.	29		Theodore A.	128
Sasser			Schwertner	
Peggy Anne	135		Esther Denham	211
Saunders			Herman	211
Annie Lee	65		Scott	
Charles Adron	126		Charles L.	36
D.L. & B.L.	139		Ella Keys	79
Golda C. Norris, Mrs.	47		George E., Sr.	20
Harry B.	216		Lester Aden	79
Infant	139		Margaret E.	121
Lewis Randolph	65		Milton L.	20
Louise B.	139		Robert	20
Margaret N.	139		William James	121
Mildred V.	216		Seale	
Rebecca E. Bell	127		Allie N.	115
Ruth E.	65		Charles H.	114
William Henry	47		Seaton	
Savopoulos			Bertha V.	120
Melvie H., Mrs.	135		Georgia Elizabeth	100
Steve	135		Joseph	35
William S.	135		Norman B.	100
Scarr			Robert Elmore	120
Harry Alan	211		Seccombe	
Schaub			Alfred Burdon	227
Carroll F.	147		Secrest	
Lilian H.	147		Larry Dale	103
Scheetz			Seekford	
John Freed	131		E. David, Jr.	129
Schmidt			Semones	
Arthur H.	107		Oden K.	158
Marie U.	107		Sensabaugh	
Schmith			Charles T.	153
Ellen May	70		Settle	
Schooley			Joseph M.	14
Audrey B.	183		Myrtle H.	15
Carl Henry	183		Sewell	
Francis B.	183		John T.	86
Schreiner			Susie B.	87
Mary Catherine	132		Shafer	
Schriver			F.W.	vi
Gloria A.	206		Timothy Michael	91
Schulke			Shaffer	
Ernest F., Sr.	16		Ruth Wilson Harrison	3
Ernest H., Jr.	15		Shawen	
Lena Jackson	16		Frances Smith	58
Schuller			Ryan Michael	223
Herbert D.	216		Sherwood	
Schulz			Clayton Benjamin	218
Helen Charlotte	128		Nannie Laycock	218

Shetter
  John W. 142
  Viola B. 142
Shiflett
  Daniel Lee 52
Shiring
  Anne Rea 229
Shorey
  Arthr Michael 211
Shreve
  Allen K., Sr. 212
Shry
  A. F. 27
  Alfred F. 27
  Andrew F. 27
  Anna Arlene, Mrs. 203
  Catherine V. 27
  Charles A. 26
  Edith Virginia 26
  Harry T. 26
  Harry Thornton 26
  J.W. 26
  James W. 27
  Judge Franklin 203
  Lillian Helen T. 26
  Marshall Franklin 203
  Priscilla E. 26
  Viola 27
  William Nelson 27
Shryock
  Charles Edward 98
  Christopher A. 61
  Irene Blanche 98
  Richard F. 61
  Samie E. 61
Shugars
  Annie Virginia, Mrs. 87
  Bertha J. 87
  Charles C. 131
  Charles Franklin 86
  Edward Preston, III 87
  Edward Preston, Jr. 87
  Edward, Sr. 87
  Lewis E. 87
  Linda K. 87
Simcox
  Eleanor A. 152
Simmons
  Elizabeth Flagg 91

  Margaret M. 21
  Martha 21
  William Perry 63
Simon
  Anna Mae 144
Simpson
  Deborah Ashley 225
  Eva R. 170
  Golena M. 206
  Howard Smoot 87
  J. Lupton 87
  John Blakely 170
  John Smith 87
  Larry D. 132
  Mary J. 87
  Michael Robey 215
  Verner Lee 120
Singleton
  Donna 154
Sisk
  Calvin C. 215
  Frances Lee 107
  Henry Lee 107
  Michael Allen 215
Skidmore
  Pactheia J. 36
Slack
  Annie Taylor 23
  Baby 20
  Clarence E. 20
Slaughter
  Homer H. 199
  Isma E. 199
Slaymaker
  Ada Fred 74
  Amos B. 74
Sloyan
  Amy Louise 111
Slusser
  Della Maude 168
  Samuel W. 168
Smallwood
  Baby Boy 170
  Harry 54
  Howard P. 54
  Mary L. 54
  Viola H. 170
Smerheim
  Fred 152

Smith		Frank Purcell, III	136
Anna Jett	39	Thelma J.	165
Annie Gregg	18	Snider	
Annie Ward	123	Elizabeth Ann Dawson	32
Baby	102	Ernest Glenwood, Sr.	32
Benjamin Harrison	39	M.F.	32
Daniel G.	vi	Marion Franklin	32
Dean S., Sr.	223	Snoots	
Douglas W.	217	Victor C.	27
Edward S.	47	Snyder	
Elizabeth Carter, Mrs.	47	Paul	126
Elizabeth Gore	146	Sobol	
Ella Hough	58	Hrefna	111
Ella P., Mrs.	18	Socks	
Ellen E.	vi	Herbert	225
Ernest W., Sr.	138	Soden	
Frances S.	39	Herman F.J.	35
Gladys M.	138	Solomon	
Gwendolyn E.	223	Bertha K.	56
John	128	C. Lester	56
John W.	39	Daisy M.	56
Joseph C.	19	E. Mason	194
Joseph D.	39	Emory Wilson	194
Joseph Lee	123	Fannie S.	56
Larry Randolph	91	John Edwin	56
Leah Faith	224	Linda Marie	194
Leah Michelle	102	M.M., Mrs.	66
Lemuel Perry	58	Matthew M.	56
Leon	182	Nancy L.	194
Linwood J.	11	Ollie Mae, Miss	56
Mabel Rumley	146	Stephen Lester	194
Margaret H.	223	William M.	56
Marvin F.	114	Sommers	
Mary B.	138	Alice McC.	108
Mildred K.	183	Harry S.	108
Myrtle	11	Southerland	
Nannie C.	34	Marjorie Louise	109
Paul Edward, Sr.	91	Sowers	
Philip Clark	11	Annie Catherine Adrain, Mrs.	13
Rhonda Joy	128	Beulah F.	12
Robert Rumley	146	Harriett Ashton Eskridge	12
Velora	142	J.E.	182
Walter Gibson	123	James Egbert	182
William B.	84	Kay E.	182
Smoot		Lavalette O'Darr	12
Betty Chamblin, Mrs.	136	Philip D.	13
Florence Anne	165	Robert J.	12
Frank P.	165	Robert L.	12
Frank P., Jr.	136	Roger O.	23

Spann			Steadman	
Katie E.	127		Dixie D.	148
Spargo			Donald C.	143
Harold Wesley	190		James	vi
Sparrow			Robert Graham	148
Leonard Kip	162		Stehle	
Mary E. Williams	162		A.A.	63
William Edward, Jr.	162		Jessie C.	64
Spelman			Richard Carson	64
Ellen B.	138		Stevens	
Spence			Leona M.	227
Ethel Altie	130		Luzenia Adeline Randolph	147
Malachi G.	225		Stewart	
Robert W.	130		Bessie Wyncoop, Mrs.	34
Spinks			Chas. Walter	35
Berkley C.	68		Esther Perry	132
Edna V.	68		Florence Miriam	35
John Daniel	50		Garnet G.	19
Lena L.	17		Gertrude Leach Cooley	34
Nancy Catherine, Mrs.	50		Harvey J.	34
William H.	17		Helen G.	37
Spitler			Mattie Benton	150
J. Quinter	228		Paul	37
Ruth W.	228		Willard E.	150
Spradley			Wilmer W.	37
Eugene Iris	6		Stickle	
Martha Evelyn	6		George Robert	1
Sprague			Virginia L.	1
Frances Fuller	195		Stillions	
Spring			Baby Boy	102
Carroll W.	154		Stocks	
Helen R.	154		Clara Cooper	33
Ralph T.	220		Helen M.	33
Springs			Infant daughter of R.W.&	
Claude Lee	54		Helen	33
Spurloch			John Preston	199
Ray	221		Mary E., Mrs.	33
Stanley J.	213		Richard Junior	199
Spurlock			Richard W.	33
Bessie Wilder	213		Stokes	
Elmo	213		William Joseph	223
Morgan Green	19		Storke	
Raymond	222		Mary Fletcher	25
Stallings			Stowers	
Charles A.	107		Doak Clinton	157
Ethel S.	107		Ella Jane	157
Stavrakas			Henry Clinton	157
George A.	54		Hiram R.	84
Ruth Hannah C.	54		Lena May	84

Roy C.	151	Everett W.	115
Terry Franklin	157	Harry Luther	93
Theresa R. Kirkpatrick	157	James H. (Dock)	185
William S.	157	Jesse W.	116
William Vance	84	Joshua Mintron	183
Strawbridge		K.G. & C.T.	17
Elizabeth	64	Kathleen G.	207
Etta Wharton, Mrs.	64	Lincoln V.	185
James Bosler	64	Mabel C.	18
Stream		Margaret R.	183
Annie R.	204	Marvin M.	183
Beulah M.	13	Maudie A.	185
Charles Frank	14	Nannie M.	93
Clark E.	204	Peggy Ann	18
James William	13	Phillie C.	183
Jessie F.	14	Roy Arnold	115
Paul Clifton	13	Steven A.	178
Strickler		Willie	183
Minnie A.	89	Sutton	
Stuart		Charles B., Rev.	73
Jessica Anne	92	Iola Estelle, Mrs.	73
Stub		Swank	
Elizabeth V.	138	Robert Edward	198
Ione Ingalls	138	Swart	
Stunkle		Benjamin F.	125
Bessie S.	124	Benjamin Franklin	78
Edgar	124	Cora Edna, Mrs.	78
Sturgill		Fannie Bell, Mrs.	60
Stephenson	102	James M.	60
Suddith		Mary J. Smith	60
George W.	17	Oliver Lee	97
Sudduth		Robert W.	60
Effie V.	17	Sweeney	
Suits		Lorna S.	120
Alice	172	Thomas B.	120
Kenneth E.	216	Sydnor	
Sukler		Charles W.	195
Baby	98	Velma W.	195
Sun		Symington	
Huai Chin, Dr.	153	Diedre Huntington, Miss	135
Sutler		James Huntington	135
Sharon Arleen	203	Powers	135
Sutphin		Symonds	
Bolden D	18	Robert	58
Clifford D.	17		
Clinton Moore	183	—T—	
Cora Lee	183		
Dorothy B.	116	Talbot	
Elijah T.	93	Charlotte Mosley	33

Helen J.	33		Eugenia C.	32
John Leland	33		Eugenia Cullimore, Mrs.	192
Talmadge			Eva Belle	100
Barbara Crooker	127		George W.	94
Tavenner			Madeline Compher	192
Benjamin E.	42		Michel David	216
Charles Welby	69		Samuel E.	100
Cloyd T.	196		Verna A.	94
Doris Ann	80		William Compher	192
Hazel A.	80		William T.	192
Henry Ashton	187		Thompson	
James Eden	42		Alex W.	22
James H. (Jimmy)	80		Annie U.	174
John C.	71		Arthur J.	151
John H.	16		Charles W., Sr.	39
John W.	42		Emily Rivers	161
John William	124		Ernest H.	201
Kathryn Orrison	196		Etta M.	24
Mary Jane, Mrs.	42		Franklin Allen	24
Mary Louise Kidwell	187		Goldie May, Mrs.	110
Minnie B.	42		Hannah Elizabeth Norris	156
Nancy Lee	16		Henry M.	174
Omar E.	42		Hugh Ashby	156
Paul Washington	42		John F.	39
Richard Wayne	220		John W.	24
Sadie R., Mrs.	72		Joseph M.	42
Viola Johnson	16		Joyce A.	72
Taylor			Laura Edmunds Conrad, Mrs.	76
Andrew Michael	209		Magnus Stribling, Col.	75
Charles Russell	214		Marguerite L.	110
Michael Eugene	115		Marguerite L., Mrs.	151
Tina Marie	103		Mary Geneva H.	24
Teates			Mary Louise	39
Christopher	90		Maud E., Miss	24
Frank W., Jr.	90		May Louise	42
Frank W., Sr.	90		Thomas Donovan	110
Tebbs			Viola	39
Charles B.	vi		Thomson	
Thayer			Jo Ann W.	206
Beatrice H.	14		Thornton	
Ethel Virginia	179		Lucille Anna	41
Gracy P.Y.	178		Thorpe	
Jack Thomas	178		Daniel Leroy	130
James W.	178		Leroy Wallace	130
James Wilton	14		Thrift	
John Thomas	178		Blanche E.	42
Sara Holden, Mrs.	179		Chester R.	42
William F.	178		Leonard E.	42
Thomas			Lucie E., Mrs.	42

Melvin P.	42	O.H.	6
Samuel	42	Titus	
Virginia R.	42	Albert Burch	6
Thyson		Annabel H.	26
William Frank	197	Blair Sumner	173
Tiffany		C.R.	8
Harry I.	188	Carrie Virginia	8
Virginia Alsip	188	Charles R., Pvt.	7
Till		Child of Albert	6
Franz	91	Clifton Ross	187
Tillett		D.T.	8
Albert L.	51	Dorothea Marie	6
C. Russell	208	Dorothy Jane	6
Eugenia Anderson	23	E.T.	6
Evelyn May	125	Edgar Tunis	6
Florence E.	51	Edward Farrell	6
Harry Randolph	23	Elizabeth Gay	184
Howard C.	51	Franklin Dunlap	6
Hugh Albert	23	G.W. & Ellen	26
Jean Berry	23	George Tunis	174
Mary L.	23	George W.	26
Orra Lee V.	23	H.L.	7
Sadie A., Mrs.	184	Harvey Brown	164
Samuel C.	23	Hattie Blanche Fadeley	163
Summerfield B., Jr.	125	Helen Ann	174
T.R.	23	Henry L.	8
Tessie Penn	208	India R., Mrs.	26
Timms		J. Nelson	158
Benjamin Franklin	150	James Eugene	163
Bruce F.	150	James Eugene, Jr.	163
Timon		John William (Bill), Jr.	122
Martin J.	52	Joseph C., Sr.	163
Tincher		Lillie May Gant	8
Garland V., Sr.	179	Lori Lynn	187
Irol Truman	179	Louis Templar	149
John Truman	179	Margaret A.	6
Mary Brown	179	Marie G.	158
Orville T.	179	Mildred M.	187
William Clay	179	Robert Gordon	7
Tipton		Roger	26
Dorothy Snead, Mrs.	68	Roy F.	174
Jerry W.	68	Susan Virginia Wenner	173
Joseph W.	68	Thomas Edward	184
Tittman		Virginia Ella (Virgie)	174
Jean Crosby	6	William F.	26
Kate T. Wilkins	6	William Richard	174
Otto Hilgard, Dr.	6	Tomlin	
Tittmann		Cyrus Smith	93
Charles Trowbridge	6	Tracy	

Lillian A.	168	Joseph Howard	71
Trail		Turner	
Dorothy S.	159	Eva Hogan	144
Roy Thomas	159	Lawrence E.	220
Treviranus		Righter	144
Angus Stewart Whitehurst	223	Robert	98
Tribby		Tynes	
Harry Franklin, Sr.	115	A. Lacy, Dr.	112
Theresa Kitts	123	Bessie Meade	112

—U—

Triman			
Child of Herman R.	57		
Triplett		Udall	
Martha Wilson	145	Ella Royston	211
Oney Charles	83	Umbaugh	
William Harrison	145	Dorothy Thayer	179
Trittipoe		Harry	197
Child	151	J. Hanson	179
Ernest Benjamin	77	Maggie A. Loy, Mrs.	50
George Wilbur	212	Underwood	
Gussie Virginia	77	Blanch A.	122
Lucy Ella	151	George Y.	122
Norma Jean Ware	221	Updegrove	
William H.	151	Earl David	142
Truehart		Upton	
Myrtle Ferne	9	Edgar Lee	196
William C.	9	Minnie B.	196
Trundle		Utgaard	
H. H., Mrs.	48	Lucille Schustron, Mrs.	63
Trussel		Myron H.	63
Willie K.	57	Utterback	
Trussell		Elsie Caylor	82
Baby Girl	166	Harry Stanley	159
Betty Jane	57	James Edgar	82
Edith Jane W.	57	Josephine Atwell	159
Emma J.	57		
Fannie M.	57		

—V—

Harry Harper	166		
Harry K.	57		
Hubert Hanes	57	Valdetara	
James H.	57	Frank C.	212
Minnie Belle Arnold	166	Vandevanter	
Roger B.	228	Armistead M.	vi
Tucker		VanDeventer	
Frederick H.	58	Albert Lee	57
Viola Frye	58	Anne Graham	57
Turley		Robert Gover	66
Alice W. Alloway	71	VanHooser	
Harry A.	71	David B.	223
John Gouldey	71	VanSickler	

Margaret C.	100	Walsh	
Vermillion		Jack	117
Alvirty	52	Kathryn Griffin	154
Vesey		Walter	
Martha Collins	107	C. Browning	131
Vinoski		Walton	
John P.	123	Steven D.	83
Virts		Want	
Dorothy Catherine	49	Dorothy Elliotte	139
Edwin Spencer	77	Elliotte Cullen	139
Garnie Craven	110	Fulton, Sr.	139
Henrietta A.	106	Ward	
Howard F.	49	Della K.	152
Nina Russell	77	Elliot Lee	156
Susannah, Mrs.	49	George E.	152
William E.	106	Henry Clay	58
William E., Jr.	49	Laurie L.	228
William Edgar	49	Virginia Steadman	156
Vogel		Ware	
George E.	78	Orma Anna	212
Margaret Miller C., Mrs.	78	Walter Justus	212
		William Arthur	220
		Warner	

—W—

Waddell		Eugene Lee	133
Margaret Newton, Mrs.	49	Gordon Edward	192
William Fontaine	49	Leonard O.	180
Wagar		Mildred M.	180
Ross L.	114	Nancy Wynkoop, Mrs.	141
Wagner		Warren	
Francis M.	124	Benjamin E.	40
George S.	124	Eva Gertrude, Mrs.	40
Richard Clark	190	Wastie	
Walker		Nanci Hallett	208
Harold B.	141	Waters	
Walter Allen	104	Susie Daniel, Mrs.	88
Walko		William Wright	88
Baby	92	Watkins	
Wall		Elizabeth Fitzhugh	160
Baby	196	Hezekiah	160
James & Ellen	196	Weadon	
Wallace		Lucille Kirby	44
Arminda E.	13	Weaver	
James W.	13	George F.	10
L.K., Mrs.	18	James H.	55
Mary E., Mrs.	18	Lula G.	10
Peggy L.	148	Lulu G.	10
Ruby Maffett	132	Webster	
Samuel Aston	132	Logan A., Mrs.	109
		Weed	

Kenneth L.	73	Williams	
Lawrence F.	69	Ada	28
Mary H.	69	Alfred W.	139
Marylee Ward	80	Alice M.	109
Weeks		Cecilia	225
Virginia Beall	25	Charles A.	77
William A.	25	Charles Ashby	77
Weiskircher		Child	35
Sylvester John	115	Earl E.	109
Welch		Eugene E.	109
Florence H.	133	Ferrell T.	225
Robert Winfred	58	Frank B.	139
Winford J.	58	Franklin Delano	59
Welsh		Harrison	186
Elinor G.	58	Helen Moore	145
Thomas Edward	129	John H.	28, 35, 77
Wenner		Joseph Ernest	28
Francie M.	197	Lottie P.	139
Vicki	154	Mary Augusta	77
Wertz		Mary Ellen	139
George Bryant	128	Mary Nelson	59
Ruth E.	129	Mary Virginia	134
Wetzel		Mattie L.	28
Gertrude	214	Michael Shane	152
Wharton		Ruth Morse	59
Louis Morgan	147	Ted Byron	139
Whetsell		William Thomas Lamar	134
Michael Burl	86	Winslow	145
Thomas L.	102	Willingham	
White		Alice Virginia	197
Doris B.	228	Joseph Herbert	197
Elijah B.	202	Roy Nathan	197
Hannah Frances	89	Willoughby	
Jennie, Miss	93	Aileen Beatty	146
Marvin P.	89	Wilson	
Whitmore		Carrie Louise Bennett	150
Joseph Shafer	8	Creola Daniel, Mrs.	211
Louise Gertrude H.	8	Ethel E.	206
Marguerite Fadeley, Mrs.	157	Frank H.	150
Michael T. & Emma S.	8	Frank H., Jr.	150
William C.	157	James Edward, Sr.	206
Widman		Joe B.	114
Harvey	68	Lloyd B.	145, 150
Wieland		Lloyd Bennett	150
Emily Lewis	228	Lloyd Bennett, Jr.	150
Wilklow		Pauline	116
John W.	36	Robert J.	168
Myrtle Virginia	36	Rose Anna, Mrs.	214
Welby Foster	36	Silence Stewart, Mrs.	150

Thomas Wayne	68		Maureen Crooks	209
Wine			Mollie W.	5
Eda Mae Jennings	204		Mrs. Geo.	4
Maurice R.	204		Richard T.	4
Ruth M.	204		Wright	
Winingder			Alva S.	220
Frank E.	229		Annie Lottie	52
Wippel			David Edgar	184
Linus W.	199		Dennis L.	221
Pauline Lee	199		Dorothy M.	211
Witt			Edna V.	82
Elsie C.	199		Eleanor L.	184
Wittman			John Thomas	172
Mary Lee Hammes	126		Katoria Rollins	172
Witul			Leonard James	207
John S.	153		Newell H.	199
Wogan			Susan Etta	199
Jesse, Jr.	180		Tersa L.	184
Wolford			William Chester	172
Elsie P.	137		William E.(Bill)	223
Gillespie Blaine	137		Wynkoop	
Virginia B.	137		Belle C.	192
Wolverton			Bessie deButts	141
Mary E.	94		James C., Jr.	141
Paul M.	94		James Cartwright, Sr., Dr.	141
Perry M.	94		James Millard	192
Womeldorph			John deB., Dr.	141
Donald E.	138		Thomas Kelley, Sr.	141
Woodruff			Wynn	
John M.	82		Margaret F.	92
Woodward			Mary Lee (Molly)	92
Brenda Sue	131			
Everett (E.J.), II	81		—Y—	
Howard Edward, Sr.	91			
Ivan C.	102		Yerovsek	
Nannie	102		Angela Nicole	129
Woodyard			Roman Frank	129
Florance May	123		Young	
Worley			Baby Girl	103
Floyd W.	151		Ronald & Carole	103
Wortman			Yowell	
Annie R. Ball	110		Odie Phillips	141
Arthur T.	165			
George E.	4		—Z—	
Henry	4			
Henry Mason, Mrs.	32		Zeiler	
Herbert Lee	109		Van Iden	118
Lenora Hurst	57		Zimmerly	
Maude P.	165		Barbara L.	121

Richard A. Zulcosky 121   Josephine A. 68

www.ingramcontent.com/pod-product-compliance
Lightning Source LLC
Chambersburg PA
CBHW070725160426
43192CB00009B/1313